Zion in Africa

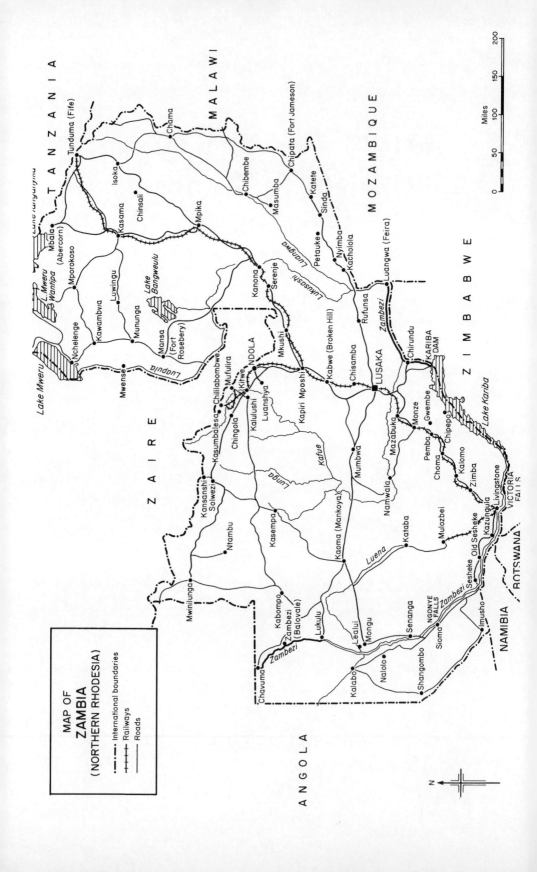

MAP OF
ZAMBIA
(NORTHERN RHODESIA)

— · — International boundaries
+++ Railways
—— Roads

ZION IN AFRICA
The Jews of Zambia

HUGH MACMILLAN AND
FRANK SHAPIRO

I.B.Tauris *Publishers*
LONDON · NEW YORK
in association with
The Council for Zambia
Jewry

Published in 1999 by I.B.Tauris & Co Ltd
Victoria House, Bloomsbury Square, London WC1B 4DZ
175 Fifth Avenue, New York NY 10010
website: http://www.ibtauris.com

in association with the Council for Zambia Jewry Ltd

In the United States and Canada distributed by St. Martin's Press
175 Fifth Avenue, New York NY 10010

ISBN 1 86064 405 8

A full CIP record for this book is available from the British Library
A full CIP record for this book is available from the Library of Congress

Library of Congress catalog card: available

Set in Garamond by Ewan Smith, London
Printed and bound in Great Britain by WBC Ltd, Bridgend

Contents

	List of Illustrations	vi
	Foreword	vii
	List of Abbreviations	ix
1	Jews on the Frontier	1
2	The Susman Saga: the Early Years, 1901–30	16
3	Jewish Networks, the Line of Rail and the Growth of Towns: 1905–39	38
4	A Wandering Jew: Moss Dobkins's Story	70
5	The Copperbelt: Boom, Bust and Recovery, 1924–39	82
6	'Land of Milk and Honey': Settlement Schemes and Immigration Debates, 1934–39	103
7	Escape from the Holocaust	120
8	Bigger Business: from the Depression to Independence, 1930–64	133
9	The Climax of the Community, 1945–70	158
10	The Galaun Story	182
11	Bigger Business Continued: Independence and After	194
12	Religion	206
13	Politics	224
14	Intellectuals and Some Professionals	259
15	Conclusion	286
	Notes and References	294
	Sources	318
	Index	330

Illustrations

1. The wedding of Harry Susman and Annie Grill, Livingstone, July 1910.

2. The Susman family at Memel, East Prussia, 1913.

3. Lusaka's first shop. Glasser's store in Cairo Road, circa 1920.

4. The Kollenberg family outside their house in 13th Avenue, Bulawayo, in 1903.

5. Harry Wulfsohn with colleagues at the Namwala Store, circa 1937.

6. Imwiko Lewanika, Litunga or Paramount Chief of Barotseland, at his palace at Lealui with Harry Susman and Harry Wulfsohn, 1945.

7. The Synagogue, Mufulira, 1947.

8. The Kopelowitz family, circa 1950.

9. Leading members of the management of the Susman group of companies at the first meeting of the board of directors of Rhodesian Mercantile Holdings, Salisbury, 1956.

10. The first Jewish mayoral service held in Northern Rhodesia, Kitwe, 1955.

11. Jack Fischer in his robes as the first mayor of the City of Lusaka, 1961.

12. Simon Zukas is welcomed by crowds of wellwishers on his return to Northern Rhodesia after eleven years of exile in London, February 1964.

13. Dennis and Maureen Figov outside their shop in Luanshya in 1989. The shop was built by Harry Figov in 1936.

14. Hanan Elkaim, of Ndola, receiving the Order of Distinguished Service (First Division) from President Kenneth Kaunda at State House, Lusaka, 1990.

15. The Sefer Torahs of the Lusaka Hebrew Congregation, including one donated by the Mendelsohn family in memory of Sam Mendelsohn.

16. History of the Jews in Zambia Project committee, Lusaka, August 1997.

Foreword

'It's just like the synagogue near my home in London – what is the history of this place?'

These words from a Jewish visitor to Lusaka being shown round the synagogue were to be the start of a fascinating project spanning several years which has finally culminated in this intriguing book. They prompted the Council for Zambia Jewry to commission a history that would provide a permanent record of the role members of the community had played in the life of the country in the twentieth century. The council was fortunate to secure the services of Frank Shapiro, who initiated the project with great enthusiasm and carried out a large number of interviews in Zambia, Zimbabwe, South Africa, Israel and the United Kingdom in 1989–90. At a later date the council was able to obtain the help of Hugh Macmillan, then a member of the History Department at the University of Zambia. He brought to the project his own wide knowledge of the history of southern Africa as a whole, and built upon the foundation which Frank Shapiro had laid. He did a large number of additional interviews, as well as extensive archival and library research, and has written the book in its present form.

Generous material help for the project came from the Council of Zambia Jewry, the Kaplan Foundation in South Africa, the Commonwealth Jewish Council, and from individuals too numerous to mention. To all these bodies and people we extend our sincere thanks.

We would also like to thank all those who people who agreed to be interviewed, sometimes on several occasions, and who provided documentary material and photographs, as well as generous hospitality to our researchers. Their names appear in the list of sources at the end of the book. It is a matter of regret that a number of elderly people who were interviewed have passed away before publication. We hope that their families and friends will find a reminder of them in this book.

The authors have made every effort to ensure that the book is accurate, but they are aware that some errors are bound to have escaped their scrutiny. This is almost inevitable when it is remembered that there are in this book three people who bear exactly the same names, that some people have spelled their names in three different ways, and that some, who shall be nameless, have had as many as three different birth dates!

Thanks are also due to the staff of the libraries and archives used by the authors, especially to the always helpful and friendly staff of the National Archives of Zambia, Lusaka, under the guidance of their Director, Mrs N. Mutiti.

Finally, a special mention must be made of Mr Malcolm Gee in London, whose untiring efforts over the years have kept the project together. Without him, the project might never have come to fruition.

We offer this book to the Zambian, and to the international, public as a contribution to the history of the Jews in the Diaspora, and to the history of Zambia and the southern African region as a whole.

Michael Galaun, Michael Bush
and Simon Zukas (Lusaka)
Edwin Wulfsohn (London)
October 1998

Abbreviations

ANC	African National Congress
BP	Bechuanaland Protectorate
BSA	British South Africa
CO	Colonial Office
CRL	Companies Registry, Lusaka
DC	District Commissioner
DO	District Officer
ExCo	Executive Committee
FO	Foreign Office
FS	Financial Secretary
Gov	Governor
LegCo	Legislative Council
NR	Northern Rhodesia
NRGG	Northern Rhodesia Government Gazette
PC	Provincial Commissioner
PM	Prime Minister
RHL	Rhodes House Library, Oxford
SA	South Africa
SACP	South African Communist Party
SAJBD	South African Jewish Board of Deputies
SPLC	Stenham PLC, London
SWAPO	South West African People's Organisation
TZI	Trans Zambezi Industries
UDI	Unilateral Declaration of Independence
UNIP	United National Independence Party
WENELA	Witwatersrand Native Labour Association
WIZO	Women's International Zionist Organisation
ZANU	Zimbabwe African National Union
ZAPU	Zimbabwe African People's Union
ZCCM	Zambia Consolidated Copper Mines
ZIF	Immigration Files in ZNA
ZNA	Zambia National Archives

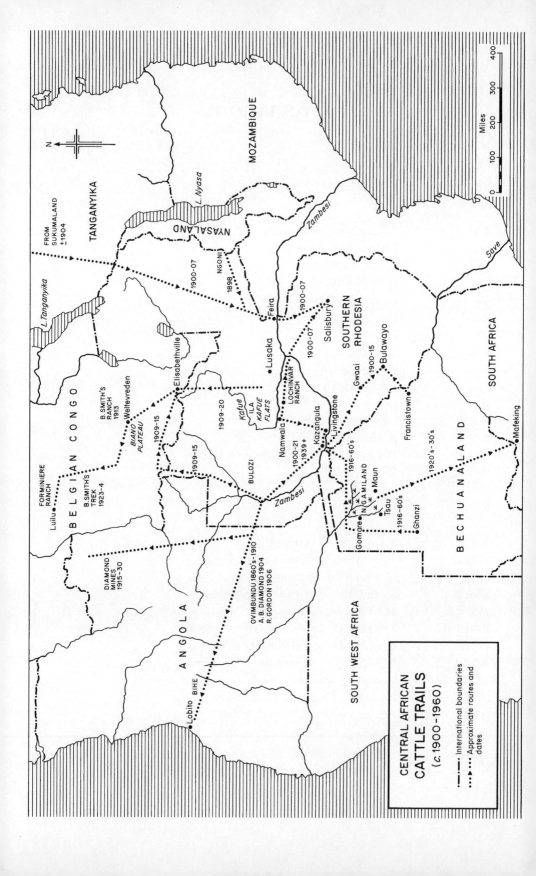

CENTRAL AFRICAN
CATTLE TRAILS
(c.1900-1960)

----- International boundaries
••••► Approximate routes and
dates

CHAPTER I

Jews on the Frontier

There is probably no definition of Jewishness which will satisfy everyone. In the final analysis there are only two definitions of what is a Jew, as of any other ethnic group. People may define themselves as Jews, or they may be defined as Jews by others. In a work of this kind, it is necessary to take the widest possible definition. A purely religious definition, emphasising maternal descent and observance, would exclude people of Jewish origin who have a significant part to play in this story such as Alfred Beit, and his family, who were converted to Christianity, or Simon Zukas, who is agnostic. It would also exclude people, such as Sir Roy Welensky and Aaron Milner, who are Jewish by paternal descent, and who value the Jewish element in their ancestry.

This study of the history of the Jews in Zambia is influenced by the view that it is important to avoid statements which attribute similar racial or ethnic characteristics to all members of any social group. We see the Jews on the frontier in Zambia as an example of a fairly common social phenomenon: an immigrant ethnic group which, through the force of historical circumstances, rather than heredity, specialises, at least for a time, in a particular field of economic and commercial activity. There have been earlier studies of such groups. The Dotsons made a pioneering study of the role of Asians in central Africa. Barry Kosmin has written an excellent book on the history of the Jews of Zimbabwe. John McCracken has written about the Italians in Malawi. It is hoped that this study may stimulate the production of histories of other immigrant ethnic groups, including African groups, and that it may shed light on the process of creating a Zambian identity which has drawn on a great variety of sources, predominantly African, but also European, Asian, and from almost every corner of the world.[1]

The Jews in Africa

It appears that there is, as yet, no general history of the Jews in Africa. This is a surprising omission. A plausible case could be made for the African origins of Judaism. In *Joseph and His Brothers*, one of the great novels of the twentieth century, Thomas Mann pointed to the possible links between Jewish

monotheism and the Pharaoh Amenhotep IV (Akhnaton)'s ill-fated attempt
to impose this theology on Ancient Egypt. Moses received the ten command-
ments in Sinai, a peninsula which links Africa and Asia. His wife was a black
African from Kush, and his marriage to her caused controversy. It is unlikely
that all Jews left Egypt with the Exodus. Correspondence survives from the
fifth century BC relating to the Jewish temple at Elephantine (modern Aswan)
on the upper Nile. This was the only Jewish temple outside Jerusalem and
was of the same size and design as Solomon's temple in that city. The recent
emigration to Israel of most of Ethiopia's black Jews, the Falashas, has
drawn attention to the long history of that community. It has recently been
persuasively argued that Judaism spread up the Nile into Ethiopia in the last
millennium BC. Jews were widely spread in north Africa from Egypt through
Carthage to the Atlantic Ocean in the later centuries of the pre-Christian era.
The Jewish Bible was translated into Greek in Alexandria in the third century
BC in the version known as the Septuagint. The great Jewish philosopher and
theologian Philo of Alexandria, a contemporary of Jesus Christ, estimated
that there were a million Jews in Egypt, perhaps one-tenth of the population.
Jews occupied two of the five quarters of Alexandria, then the greatest city
of the ancient world. After the Jewish revolt against Roman rule in Cyrenaica
in AD 115, there was a diaspora westwards, and into the Sahara.[2]

Legend has attributed the origins of the great empire of Ghana to these
refugees. There is no doubt that Jews were, together with Kharajite Berbers,
among the founders of Sijilmasa, the main northern terminus of the trans-
Saharan trade in gold from Ghana. Jews were almost certainly settled south
of the Sahara, where they may have been the earliest goldsmiths, before the
end of the first millennium AD. The earliest maps of this region, including
one which provides a famous portrait of Mansa Musa, the great ruler of
Mali, were drawn in 1375 by Majorcan Jewish geographers at the court of
King Charles V. Jewish traders were expelled from Timbuktu by its Muslim
rulers at the end of the fifteenth century, but they must have been allowed
to return later, for such traders were recorded as arriving with caravans from
the Sahara at Oran in 1626, and were actively involved in the trans-Saharan
trade in its last period of prosperity in the mid-nineteenth century.[3]

Many Jews from Spain and Portugal took refuge in Muslim north Africa
at the end of the fifteenth century. They were fleeing persecution by the
Inquisition which was intended to rid Spain and Portugal of Jews, Muslims
and heretics, and to make it a 'Christian country'. Others travelled as far east
as the Ottoman empire, which had taken control of Constantinople from
the Byzantine Christians in 1453. The Ottoman Sultan was unable to understand the madness of the Spanish monarchs who sought to rid their country
of such useful citizens. They became the 'Ladinos', Spanish-speaking Jews,
some of whose descendants reached the Congo and Northern Rhodesia
from Rhodes and Smyrna in the twentieth century. Portuguese Jewish children,
who were victims of the Inquisition and unwilling converts to Christianity

– the so-called 'New Christians' – were settled on the island of São Tomé, off the shores of Gabon, before 1500. It was reported in 1632 that the 'Marranos' were so numerous on the island that they were able to practise their old religion 'almost openly'. 'New Christians' from São Tomé were among the founders of Luanda, and of Portuguese Angola, in the sixteenth century. Even there they did not escape the Inquisition. Recent publications have documented an investigation by the Inquisition of the 'New Christians' of Angola at the end of the sixteenth century. Among the crimes alleged against them were over-familiarity with the 'natives'. It is hardly surprising that they welcomed the occupation of Brazil and Angola by the somewhat more tolerant Protestant Dutch in the early decades of the seventeenth century. Portuguese-speaking Jews formed the nucleus of the substantial Jewish population of Amsterdam.[4]

There were Jewish mathematicians and astronomers at the court of Prince Henry the Navigator, and King John II, the Portuguese sponsors of west African exploration. They produced the tables of solar declination which made navigation south of the equator possible in the second half of the fifteenth century. There were also Jews among the companions of Vasco da Gama. The best-known of them, Gaspar da Gama, took his patron's name.[5] Jews were, however, excluded from settlement at the Dutch colony of the Cape of Good Hope on its establishment in 1652. The first people of Jewish origin to settle at the Cape were soldiers in the Dutch East India Company's service, who arrived in 1669, and were baptised as Christians at the Cape. Adam Tas, one of the leaders in 1705–6 of the first settler-led protest movement against the Dutch East India Company's administration, and the author of a famous diary, was of Jewish descent. Although settlement was prohibited, Jewish financiers were among the major backers of the Dutch East India Company, and provided directors of the company in the eighteenth century. It was only after the British occupation of the Cape in 1795 that Jewish settlement was officially allowed. There were Jews among the 1820 settlers, but it was not until 1841 that a *minyan* could be formed at Cape Town. There were only sixty Jewish families in the Cape colony outside Cape Town in 1859. Most of them were traders of British or German origin, but there were also doctors and civil servants.[6]

The British South Africa Company

There was further immigration following the discovery of diamonds in Griqualand West in 1869. There were probably no more than 500 Jewish families in South Africa when the Governor of the Cape, Sir Henry Barkly, spoke at the laying of the foundation stone in 1875 of the first synagogue at Kimberley which was to serve its Jewish population of 120. It was from Kimberley that British expansion into central Africa was planned. The profits of Kimberley diamonds, and of Witwatersrand gold, financed the British

South Africa Company which was granted a charter in 1889 for the administration of what eventually became Northern and Southern Rhodesia. The prime
mover behind this company was the man who gave his name, for a while,
to the two countries. Cecil Rhodes became, in partnership with Alfred Beit,
a converted Jew from Hamburg, the monopolist of the Kimberley diamond
fields. The instrument of their monopoly was the De Beer's Consolidated
Mining Company. Rhodes, who was soon to become Prime Minister of the
Cape Colony, was almost unknown in London in 1889. It was a financial
reference from Nathaniel, first Lord Rothschild, merchant banker and leader
of Britain's Jewish community, which convinced the Prime Minister of the
day, Lord Salisbury, of his bona fides.[7]

Rhodes's interest in central Africa did not simply lie in 'painting the map
red' from the Cape to Cairo, but in the belief that the gold reef of the
Witwatersrand might extend to Zimbabwe and Katanga. It was this belief
which prompted him to finance British expansion into an area north and
south of the Zambezi river which would otherwise have fallen to the
Portuguese in the Scramble for Africa. His dream of another 'Ophir' in
central Africa was not realised. While there were outcrops of gold-bearing ore
in Southern Rhodesia, there was no great reef. The BSA Company was not
a financial success and paid no dividends during its period of administration
which ended in 1923. A Jewish trader, Daniel Kisch, had been settled at
Bulawayo, the Ndebele capital, as early as 1871, and acted as secretary to King
Lobengula. He was, perhaps, the first example in southern Africa of the
'Court Jew'. He was the nephew of Aaron de Pass, a pioneer of the whaling
and guano industries of the Cape, and one of the founders in the 1840s of
Cape Town's Old Synagogue. There was a handful of Jews in the Pioneer
Column of settlers which, by-passing Matabeleland, occupied Mashonaland in
1890. Hebrew congregations were established in Bulawayo and Salisbury in
1894 and 1895 respectively.[8]

It was not until after 1900 that administration was fully established in
Northern Rhodesia. Until 1911 this vast area was divided into two halves,
North-Western and North-Eastern Rhodesia, and was governed from two
capitals, Kalomo and, from 1907, Livingstone in the west, and Fort Jameson
(Chipata) in the east. The British protectorate over North-Western Rhodesia
had been negotiated in 1890 by agents of the British South Africa Company
with King Lewanika, whose domain was known to his own people as Bulozi
and to the British as Barotseland. Like Khama the Great of Bechuanaland,
he sought protection from the Ndebele who raided north of the Zambezi.
The intermediary in these negotiations was François Coillard, a French
missionary and head of the Protestant Paris mission, which had been allowed
into Barotseland through the intercession of George Westbeech, an English
ivory trader, who settled at Pandamatenga, just south of the Zambezi, in the
early 1870s. Among Westbeech's employees was Jan Africa, said to be of
mixed 'Hottentot', though probably Griqua, and Jewish parentage. He was

born in 1844 and entered Westbeech's employment in 1872. He is the first person of Jewish descent who is known to have entered the region which is now Zambia.[9]

The BSA Company ensured that Lewanika did not get such a good deal as Khama, but Barotseland always had a special status within the protectorate. Lewanika and his successors did preserve a measure of control over the natural resources of the area, such as ivory, game and fish, which were denied to the chiefs of less prominent pre-colonial states. There were also tight restrictions on land alienation within Barotseland. The Lozi rulers were also paid a royalty for minerals extracted in the Copperbelt – an area which lay far beyond the real boundaries of their dominions.

Access to North-Eastern Rhodesia was by steamer up the Zambezi and Shire rivers and through Nyasaland. The trade of the region was dominated by the Glasgow-based African Lakes Corporation. Scottish missionaries, traders and engineers continued to play a major role in Nyasaland and North-Eastern Rhodesia until the 1950s. They faced stiff competition from the 1890s onwards from Eugene Sharrer, a German Jewish entrepreneur from Hamburg, who founded Sharrer's Zambezi Traffic Company. He was encouraged to set up in competition with the African Lakes Corporation by the first administrator of British Central Africa, Sir Harry Johnston – later known as a gentile Zionist. Sharrer was responsible, with the help of the British government, for the construction of the Shire Highlands Railway. His company was also involved for a time in transport along the Stevenson Road, the route from the north end of Lake Nyasa to Lake Tanganyika which had been pioneered by the African Lakes Corporation in the 1880s.[10]

Rhodes was kept out of British Central Africa, now Malawi, as a result of a campaign orchestrated by the Scottish missions which were doubtful about his South African links. He also met some problems in establishing his claims in North-Eastern Rhodesia as a result of the activities of a German adventurer, Carl Wiese, who was established on the middle Zambezi, and in the Luangwa valley, as an ivory and rubber trader from the late 1880s. He obtained extensive concessions covering parts of Mozambique and North-Eastern Rhodesia from the Ngoni King, Mpezeni, at whose court he lived for some time. He sold them to a company which was controlled by Libert Oury, a financier of British citizenship and Belgian birth.[11]

These claims were so substantial that the British government compelled the British South Africa Company to recognise them by the grant to Oury of the North Charterland Concession, covering 10,000 square miles of what is today the Eastern Province of Zambia. Wiese himself was employed by this company on its concession in the late 1890s and helped to precipitate the attack by British troops from Nyasaland on Mpezeni's Ngoni in 1898. His main interests were, however, in Mozambique where he had married into one of the Afro-Portuguese prazo-holding families. He was given control in 1890 of the Massingire prazo and became something between an African chief and a feudal lord. He was clearly well-educated and a remarkable linguist. He was the author of a substantial ethnographic study of Mpezeni's Ngoni which was published in Portuguese. Sir Harry Johnston described him a little ambiguously as 'a conscienceless and intriguing German', as 'little less than a slave-trader', and as a man of 'dubious antecedents'. The historian Lewis Gann was certain that these antecedents were Jewish. Wiese was certainly part of a German Jewish trading network, and in 1900 gave his addresses as 'Chiromo and Hamburg'.[12]

The Rubber Frontier

Carl Wiese's main backer was Ludwig Deuss, of Hamburg, who had branches of his trading business at Quelimane and Chinde on the Indian Ocean coast of Mozambique from the 1880s onwards, and established a network of stores on Lake Nyasa and on the Stevenson Road in the 1890s. Deuss's firm, like Sharrer's, and the African Lakes Corporation, was involved in the export of wild rubber from the Congo and Northern Rhodesia during the short-lived rubber boom at the turn of the century. Deuss was also the main backer of Gustav Rabinek, an Austrian, who was also of Jewish descent. Rabinek created a rubber and ivory trading empire in the area to the west of Lake Tanganyika at this time, and chartered a steamer from the African Lakes Corporation for trade on that lake. He was arrested by the Congo Free State authorities in 1901 while on board another of their steamers, the *Scotia*, on Lake Mweru. He had a concession from the Katanga Company for rubber collecting in the Congo, but this was cancelled, and he was tried and sentenced to a year's imprisonment for illegal trading. He died in detention while on his way to the Congo Free State capital of Boma to appeal against this sentence.[13]

Rabinek's death became a *cause célèbre* and was used by E. D. Morel, the author of *Red Rubber* and other works, in his campaign against King Leopold's rule in the Congo. Correspondence relating to the circumstances of his arrest and death fills a volume of the British Foreign Office records. The furore over his death coincided with the Dreyfus Affair in France and it is probable that his Jewish origins were deliberately played down. Morel's informant in this case was Mauricio Teixeira de Mattos, who been involved with Wiese in Mozambique in the late 1880s, and with Deuss and Rabinek in the Congo and 'Barotseland' rubber trades at the turn of the century. De Mattos was described by a contemporary observer as 'a big breezy Dutch-speaking Portuguese Jew, almost as original as his nationality'. Known to his friends and acquaintances as 'Moses', he turns up all over the region. He protected the British explorer Joseph Thomson from Mpezeni's Ngoni in 1891, was later involved in the supply of food to the Tanganyika Concessions Company's Katanga mines, was at the north end of Lake Nyasa in 1907, at Dilolo on the border between the Congo and Angola in 1908, and was trading rubber from west of the Lualaba to Deuss at Broken Hill on Northern

Rhodesia's newly-opened railway line in the same year. He was running a successful business in prefabricated houses at Elisabethville in 1913 when he disappears from the records.[14]

The Russian Empire

Sharrer, Deuss, Wiese, Rabinek and de Mattos represented, directly or indirectly, German Jewish mercantile capital, and relied for the most part on access to the region by steamer along the rivers and lakes of east central Africa. They had their heyday during the Scramble for Africa when they traded not only in commodities, but also in treaties and land concessions. They were rugged individualists who played no part in the establishment of a Jewish community. It was in the west that larger numbers of poorly-capitalised Jewish immigrants from the Russian empire first made their appearance, and laid the basis of a Jewish community. Access to North-Western Rhodesia was, until the opening of the Victoria Falls bridge and the arrival of the railway north of the Zambezi in 1905, by the arduous wagon route from the south. The railhead reached Mafeking, 800 miles to the south in 1894, and Bulawayo, 300 miles to the south, in 1897. Jewish migrants first made their way into North-Western Rhodesia in small numbers along the Hunters' Road from Francistown in Bechuanaland. These were among the most adventurous, and possibly the most desperate, of some three million Jews who left the Russian empire between the 1880s and the First World War.

This emigration was set off by the wave of pogroms which followed the assassination of Tsar Alexander II in 1881. Many Jews were also compelled to leave as a result of a new wave of pogroms which started in 1903, and in the wake of the failed revolution of 1905. The great majority of these emigrants went to the United States, but significant numbers also went to western Europe, Palestine, South America and South Africa. There were estimated to be 50,000 Jews in South Africa in 1911. The great majority of the new immigrants were attracted to Johannesburg and the mining towns of the Witwatersrand and were engaged in trade. Three-quarters of them originated in the Russian empire. As many as two-thirds of these may have come from the Kovno Province (today's Lithuania) while most of the remainder came from the neighbouring province of Kurland (now Latvia), and from Byelorussia. In their home country they were excluded from land ownership and from many of the professions and crafts. The majority of them came from rural *shtetls*, small towns and villages, where they were forced to earn their living as traders, artisans or labourers. Many of them were butchers and cattle traders, though milling and inn-keeping were also permitted activities. They formed a distinct ethnic group with their own language, religion and schools. They occupied an intermediary position as traders in a society which was sharply divided between a Polish, or Russian, aristocracy and a Lithuanian, or Latvian, peasantry. It has been suggested that Jews on the frontier in southern Africa were able to re-create for a while the social situation which they had occupied in their home regions, though they were now commercial intermediaries between a British ruling class and an African peasantry.[15]

The Jews of Lithuania were known for their poverty, piety and devotion to biblical scholarship, but also for their tendency towards religious sectarianism. Vilna (now Vilnius) was, with its ninety synagogues, described as 'the Jerusalem of the North'. The better-educated emigrants found new homes for themselves in Europe, especially in Germany, and became assimilated members of the German and French intellectual elites, but the less well-educated were forced to move further afield. Many of the Jews who became frontiersmen in the Rhodesias were latecomers who, moving to South Africa in the 1890s, found the most obvious commercial niches on the Witwatersrand already over-subscribed. It was necessity, as much as a love of adventure, which drove them north. The average age of Jewish immigrants at this time, almost all of them men, was very low, not more than the mid-twenties, and the expectation of life was short. The greatest danger was blackwater fever – a complication of malaria which was induced by its antidote, quinine. According to a well-informed source, death rates at this time were comparable with what would be expected among soldiers in a major war.[16]

The Wild West

The story of Northern Rhodesia's 'Wild West' is not well known. Following the great rinderpest epidemic of 1896–97, which killed 90 per cent of the cattle of Southern Africa, there was a serious shortage of stock. This shortage was intensified by the outbreak of the Anglo-Boer War in 1899 which greatly increased the demand for beef, and for draught oxen, in the region. Owing to some accident of geography and epidemiology, much of Barotseland escaped rinderpest, and the area provided an important source of cattle for the south.[17] The first traders to exploit these cattle reserves were Ovimbundu traders from Angola who had been trading between Bulozi and the Atlantic coast since the mid-nineteenth century.[18] From 1900 onwards, traders entered Bulozi from the south seeking cattle for the Bulawayo market. They came from a variety of nationalities, and included Afrikaners and Scots as well as Jews. Cattle trails were developed southwards from Barotseland, as well as from the Ila who also had large herds. The trail from northern Barotseland to Bulawayo extended for 700 miles, and from the Ila country for 500 miles.

The main cattle trails led from Barotseland to the south. People driving cattle south would sometimes meet transport riders with wagons bringing mining machinery or trade goods in the opposite direction. The extension of the railway to the Zambezi did not put an immediate stop to the cattle trails which now terminated at the railhead. Before the outbreak of the First

World War, new trails were opened up from Barotseland to the north. The development of copper mining on the Congo side of the border, with the rapid growth of the town of Elisabethville, created a new demand for beef. Another trail led north-westwards to the newly-opened diamond fields of Angola and to construction camps on the Benguela railway.

The first Jewish participants in the Barotseland trade were Robert 'Zambezi' Gordon and Fishel Levitz who arrived in 1900.[19] They were joined in 1901 by the brothers Elie and Harry Susman, Joseph Finkelstein, and Wolf Levin. Max Kominsky, Isadore Pieters, the Diamond brothers, David Wersock, the Peimer brothers and Egnatz Snapper were also among the Jewish traders who arrived in the very early years of the century. There were some cattle traders in the area of different origins such as the Scots George Findlay, George Buchanan and Sam Haslett, and the Afrikaner N. M. Human, but Jewish traders acquired an extraordinary hold over the trade.[20]

Robert Coryndon, the British South Africa Company's first Resident Commissioner in North-Western Rhodesia, who was based at Mongu from 1897, noted in his first report on the territory in 1902 that about 1,800 cattle had been exported to the south in the course of the previous year. He referred in coded language to the presence at the Lozi capital, Lealui, of traders 'of a certain influence', by which he meant Jews. He estimated that cattle exported from Barotseland in the previous year had been sold at Bulawayo for an average of £14. 10. 0. per head. He reckoned that a similar number of stock had been exported to the west by what he called 'half-caste' Portuguese traders. He had no control over them as the border with Angola was not yet defined.[21] Writing from Lealui in February 1901, Colin Harding, Commander of the British South Africa Company's Barotseland Police, had earlier reported that as a result of the demand for cattle from Southern Rhodesia in the previous year, local prices had risen from £4. 5. 0. to £6. 15. 0. per head. He noted not only that prices had increased 'with these gigantic strides', but that the 'natives' now had so much gold in their possession that they refused to sell cattle 'unless there is a certain amount of trade material included in the transaction'. He also commented on the presence of 'Mambari', or Ovimbundu, traders from Angola and observed that, with the export of cattle to the south and west, cattle stocks were being depleted.[22] From other sources it is clear that King Lewanika had in the past sought to control cattle exports by insisting that only oxen, and not breeding stock, should be allowed to leave his country.[23]

Frank Sykes, the District Commissioner at Victoria Falls, reported early in 1902 that most of the cattle traders were Jews from Bulawayo and Francistown. He had collected £85 in licence fees in the early months of 1902, suggesting that between twenty and thirty traders had entered the area. He thought that there would be keen competition and that the trade would not be as profitable a speculation as it had been in the previous year. He thought that Lesser and Company of Francistown, a firm in which Robert Gordon

and Fishel Levitz were partners, had taken out the majority of cattle from
the Barotse area in the previous two years. He noted that they were, in April
1902, about to build a permanent trading store at Sesheke which would be
'of considerable convenience to the district'. He also noted that a number of
'Mangwato and Shangaan' traders had been in the area.[24]

Anti-Semitism

Many of the early officials of the British South Africa Company shared in
the anti-Semitism which was endemic among white settlers in southern Africa
until after the Second World War. Anti-Semitism was clearly an important
factor in defining and maintaining a distinct Jewish identity in the early years
of the century. Many people saw Jews not only as of a different 'influence'
or 'persuasion', but also as of a different 'race'. Jews were seen by some as
not quite 'white' and as occupying an intermediate space between 'whites'
and 'Africans'. There was a frequently expressed fear that Jews on the frontier
might become too familiar with Africans and undermine the deference
towards whites which Africans were expected to display and which many
whites saw as essential to their security. Jews and Africans were both the
objects in differing degrees of racism. This was symbolised by references in
the literature to 'Jew boys'. Jewish men were, in common with African men,
frequently denied the status of adulthood. J. B. Thornhill, a mining surveyor,
who spent several years in Northern Rhodesia and the Congo in the early
years of the century, reported an incident involving Frank Sykes which
provides a good illustration of contemporary attitudes. He noted that Sykes
had 'some very bad luck':

> Like all sound men on the advance, he was very strong on the subject of
> upholding the European prestige. A Jew trader, in order to get favours from
> Lewanika, the king of the Barotsi [sic] nation, prostrated himself on the ground
> and clapped his hands – the native form of salutation – to one of Lewanika's
> sons. Sykes took absolutely the right course, arrested the Jew boy, and deported
> him over the border. A skilful lawyer took up the case and succeeded, I under-
> stand, in getting a tidy penny out of both Sykes and the Chartered Company.[25]

Thornhill was not alone in having strong views on the question of
handshakes. He strongly deprecated what he saw as the west African practice
of shaking hands with Africans which was 'totally opposed to all the ideas
of South Africans, who insist on the native making whatever is the recognised
salutation they give to their great chiefs'. For a white person to shake hands
with an African was in itself unacceptable, but to recognise the authority of
an African ruler by prostrating oneself in this way involved a shocking reversal
of roles. This story says a good deal about the attitudes of both Sykes and
Thornhill to Jews and Africans, and the relationship between them, but it is
by no means unique. The question of handshakes was taken very seriously

by the administration itself. For many years the Governor and other officials in Northern Rhodesia were permitted to shake hands with only two of their African subjects, the Litunga of Bulozi and his heir.

Percy Clark, who reached the settlement at the Old Drift on the north side of the Zambezi near the Victoria Falls in 1903, provided plenty of evidence of prevailing prejudices. He described a Jewish trader who saved the life of himself and his companion by providing them with water on their way north to the Zambezi as 'the Gargantuan Hebrew' and 'our Transjordanic and bulky friend'. He included a stereotypical account of a Jewish cardsharp or 'trickster' and gave the following account of a Jewish trader whom he met on the upper Zambezi in 1903:

> When I came on him he was eating with his native boys, a thing which whites regarded as pretty low down. He complained that he could not get his boys to do anything. They went their own way and would take no notice of anything he said. 'They simply laugh at me', he whined. He was nearly crying with self-pity. 'What do you expect when you treat them as equals?', I replied. 'It serves you dam'well right!' This chap lived on as a trader in Barotseland for nearly thirty years and he died there. He had several wives and a host of pepper-and-salt children. It is hard enough to keep the respect of natives as things go, but there is nothing lets the white man down so readily as this sort of behaviour.[26]

The reference was to Egnatz Snapper, who reached Barotseland in 1902 and was based at Kanyonyo, near Mongu, for many years. His origins are obscure, but he had relatives in London and was naturalised after service in the British army during the Anglo-Boer War. He had three Lozi wives and among his 'pepper-and-salt' children, of whom Clark was clearly so dis-approving, was Dick Snapper, who was to play a prominent part in central African 'Coloured' pressure groups in the 1950s. Another son, John, served in the Second World War and worked for many years as a store manager for Susman Brothers and Wulfsohn. Egnatz Snapper's nephew, Sid Diamond, also features later in this story as one of the most successful of the Copper-belt shopkeepers. Snapper remained in business at Kanyonyo until the 1940s. He was buried in the Jewish section of the Livingstone cemetery where a tombstone was erected in the 1970s by his children and grandchildren.[27]

Fear of miscegenation, and its alleged consequence of racial degeneration, was as widespread on the frontier as miscegenation itself, and had an influence on the British South Africa Company's policy on the issuing of trade licences. According to L. H. Gann, it was official policy by 1908 to encourage the 'wealthier storekeeper, as against the small hawkers, in order to protect the Africans against known bad characters, to prevent European prestige being lowered by poor men becoming too familiar with the Africans, and to avoid cut-throat competition'.[28] The Barotseland frontier was at this time a place of high profits and high risks. Bankruptcy was a more common occurrence than spectacular success. Percy Clark commented on the basis of his own

experience, but with a touch of hyperbole, on the gold rush atmosphere of
the time:

> The profits on trade goods were enormous in those days. Cups and saucers –
> the sort one got with 'A present from Margate' on them – fetched ten shillings
> each. Spoons went at the same ratio, three-halfpenny spoons for a shilling a
> piece. Japanese silk fetched ten shillings a yard. Yes, trading was a great game in
> Barotseland in 1903, but the money made at it was generally soon spent.[29]

Gordon and Levitz

The frontier did, of course, attract adventurers and there were undoubtedly
some bad characters among them. One of the first partnerships involved in
the Barotseland cattle trade ended in acrimony, charges of conspiracy and
fraud, and bankruptcy. Robert 'Zambezi' Gordon – a Lithuanian Jew despite
his Scots-sounding name – disappeared with over 500 head of cattle into
Angola in 1906 and was last heard of in the Bihe district, not far from the
Atlantic coast. It is not certain where he disposed of the cattle, some of
which he had undertaken to sell for King Lewanika and the Lozi Queen, the
Mulena Mukwae of Nalolo, though it is possible that they were delivered to
the contractors who had begun the construction of the Benguela railway
from Lobito Bay to Katanga in 1904.

His partner, Fishel Levitz, claimed that Gordon had swindled him by
selling their firm's goods in exchange for cattle to David Wersock, a former
employee, who had set up in business at Mongu on his own account in 1904.
Levitz returned to Lealui after a trip to Bulawayo to buy goods for King
Lewanika and found that their store, which had contained stock worth £2,000
when he left, was empty, while Wersock's store was full. Gordon himself had
disappeared with the firm's books. Wersock, whose books had conveniently
been burnt in a fire which spared his stock, said that he had bought the
goods from Gordon for £1,700, and paid him in cattle. Wersock was also
accused of swindling Egnatz Snapper by informing him that Gordon was
dead, and persuading him to accept £1 a head – about one-third of their
true value – for forty cattle which Gordon had undertaken to sell on Snapper's
behalf.[30]

Whether or not the allegations against him were true, Wersock prospered
and became a property-owner in Livingstone, though he was later based at
Mafeking and, ultimately, in Salisbury. Fishel Levitz formed another partnership with Max Kominsky, but was declared bankrupt in 1912. He, nevertheless,
remained in business at Sesheke and Mongu until the 1930s. Joseph Finkelstein,
another pioneer of the trade, was probably brought up in England, and acted
as an interpreter from Yiddish to English in this case. He traded at Lealui
and Sesheke until his death in 1943. He was a prominent Zionist and became
a respected senior citizen.

Among those mentioned in the case, and alleged to have knowledge of the truth of the matter, was Aaron Barnett Diamond, who was a naturalised British citizen, and had come to Africa from Ireland. He was at Nalolo in 1902 and remained as a trader and cattle dealer at Lealui for some years. He is acknowledged as the Jewish pioneer of the route to Lobito Bay, a journey of over 1,200 miles, which Robert Gordon followed in 1906. A few years later, in 1909, he opened up a tsetse fly-free route to the Congo. He had been a prominent member of Bulawayo's small Jewish community before the turn of the century, and became the first president of the Elisabethville Hebrew Congregation in 1911. He returned to Northern Rhodesia and, as we shall see, farmed for some years near Lusaka. A. B. Diamond's son, W. H. Diamond, who died in 1932, and his brother, Louis Solomon Diamond, were also in business at Mongu for many years. The latter was, as we shall see, trading at Tara Siding and at Katengwa, near Namwala, in the mid-1930s and died at Livingstone in 1941.[31]

Max Kominsky and Isadore Pieters were among the pioneers of the Barotseland cattle trade who remained in the area for a relatively short time. Kominsky was an intellectual who had trained as a chemist in Moscow and Berlin, and was based in Northern Rhodesia until he left Livingstone for Bulawayo in 1911. According to his daughter, Zena Berold, he was sent out to South Africa by his father to rescue a sister from the disgrace of a divorce. He failed in that objective, but never returned to Europe. He did research work as a chemist in South Africa during the First World War, and developed a process for extracting cyanide from gold slimes. He was a trader in the Congo after the war, but died of blackwater fever in Bulawayo in 1926.[32] Isadore Pieters was settled as a cattle trader at Kalomo in North-Western Rhodesia by 1903, but died there of blackwater fever in 1906. He was a partner in the Bulawayo firm of A. and I. Pieters, which survived for some years after his death. A number of other Jews died north of the Zambezi in the early years of the century. Among the names that were remembered by the Reverend Moses I. Cohen, minister for many years of the Bulawayo Hebrew Congregation, were those of Dantziger, Gelman, Natkin and Salant.[33]

There were a number of Jewish businessmen who became prominent in Southern Rhodesia, but whose fortunes were based on the profits of the Barotseland cattle trade. Jack Goldberg, a Londoner, moved on to be a founder of the Matabeleland Trading Association, the first Jewish-backed 'kaffir-truck' wholesaling organisation, and managing director of the Manchester Trading Company. He owned hotels in Salisbury and Gatooma before investing in chrome mines and mica deposits. He became president of the Salisbury Hebrew Congregation, but went into tobacco farming and was bankrupted by the combined effects of the tobacco crash of 1928, and of the great depression, which wiped out his mines a few years later. Louis Braude and his brothers came from Lithuania and started trading from

Francistown. They were among the backers of Gordon and Levitz before moving to Bulawayo in 1905. Louis Braude, who was also a director of the Abercorn Trading Company, became president of the Salisbury Hebrew Congregation, and was deputy mayor of the town for three years in the 1930s. The four Landau brothers, who came from Manchester, were also involved in the Barotseland cattle trade, though possibly only as providers of goods and credit, and became prominent Bulawayo wholesalers.[34]

Perhaps the most remarkable of the people whose fortunes were based, at least in part, on the northern trade, though they were never personally resident north of the Zambezi, were the Hepker brothers. The eldest of them, Hermann, came from Goldingen, Latvia, and reached German South West Africa in the mid-1880s. He was followed by his brothers, Julius, Adolph and William. They moved through Kimberley to Bechuanaland and Southern Rhodesia, and were settled by 1896 in Bulawayo where they established the Chartered Butchery. Their major source of cattle in the years before the First World War was Barotseland. The Hepkers went on to establish a substantial saw mill at a railway siding sixty miles north of Bulawayo and their company, Rhodesian Native Timber Concessions, extracted timber further north in the Nyamandhlovu district. They became the centre of an extensive commercial network which extended to South Africa and the Congo. A number of their relatives reached Northern Rhodesia and feature later in this story.[35]

Early Jewish traders who penetrated to the remoter corners of North-Western Rhodesia included some rough characters. Harry Stern, also known as 'Kapatamatunga', had a store, in partnership with W. Frykberg, at the Kansanshi mine near the Congo border in Kasempa district in 1908. They were also involved in ivory poaching, and in the recruitment of Kaonde workers for the mines in Southern Rhodesia. It was reported that 100 workers, out of 400 recruited in 1909–10, failed to return home and were presumed dead. Stern was said to have been 'murdered by natives in the Balunda district' in 1911, but was reported six months later to be alive and well and living in the Mwinilunga district. Another remote mine store owner was Robert Glasstone, a Scots Jew, who ran the store at the Sable Antelope mine in the Mumbwa district, and later at Kansanshi, before moving on to the Congo where he and his family remained for many years.[36]

A number of Jews were also active on the cattle trail from Sukumaland in central Tanganyika to Salisbury which passed through Fife (Mwenzo), Kasama, Mpika and Mkushi crossing the Zambezi at Feira (Luangwa), its confluence with the Luangwa. Feira was a busy place with two hotels and a billiards saloon at the height of the cattle boom. Ludwig Deuss and Gustav Rabinek were both involved in this trade. One of Rabinek's agents, an English-speaking Asian called Naicker, reached the Kafue–Zambezi confluence with cattle from the Mambwe people on the Tanganyika border in 1900. Deuss had a store at Feira by 1903, and was operating a free ferry across the Zambezi in 1907. He had also established branches at Mpika and Fort Jameson (Chipata) which may also have been involved with the cattle trade. His career in Northern Rhodesia seems to have ended with the First World War when, as a German citizen, he would have been regarded as an enemy alien. An account from 1904 describes the plight of one Goldschmeidt (sic), an Austrian Jew, who was encountered on the North-Eastern Rhodesia/ Tanganyika border at Fife (Mwenzo) with 200 very sickly cattle. He had been on the trail for three months and it would take him a further three months to reach Salisbury.[37]

The main focus of Jewish traders was, however, Barotseland. The early cattle traders who play the major part in this story are two enterprising brothers, Elie and Harry Susman. They are remarkable not only for their role as pioneers of the cattle trade, but for their long-term commitment to trade, agriculture and industry in the country, as well as for their significant contribution to the development of the economies of Southern Rhodesia and South Africa. It is to an account of their early years in Barotseland that we now turn.

CHAPTER 2

The Susman Saga: the Early Years, 1901–30

Harry (short for Harris) Susman was born in 1876 in the *shtetl* of Riteve in what is now Lithuania. His brother, Elie, was born there four years later. They were among the five surviving children of Behr and Taube Susmanovitch. Their father was a restless soul who, according to family legend, left Riteve at least four times. A period in America in the 1880s was not a success. He was strictly orthodox and was unable to come to terms with the modern world as he saw it in the United States. He set off again for Africa in company with two friends, Marcus Grill and Isaac Levine. They could not leave the Russian empire legally, and had to bribe the border guards to let them cross. The guards fired on them and one of their companions was killed. On arrival in South Africa, they worked their way from Cape Town to Johannesburg and reached Bulawayo by 1896. Their arrival coincided with a depression which was caused by the impact of the rinderpest epidemic. Behr Susmanovitch was employed for a while on a poor relief scheme which involved the laying out of a public park. His piety was sufficient to persuade a British South Africa Company official to release him from work on the Sabbath – to the apparent annoyance of other workers. He did not, however, stay long in Southern Rhodesia. He returned to Riteve, where his wife kept an inn, but he encouraged his elder sons to try their luck in Southern Africa, where his companions, Marcus Grill and Isaac Levine, remained.[1]

They set off for South Africa soon after his return to Lithuania in 1896, though they appear not to have travelled together. According to one account, they arrived at Cape Town with a few shillings between them, and peddled goods around the Boland. This might explain Harry Susman's apparent fluency in Afrikaans which is said to be closer to Yiddish than to English. They eventually made their way up to Bulawayo where they sold ginger beer on the railway station platform soon after the arrival of the first trains in 1897. It was in Francistown, in Bechuanaland, that Elie Susman first became involved in the cattle trade. Among his friends and partners there was Max Sonnenberg who was in business in Francistown and Bulawayo on behalf of his uncle's firm, C. Solomon and Co. of Vryburg. Sonnenberg noted in his memoirs that the major source of beef for Bulawayo in the early years of the century was from north of the Zambezi. The Susmans were almost certainly among his suppliers and it may have been with his encouragement that they went north.[2]

The Barotseland Trading Expedition

The Susman brothers set off from their base at Plumtree, on the Southern Rhodesian side of the border with Bechuanaland, early in 1901. Elie described their venture in a will which he wrote in July 1902 as 'the Barotseland trading expedition'. According to their nephew Maurice Gersh's acccount, they did not have the £100 capital required to pay for a wagon and oxen, and were compelled to hire one. They travelled by the Old Hunters' Road through Wankie (Hwange) and crossed the Zambezi in April 1901 at the drift at its confluence with the Chobe river at Kazangula. This is still the crossing point for road traffic entering Zambia from Botswana.[3] According to a somewhat embroidered account, based on an interview with Harry Susman, there were eight wagons in the expedition, and a number of other traders in the party, of whom only Joseph Finkelstein and Wolf Levin reached Barotseland. When they reached Kazangula, they were not much more than halfway to their destination, as King Lewanika's capital, Lealui, on the Zambezi flood plain, lay more than 250 miles further north. They still faced an arduous boat journey, with porterage around the rapids at Sioma, to Lealui.[4]

The earliest documentary evidence of their presence north of the Zambezi, and the only evidence of the success of their first expedition, is a letter from Frank Sykes, the District Commissioner at the Victoria Falls, to Elie Susman which is dated 4 October 1901. In the letter Sykes indicated that he had detained 135 cattle which Susman's 'boy' wanted to ferry across the Zambezi, probably at the Old Drift, a few miles above the Falls. He pointed out that Susman needed a licence to trade in North-Western Rhodesia, and suggested that he return to see Coryndon who would be at the Falls in a few days' time. He presumably did return because trading and gun licences are stamped on the back of the letter and dated 11 October 1901.[5]

The brothers returned for a second trading expedition in 1902. It was on this expedition that Elie Susman became desperately ill with blackwater fever at Nalolo and wrote a will, dated 28 July, which is the earliest surviving document to have been signed by either of the brothers. It is a unique contemporary source and sheds a little light on their financial circumstances. It was written in English in an almost indecipherable scrawl and was witnessed by A. B. Diamond, whose career has already been outlined, and by N. M. Human, who was a trader in Barotseland for many years. Elie appointed as his executors his brother Harry and David Landau, a partner in the firm of Landau Brothers in Bulawayo. His role as an executor suggests that the firm may have been backers of the Susmans' early ventures. Elie listed his assets as a two-thirds share in the capital and profits of the 'Barotseland trading expedition', and a two-thirds share in the capital, with profits already amounting to £150, of a Francistown business venture. Elie left half his property to Harry, and the other half to his father, mother, younger brother and sisters, then in Lithuania. Elie, though younger than Harry – he was only twenty-one when he crossed the Zambezi for the first time – was the major partner in the Barotseland venture.[6]

They clearly regarded their first two trips to Barotseland as 'expeditions' and did not initially contemplate settlement or the establishment of a permanent business. Elie was naturalised as a British subject in Southern Rhodesia in April 1903 and negotiated in the same year to take a partnership in a hotel and store at Sebakwe in the Gwelo (Gweru) district. This project would have involved him in the full-time management of the business, and in the investment of £5,000, but it seems to have fallen through.[7] In July 1904 he negotiated successfully for the purchase for about £1,500 of the buildings and stock of Robert Gordon's store at 'Sheake', presumably Sesheke. Also known as Mwaandi, this was forty miles east of modern Sesheke and thirty miles west of Kazangula.[8] Percy Clark rather ruefully recalled in 1936 that he had agreed to buy the same store in 1903, probably from Lesser, the original partner of Gordon and Levitz, who was anxious to leave the country for the sake of his health. Clark had agreed to pay for the store from the proceeds of future sales, but left after a few days:

> when another Jew came along, and I was told that this second fellow was to help me in running the store. No such assistance was needed and I became indignant. I told the owner that I was not going to be watched and he could go and eat coke. Then I walked out. The storekeeper departed a day or two after that, and the second Jew was left in charge. Perhaps I needn't say that every bob he took while running things was a prisoner. Much later the same store was taken over by two brothers of the same persuasion. Today these two men are about the richest in Northern Rhodesia.[9]

The two men to whom he referred were, of course, the Susman brothers. From this time onwards they were permanently settled north of the Zambezi.

Lewanika's Kingdom

At this time the colonial administration was barely established, consisting of little more than Robert Coryndon, the BSA Company's Resident, who was based at Mongu, Colin Harding, who commanded the Barotseland Mounted Police, and Frank Sykes, the District Commissioner at the Victoria Falls. Traders entering Barotseland may have required licences from the British South Africa Company, but they also required King Lewanika's permission to enter his kingdom and to establish stores. The rather curious licence issued by the BSA Company to Elie Susman for the Sesheke store in January

1906 cost the substantial fee of £10 and either entitled, or committed, him to keep in stock £200 of 'whitemen's provisions' and further provisions for the African trade. In September of the same year Elie Susman secured from Prince Litia, King Lewanika's eldest son and heir, a letter which gave the king's consent to the Susmans' occupation of the Sesheke store site.[10]

Cattle trading in Barotseland at this time was an intensely political activity. Cattle ownership was very uneven in a society where the king, his family and the aristocracy owned most of the livestock and, indeed, many of the people, as slavery was not legally abolished until 1906. Large herds were held at royal cattle posts in different parts of the country. Many cattle were lent to commoners by the king under the system known as *mafisa* which regulated their use. Cattle lending was a method used by the king to cement political alliances. He had used it to extend his influence in the southern part of the country, which had been affected by rinderpest, and where cattle stocks had been seriously depleted. In this political context, good relations with the king and the queen, the Mulena Mukwae, who had her own capital at Nalolo, were essential to successful trading. Many cattle were bought directly from the dual monarchs – they were brother and sister, not husband and wife – and their courtiers. King Lewanika was himself a major participant in the cattle trade. John Smith, a veterinary officer employed by the BSA Company, estimated the royal cattle herds on the Barotse Central Plain alone in 1913 at 15,000 head. According to J. B. Thornhill, Lewanika had offered to sell 4,000 cattle, which he had been forced to withdraw from Angola after the declaration of the new boundary in 1905, to George Grey of Tanganyika Concessions, which was opening mines in Katanga, for £8,000.[11]

In these early years the Susmans had to spend many months at Lealui and Nalolo. They are said to have established cordial relations with King Lewanika. The relationship may have been fostered by their role in organising the construction and importation of a mule-drawn cab, or 'growler', which had reached Barotseland by 1904. King Lewanika had paid a visit to London in 1902 to attend the coronation of King Edward VII, and was very impressed by what he saw. He returned with the full-dress uniform of a British admiral, given to him by King Edward, with Liberty print dresses for the ladies of his court, and with a desire to own a vehicle of the kind which he had seen on the streets of London. The cab was made to Elie Susman's specifications, including liberal applications of gilt paint, by coach builders in Bulawayo. It was paddled up the Zambezi on canoes and barges from Kazangula to Lealui. King Lewanika's confidence in the Susmans may have been reinforced by the financial loss which he incurred at this time when he entrusted about £700 to the African Methodist Episcopal Church missionary, Willie Mokalapa, and asked him to import wagons, boats, carriages, and a scotch cart.[12]

The Susmans also forged at this time important and lasting links with King Lewanika's successors. They had close business ties with his heir, Prince Litia, who had been in charge of the royal headquarters at Sesheke since the early 1890s. Elie Susman lived at Sesheke for five years from 1904 to 1909, and was in frequent contact with him. Litia had a few years' education at a Paris mission school and had some modern hobbies, including photography and motor cycles. He succeeded his father in 1916 and took the title of Yeta III. He was replaced as chief at Sesheke by his younger brother, Imwiko, who also had close ties with the Susmans. Imwiko succeeded Litia, who had been incapacitated by a stroke, as Litunga in 1944 and died in 1948. His successor, who took the title Mwanawina III, was yet another son of King Lewanika. The Susmans also had close business dealings with Mukwae Akananisa, known to whites as the Little Mukwae, a junior queen who had her own headquarters at Sesheke. King Lewanika's grandson, Akashambatwa Mbikusita-Lewanika, has no doubt that the Susmans' ties with the royal family were of profound importance to their commercial success. He also maintains that King Lewanika was very selective as to the traders whom he favoured. It is, perhaps, not too fanciful to suggest that the Susmans fulfilled for King Lewanika, and his successors, a role which was similar to that of the 'Court Jews' who were so important in the principalities of Germany in the eighteenth century. The usefulness of the Susmans, and of some other Jewish traders, to the Lewanikas lay in their role as impartial middlemen. They were not necessarily identified as Jews, but as white men who, as traders, were neither colonial officials nor missionaries.[13]

Hazards

There were many risks involved in the Barotseland cattle trade. Tsetse fly belts intersected some of the trails, and cattle could most safely be driven through them at night, and in the cold season. Cattle herds were sometimes stampeded by marauding lions. Cattle crossing the Zambezi had to be lashed to barges and were liable to attack by crocodiles. Stock lost weight and condition on journeys lasting months, and some deaths were inevitable. As time went on, cattle driving became less of an adventure and more a matter of routine. George Sterling, a Jewish native of Vilna, who had served in the United States army in the suppression of the Boxer Rising in China, later recalled his experience of the cattle trails. He had accompanied A. B. Diamond on his first journey to the Congo in 1909, and was employed by the Susmans for several years before the First World War as the supervisor of cattle 'mobs' on the trail from Barotseland along the Angolan border to Elisabethville. They had African herdsmen who knew their job, and a number of gunmen to guard the cattle in case of attack by wild animals such as lions, leopards and wild dogs. He remembered cattle driving as a well-organised business. A great deal of attention was paid to the comfort of the supervisors. He recalled that 'we carried enough food for all', and, 'as for myself I was provided with a small portable tent, camp stretcher, iron rations, tin milk, oatmeal etc', as well as a personal cook and assistant.[14]

The greatest danger to the traders in the early years was malaria and subsequent blackwater fever. As we have already seen, Elie Susman was seriously ill with fever at the end of his first expedition in October 1901, and was desperately ill at Nalolo, the capital of the Mulena Mukwae, in July 1902. His life may have been saved on that occasion by a detailed prescription for the treatment of the disease which was sent from Mongu by the Resident Commissioner, Robert Coryndon, himself. He not only sent instructions on treatment, but also provided medicines and a bottle of champagne which was then thought to be essential to recovery from this killer disease. Coryndon's generous intervention was, perhaps, an indication that the Susmans had already established their bona fides in the eyes of a colonial administration which was inclined both to social snobbery and to anti-Semitic prejudice.[15] On one of these occasions, King Lewanika is also said to have intervened to save Elie Susman's life, providing a boat, paddlers and carriers to ensure his speedy evacuation to the south. Harry Susman attributed his recovery from a serious attack of blackwater fever in the Gwaai river marshes, 150 miles south of the Zambezi, to the action of his headman in building a hut around him where he lay, and forcing him to sweat out the fever through drinking gallons of millet beer. It was widely believed at this time that it was fatal to move a person who was suffering from blackwater fever.[16]

Lobengula's Treasure

The Susmans would not have been in Northern Rhodesia if they were not risk-takers, but not all their gambles came off. It was Harry who fell for one of the first of a long line of confidence tricksters to try their luck in Zambia. Harry, a small man of great strength, was the more physical of the two brothers. He was said to be capable of tossing 200-pound bags of maize, and of wrestling recalcitrant oxen to the ground. He was never able to write in English, but kept notes of his transactions in Yiddish. He had a remarkable memory and was able to recall every detail of a day's cattle sales. He was a generous and much-loved person, but he could be gullible. In 1908, when he was based at Lealui, he joined with a number of German and Afrikaner speculators in sponsoring an expedition to search for the treasure of the Ndebele king, Lobengula, which was said to have been hidden in Angola. The expedition had the support of King Lewanika, who provided an armed escort. It was guided by John Jacobs (also known as Witbooi), who either was, or claimed to be, Lobengula's former secretary. The treasure was alleged to consist of thirteen wagon-loads of gold, ivory and precious stones. Harry provided oxen and wagons and personally participated in a three-month trek which took the party into Angola beyond the Chavuma Falls – about 200 miles north of Lealui. The expedition not only encountered cannibals, but one of the last of the Ovimbundu slave-trading caravans.[17]

Harry eventually returned empty-handed, out of pocket to the tune of

£500, and without wagons or oxen. He was always inclined to be hot-tempered, and flogged his misleading informant. He was fined £10 by the magistrate at Mongu for the offence, but Jacobs was deported from the Rhodesias. He returned to Northern Rhodesia on another attempt in 1916 with Bishop S. J. Brander, the leader of an African independent church, the Ethiopian Church in Zion, and Samuel Glass, a Jewish adventurer. Harry Susman was able to ensure that Jacobs did not on this occasion travel beyond Livingstone.[18]

Success

By most accounts, the astute financial brain behind the success of the brothers' enterprise belonged to Elie Susman. It was only in 1907 that the title 'Susman Brothers' replaced 'E. Susman' on the firm's letterhead. The difference between the brothers was neatly encapsulated in an anecdote which asserted that, as their parents had been too poor to send both brothers to school, they had to toss a coin to decide who would go – and Elie won. They had established permanent trading stores by 1908 at Lealui and Nalolo, as well as at Sesheke. By that time they were sufficiently well-established for Elie to write a complaint to the *Livingstone Mail* about unfair competition from under-capitalised hawkers who did not have to bear the expense of permanent buildings.[19] Their activities then included, as their letterheads and advertisements indicated, cattle trading, grain dealing, curio selling and trans-port contracting. Of these, cattle trading was clearly the most important.

From an unbroken sequence of balance sheets which survive from 1907 to 1912, it is possible to get some idea of the nature, development and scale of their activities.[20] Between June 1907 and May 1912, the capital employed in their business grew from £6,000 to £33,000, and their assets grew from £10,000 to £60,000. From their accounts for these years it is possible to get some idea of how their business was financed. In May 1912 they owed over £20,000 to suppliers in bills of exchange and on open accounts. Their major creditors were the Matabeleland Trading Association, Landau Brothers, Meikle Brothers, I. Pieters and C. Salomon, all of Bulawayo, to whom they owed over £2,000 in each case. They also owed smaller sums to Mosenthals, and to Dunell, Ebden of Port Elizabeth, and to W. Bolus of London. The latter firm was an importer of ivory, hippo strips and skins. Their only debt to a bank was of about £2,000 to the Standard Bank in Livingstone. Among their major debtors were King Lewanika, Prince Litia and the Lozi Queen, the Mulena Mukwae, who owed over £1,000 between them. They were also owed a significant sum by A. B. Diamond who had recently set up in business as a butcher in the newly established township of Elisabethville in the Congo.

Between 1907 and 1912 they had reinvested profits and accumulated capital at an average rate of £5,000 a year. The proportion of their assets tied up in cattle, which had been as high as two-thirds in 1907, had tended to decline, while they had diversified their trading activities with the purchase of the Pioneer butchery, bakery and general dealer's business in Livingstone. Farming and ranching were beginning to emerge as activities in their own right, and were not merely incidental to cattle trading. In addition to farms at the Gwaai river and at Kalomo, they were negotiating in 1912 for the acquisition of the 25,000-acre Leopard's Hill Ranch near Lusaka. They paid very little for the land, but the grant was made on the understanding that they would spend substantial sums on its development.

The Susmans had clearly accumulated capital rapidly from the profits of their first ventures. Cattle in Barotseland were, owing to their distance from the main markets, relatively cheap. Prices in 1908 were estimated at an average of £3–£4 for the cattle in a 'mob' with a range from 30 shillings for young stock to £6 for an exceptional beast. Prices were clearly much lower than they had been in the boom years at the turn of the century. They were roughly the same in 1912 as in 1908, and compared with the average price of £5 a head which was obtained for cattle from Bechuanaland which were sold in Johannesburg in the same year.[21] It has, of course, to be remembered that the prices paid by traders were not as high as they seemed. They usually bought cattle in exchange for goods, and the prices included a substantial profit margin. If they did not buy for goods, they often bought for cash which was then spent in their own stores. The situation was nicely summarised by the trader who responded to a question from John Smith as to whether the bullocks which he was buying for £5 a head in 1914 were cheap: 'No, they're damn [sic] dear, but then so are my blankets!'[22]

The secret of the Susmans' success lay in controlling the costs, and stock losses, involved in getting cattle to market over very long distances. A factor in this success may have been the establishment of holding camps where cattle could be rested and fattened on route. J. B. Thornhill has left a vivid description of life at a cattle camp on the Gwaai river marshes where he spent six weeks early in 1909 preparing a herd of nearly 1,500 cattle for a sale. He was working for the Hepkers, and not for the Susmans who also had a base there, but his description must be representative of the scene at a place where they also had a camp. The place played an important role in the Barotseland cattle trade, with buyers coming up regularly on the Zambezi Express from Bulawayo. He found the cattle in poor condition when he took over their management, and was pleased by the improvement which, with care and attention to detail, he was able to achieve.[23]

It seems improbable that the Susmans would have been able to develop the rapport that they did with King Lewanika, or to have established such a dominant position in Barotseland trade, if they had not been regarded as fair traders. They were also on very good terms with the French missionaries of the Paris mission, who would not have taken kindly to unscrupulous businessmen. Their business was regarded by officials from as early as 1908 as the best financed and supplied in the area.[24] Their early stock in trade consisted of cloth, beads, blankets and salt. They prided themselves on their refusal to sell either guns or alcohol. This was a policy which was followed by their business throughout its history. Exports from Barotseland to the south of up to 10,000 cattle a year, in the years before the First World War, indicate that the prices offered were sufficient to encourage significant sales from cattle stocks which are unlikely to have exceeded 350,000. Encouragement to part with stock was given by the introduction of hut tax by the colonial government from 1906. Barotseland's probable annual income from cattle sales of about £30,000 in the years to 1912 was greater than the total revenue collected in the area. Information on the scale of the trade is hard to obtain. In 1911 and 1912 cattle exports were estimated at about 8,000 head, and 10,000 head, respectively.[25] It seems probable that at least half of these exports were in the Susmans' hands.

It was in 1912 – a year which marks the first peak in the expansion of their business – that the Susmans, who had been sending cattle up to the Congo for a year or two, established themselves in Elisabethville through the purchase of the butchery of Adolph Ullman, also known as 'Tambalika'. He had entered North-Eastern Rhodesia in 1900 from the east and had been involved in the transport of mining machinery to the Congo for the Tanganyika Concessions Company. He had also kept a store at Kapopo's, where the wagon route to the Congo from Broken Hill crossed the Kafue river at a point just north of the Lukanga Swamps, in the years before the extension of the railway. He had also been involved in the rubber and ivory trades and had brought in a number of his brothers and cousins. He had reached Elisabethville by 1909 and was a founder member of the Hebrew Congregation there. The Susmans' move into retail trade in the Congo was not a success as competition in the butchery business there was exceptionally fierce. There were at least five butcheries there in 1911, two of which, A. B. Diamond's and Ullman's, had been founded by people who brought their first stock up from Northern Rhodesia. A third butchery, which was to become the dominant one, was founded by Barnett 'Bongola' Smith who had arrived from Southern Rhodesia in the previous year, and who was, as we shall see, to play an important part in the post-war development of the Susmans' business.[26]

It was also in 1912 that the Susmans began to forge new links with Bechuanaland. A letter written on 23 October 1912 to Elie Susman by Captain H. P. Eason, the acting Resident Magistrate at Kazangula, on the Bechuanaland side of the Zambezi, sanctioned the opening of trading links between the Susmans and C. Riley of Maun, Ngamiland. This letter marked the beginning of a relationship between the Susmans and the Rileys of Maun which was to last for fifty years. It was a relationship which was soon to assume great importance for the Susmans and to offer their business a lifeline in the greatest crisis which it had yet faced.[27]

Disaster

The *Livingstone Mail* reported on 28 December 1912 the imposition of a ban on the import of cattle from Sesheke to Livingstone except in the cold season and for slaughter. The report referred to the need to prevent the spread of 'Sesheke sickness' to the Batoka plateau. This may be a reference to an outbreak of anthrax, or to a fly-borne disease, which killed thousands of cattle and marked the beginning of the end of the Barotseland 'beef bonanza'. It was followed in 1915 by an outbreak of bovine pleuro-pneumonia, commonly known as 'PP' or the 'snot-sickte', which caused further devastation to Barotseland cattle stocks and resulted eventually in the end of the export trade to the south.

The Susmans are said to have been indirectly involved in the outbreak of the latter disease. Harry Susman recalled that they had sold a large number of wagons with trained oxen teams to King Lewanika. He sold some of these to the Anglo-Portuguese Boundary Commission which had come to survey the country's western border with Angola. The commission took these teams into Angola and, ignoring a ban on the import of cattle from the west, brought diseased animals back into the country in November 1914. According to John Smith, the real blame for the outbreak lay with a District Officer who mistakenly granted a permit for the cattle to be brought back into the country from Angola. Whatever the facts of the case, Harry Susman evidently appreciated the irony of a big sale which had the unintended effect of undermining the foundations of a profitable business.[28]

There does not, unfortunately, appear to be any contemporary documentary evidence for the impact of this crisis on the Susmans' business. There is a gap between 1912 and 1915 in the sequence of balance sheets which provide some information on its earlier growth. We do know that the capital employed in the Susmans' business was reduced between May 1912 and December 1914 from £33,000 to £18,000. This suggests that the brothers sustained losses in the years 1913 and 1914 amounting to £15,000 or almost half of their total capital. John Smith's letters indicate that the Barotseland cattle trade was already severely depressed, as was the economy of the Rhodesias in general, before the outbreak of 'PP' in April 1915. He told his parents in February 1915 that:

> The outlook for our market in cattle is rapidly getting worse. Yesterday, movements of cattle were stopped from Northern Rhodesia to the south, whilst the Congo market is almost non-existent, as most of the Belgians have left to go back to Europe, and those remaining are almost bankrupt. So the outlook for our traders is grim.[29]

The new disease broke out at a time when the traders had brought their stocks of trade goods up to Barotseland, and had begun to purchase cattle in anticipation of the opening of trade with the area which came to be

known colloquially as the Line of Rail on 1 May. Some traders sought to cut
their losses by driving their herds, including sick animals, towards Senkobo,
a halt on the Line of Rail a few miles north of Livingstone, thus spreading
the disease into the Southern Province. 'PP' was only driven back and
confined to Barotseland by a ruthless policy of slaughter which was carried
out along the cattle trails and supervised by Smith. Thousands of cattle were
killed without compensation, and very heavy fines were imposed on traders
who broke the stringent regulations which were imposed. It is perhaps a
tribute to the good sense of both parties that, in spite of his role at this
time, Smith and the Susmans became life-long friends. They apparently
appreciated that his actions, which helped to bring them to the verge of
bankruptcy, also had the effect of stopping the disease from becoming
endemic along the Line of Rail, and of safeguarding their ranching interests.
Smith was certainly conscious of the traders' predicament. He wrote to his
parents on 16 May 1915:

> The traders whose cattle have been stopped are in a bad way, and I feel very
> sorry for them. They buy all their supplies 'on tick' and depend on selling their
> cattle as soon as they arrive down south to pay these bills. Now, the cattle are
> stopped and many may die, so there will be no funds to meet these com-
> mitments.[30]

Elie Susman recalled that they struggled to keep themselves afloat at this
time by the export of the hides of dead cattle. They encouraged people to
bring them to the river banks in both Barotseland, and the Ila country,
where they were bought for a few shillings and exported by boat. Robert
'Katembora' Sutherland, who arrived in the area in 1914, recalled that 'at the
height of the epidemic the country reeked of dying cattle. Boats and barges
that had once been piled high with merchandise went hurrying down the
river piled high with hides.' Sam Haslett told his fellow Scot, Sutherland, that
he had been camped at this time at the Machile river with 600 apparently
healthy cattle. Harry Susman came along and offered him a price for the lot.
He took it and heard the next day that disease had broken out in the herd.
'By evening they were all dead.' Harry Susman's gamble, if Haslett's story is
to be believed, may have contributed to the near collapse of their business.
    It is not clear whether formal bankruptcy proceedings were instituted, but
family tradition recalls that the brothers were summoned to a meeting of the
Bulawayo merchants who were their major suppliers and creditors. Elie
Susman recalled that the meeting was going badly for them when Tom Meikle,
one of their principal creditors and a major buyer of Barotseland cattle for
his Shangani River ranches, walked into the room. He said indignantly: 'You
can't break these boys. They're workers. They must have another chance.
They'll come out on top if they get another chance.' He backed up his
words with a substantial unsecured cash loan. This practical demonstration
of support, and his advocacy with the other creditors, saved the brothers

from bankruptcy.[31] A number of other Barotseland traders, including George Findlay and Gabriel Epstein, were bankrupted at this time. There seems to have been an affinity between Scots and Jews on the frontier. This may have stemmed from their shared interest in the Bible, and the similarities between the Jewish and the Protestant work ethics, as well as from the similarities in their ethnic stereotypes. Meikle, who built up one of Southern Rhodesia's biggest businesses, including Salisbury's most famous hotel, had provided a room in his Bulawayo store for some of the first Jewish religious services which were held in the region in 1895.[32]

Recovery

In spite of the severity of the crisis, recovery seems to have been quite rapid. The balance sheets show a surprising profit of £600 for the first six months of 1915, though the full impact of the crisis may only have been reflected later, and of over £5,000 for the period from January 1915 to April 1916. It is a little difficult to square this apparent level of profit with bankruptcy, though it may have been insufficient to enable the brothers to meet their outstanding obligations. Recovery coincided with a general upturn in the Rhodesian economy. Expenditure on the war effort in East Africa led to a new buoyancy in the economy, though it was accompanied by the onset of a new phenomenon – inflation. It was not until 1918, when the profits of the firm were over £6,500, that the capital employed in the business returned, at least on paper, to the level of 1912. If allowance is made for the impact of inflation, it was not until several years after the end of the war that recovery was complete.

The brothers had clearly responded to the crisis with the resourcefulness and speed which must explain their long-term success. The base of their business remained in Livingstone where they continued to live, but they turned their attention back to their trading roots in Bechuanaland. Within a year or two of the partial closure of Barotseland, and the subsequent closure of their southern export markets, they had entered into a partnership with the Rileys of Maun. They initiated a joint venture under the name of Susman Brothers and Riley, and opened branches at Maun, Tsau and Gumaree (Gomare) in Ngamiland. They employed several European managers, and an army of African cattle buyers, and developed cattle trails from Maun and the Okavango area to Kazangula. Their trails soon extended from Maun as far as Ghanzi on the western boundary of Bechuanaland with South West Africa. This was over 400 miles in a straight line from Livingstone and about 1,000 miles from Elisabethville. Cattle imports into Northern Rhodesia from Ngamiland were periodically stopped on veterinary grounds, but the development of this source did mark a significant diversification of their business. Harry Susman played a major role in the development of the Ngamiland trade. He acquired a remarkable knowledge of the complex geography of the region and became an important source of information for explorers of the area. Among those whom he introduced to Ngamiland and the Kalahari was Laurens van der Post, the man who first put the area on the literary map.

Cattle could still be driven north from Barotseland to the Congo and to the Angolan diamond fields. Harry Susman is himself said to have been involved in driving 2,000 head of cattle through Angola to the Congo in 1913, and to have encountered serious problems with the Portuguese authorities in the process.[33] But the opening of the railway to Elisabethville soon made the long drive to the Congo unnecessary. The real problems for the Susmans were the depletion of Barotseland cattle stocks, restrictions on movements of cattle within Northern Rhodesia and the closure of the Southern Rhodesian market. Cattle movements from Barotseland to the Line of Rail were briefly resumed at the end of the war, but there was a complete ban from 1921 onwards after an outbreak in the Livingstone area. This was stamped out after a further mass slaughter and the area was restocked from Ngamiland. In 1921–22 a 500-mile cordon fence was constructed to make possible the exclusion of Barotseland cattle from the rest of the country.[34]

The decline of the Barotseland cattle trade, and the drastic depletion of Lozi cattle herds which were reduced by at least two-thirds, had devastating effects on the economy of the area. By 1915–16 there was a dramatic decrease in the levels of revenue from taxation. People who had previously paid tax through cattle sales were forced to liquidate their gold reserves and were driven on to the labour market. The Rhodesian Native Labour Bureau had been active in the area since before the outbreak of the First World War, but it was only during the war that recruitment levels became very high. Many men were forced to go south to the farms and mines of Southern Rhodesia. The Wankie Colliery, which was less than a hundred miles south of the Zambezi, was the most important single destination for migrants from North-Western Rhodesia. Labour migration caused great hardship to the men, and some women, who were forced to walk long distances to work for low wages in often dangerous conditions, and to endure long periods of separation from their homes and families. Fees paid for the recruitment of labour, and sales made to returning labour migrants, were to be the mainstay of Barotseland trade until the 1960s.[35]

Diversification

The Susmans had begun to diversify their activities before the crisis of 1913–16. They were already in the process of developing new markets and new sources of cattle before the crisis broke. They had also begun to convert some of the profits which they had obtained from trade into farming assets. This process continued during the war with the development of Kabulonga farm and the Leopard's Hill ranch near Lusaka. Their intention was clearly to develop sources of cattle within the newly unified country of Northern

Rhodesia, but outside of Barotseland. What they later termed 'local' as opposed to Barotseland supplies were to be increasingly important for the Congo trade in the early 1920s, and for the Northern Rhodesian Copperbelt when it began to be developed in the later 1920s.[36]

In a strategy which was clearly intended to provide yet another source of cattle, they established at the end of the First World War a 50,000-acre ranch in the Plumtree (Bulalima-Mangwe) district of Southern Rhodesia. This was in addition to the 8,000 acres which they continued to use as cattle holding grounds at the Gwaai river. The Brunapeg ranch, named after Elie's daughters, was close to the border with Bechuanaland and was stocked from there. By the early 1920s they had access to half a dozen different sources of cattle: Barotseland (though only for trade with Angola), Ngamiland, the Ila cattle country in the Namwala district, farms and ranches on the Line of Rail within Northern Rhodesia, as well as the Plumtree ranch which could draw from central and southern Bechuanaland. These varied sources provided them with some insurance against the vagaries of the Southern African cattle trade.

Elie Susman's Diary

An idea of the new post-war diversity in their operations can be obtained from a unique source. This is the diary which Elie Susman kept for most of a single year – 1920. It is not an introspective diary, though it does shed a little light on his personality and family relationships. It is, for the most part, the diary of a highly successful businessman at the height of his powers. It provides a record of his continuous movements along the Line of Rail between Cape Town in the south and Elisabethville in the north. He was away from home for at least four months of the year with two lengthy business trips to Elisabethville, two week-long visits to the Lusaka farms, two stays in Bulawayo, a ten-day trip up the Zambezi to Sesheke, and a three-week journey to Cape Town.[37]

References to travel by motor car, and even by aeroplane, show that the Wild West days were coming to an end. Rail travel was, however, not without incident. There were numerous derailments on one trip from Livingstone to Elisabethville which took five days. Elie expressed real concern at the terrible suffering of the cattle on this trip. They were kept without food and water for five days and some were killed by the overturning of a truck. His return from the Congo on his first trip was delayed by a long strike of railway workers – prompted by white South African railwaymen who suffered at this time from the withdrawal of the British pound from circulation, and from payment in devalued Belgian francs. It is, nevertheless, the ease and speed of travel which is most impressive. The diary demonstrates the way in which the extension of the railway had within a few years created an economic region. It is only when he makes a side trip to Sesheke that we are back for a moment in the pre-war era. The journey begins with a fast drive by car to Katembora, but this is followed by three days in a boat with nine paddlers struggling against the current to Sesheke. The travel event of the year was his first twenty-minute flight over the Victoria Falls on 21 July. He had witnessed the arrival in Livingstone of the first aircraft to reach Northern Rhodesia – a Vickers Vimy which was flown from London to Cape Town by Pierre van Ryneveld – a few months earlier on 5 March. He described his flight as 'the event in my life ... It was beautiful and very exciting. I really cannot describe the sensation. The Falls was a sight for the Gods.'

In the course of the year he attended cattle sales along the Line of Rail at Kalomo, Monze, Pemba, Mazabuka, Kafue and Lusaka. He was continuously buying and selling cattle and making arrangements for their movement. On his two trips south to Bulawayo he arranged purchases of stock for the Barotseland stores at Sesheke and Kanyonyo. On his trip to Cape Town he stopped over at Mafeking and had consultations there with the elder of the Rileys who had brought down 600 head of cattle, in which the Susmans had an interest, from Ngamiland for sale to Johannesburg. This was at a time when cattle movements from Ngamiland into Northern Rhodesia were temporarily stopped. He made regular visits to the farms and ranches at Sinda, near Livingstone, at Kabulonga and Leopard's Hill near Lusaka, as well as at Gwaai river, where the manager, J. A. Chalmers, was producing half a ton of butter a month. Elie was organising at this time the concentration of cattle holdings at Leopard's Hill, bringing in cattle from Lochinvar, Monze and Kalomo. He noted that there had been heavy losses at Leopard's Hill during the year and hoped that the replacement of the manager would have beneficial results. He did not visit the Brunapeg ranch at Plumtree during the year, but noted that an outbreak of East Coast Fever at Figtree would delay the stocking of this new acquisition.

'Bongola' Smith and the Congo Cattle Trade

Elie's major commercial preoccupation in 1920 was with the Congo cattle trade. On his two trips to Elisabethville, he was engaged in negotiations with Barnett 'Bongola' Smith, the dominant figure in this business. The Susmans and Bongola must have had earlier dealings, but it was in 1920 that they entered a formal partnership with him for the supply of cattle from Northern Rhodesia and Ngamiland. Bongola was one of the great characters of the central African frontier, and appears to have made an indelible impression on all whom he met – especially on children. He was not tall, but was, like Harry Susman, reputed to be immensely strong, and of a volcanic temperament. According to one source, 'he was hard on others, but even harder on himself'. He was alleged to be unable to read or write in any language, but this handicap did not prevent him from becoming the most formidable player in the central African cattle trade. He was born at Riga, Latvia, in the early

1870s, and, as a teenager, followed his father to London, where he worked at first as a trouser presser in an East End sweatshop. He reached South Africa, with his wife and the first seven of his eight children, during the Anglo-Boer War. He probably acquired his nickname – *bongolo* is the Zulu word for donkey – as a result of his involvement in the sale of horses and donkeys to the British army at that time. He is said to have lost several fortunes in South Africa through unfortunate speculations – at least one of them in the ostrich feather business. He became an itinerant wagon trader (a *smous*) in the Cape and the Transvaal, with bases at various times in Middleburg, Frankfort and Krugersdorp. He reached Southern Rhodesia in 1909; his wife ran a restaurant in Salisbury while he moved north to Elisabethville in 1910. He must have trekked north, as he took mules and oxen to the Congo, and was involved in transport riding, before turning to the butchery business.[38]

He is said to have arrived in Elisabethville 'poor in money, but rich in energy and experience'. There were no indigenous cattle in Katanga, and his first great coup was the successful establishment by 1913 of a ranch, known as 'Weltevreden', on the Biano plateau, which is north of Kambove and Likasi, and high enough to be free of tsetse fly. His original breeding stock of a few hundred animals was selected from cattle arriving in Elisabethville from the south by rail for slaughter. He later bought the entire stock of the Lochinvar ranch, near Magoye, from Major Robert Gordon, and had the cattle driven up from Northern Rhodesia to the Congo. By 1918, or soon afterwards, he had 4,000 head of cattle on his ranch which was the largest herd in the country. He had established his wife, who was also a formidable personality, and some of his children in a corrugated-iron house on the ranch, while he concentrated on the expansion of his butcheries, dairies and numerous other enterprises in Elisabethville, Kambove and Likasi. His scotch cart, drawn by four mules, was a familiar sight in the new town of Elisabethville. He kept a small number of dairy cattle at his home in the centre of the town – his favourite and most productive cow, 'Morgenzon', was said to be given 'drinks' of eggs and whisky.

His initial capital was provided by the leading representative in Katanga of the Catholic Church, Monsignor de Hemptinne, a Benedictine monk who was Apostolic Prefect, and, later, Bishop of Katanga. The Benedictines also established a ranch, with Smith's help, and this rather improbable duo frequently travelled together by bicycle in the region of northern Katanga beyond the railhead. He also had the support of a senior government official, Gaston Heenen, who later became Governor of Katanga. Bongola did not apparently have much knowledge of French, but his fluency in Afrikaans must have enabled him to communicate with Flemish-speaking Belgians.

He bought farms in Northern Rhodesia, probably during the First World War, which he used as holding grounds for slaughter stock for the Congo market. When he applied for naturalisation as a British subject in Northern

Rhodesia in 1922 – it was quickly granted – he described himself rather
modestly as a Mazabuka farmer. In 1923–24, he drove several thousand
cattle by a circuitous, and tsetse fly-free route, from the Biano plateau to the
Kasai province to stock a ranch on a plateau there for Forminière, the
diamond mining company. He was thus largely responsible for the provision
of the first breeding stock, drawn from Lozi, Ila and Ngamiland sources, to
both of the Congo's southern provinces. He did a deal in 1925 with Belgian
banking interests as a result of which his varied businesses in the Congo,
and the two Rhodesias, were brought together, as we shall later see, in a
Brussels-based holding company known as Elakat.

The Susmans and Smith

Elie Susman's major deal in 1920 was the agreement to supply Smith with all
his cattle requirements. He had been cut off from his Southern Rhodesian
sources by the closure of Northern Rhodesia to cattle imports by rail from
the south. Negotiations went on between February and April, and involved
trips by Elie to Elisabethville and by Bongola to Livingstone. Smith also
employed a number of Scots managers and agents, including Robert Boyd
and Sam Haslett, as intermediaries. Elie's own representative in Elisabethville
was J. R. Rollnick, who had previously been a trader at Kalomo, Lusaka and
Broken Hill. Elie confided to his diary after talks with Smith and his son-
in-law, Abe Gelman, on 19 March: 'They are too greedy and want too much.'
He soon, however, agreed to a price which, with cattle weighing an average
of 400 pounds, worked out at about £10 per beast, payable in Livingstone.
Smith needed 800 cattle a month to meet his Belgian government and mining
company contracts, and the business was then worth nearly £100,000 a year.
The Susmans saw this as a joint venture and in May 1921 they had £14,000
invested in the enterprise. Profits in the previous year had come to nearly
£9,000 which was by far the largest single item in a gross profit on all
branches of the business of £24,000. The net profit for the year was estimated
at just over £4,000, but this was after allowing for expenditure on the
development of farms and ranches, including Leopard's Hill.[39]

Elie Susman's diary for 1920 refers to a number of farmers' meetings
which he attended in the course of the year. These usually coincided with
cattle sales. The major issue under discussion was whether or not to reopen
Northern Rhodesia for the transit of cattle to the Congo from Southern
Rhodesia. This was in theory a veterinary issue, but it is clear that at this
time the farmers had an overwhelming say. The country remained closed to
Southern Rhodesian cattle throughout the year. Elie Susman welcomed this
closure because it prevented Smith from bringing cattle in from the south,
and forced him to depend on supplies from Northern Rhodesia and, to a
lesser extent, Ngamiland.

It was impossible for the Northern Rhodesian farmers on the Line of

Rail to meet the demand from the Congo entirely from their own resources. They resolved in February to allow some movement of cattle from Barotse-land through Kalomo to the Congo. Outbreaks of 'PP' were still a matter of concern. At one point Elie was informed by a veterinary officer of fresh outbreaks of the disease in 'the valley' and expressed the hope that his stock had been moved in time. Towards the end of the year the farmers resolved to allow the importation of some cattle from Ngamiland. In October Elie arranged to bring in 1,000 head of cattle which had been delivered to Kazangula by Jim Riley of Maun. The Susmans were also involved in the Ila cattle trade from Namwala. They were in partnership there with Abraham Wacks, to whom they supplied bangles, probably of ivory, and cash, but it was clear that without imports from Ngamiland they would be unable to satisfy Bongola's requirements.

The Susmans' relationship with Bongola was profitable until 1922. In that year, the transit of cattle from Southern Rhodesia to the Congo was once again allowed and the demand for local and Ngamiland stock was greatly reduced. A severe depression hit the worldwide cattle trade and the Susman Brothers' business recorded a loss of over £1,000 for the year to 1923. There were substantial losses on Barotseland trade, especially at Kanyonyo, and the collapse of beef prices forced them to write down the value of the cattle stocks on their ranches. By the middle of the decade, they were back in profit. Resumed cattle exports from Ngamiland to the Congo, as well as exports from Barotseland to Angola, contributed to profits of over £12,000 in 1925 and of over £20,000 in 1926. Their profits were also helped by a number of joint ventures in which they participated from the early 1920s. These included the Zambezi River Transport Company, in which they co-operated with Robert Sutherland and W. Shelmerdine. They had a minority share in R. F. Sutherland Ltd, a trading company which was set up in 1924, and in the Mapanda Transport Company. They were also involved in a joint venture with George Buchanan in the export of cattle from Barotseland to the Angolan diamond fields. Buchanan personally drove cattle on this trail, taking as long as nine months for the journey on one occasion. Complications with the Portuguese authorities involved Elie in an adventurous drive by motor car into Angola in the mid-1920s.[40]

By 1925 Northern Rhodesia's cattle exports accounted for only a quarter of the Congo market, with Southern Rhodesia taking half. Ngamiland also kept a share of the market. This was very largely due, as the government of the Bechuanaland Protectorate later recognised, to the special relationship which existed between Bongola Smith and the Susmans. Maurice Gersh, who worked for his uncles in Livingstone from 1924, recalled the thousands of cattle which he shipped from Livingstone to Bongola in the 1920s.[41] By 1930 Northern Rhodesia and Bechuanaland had both been cut out of the Congo trade. Northern Rhodesian and Bechuanaland producers were protected for a little while by the new demand created by the construction boom on the

Copperbelt. This development, and the impact of the depression on the Susmans' business, will be considered in a later chapter.

Family Life

It is not easy to get an idea of the Susmans' social life in their bachelor days in Barotseland. An attractive glimpse of the brothers at ease is, however, provided by a paragraph in the *Livingstone Mail* which appeared under the heading 'Sesheke Notes', and was dated 1 February 1909:

> To-day being the anniversary of both H. and E. Susman's birthdays (they are 31 and 28 respectively) they invited all their friends to dinner, and as there are quite a number of traders passing through just now no less than fourteen sat down. After a most excellent repast the remainder of the evening was devoted to music. Songs were contributed by several of the guests, the gramophone filling in the intervals. Mr Levitz, on the flute, and Mr Epstein, on the violin, provided the instrumental portion of the programme, and quite a surprising amount of talent was brought to light. Toasts were numerous, and if good wishes count for anything the firm of Susman Brothers should prosper.

On 2 July 1910, a year after the brothers' settlement in the new town of Livingstone, Harry married Annie Grill, the daughter of Marcus Grill, who was one of those who had accompanied Behr Susmanovitch to Africa in the 1890s. Theirs was the first Jewish wedding to be celebrated in Northern Rhodesia and was conducted by the Reverend M. I. Cohen, minister of the Bulawayo Hebrew Congregation since 1900, and a major figure in the history of the Rhodesian Jewish community. According to the *Livingstone Mail*: 'Last Sunday was a red-letter day in the history of Livingstone, for the first Jewish wedding was not only solemnised but celebrated in a style which will be long remembered.' After a detailed description of the service the newspaper continued: 'Thereafter there were congratulations from all present, and the guests adjourned to the next room where long tables had been spread with light refreshments. Champagne was the only drink, and it was lavishly supplied. Everyone was in the best possible humour, and it seemed as if they were all talking at once.'

The first child of the marriage, Joseph, was born in the following year. According to Harry Susman's much later account, it was soon afterwards that H.R.H. Prince Arthur, Duke of Connaught, a son of Queen Victoria, paid an official visit to Livingstone. King Lewanika came down from Barotseland to pay his respects to the visiting dignitary, and was invited to lunch at Harry's house with a party of chiefs and headmen. When news spread that the king was there a large number of his subjects gathered at the house. After lunch King Lewanika took the baby in his arms and told the assembled crowd: 'This child is going to be your trader. You can always trust a Susman ... The man who does not know Susman is not a Barotse.'[42] It is a good story, but, sadly, the dates do not fit. The Duke of Connaught visited Livingstone in November 1910 and Joseph Susman was not born until April 1911. It is, however, possible that Harry Susman was remembering a later visit by Lord Gladstone, the first Governor General of the new Union of South Africa.

In 1913, alarmed by the threat of war in Europe, Harry Susman travelled with his wife to Memel in Prussia with the intention of bringing back to Africa his parents and the younger members of their family. The brothers had, following the early success of their business, sought to persuade Behr Susmanovitch to come to Africa in 1905. He had then refused to do so, but had emigrated with his wife, Taube, and their daughters, Dora and Marcia, to Palestine. He did not go there as a Zionist, but as a devoutly orthodox Jew who saw it as his duty to live and die in the Holy Land. He and his wife were among the early Jewish settlers at Tel Aviv where they had a house in Lillienblum Street. Their daughter, Marcia, married a Lithuanian-born rabbi, Emmanuel Gershowitz, in Palestine and they had two children, Maurice and Harry Gershowitz, later known as Gersh, who were born in 1906 and 1908. Following Emmanuel's death in Vienna in 1910, one of the elder Susman brothers had visited Tel Aviv with the intention of persuading the family to come to Africa, but they returned to Lithuania.[43]

Harry had left the Russian empire in the 1890s illegally and could not in 1913 cross the border from Memel. The elder Susmanovitches and their daughter were free to leave, but the two boys, Maurice and Harry, had to be smuggled out, lying under coats on the floor of a cart, as it was illegal for them to emigrate before they had done military service. The family travelled to London, where Marcia was left at school, and took the Union Castle mail boat from there to Cape Town. Marcia later travelled to South Africa and married Louis Rubinstein who was in business in Bulawayo. Behr and Taube Susmanovitch lived together with Dora Gershowitz, and her two young sons, in Cape Town for the next seven years. The Gersh boys were sent to school at Cape Town Normal College.

Oscar Susman, the younger brother of Harry and Elie, also reached Africa in 1913, but travelled separately. He became a junior partner in the Susmans' business in 1914 and applied for British naturalisation in Northern Rhodesia in the following year. He joined the Rhodesia Rifles and served in the East African campaign against Von Lettow Vorbeck. He suffered from blackwater fever, was invalided out of the army, and spent some time in the Wynberg Military Hospital at Cape Town. He was trading in Barotseland early in 1918, and was in Livingstone early in the following year. He was an enthusiastic Zionist and was on his way to Palestine when he died in London in March 1920 at the age of thirty. His involvement with Zionism is considered in a later chapter.

Meanwhile, Elie Susman had married Bertha Lewinson in Johannesburg in 1914. She had been born in Johannesburg in 1891. In December 1916,

Elie applied for passports to enable his wife, their young daughter, Bruna, and an English nurse, Miss Brattle, to travel to Mombasa and Nairobi to visit her family. Her father was at the time running a hotel at Londiiana, Kenya. One of her brothers was in the colonial civil service while two others were serving in the East African campaign. Miss Brattle, the nurse, was still employed by the family in 1942.[44]

Some insight into Elie's relations with his family is provided by his 1920 diary. At the beginning of the year his father, Behr, then in his mid-sixties, was visiting Livingstone. He left for Cape Town with Bertha early in February. Ten days later Elie noted that 'it is miserable at home without Bertha'. In the following month, on 24 March, Elie recorded that he was without words to express his sorrow at the news of the death in London of his younger brother, Oscar. Elie was in Elisabethville at the time and was in the thick of negotiations with Bongola Smith. On 15 July he noted with the celebratory comment in Yiddish, 'Mazeltov, Mazeltov', the birth in Livingstone of a third child, Osna, who followed Bruna and Peggy.

Ten days later he left for Cape Town to see his parents and attend to the administration of his brother's estate. He was 'heartbroken' at leaving his wife and child so soon after the birth, but he had to see his 'dear parents' and sort out his brother's estate. On 8 August his parents left Cape Town for Palestine via Durban and Port Said. They never returned to Africa, but lived for many years in Tel Aviv. Their sons later added a number of flats to their house in Lillienblum Street, hoping that the rent would provide them with extra income. When Harry visited them in the mid-1930s he found that the flats were occupied by rabbinical students from whom Behr demanded no rent.[45] Elie visited Tel Aviv later in the decade with his wife and their older children. The youngest child, David, who was born in 1925, was left at home. Taube died in 1938. Behr survived her by three years, dying in 1941 at the age of eighty-seven.[46]

Social Life and Religion

Elie's diary also sheds some light on his social life and network of friends. While much of his time was spent with business associates such as Haslett, Boyd, Rollnick and Bongola Smith, his trips to Bulawayo brought him into touch with people who were friends as well as business partners. They included Louis Landau, Henry Ellenbogen, both Bulawayo wholesalers, and Cecil Jacobs, a young lawyer. All three of them were to play an important part in the life of Southern Rhodesia's Jewish community, and in political and public life, for several decades. Elie travelled to Cape Town with Louis Landau and his diary records visits with him to the 'bioscope', theatre and the Opera House. Elie does not seem to have been involved at this time, anyway, in the poker games played for high stakes which are said to have delayed the departure of trains on Northern Rhodesia's Line of Rail. His diary does record his enjoyment on the train, and in Cape Town, of a few games of bridge.

While Elie had many gentile friends and business partners, such as Robert Sutherland, George Buchanan, Sam Haslett and Robert Boyd, who were, incidentally, all Scots, it is probable that his closest friends were Jewish. It is not easy to get an idea of his attitudes towards either Judaism as a religion or Jewishness as an identity. If his diary is anything to go by, religion was not in itself important to him at this time. In the course of 1920 he attended synagogue only once when he visited the Cape Town 'Shool' with his intensely orthodox father to say prayers following the death of his brother. Attendance at synagogue may not be a fair indicator of his attitude towards religion, as there was no synagogue in Northern Rhodesia at this time. He was himself to lay the foundation stone in Livingstone in 1928 of the first synagogue in the country. From other evidence, however, it would appear that he had rejected his father's orthodoxy, but saw the importance of maintaining links with his ancestral religion.

There is rather more evidence in the diary of his interest in Palestine and Zionism. In his second will in 1909 he had left money to the Palestine National Fund.[47] It was found on his brother Oscar's death that he too had left the proceeds of an insurance policy to the fund. Following Oscar's death, money was subscribed in Livingstone to plant trees in Palestine in his memory. In February 1920 Elie attended a lecture on Palestine in the Guild Hall in Bulawayo. It is not clear who gave the lecture, but this was at a time of gathering excitement in Zionist circles over the assumption by Great Britain of the mandate over Palestine, and of hopes for the fulfilment of the promise made in the Balfour Declaration of 1917 on the establishment of a Jewish National Home. On the train back from Cape Town in August, Elie met Mark Abrahams, South Africa's leading Zionist, who told him of his experiences in Palestine, expressing the opinion that 'if we get plenty of money to run the country it will be a success'. It seems that the Susman brothers may best be described as 'traditional' Jews for whom the sense of Jewish identity, increasingly expressed at this time through Zionism, was more important than Judaism.

CHAPTER 3

Jewish Networks, the Line of Rail and the Growth of Towns: 1905–39

The coming of the railway transformed communications and commercial life in Northern Rhodesia. The area known as the Line of Rail became the new focus of commercial activity. Towns gradually grew up which attracted an ever-increasing proportion of the country's population – so much so that Zambia has been known since the 1960s as one of the most urbanised countries in Africa. In the years before the Second World War, the towns were not large, but they were growth points, and harbingers of what was to come. It was not a coincidence that the railway line passed by three potential mining centres – Wankie in Southern Rhodesia, Broken Hill, and Bwana Mkubwa, near Ndola, in Northern Rhodesia – and terminated on the Congo side of what was already becoming known as the Copperbelt. It was, however, a coincidence that the railway also passed through the Batoka plateau, now in Zambia's Southern Province, which had been identified by David Livingstone in the 1850s as the area of central Africa which was most suitable for white settlement. African peasants responded quickly to the opportunities provided by the building of the railway, but a strip of land on both sides of the railway was soon alienated to settler farmers, and the peasants were gradually pushed up to twenty miles away from it. It was the economy created by African peasants, settler farmers, mining companies, and by mainly Jewish traders, which created the Line of Rail as an economic region. This chapter will examine the role of Jewish traders and entrepreneurs, and of Jewish credit and kinship networks, in laying the foundations of modern commerce, and of towns, in this region.

The situation of the Jewish traders on the frontier was well summarised by the Reverend Moses Isaac Cohen, the best-informed, and most articulate, spokesman for the Rhodesian Jewish community, who wrote in 1929:

> The Jews certainly created the kaffir truck business in Rhodesia. They opened their stores in every part of the country, shared in all its pioneering hardships, and helped materially to develop its commercial life. The early settlers for the

most part knew little English, they could not obtain jobs, and were practically forced into the one line of business.[1]

Nearly twenty years later, another acute observer, Wolf Rybko, a Zionist emissary and writer, who had first visited the region in 1928, summarised their history in a similar way. He wrote: 'Jews came to Northern Rhodesia, not for farming, but to open up trading stations. Jewish wholesalers in Bulawayo assisted their relatives and *landsleit* (countrymen) by giving them goods and oxen so that they could go to the new territory to open shops at railway stations and sidings.'[2]

It has frequently been noticed that immigrant ethnic groups perform the role of middlemen and entrepreneurs in frontier zones. The Jews were not the only such group on the frontier in Northern Rhodesia in the early twentieth century. There were similar groups, such as the Scots and the Greeks, and they were followed by larger numbers of Asians. They were, however, in the early years, and especially in the western half of the country, the most important of these groups. It was not the teachings of any particular religion or sect which made these ethnic groups flourish in trade; what Jews, Scots, Greeks, and later Hindus and Muslims, had in common was not so much a similar creed as a solidarity which came from tight-knit families, and shared membership in a minority ethnic group.

The Jewish traders on the frontier brought with them very little capital in the form of goods or money. They did, however, bring with them a good deal of 'non-material' capital.[3] This included a high level of motivation derived from their status as economic, religious or political refugees with no home to which they could easily return, and their membership of kinship networks which functioned as channels for recruitment, credit, supplies and commercial information. They also brought with them some prior experience of trading – often for cattle and grain. Their accounting skills were not always sophisticated, and their accounts were often kept in Yiddish, but they had the vital abilities to distinguish between capital and income, and to limit consumption to a bare minimum. As a commercial traveller, Arthur Kaplan, whose knowledge of these traders dates back for over fifty years, recalls: 'They knew how to live on nothing.'[4]

The turnover of shopkeepers on the frontier was generally small, and was insufficient to generate a large income. The average rewards were almost certainly less than would have been expected by white artisans in the region. The risks in terms of material loss, and loss of life, were high. There were a few spectacular success stories, but, for every one of these, there were many failures: bankruptcies, deaths from blackwater fever and suicides. Inevitably, the main focus in this book is on the successful traders, because they set up businesses which endured. It has always to be remembered, however, that they were exceptional – and lucky. For a few people, escape from the restrictions of the *shtetl*, or the ghetto, provided opportunities in which they were able to flourish.

The railway reached Bulawayo in 1897, and paused there for six years which coincided with the aftermath of the rinderpest epidemic. Francistown, Plumtree and Bulawayo all served as centres of credit and supply for the Barotseland traders, but in the end it was Bulawayo which became dominant. There was, as we have seen, a symbiotic relationship between the development of Jewish wholesaling businesses in Bulawayo and the Barotseland trade. These traders were themselves initially financed by importers, such as the Mosenthals, who were based at Port Elizabeth in South Africa. Moses Cohen noticed that it was the Anglo-Boer War which enabled Jewish traders in Bulawayo to gain their independence from the Port Elizabeth merchants, and to enter into direct relationships with London shippers.[5] It was almost certainly also the profits of the Barotseland trade which enabled them to establish this independence, and in the case of some firms, such as Landau Brothers, to set up their own London offices, or, in the case of other firms such as Charelik Salomon, later Salomon and Kaufman, to appoint their own London agents.

Bulawayo became the 'distribution' centre, to use the language of the railway companies, for Northern Rhodesia. For most of the colonial period, railway rating policy was used to reinforce the dominance of the Bulawayo wholesalers over their Northern Rhodesian clients. Railway rates were designed to make it cheaper to consign goods from the coast to Bulawayo, and to send them on from there to Livingstone or Lusaka, than it was to ship directly from the coast to Livingstone. Some stations in the north, such as Livingstone and Lusaka, eventually became distribution centres on their own account. These subsidiary centres found it very difficult, however, to escape completely from the dominance of the Bulawayo suppliers. Only the larger businesses were usually able to get direct access to South African and London suppliers. Although there were a few wholesalers who managed to establish themselves in the north, the relationship of dependency on the south was not really broken until after Zambian independence.[6]

Rhodes's Cape to Cairo rail and river route was originally intended to run northwards from Bulawayo to Salisbury, cross the Zambezi at Kariba, and terminate at the south end of Lake Tanganyika. The discovery of copper in Katanga by Robert Williams's Tanganyika Concessions Company made the extension of the railway to the Congo more urgent. The discovery of vast coal deposits at Wankie in Southern Rhodesia, and of lead and zinc deposits at Broken Hill, determined the eventual route of the railway north of Bulawayo. The man behind the Wankie and Broken Hill mines, and the main influence on the path taken by the railway, was a controversial London-based entrepreneur, Edmund Davis. Born in 1861 at Toorak, Melbourne, Australia, and said to have been of French Jewish descent, he began his business career in his early twenties with the exploitation of guano deposits on islands close to Cape Town. In the early years of the century, he was the major promoter of the Wankie Colliery Company, and of the Northern Copper

Company which developed a number of small mines with picturesque names, such as Silver King, Sable Antelope and Crystal Jacket in the area then known as the Hook of Kafue. These mines exploited the exposed seams of copper oxide ores, but they were handicapped by the difficulty and cost of transport to and from their remote locations. Davis was the major promoter of mineral development within the BSA company's dominions, but he was said to venture little money of his own. He was a master manipulator of share issues.[7]

The railway was extended northwards to Wankie in 1903, and reached the Victoria Falls in 1904. It was pushed on beyond the Zambezi and had reached Kalomo, 100 miles to the north, before the completion of the spectacular Victoria Falls bridge over the Zambezi in September 1905. The line reached its next major stop at Broken Hill in January 1906, and paused there for three years. It had been thought that the railway would pass through British territory to Kansanshi mine, near modern Solwezi, and cross the border into the Congo there. But, as most of the funding came from Belgian sources, a route was chosen which involved the shortest possible distance in Northern Rhodesia, and the longest possible distance in the Congo. The railway passed close to the Bwana Mkubwa mine and entered the Congo at Sakania. It reached Elisabethville which was close to the Etoile du Katanga mine late in 1910. A copper smelter came into production there in the following year.[8]

The construction of the railway was itself a stimulus to trade. The main contractors employed a large number of sub-contractors, and an army of workers, both black and white, had to be fed. Paradoxically, railway construction provided a great, though temporary, stimulus to transport riders who carried supplies ahead of the line. They were also involved in the moving of materials and supplies for the construction of the small mines of the Hook of Kafue area. Jewish traders followed, and, in some cases, went on ahead of the construction work, buying cattle and maize to supply the contractors, and selling goods to the workers.

Jewish traders were not, of course, the first traders in the region. A number of African peoples, including the Ovimbundu, the Bisa and the Yao, had previously specialised in trade. Jews were, however, among the first people to become settled shopkeepers. Although much of their trade was carried on by barter, and on credit both from suppliers and to customers, they played an important role in the introduction of a money economy. As middlemen, they were in closer contact with the African population than most settlers. It was often noted that they could communicate better in vernacular languages than they could in English. Conversely, it was, as Moses Cohen noted, often their inability to speak English well which had driven them into African trade in the first place.

Livingstone

The first modern town in Northern Rhodesia was Livingstone which was laid out in February 1905. Its site was about six miles from an earlier informal settlement, known as the Old Drift, which had been set up close to the Zambezi river, and above the Falls, in 1898. The capital of North-Western Rhodesia was at Kalomo until 1907 when it was transferred to Livingstone. The moves from the Old Drift and Kalomo were both made in an attempt to reduce the death rate from blackwater fever. In 1911 Livingstone became the capital of the united country of Northern Rhodesia. In 1910 it was estimated that there were 260 white residents in the town, of whom thirty-eight were said to be Jews.[9] When Elias Kopelowitz arrived three years later, he found that there were eight Jewish families and ten bachelors in the town. There were probably not much more than a hundred Jews in the whole country at that time. The Jewish element in the small white population of Livingstone was about 15 per cent.[10] This was a significantly higher proportion than would have been found in Bulawayo or Salisbury, or on the Witwatersrand, where Jews did not exceed 6 per cent of the white population.

The population of Livingstone in the early years was a shifting one. The British South Africa Company administration and Mashonaland Railways were the largest employers, but their staff did not usually stay long. The most prominent trader in the town was Frederick J. 'Mopani' Clarke, who had first established his Zambezi Trading Association at the Old Drift in 1898. He developed branches of his business, which specialised in the sale of goods for the European market, and in agricultural machinery, along the Line of Rail, and later moved to Kalomo. He then became a rancher on the Kafue Flats, though he retained control of his trading business. Another 'Old Drifter' who moved to Livingstone was Leopold Moore, the pharmacist, who had arrived in 1904 after going bankrupt in Bulawayo in the previous year. He was the founding editor and proprietor of the *Livingstone Mail* from 1906 and became a settler politician and leader of the unofficial members of the Legislative Council. Both Clarke and Moore were regarded as anti-Semitic. A certain piquancy was added to Moore's frank anti-Semitism by the widely-held belief that he was himself of Jewish descent.[11]

Before, during and for some time after the First World War, as many as two-thirds of the general dealers' licences issued in the town were held by Jews. This commercial dominance was resented by some visitors to Livingstone in the years before the First World War, and was the pretext for some thinly-veiled anti-Semitism. Many examples of this could be quoted from contemporary literature. The comments of Charlotte Mansfield, author of *Via Rhodesia*, an undated travel book, which describes the situation as it was in about 1908, are typical. She wrote after a visit to Livingstone:

With regard to the Jews, I have no grudge against the Jew or the foreigner, but

I should like to see a few Englishmen make money. At present the Jew and the foreigner seem to be collecting all the plums. Great credit is due to them for their energy and enterprise in superintending labour, and building their own fortunes, but, oh, you Englishmen, what a chance you are missing by leaving the trading to others.[12]

She noted that the silver threepenny piece was, as was still the case until the mid-1930s, the smallest unit of coinage, and that there was very little cash trade. It was, in her view, 'time that the tin shanty in Rhodesia should vanish from the land, and in its place well-built stores be erected, and business be carried on with less credit and with more sound business principles'.[13]

There was some truth in her comments. Most stores on the frontier were tin shanties, or pole and dagga hovels. But the majority of Jewish traders were struggling to survive. The intermediate position of Jews in the early towns is vividly demonstrated by their dual role as victims of anti-Semitism, though on a much lesser scale than in their home countries, and as, to some extent, the agents of white racism against blacks. Charlotte Mansfield demanded commercial segregation and the construction of separate stores for 'Native' trade. This is, of course, an indication that the early stores were not segregated. There is, however, evidence that some traders in Livingstone were already beginning to respond to this demand. In opening their new store at about the time of her visit, Messrs Jacobson and Kiehl assured potential customers that their shop would cater for 'None but white trade; ladies will not be required to rub shoulders with a crowd of clamorous and odorous natives'.[14] Commercial segregation became the norm only after the First World War, and was probably related to the arrival of larger numbers of white women. It was then that the practice of serving black customers through hatches at the side of shops became commonplace in Livingstone. It was later extended to Lusaka and to the Copperbelt.

Early Jewish Settlers

From the advertisements in the *Livingstone Mail*'s short-lived predecessor, the *Livingstone Pioneer and Advertiser*, which was published in the early months of 1906, it appears that the first Jewish traders, or artisans, in the town were Isadore Aberman, 'general merchant', Messrs Berger and Cohen, 'retail merchants', Bloch Brothers, 'general dealers', and R. J. Bernstein, builder. The Peimer brothers, Samuel and Michael, formerly of Barotseland, moved their store from Maramba siding to Mainway in February 1906. Messrs Jacobson and Kiehl, who had also been involved in the Barotseland trade, and had been unable to withstand competition from the Susmans at Nalolo, arrived a year or two later.[15]

The majority of these people fade from the scene with the First World War. The most significant of them was Isadore Aberman, from Romania, who arrived in 1905. It is probable that he was financed by Charelik Salomon, who was then the most important of the Bulawayo wholesalers. Aberman's career is typical of many, both for its vicissitudes and for his movements along the Line of Rail. After eight years in Livingstone, he was able to take a trip home with his family. He was there caught up in the First World War, enlisted in the Romanian army, and was unable to return to Northern Rhodesia until 1920. He then went straight to Lusaka where, as we shall see, he established a shop in Cairo Road.[16]

Only one of the other Jewish founders of the town had a lasting significance. This lay not so much in himself, though he was literally a builder of the new town, as in his progeny. Abraham Gelman, who died in June or July 1905, was a brickmaker. His grave is the first in the Jewish section of Livingstone's new cemetery. The sale of his effects, which included eighty-three cattle, three scotch carts, twelve bucksails, a township stand, and 50,000 bricks, was reported in January 1906. He came from a family of brickmakers in Warsaw, Poland, who had transferred their skills to Bulawayo by way of Hull, England. His son, also Abraham Gelman, has already featured in this story as a key figure in the cattle trade of the Congo, and will appear again as a contributor to the development of secondary industry in Livingstone.[17]

The Susmans and the Grills

The greatest single asset of the Jewish traders in Livingstone, and the other new towns on the frontier, lay in their kinship and credit networks. It makes sense, therefore, to focus on the way in which these were built up. The Susman brothers were not among the first Jewish settlers in Livingstone, but, as the most successful of the Barotseland traders, they played the key role in the development of the town as a regional distribution centre. They were, as we have seen, based in Livingstone from 1909 onwards when they took over the Pioneer Butchery and Bakery in partnership with Frank Davis. They made the town the centre of a business which eventually extended over much of Northern Rhodesia and into northern Bechuanaland, Southern Rhodesia, Angola and the Congo. Livingstone is not far from Kazangula, where, uniquely in the world, the boundaries of four countries, Zambia, Zimbabwe, Namibia and Botswana, meet at one place. The boundary with a fifth country, Angola, is not far away. For a period of about sixty years, the Susmans were able to exploit the geographical position of Livingstone, and the usual lack of restrictions on cross-border trade, to carry on business on a regional basis. They became the most prominent members of the Jewish community, and provided it with an element of stability. They brought many people to Livingstone as relatives, friends or employees. The Grills were the largest, and longest-staying, of the families which were brought to Livingstone through the Susman connection. Harry Susman's future parents-in-law, Marcus and Faiga (also known as Fanny) Grill, moved up from Bulawayo in September 1909. Most of their eleven children lived in Livingstone at one time or another, and the Grill family made a lasting contribution to the life of the town.

Marcus Grill had, as we have seen, left the Russian empire in company with Behr Susmanovitch in 1895.[18] He was born at Vorne in Kovno province, and married Feiga Bruch at Plungyan in 1887. He ran a mill, and later an inn, at Medingyan. He was driven to emigrate as a result of an edict that Jews could no longer sell liquor. When Behr Susmanovitch left Bulawayo in 1896, Marcus Grill remained. He built himself a small store out of old packing cases and sent for his family who arrived in Bulawayo in December 1901. He had some rabbinical training and was able to supplement his small income from trade by assisting at services on the High Days and Holy Days. A few years later he gave up retail trade and rented a boarding house.

Marcus Grill's departure for the north was prompted by a crisis which was typical of the struggle for survival of Jews on the frontier. According to family tradition, he was a kind-hearted man who was too tolerant of non-paying guests. His son, Natie, recalled an incident in which Marcus was slashed with a razor by a guest when he asked for three months' overdue rent. The *Bulawayo Chronicle* reported in December 1908 a subsequent case in which Isadore Herman claimed that Marcus had attacked him with the razor. He alleged that he had used 'such language as only a dirty Peruvian would make use of'.[19] 'Peruvian' was a derogatory term used at the time by both Jews and gentiles to describe unsophisticated Jews from the Russian empire. The magistrate dismissed the case, but this did not save Marcus from eventual bankruptcy and the sale of his household effects. He was saved from destitution by his daughter's engagement to Harry Susman who helped to set him up in business in Livingstone with a loan of £200, but even there he struggled to feed and clothe his large family. Natie Grill remembered occasions when some of the children were sent home from school because they had no shoes.

The story of the Grill family illustrates the role of Jewish entrepreneurs as innovators in new service industries, and also the dynamic role of Jewish women as entrepreneurs. Marcus Grill, and his eldest son, Solly, were the promoters in 1919 of Livingstone's, and indeed Northern Rhodesia's, first cinema. This was moved from a site in Queensway to Mainway in 1921. At first the cinema's patrons sat outside, but in the following year Grill's Kinema was built with an indoor stage, lounge bar and dance hall on the same plot. In the days of the silent movies, the cinema had its own pianist and was the town's social centre.

The eldest of the Grills' many children was their daughter Gertrude, known as Gertie, who became one of Northern Rhodesia's first modern businesswomen. She married Joe Merber in Livingstone shortly before the First World War, and was widowed when he was posted missing in action in France. She never remarried and had no children. She was regarded as both astute and tough. She managed the first cinema and was largely responsible for the construction of a new one, the Capitol Theatre, which was opened in 1931. This is still one of Livingstone's architectural landmarks – in an interesting amalgam of Cape Dutch and Art Deco styles. The name of the new cinema was inspired by the debate over Livingstone's status as the capital of the country. Gertie Gerber was also involved in another new service industry which emerged after the First World War. She managed the town's first garage, the Livingstone Motor Works, and later Kohler's garage. She also developed her own furniture factory.[20]

The Grills' youngest daughter, Bella, was also a formidable organiser. She was very active in Jewish communal organisations, and other public works, though latterly immobilised by illness. She had musical and dramatic talents and first appeared on stage in Livingstone in 1912 at the age of three in *Ali Baba and the Forty Thieves*. She started to produce musicals before she was fifteen – the first was *American Girl* – and at seventeen she was running her own dance band. In 1935 she married Harry Sossen who, as we shall see, was to become an important figure in the business of the town after the Second World War. Of the other Grill girls, Hannah trained as a nurse and caused a temporary crisis in her strictly orthodox family by marrying out of the faith. Her husband was Trevor Wright and their son, Patrick, still lives at Chisamba. Hannah served for many years as sister-in-charge of the Choma Hospital. Tilly was also a nurse. She became matron of Gwelo (Gweru) Hospital, and lived into her nineties. Lily became a secondary school teacher and married Willy Fredman. They had a shop in Livingstone between the wars.

The Grills' five sons – Solly, Natie, Bennie, Harry and Abe – all lived for some time in the town. Natie left school at twelve and started work in his father's store. He joined the Northern Rhodesia Regiment soon after the outbreak of the First World War, and was invalided out of the army after a severe attack of malaria. He was advised that it would be unsafe for him to continue to live north of the Zambezi, and had a successful business career in Namaqualand and Bulawayo. Harry Grill worked as an underground miner at Mufulira before the Second World War, and later ran a brickworks in Livingstone, before moving to Bulawayo where his widow, Laura, still lives. Marcus Grill died while on holiday in Cape Town in 1936. Faiga Grill lived on for another thirty years, dying as a feisty old matriarch in Bulawayo in 1969 at the age of ninety-nine.

Two of Marcus Grill's nephews – another Harry Grill and Hymie – reached Livingstone in the mid-1920s and took over the Public Services Association's store, which was known as the PSA, and a mineral water factory. Hymie died young in 1934, and Harry was compelled to leave Livingstone after a tragic liaison with a cousin. Their business interests were taken over by Harry Sossen. Their sister Annie married Joe Furmanowsky, who had a shop and ran the town's first taxi from the early 1930s until after the Second World War. Another member of Marcus Grill's extended family who lived in

Livingstone from 1928–1935 was Hymie Wolffe, his nephew, who worked there for a firm of auditors. He was for a while secretary of the Livingstone Hebrew Congregation. He was recruited by Elie Susman in 1936 to work for Woolworths, and has done so for over sixty years. He is, at the time of writing, alive and well and living in Cape Town.[21]

The Shapiros, Feigenbaums and Wassersons

Another family of Lithuanian origin, which was drawn to Livingstone by the Susman connection and then proliferated, was headed by Max Shapiro. He was born in Popolan in 1878 and came to South Africa before the Anglo-Boer War. He had met and married his wife, Jenny Feigenbaum, on a holiday visit to relatives in Manchester in 1903–4. After trying his luck in Mafeking and Bulawayo, he was encouraged by the Susmans to set himself up as a watchmaker and jeweller in Livingstone in 1908. In the late 1950s, he described himself as a merchant and, a little improbably, as a furrier. He was a man of unusual piety who, despite a strong physical resemblance to Joseph Stalin, laid *tefillin* (put on phylacteries) to pray daily. The Shapiros remained in Livingstone for over fifty years, celebrating their golden wedding anniversary there in 1954.[22]

A number of members of Jenny Shapiro's family followed her to Africa. Her sister, Ethel Feigenbaum, married Harry Wasserson at Harry Susman's house in Livingstone in 1922. They had met and become engaged in Manchester, where Harry was born to Polish immigrant parents. He had served in India during the First World War and came to Livingstone in 1920. The Wassersons set up a curio shop next to the Shapiros' store and also ran a tearoom which catered for the tourist market. They remained in Livingstone for many years and were, with their family, prominent members of the Jewish community. Their daughter, Norma Davidov, recalls her father's love of Africa and the liberating effect which it had upon him after an impoverished upbringing in Manchester. Ethel Wasserson's brother, Bill Feigenbaum, was one of a number of other members of her family who came to Northern Rhodesia. One of her nephews, Alan Feigenbaum, has been for many years the president of the Bulawayo Hebrew Congregation. A number of members of Harry Wasserson's family, including a brother, Jack, and two sisters, also followed him to Africa.[23]

The Jacobs Brothers

Lewis and Michael Jacobs, who came from Kupiski, Kovno, seem also to have been brought to Livingstone through the Susmans' Lithuanian connections. Michael (also known as Jehiel) Jacobs produced their accounts in a fine copperplate hand in 1911–12. They were among the pioneers of secondary industry in Northern Rhodesia. They were, with Aristotle Hippocrates (known to his friends as 'Hippo') Troumbas, from the island of Samos in Greece, the founders of the Livingstone Saw Mills. The business was set up in 1911 as the Dimitra Saw Mills and was producing 100 railway sleepers a day in the early years of the war. It was taken over in the mid-1920s by W. E. Tongue and C. S. Knight, who became Livingstone's first mayor and a member of the Legislative Council. It was incorporated in 1927 as Zambesi Saw Mills Ltd, and was greatly developed by them in cooperation with Rhodesia Railways in the later 1930s. The firm was, as we shall see, eventually taken over by the Susman brothers, who had always been closely associated with it, as transport contractors, timber suppliers and agents. After the takeover of the timber business, the Jacobs brothers concentrated on their Livingstone and Barotseland trading businesses. Michael Jacobs lived in Livingstone, but kept his distance from the town's Jewish community.[24]

Meyer Rubin Flax was a partner of the Jacobs brothers in the 1920s and 1930s. He was born in Kovno province in 1896, and arrived in Livingstone from the Cape in December 1918. Apart from a six-year absence in Lithuania between 1925 and 1931, he was to remain there until his death in 1979. In the early 1930s he was a half-share partner with Michael Jacobs in stands and buildings in Mainway and Queensway. A police report written in 1933 sheds an interesting light on a man who was later to be known as a successful businessman as well as an eccentric and recluse. It was reported that: 'On his return from Lithuania Mr Flax showed a great tendency to propagating Bolsheviki [sic] cause, and numerous natives to whom he had spoken subsequently appeared in Livingstone wearing button-hole badges emblematic of their favourable attitude to the cause, which undoubtedly they fail to understand.'

The police do not appear to have taken a very serious view of this first example of the spread of Soviet propaganda in Northern Rhodesia. It was reported that 'a hint dropped in the Jewish quarter seemed to have the effect of causing Mr Flax to desist from his public statements in connection with the European political situation'. It was also reported, a little paradoxically, that he, like his partner, Michael Jacobs, did 'not fraternise with local Jewry'.[25]

Elias and Henne Kopelowitz

The most remarkable example of family network-building is provided by the Kopelowitz brothers. Paul Kopelowitz arrived in Livingstone from Ezherene, Kurland (later Latvia), in about 1910 and was followed by his brother, Elias, who arrived three years later at the age of twenty-one. (Another brother went to America and a radical sister stayed at home and played an active part, as a Bolshevik, in the Russian Revolution.) They were, at first, involved in the Barotseland trade, but they were not cattle traders. They dealt in the usual imported trade goods, and in a variety of local products including hides, skins, ivory, beeswax and curios. Paul died in the early 1920s, but Elias, who had spent long periods in Barotseland, remained in business in Livingstone for many years, and was a prominent figure in the town until his death in the late 1960s. He was one of the few businessmen in Livingstone who was able to establish himself as a wholesaler. He had a large warehouse and supplied goods to independent white, and later Asian, traders, as well as to African hawkers throughout Barotseland and the Southern Province. He later became a supplier of goods to the copper mines and was involved through his close relatives, the Tow brothers, in the development of secondary industry in the town. He was a leading member for many years of the Chamber of Commerce and was at various times president of the Hebrew Congregation and of the Herzl Zionist Society. He was also a benefactor of the Catholic convent and girls' school. He was an intellectual whose range of friendships extended from 'Chirupula' Stephenson to Kenneth Kaunda.[26]

Known to his relatives as 'Old Man Kop', Elias Kopelowitz eventually became the centre of an extensive web of kinship which had its roots in Latvia, but which came to involve families of Lithuanian and German origin. His network eventually included members of the Fischer, Illion, Iljon, Tow, Kollenberg, Scher, Schlesinger, Behrens, Guttman and Rowelsky families, and covered much of Northern Rhodesia. His sister, Rosa, married Zalkind Scher, a prominent Jewish resident of Livingstone and, later, of Kalomo. He was a religious man and a *shochet*. Their daughter Cilla married Heinz Behrens, a German refugee who was later also in business in Livingstone and Kalomo. Elias's cousin, Sam Fischer, arrived from Latvia in 1920 and moved two years later to Lusaka, where he was to play an important part in the development of the future capital city. Sam's half-brother, Philip, and other siblings, soon followed. Philip became, as we shall see, a prominent trader in Mazabuka.

Elias Kopelowitz visited his home in Latvia soon after the war and returned with a wife, Henne Illion. She came from a rabbinical family in Libau, and was to play an important role in the development of the Hebrew Congregation. Several of her brothers, including Uri, Eli and Lazar Illion, arrived in the country soon afterwards. Uri Illion came in 1926 and set up a branch of the Kopelowitz firm in Mazabuka. He soon moved on to Lusaka, and eventually settled, with one of his brothers, in Mufulira.

To focus on families and networks places a possibly undue emphasis on traders who stayed for a long time, and put down roots. It also tends to emphasise the role of the 'notables', and to obscure real class distinctions which existed within small communities. It leaves out of account some of those who stayed for a long time, but who did not, for one reason or another, produce large extended families. There were always more Jewish men than women on the frontier, and there were many men who remained bachelors. An example is Smerl Naparstock, who came from Lithuania and worked for the Susmans for many years in the Barotseland cattle trade, and in Livingstone, but had no obvious family ties. Many young men who arrived from Lithuania and Latvia in the 1920s and 1930s, such as members of the

Benigson and Katz families, worked in Livingstone as shop assistants. The
Livingstone shops were a training ground for them and a gateway to the
Copperbelt. In addition to the shop assistants, there was in the early days a
small group of itinerant Jewish traders, the hawkers and *smous*, who are
almost inevitably anonymous.

Throughout the whole history of the Line of Rail region, from its
formation until Zambian independence, an important but almost totally
unrecognised role was also played by the commercial travellers – most of
them Jewish – who worked for the Bulawayo wholesalers, and the manufacturers' agents who worked for South African and, later, Southern Rhodesian
clothing manufacturers. The arrival of the representatives of Salomon and
Kaufman, and Landau Brothers, on the twice weekly 'mixed goods' train from
the south, was noticed by an observer who described the scene at Kafue as
early as 1912. The presence of a large number of 'commercials' at Lusaka in
the following year was taken as a sign of the prosperity of the new township.
At a later date, certainly after the Second World War, these travellers came by
car. Arthur Kaplan describes, from that time, the three month-long journeys
a year which he made for nearly twenty years from Bulawayo to the Copperbelt, as a representative of the clothing manufacturers. He describes the nights
spent in cheap hotels, and the setting up of 'sample rooms' to which European
and Asian traders would come at different times to inspect goods and make
their orders. They clearly played a very important role in the extension of
trade, in the spreading of fashions and in the provision of credit.[27]

The Depression

Jewish traders did not, according to Hymie Wolffe, suffer any great hardship
during the depression, though it was reported in 1933 that there were many
unemployed people and great distress in Maramba, the town's 'Native' location. Livingstone did, however, suffer two blows to its status during the
1930s. The first of these was the transfer of the headquarters of the railways
to Broken Hill in 1932. The second and more serious blow was the transfer
of the capital to Lusaka in 1935. The move occurred in spite of the determined
opposition of Leopold Moore who never tired of describing Lusaka as a
desolate and wind-swept stop on the railway. The move almost halved the
white population of the town, which had reached 1,600 in 1931, but was still
only 1,300 in 1946. The black population was approximately 10,000 in 1931
and 13,000 in 1946. The town today remains very much as it was in the 1930s
– a colonial time warp.[28]

Apart from the African Lakes Corporation – Mandala Stores – which
opened a branch in 1906, Jewish traders in Livingstone had no serious
competition in African retail trade until the mid-1930s. For reasons which
remain obscure, but which may relate to the depression and the move of the
capital, as well as to the opening of the Great East Road, it was only then

that Asian traders began to present real competition. It is probable that the depression squeezed profit margins in retail African trade to the point where established Jewish traders, with relatively large overheads, could be undercut by newly immigrant Asian traders. According to the Dotsons, they were probably making average net profits in the 1930s of no more than £10 a month.[29] It is also clear that there was, from the late 1930s onwards, increased competition in rural retail trade from licensed African traders, and from hawkers, both licensed and unlicensed. Elias Kopelowitz recalled that there were a few Asian hawkers and market gardeners in the town when he arrived in 1913. It was only in the early 1920s that trading licences for shops were granted to Asians in what became the second-class trading area of Queensway. It was not until the mid-1930s that they penetrated the 'soft goods' or textile business. By 1938, there were fifteen Asian shops in Livingstone, and they provided such stiff competition in African retail trade that by the end of the Second World War Jewish traders had been forced to withdraw into wholesale trade, the more specialist European market and, most significantly, the development of secondary industry. There was a sense in which Asian competition did Jewish traders a favour by forcing them upmarket and into more dynamic sectors of the economy. The replacement of the Jews by Asians in African retail trade in Livingstone is an early example of what has been called 'ethnic succession' – the tendency for ethnic groups to replace each other in specialised commercial activities.[30]

Broken Hill

In terms of chronology, though not of present-day geography, the next major stop on the Line of Rail was Broken Hill, which is nearly 400 miles north of Livingstone. It was to become the second modern town in Northern Rhodesia. The railway reached the Broken Hill mine in January 1906. Pauling's, the contractors, were working so fast at the time that they laid almost six miles of track in a single day, breaking a world record in the process. The last half-mile of rail was laid from a slowly moving train – a remarkable feat. The mine was closed at the time, and there was no crowd to witness this event, but it was recorded on cine film by Pathé News, apparently the first time that an event in central Africa had been filmed. Owing to a shortage of capital, Broken Hill remained the railhead until 1909 when construction began again. Railway building created boom conditions, but delays in construction created slumps. J. B. Thornhill described the scene at Broken Hill in 1908 where 200 unemployed and destitute white workers were waiting for construction to recommence. In what he saw as a kind of degradation, these men were living on maize meal (*nsima*). The administration had to introduce border controls at Livingstone to stop the influx of white work-seekers.[31]

Edmund Davis was initially opposed to the establishment of a public township close to the mine. He sought to limit trading to mine property and

gave concessions to two companies, the African Lakes Corporation, and
Salomon and Rollnick, which was probably a partnership between Charelik
Salomon, of Bulawayo, and J. R. Rollnick, who had come up as a trader with
the railway. The mining company's resistance to the laying-out of a township
was eventually overcome, though it insisted on the allocation to itself of
many of the best stands. Development of the commercial township began
before the outbreak of war in 1914, but the town as a whole was to remain
somewhat disjointed, with a mine township, a railway township, and an
administrative centre, the Boma, which was built in 1907. Edmund Davis
campaigned in 1930 for Broken Hill's selection as the new capital, but one
of the arguments against it was its lack of a planned centre.[32]

Jewish traders became dominant in Broken Hill in much the same way as
they had done in Livingstone, but it never became a centre for family
networks, and did not produce many prosperous or long-staying families.
This was largely due to the fact that the prosperity of the town was dependent
on the mine which went through many vicissitudes. The town reached the
height of its importance in the late 1920s when the lead and zinc produced
by the mine were, for a time, Northern Rhodesia's major exports, but it
suffered badly during the depression. Apart from Salomon and Rollnick,
which was Bulawayo-based, one of the first Jewish businesses at the railhead
was Ludwig Deuss's Northern Rhodesia Trading Company which was in the
district by 1906.[33] For a brief period in 1906–7 there was a branch of his
business at Mpika on the route northwards to the Tanganyika border. The
move to the Line of Rail may have been influenced by its usefulness as an
export route for rubber from the Congo. His business partner, Mauricio
Teixeira de Mattos, was exporting rubber from west of the Lualaba through
Broken Hill in 1908.[34]

The Beemer Brothers

The Beemer brothers, Harry and Joseph, had established the Broken Hill
Trading Company by 1913. They were Bulawayo-based and at least one of
them, Harry, had been involved in the Barotseland trade in the early years
of the century. Although they developed quite extensive trading interests in
Northern Rhodesia, they do not seem to have been ever permanently resident
in the country. During the First World War, they had a trading network
which extended at least as far north as Mpika, where they had four outlying
stores under African managers. They also had stores for a time in the Lusaka
district, and at Mumbwa, Bwana Mkubwa and Ndola. Joseph Beemer died
during the great influenza epidemic of 1918. Harry Beemer is said to have
died of blackwater fever at about the same time. Joseph Beemer's daughter,
Hilda Kuper, the distinguished social anthropologist, was born in Bulawayo
in 1910 and was brought up there. She never lived in Northern Rhodesia,
but she did recall her family's northern business connections. Her elder sister,

Sonia, married Cecil Jacobs, a leading member of the Southern Rhodesian Jewish community, and still lives in Bulawayo.[35]

Their Northern Rhodesian business was taken over at the end of the war by Isaac Rosen, a native of Moldavia. He had been in the town for some time and was probably a former employee. He sold the business in the late 1920s to Louis Glasser, son of Benjamin Glasser of Lusaka, but he left Broken Hill and returned to Lusaka in 1933 following the closure of the mine. There was mass unemployment and destitution in the town at the time and, as Goody Glasser recalls, 'it was not a very pleasant place to be in business'.[36] Isaac Rosen remained in the town until the 1940s, and may have resumed control of his former business. One of his sons studied medicine and was working in Broken Hill as the Rhodesia Railways doctor in the later 1940s. Meyer Jacobson, from Riga, was also brought to the country to work for the Beemers. He set up his own business in the town after the First World War and ran it until his death in the late 1930s. Members of his family, including his son Gerald, remained in the town until after the Second World War, when the business was taken over by Josef Rotter.[37]

As was the case in the other towns, these traders all brought in young Jewish men as shop assistants. One of Isaac Rosen's assistants, Shim Lakofski, whose spectacular career as a trader during the Copperbelt construction boom is described in a later chapter, reached Broken Hill in 1924. He had been recruited through a cousin, Isaac Osrin, who worked as a commercial traveller for one of the Bulawayo firms. Shim's reminiscences shed some light on the business life of the town in the late 1920s, and also show how the lucky, and hard-working, few were able to accumulate capital and make the transition from shop assistant to shopkeeper. When Louis Glasser took over Isaac Rosen's business, he invited Shim to become a partner. Shim did not have sufficient capital to do so, but he agreed to work with him on a commission basis. Within two years he had greatly increased the store's turnover and was earning over £50 a month. He had a number of trading ventures on the side. He had a motor cycle and went out on Sundays into the villages around Broken Hill to buy maize from peasants for delivery to the shop and mill on Monday mornings. This is evidence that there was still in the mid-1920s a lively peasant economy which had been built up by the Lenje people in response to the demand for food created by the mine and the growth of the town. It was curtailed from 1930 onwards by the forced removal of many people into reserves which were at least twenty miles from the town. This was to make way for settler farmers who did not in fact arrive until after the Second World War. The mine's decision, in the late 1920s, to provide five-acre plots on which its black employees could live and support their families also reduced the market for peasant produce. The mine adopted this strategy as a way of coping with the competition for labour which arose from the construction boom on the Copperbelt.[38]

In addition to buying peasant produce, Shim also bought and sold motor

cycles and cars. One of his deals provides a surprising link with Northern
Rhodesia's pre-colonial past. Among the cars which he bought and sold
several times over was a Citroën which belonged to James 'Changa Changa'
Harrison Clark. He had established himself as a chief and slave-trader, in
competition with Carl Wiese, in the lower Luangwa valley in the mid-1880s.
After the establishment of colonial rule, he was reduced to the role of
manager of the beer hall at the Broken Hill mine. He was advised by his
doctor that he should sell his car and get more exercise. He sold his car, but
died soon afterwards in 1927.[39]

The Hochsteins and the Thals

The Hochstein family probably had the longest continuous association with
the town and provided an element of continuity to the Jewish community.
Chaim Hochstein (later known as Harris Hockstein) came from Kiev in the
Ukraine, by way of London. His wife, Rebecca, was brought up in the East
End of London, and was the aunt of Moss Dobkins, who features in a later
chapter. The Hochsteins had reached Kalomo by 1905, but moved to Living-
stone in 1910. They had additional stores at various times at Kalomo, Choma,
Mazabuka and in the Lusaka district. Chaim Hochstein moved north to
Broken Hill in 1923, and members of his family, including his two daughters,
remained in business there until the late 1960s. One of his daughters married
Myer Brin who had arrived from London in 1925 and worked for Isaac
Rosen. Chaim Hochstein's son, Lewis, remained in Livingstone where he was
employed by the Susmans as an accountant and manager for many years.[40]

The most interesting member of Broken Hill's small Jewish community in
the 1920s and 1930s was Maurice (Moshe) Thal who was president of the
Hebrew Congregation for a number of years. With his younger brother,
Max, who moved on to the Copperbelt, he ran a general dealer's store in the
town from 1924 to 1935. He came from a family with a strong scholarly
tradition and was born at Thalsen in Kurland in 1876. His father, Louis
Thal, had emigrated to South Africa on his own in 1890, but died near
Middelburg in the Transvaal in the following year. Maurice reached South
Africa in 1894–95 and worked his way up through Namaqualand and the
Transvaal to Southern Rhodesia. He spent some time at the Lonely mine,
near Selukwe, where he ran a store in partnership with Willie Hepker, who
married his sister, Rebecca. They feature later in this story. He himself married
Celia Rubinstein, a talented musician, who was born in Ireland. She was well
connected in central Africa. One of her sisters married David Landau, of
Bulawayo, and another married Herman Blumenthal who became a prominent
businessman in Elisabethville.[41]

Broken Hill was in the mid-1930s a centre of activity by the British Union
of Fascists, remembered as the Black Shirts. They exploited the frustrations
of the impoverished and discontented white working class. According to

Roy Welensky, who moved to the town as a railwayman in 1933, at least one Jewish shop was closed down by a boycott at this time. Maurice Thal's daughter, Sheilagh Matheson, confirmed Welensky's account, and suggested that a boycott of Jewish shops was organised by the leader of the local fascists, a Dr Brown. It was partially effective, and depressed business so much that her father was forced to close his shop and leave the country with his family in 1935. This was one of the first organised shop boycotts in Northern Rhodesia and may have formed the model for later African boycotts of Asian shops in Broken Hill and Luanshya in the 1940s, and of Jewish-owned Lusaka and Copperbelt butcheries in the 1950s.[42]

Maurice Thal was one of those Jewish shopkeepers who was a trader by day and an intellectual by night. Surviving fragments of his journals and other writings give a remarkable insight into his thoughts about Judaism, Zionism and his own predicament, which was already touched by the rise of fascism. His writings reveal a deep knowledge of Jewish intellectual and political history from the time of Moses Mendelssohn, the leader of the German Jewish *Haskalah*, or Enlightenment movement, of the eighteenth century, to Theodor Herzl. As he prepared to leave Broken Hill in September 1935, he was troubled not only by the rise of fascism and its impact on his own family, but also by the divisions in the tiny Jewish community of Broken Hill which made it impossible at that time to gather a *minyan*. He resigned from the presidency of the Hebrew Congregation on 22 September 1935. Four days later he wrote in his journal:

Tonight is Kol Nidre night. No shul, no minyan. We shall just meet at Hochstein's house and say Good Yomtov to one another. A quarrel with Harris Hochstein made it impossible to have a minyan. The little petty quarrels of the small congregation is a reflection of what takes place in all Jewish matters, no Unity, no Forbearance. 'Am keeshai avrer' – a stubborn nation without Humility, no discipline. How will we succeed to build up a new nation? Our prophets said hard things about us, our poets said sweet things about us. We are God's chosen people, we have survived cruel masters, we have survived innumerable Hamans, our martyrs have been thrown to the lions, burnt at the stake. We have a modern Hitler. He has sworn the destruction of our nation. And yet it is necessary to whip us from one end of the world to the other, to send messengers among us, to preach to us, to appeal to our selfish natures, that the fire of anti-Semitism will overtake us, like a grass fire, that the fate of German Jewry will be our fate.[43]

A few days later he wrote:

Rosh Hashana 5696 is over. We are two days in the New Year. Soon I shall have to leave my home, and my town. We have spent more than eleven years here. Financially our stay here was far from successful, still we spent many happy days here – it is strange that one gets attached to a place. It was a mistake to stay in Broken Hill all these years. I might have been better off if I had left the

place four years ago. It is easy to judge when one looks back. One does not like
to break up a home and rush into bankruptcy. Breaking up a business means
bankruptcy, and when the family were all young, the responsibility was greater.
One always hopes things might improve. One does not reckon on things going
from bad to worse.[44]

Maurice Thal's journal clearly shows that there are different kinds of
profit. He had placed the maintenance of his family above the preservation
of his capital. He had stayed in Broken Hill through the depression because
he feared that the closure of his business would result in the break-up of
his family. By 1935 they were old enough to go their own separate ways and
they did. His wife and daughter, Sheilagh, went to the Cape. His sons stayed
on in rooms in Broken Hill, and he went into what he called 'exile' in
Bulawayo, where he ran a fruit shop. He died less than two years later, in
May 1937 , at the age of sixty. His four sons all served in the British forces
during the Second World War. The third son, Basil, joined the Rhodesia
Regiment and was killed in action in Somaliland in August 1940. The daughter,
Sheilagh, settled in Zimbabwe. Her daughter, Moira, married Ze Forjaz, a
radical architect and member of Frelimo, who became a member of the first
post-independence government of Mozambique. Moira was a close friend of
Ruth First, and has made a career for herself as a maker of films. She is
currently running an art gallery in Lisbon.[45]

Maurice Thal was one of many victims of the depression. Eileen Bigland
has left a graphic description of the decayed state of Broken Hill in 1938.
It was then known to its inhabitants as 'Busted Hill'. She is also rather
scathing about the quality of the food served in the town's Great Northern
Hotel which was run by Bill Feigenbaum, a member of Max Shapiro's
extended family.[46] Broken Hill seems never to have recovered the economic
buoyancy which it enjoyed in the late 1920s. Jewish traders also had to
contend with the arrival of Asian trading competitors from about 1936
onwards – apparently as a result of the opening of the Great East Road.
There were ten Asian traders in the town in 1938 and, as was the case
elsewhere, they tended to take over African trade.[47] They were drawn to this
branch of trade for precisely the same reasons that had originally forced
Jewish immigrants into it. These included lack of proficiency in English and
shortage of capital.

Lusaka

Apart from Ndola, the third town to emerge along the Line of Rail and to
attract a Jewish community was Lusaka. It is one of only two major towns
in Zambia which Jewish traders could claim to have founded. The other is,
as we shall see, Kitwe. The origins of Lusaka are very different from those
of Livingstone, Broken Hill or Ndola. Livingstone emerged as a railway and

administrative centre, and as the gateway to the north. Broken Hill and Ndola had their origins as railway, mining and administrative centres, but Lusaka's origins were purely commercial and agricultural. Although it eventually became the capital of the country, it was not even a local administrative centre until 1930 when the Boma, or district headquarters, was moved from Chilanga, a railway halt about ten miles to the south. It was never a railway centre, apart from the siding which eventually became a station, and its only link with mining was as a supply point for the mines in the Hook of Kafue.

Two traders, Benjamin Glasser in 1908, and Edward Kollenberg in 1909, were to lay the commercial foundations of the town which would be declared Northern Rhodesia's capital a quarter of a century later. There is some dispute between the two families as to which of them reached Lusaka first. It is probable that J. R. Rollnick was, for a brief period in 1906–8, the first trader in Lusaka, before selling his pole and dagga store to Benjamin Glasser. Rollnick had been in business in Kalomo in 1905, and moved on with the railhead to Broken Hill, where he stayed for a few years, and then to the Congo.[48]

It is clear that the early traders bought maize and cattle from local peasants, though some maize had initially to be brought in from the south to supply the needs of the railway contractors. The area was naturally well endowed with fertile soils and water resources, and soon attracted relatively large numbers of settler farmers. Some of these were wealthy men from Britain, like H. St A. Gibbons and Boyd Cunninghame, while others were railway engineers like R. B. Dean and P. S. Miller, who had the opportunity to select the most attractive farms. There was also an influx of Afrikaner trekkers, who took up small holdings on land which was sold for sub-division by Edmund Davis's Northern Copper Company, and who almost immediately constituted a 'Poor White' section of the community. Although it was not a mining centre, Lusaka had an abundance of limestone, and the quarrying and burning of limestone provided the first new industry in the district. An Italian entrepreneur, G. B. Marrapodi, was in business in Lusaka in 1909, and he was soon followed by Percy Morton and his partner, Rosazza, who produced lime for local farmers, and for a market which extended from Southern Rhodesia to the Congo.[49]

The Glassers and the Kollenbergs

Some idea of the quality of life, and the experience, of these first traders at Lusaka can be gleaned from the stories of the Glasser and Kollenberg families. Benjamin Glasser was born at the *shtetl* of Ponovese in Kovno Province, later Lithuania. While most of his brothers emigrated to America, he came to South Africa, where his wife's brother was already living in Cape Town. Benjamin became a pedlar of second-hand clothing and travelled great distances through Bechuanaland and Southern Rhodesia, riding a bicycle

and towing a trailer. He obtained a trading licence in 1908. He later supplemented his income from trading through capitation fees on workers recruited
for the farms and mines of Southern Rhodesia. After a five-year separation,
he brought his wife, Frieda, and their children up from Cape Town in 1913.
Their son, Goodman, better known as Goody, was born in Lusaka in 1914,
and was claimed – in the days when such things seemed important to the
settler community – as the first Jewish and, a little improbably, as the first
white child to be born in the settlement.[50]

Life was especially difficult for Frieda, who was devoutly orthodox and
observant. In 1947 she gave Wolf Rybko a graphic description of her early
days in Lusaka. She observed: 'There were neither people nor houses, only
trees, rocks and God.'[51] She arrived in October, the hottest month of the
year, and her greatest problem was to get a supply of fresh water. Every
morning she sent two 'Natives' with a washing basin to a distant pool. Every
evening they returned with the tub from which most of the water had
escaped as they carried it. Twice a week a train passed the siding and her
husband got two bottles of oily water from the engine. Despairing of being
able to feed or water her young family, she decided to return to Europe –
only to find that the clothes in her unopened luggage had been eaten by
white ants. Lusaka's first resident policeman, Sir Percy Sillitoe, later London's
Metropolitan Police Commissioner, recalled his efforts to solve the water
crisis at this time by digging a well.[52] Lusaka was, because of its limestone
base, not only prone to serious dry season water shortages, but also to
floods – so much so that residents were said to need boats for use in the
rainy season.

Frieda was unusual among immigrant Jews at the time in her insistence on
a kosher diet. Meat brought up from Bulawayo by train was often inedible
on arrival. Her situation was relieved by the later arrival from Cape Town of
her brother, Chaim Bloch, who was a trained *shochet*. She had by then opened
her own bakery and dairy. She claimed that she was the first person to
produce and sell a bottle of milk or a loaf of bread in Lusaka or, indeed,
anywhere on the Line of Rail between Livingstone and Broken Hill. The
inspiration of this enterprise was the need to feed her own children. She was
worried about the education of her elder children. All the other white children
in the area were Afrikaans-speaking, and there was some dispute about the
medium of instruction. Her husband eventually persuaded the District Commissioner to open an English-medium school, and the Glasser children shared
their lessons with the first teacher's two children in a corrugated-iron shed.

The Glassers were not part of an extensive family network, but Frieda
Glasser's brother, Chaim Bloch, remained in the town for a number of years.
A neighbour in Lusaka, Max Maisel, who stayed until 1928, also came from
the *shtetl* of Ponovese, and may have been a relative. The Kollenbergs were,
by contrast, a large family which was eventually spread widely through central
Africa. Edward Kollenberg began his trading career as a horse dealer in the

shtetl of Sassmachen in Kurland, later Latvia. As was the case with Benjamin Glasser, many of his family emigrated to America. His brothers in Michigan sent him money for the journey to America, but it was not enough for the trans-Atlantic fare from London. With a friend, he took a year's contract on the Transvaal gold mines which paid his fare to South Africa. After an unsuccessful trading venture into Bechuanaland, allegedly thwarted by Chief Khama's opposition to Jewish traders, they built a mud brick store at Mangwe on the Rhodesian side of the border, and then moved the short distance to Plumtree. In 1897 Edward sent for his wife, Glicka Hirschfeld, and some members of their large family.[53]

Edward Kollenberg's business prospered. He became a maize and cattle buyer for the South African mines and by 1908 he had extended his operations into Northern Rhodesia. In that year he was a major buyer at a famous auction in Kalomo at which Sam Haslett sold over a thousand head of cattle for the Susmans on one day. He attempted to break into the Congo trade, and established a branch of his business under the management of his son, Henrie, in Elisabethville. While Herman remained in Bulawayo, Edward himself opened a new store at Lusaka in 1909. He opened a mill in the following year which was one of three running in the 'village' at harvest time in 1912.[54] Within a few years the family had closed their stores in the Congo and Southern Rhodesia and concentrated their business in Lusaka. Their store, and their greatly expanded mill, remained the core of their business until the early 1930s.[55]

Three of the Kollenbergs' sons – Herman, Henrie and David – were directly involved in the Northern Rhodesian business. Herman was involved in the expansion of the business into the Copperbelt in the late 1920s, but died in tragic circumstances at Nkana in 1938. David, who had trained as a lawyer and served in the First World War, then took control of the Copperbelt business which he ran until his death in the early 1960s. Henrie Kollenberg, who was primarily a farmer and cattle trader, remained in Lusaka until shortly after the Second World War.[56] The only member of the family to remain in Southern Rhodesia was the youngest son, Isadore, who, after education in Russia, became a prominent rancher and cattle trader in Matabeleland. He features later in this story as one of the promoters of two companies which set up hotels, butcheries and bakeries on the Copperbelt in the early 1930s. The Kollenbergs' daughter, Johanna, did not reach Northern Rhodesia until 1928, and then settled with her husband in Mazabuka. At least one member of Glicka Kollenberg's own family followed her to Northern Rhodesia. Her nephew, Isadore Hirschfeld, was a partner with Philip Berelowitz, from Kovno, in a number of stores at Magoye and Monze before and during the First World War. He moved on to the Lusaka district, and remained there as a farmer for a while. Edward Kollenberg died in 1933, and the original Lusaka store was sold to Louis Glasser, who ran it until the end of the Second World War when he left the town.[57]

Jewish Ranchers and Farmers

The Glassers and the Kollenbergs were soon joined by a third Jewish trading family, the Lipowskys, who established the Lusaka Trading Company in 1912, and held a party to celebrate the occasion. They do not, however, seem to have stayed for long.[58] More important for the long-term prosperity of Lusaka, however, was the arrival from a very early date of Jewish cattle ranchers and farmers. It was, of course, difficult to tell the difference between traders and farmers, as all of the early traders in Lusaka were involved in one way or another with the maize and cattle trades, and had to keep oxen for transport purposes. They were also involved in elementary forms of secondary industry, such as milling and baking.

The Susman brothers negotiated for the purchase of a 25,000-acre ranch at Leopard's Hill, about ten miles from Lusaka, in 1912, and began almost immediately to invest money in it. They saw it as a holding ranch for the Congo cattle trade, but they were also interested in improving the quality of their stock. They imported pedigree Aberdeen Angus bulls, and carried out breeding experiments. These were not initially successful, but they eventually developed a strain of Afrikander/South Devon stock, and kept as many as 4,500 cattle on the ranch. Never people to let anything go to waste, they exploited the bat guano resources of Leopard's Hill caves for nitrogenous fertiliser, and pioneered wheat cultivation at Leopard's Hill in 1920. About 200 acres were planted in that year, and they used a McCormick reaper and binder to bring in the harvest in October.

In 1927 Elie Susman negotiated with the colonial government for the addition of a further 25,000 acres to the ranch. After riding for ten days over the first area allocated, most of which he described as useless, he reduced the application to 14,000 acres. He said that additional land was essential for the expansion of their ranching activities. The Susmans never lived permanently at Leopard's Hill, but they still owned the ranch in the late 1930s. It is not clear when they parted with it, but the area is still known in the vernacular as 'Susman's farm'. They had also bought Kabulonga farm which was closer to the commercial centre of Lusaka. They began the production of Virginia tobacco there in 1926, but they were caught by the collapse of tobacco prices two years later. They then sold the 4,000-acre farm for £1,500. Although parts of it were sub-divided for small holdings in the 1930s, it was not until the 1950s that it began to be developed as Lusaka's most expensive, and exclusive, suburb.[59]

Another of the pioneers of the Barotseland cattle trade, A. B. Diamond, bought land near Lusaka. His farm, Diamondale on the Ngwerere river, is still well known. He had set up a butchery at Elisabethville in about 1909, but must have moved south again before the outbreak of the First World War. He died at Diamondale in 1917, allegedly of a broken heart, and was buried there. His herd of cattle had been compulsorily destroyed after an outbreak of disease. Members of his family remained in the country for many years. His son, Victor Solomon Diamond, set up one of Lusaka's first garages, the Central Garage, probably in 1920. He was selling Chevrolet cars, and Triumph and Douglas motor cycles in 1925, but he went bankrupt in 1930. By that time there were several garages at the north end of Cairo Road and the area was referred to as Motor Town. Lusaka's wagon works had closed down in 1922, and by the end of the decade the town's fifteen motor mechanics outnumbered its wagon and wheel wrights. Victor's sister, Cissy, married Nicholas Rosenfield in Lusaka in 1917. He came, as she did, from Ireland. The Rosenfields remained in the town, where they ran a café and an agency business, until 1937 when they moved to Luanshya. They stayed there for a further thirty years and left the country in the early 1960s.[60]

Developments in the 1920s

There were two important new arrivals in Lusaka's Cairo Road after the First World War. The Glassers and the Kollenbergs were joined by two traders with Livingstone connections. Isadore Aberman returned to the country from Romania in 1920, and, sensing the line of future development, moved immediately to Lusaka. Ten years later, he was one of the most prominent traders in the town and had fourteen subsidiary stores in the surrounding rural area. He extended his business to the Copperbelt during the construction boom, and was very badly hit by the depression – a disaster from which his fortunes never recovered. He and his wife left the country in 1937, and settled with their daughter, Adella, a talented musician who ran a jazz dance band in Lusaka in the early 1930s, in Bulawayo. In 1947 he was interviewed by Wolf Rybko, who found him living, and presumably trading, at Shabani, a mining town in Southern Rhodesia.[61]

The arrival of Sam Fischer in 1923, at the age of twenty-three, was of greater long-term significance for the development of the town. He was, as we have seen, a member of Elias Kopelowitz's extended family, and was, presumably, 'staked' to some extent by him. He had arrived from Libau, Latvia, with his first wife, Assia, only two years previously. He recalled that when he reached Lusaka there were only five Jewish families, and a number of bachelors, in the town which had a white population of not much more than 100. He noted that the population began to grow quite rapidly from the mid-1920s onwards. His first house, a very attractive building, was behind his shop on a site opposite the present Cairo Road post office. It is one of central Lusaka's few architectural features, but is now derelict and appears to be in danger of demolition. It is difficult to imagine today that there was once a tennis court in the garden of this house which stands at the very centre of the city of Lusaka. It was built in about 1928, and was the first house in the town to have electric lights.[62]

Fischer sold his general store in about 1930 to Major Hugh McKee, who later became a prominent settler politician, wartime Controller of Civil Supplies, and Commissioner for Northern Rhodesia in London. His shop, Kee's, moved its site several times, and was the predecessor of ZCBC Ltd, the parastatal shop which occupied a prime site in Cairo Road from the late 1960s until 1995. Sam Fischer did not entirely abandon retail trade, but opened a furniture shop which also sold carpets, mattresses and firearms. He devoted much of his energy from the late 1920s onwards, however, to property development.

Jewish commercial dominance in Lusaka was so strong that in 1928 it was reported that on the Jewish New Year only one shop in the town centre opened.[63] About half of the trading licences issued in the district at this time, and of the township stands in private occupation, were held by Jews. The trade of Cairo Road, which was built up for less than half its present length and on the west side of the road only, was dominated by the quartet of stores: Glasser's, Kollenberg's and the post-war arrivals, Aberman's, and Fischer's. This dominance was not always welcomed by other settlers and members of the colonial civil service. The comments of a young veterinary officer, A. J. Wakefield, who reached what he saw as a 'Wild West' town in 1924, echoed the earlier comments of Charlotte Mansfield in pre-war Livingstone, and were probably typical of contemporary settler opinion: 'The Jews are collected from Russia, Roumania [sic] and anywhere but Palestine – all of them arrived without a bean, and now, the stranglehold they have over the smaller farmers, especially the Dutch community, speaks for itself.' He quoted a local saying that the 'ox is cultivated for the benefit of the tick, the Jewish dealer, and other local parasites'. He felt that to be addressed by Jewish shopkeepers as 'Mr Vackveld' was 'a bit of a trial'.[64]

There were soon, however, to be changes. Benjamin Glasser died in 1929 and his business was, at first, carried on in a very small way by his widow, Frieda. After Isadore Aberman's withdrawal from Lusaka in 1937, only one of the original quartet of Cairo Road stores survived, and even it, Glasser's, was not in its original place. The depression of the early 1930s, the introduction of commercial segregation in Cairo Road, and the simultaneous development of the second-class trading area in Kamwala, all had an impact on the old-established businesses. From the early 1930s onwards, African customers who wished to buy from shops in the town centre were not allowed to enter the shops, but were served through hatches.

Asian traders began to arrive in quite large numbers in the mid-1930s. They were excluded from Cairo Road and were confined to the second-class trading area. By 1938 there were twenty-six Asian store-owners in Lusaka, many more than there were Jewish shopkeepers. Their average turnover was, however, small, and they were heavily dependent for credit and supplies on Jewish wholesalers, but, as elsewhere, they took over much of the African retail trade.[65] The decline of the general dealers signalled the arrival of more specialist shops intended to cater for the European market. This created new niches which were largely filled by German Jewish refugees who set up shops before, during and after the Second World War.

The New Capital

These changes came almost simultaneously with the emergence of Lusaka as the new capital of Northern Rhodesia. The decision to move the capital was stimulated by unhappiness with the climate and the peripheral situation of Livingstone. The eventual choice of Lusaka was based on its central location and its climate. Although it was a significant farming and commercial centre, it was still in 1931 not much more than a village, with a total population of about 2,500, of whom less than 500 were white. The proportion of Jews in the settler population was much larger than in Broken Hill, though the actual size of the population, and its wealth as gauged by contributions to the Zionist cause, was in 1928 similar. Jews in Lusaka in 1931 may still have made up as much as 10 per cent of the settler population.[66]

The choice of Lusaka in 1931 as the site for the new capital was clearly of benefit to the Jewish traders who were already there. They, however, saw the original plans, which required the moving of the commercial centre to a new site close to the junction of the Ridgeway (now Independence Avenue) and Church Road as more of a threat than an opportunity. The Lusaka Chamber of Commerce was formed in 1933 in order to fight this proposal. The government offered free stands in the new centre as an inducement to traders to move, but they demanded £30,000 – a probably generous estimate of the value of their buildings – as compensation for their existing Cairo Road premises. The government was unable, or unwilling, to find the money and the commercial centre remained where it was on the other side of the railway tracks from the new administrative capital. This explains why Lusaka is probably the only capital in the world in which the central business district is still on the edge of the town and adjacent to large areas of undeveloped bush and rock.[67]

The Jewish entrepreneur who benefited most directly from the development of the new capital was David Shapiro. He was born and educated in Palestine, and arrived in Lusaka in 1923 at the age of twenty-three. He started as a general dealer, but branched out into the grain and cattle trades, and was also a clearing agent. He bought a farm from the Susman brothers in 1929 and started a tile and brick works on it. In 1933 he secured the contract for the supply of all the bricks for the new town. His monopoly, which he apparently acquired on merit, was a source of contention among other potential brick-makers. The millions of bricks and tiles which he produced have lasted well and are still to be seen in the many buildings of Lusaka's 'garden city' development. The new capital was officially opened in 1935, but he continued to make bricks until after the Second World War. In the later 1930s he also entered the milling business. He was not at the centre of a large web of kinship, but his brother, Absolom, and his cousins, David and Shoshanna Pinhassovith, followed him to the country from Palestine. In the early 1930s he married Ivy Diamond, the Australian-born daughter of Livingstone's first resident rabbi.[68]

Another major Jewish beneficiary of the new capital project was Sam Fischer. He turned his attention from retail trading to property development and cinemas. He was for many years Lusaka's leading landlord, and a long-term member of the Lusaka Township Management Board, and later the Town Council. He erected Lusaka's first two-storey structure, Fischer's Building, which still stands in a prominent position facing the Church Road fly-over bridge. Part of the shopping arcade which he also built has been demolished to make way for Society House, but the rear section remains. He later built, rented and sold other shops in Cairo Road and in the second-class trading area, which was developed after the opening of Kamwala market in 1928.[69]

He also moved into the world of entertainment and became the proprietor of the Carlton cinema. He took it over in a half-finished state from Sam Wolpowitz who had arrived in the town in the mid-1920s. Wolpowitz was by all accounts an attractive and kindly character who was born in Lithuania and had been in America before coming to Africa. He ran a butchery, and also owned the Palace Hotel and the town's first cinema, which was associated with it. Sam Wolpowitz built another cinema in the mid-1930s on the site of the Anglican cathedral. This was the only building erected in what was intended to be the commercial centre of the new town. In addition to being built in what turned out to be the wrong place, Wolpowitz's cinema was structurally unsound and was closed down after a short time. According to legend, the front of the new cinema collapsed while its wiring was being inspected by the Clerk of Works. Wolpowitz lived on in Lusaka until his death in 1943.[70]

In the days before television, the cinema was the main source of entertainment for Lusaka's rapidly growing white population. It is hard for anyone who lived in Lusaka between the mid-1970s and the mid-1990s to believe that, from the 1930s to the 1960s, the South African Schlesinger Organisation and its successors supplied three new films a week not only to Lusaka, but to cinemas as far north as Nairobi. Films arrived by train and had to be sent on northwards, often in the early hours of the morning, after their last Lusaka showing. Attendance at Sam Fischer's cinema was, as his nephew Jack Fischer recalls, a major social event. Patrons were expected to wear dinner jackets and long dresses on Saturday nights. They might not be able to see the film, if they were placed behind a pillar, or hear it, if the sound of the film was drowned by rain falling on the corrugated-iron roof. Special seats were reserved for the Governor and his party. Many people had a permanent booking for the first night of every new film, and paid for their seats on account at the end of the month. The cinema was run in conjunction with a bar, and drinks were served in the frequent and long intervals. Asians were permitted to sit at the back of the cinema, but the African population was excluded by the censorship laws, as well as by the segregationist practices of the time.[71]

New Arrivals

At the bottom of the depression in 1932–33, Lusaka, with its new capital project, was the only potential growth point in the country, and was a magnet for unemployed white people from the Copperbelt. Building work was stalled until the middle of 1933, and there were before then 400 unemployed people camping in 'shanties' on the edge of the town.[72] A number of Jewish traders were also attracted to Lusaka at this time. They included Samuel Barnett, known as 'Tubby', Wulfsohn, from Froneberg, Kurland, who withdrew from the Congo during the depression. He had previously been at Kalomo at the beginning of the First World War and had then moved north. His wife, Floretta, was the daughter of Robert Glasstone who had also moved on to the Congo where he became a prominent member of Elisabethville's Hebrew Congregation. 'Tubby' Wulfsohn became a partner in a variety of cattle trading, butchery and other businesses, while his wife ran a tiny shop. His sister Miriam (Mary) and her husband, Henry Herbstein who came from Romania, also withdrew from the Congo at this time. They settled in Broken Hill where they invested the small amount of capital which they had been able to salvage from the depression in a mineral water factory.[73]

Other new arrivals in Lusaka included Sam and Annie Mendelsohn who were, with their family, to play a prominent part in the Jewish community until the 1960s. Sam Mendelsohn was born in Warsaw, and came to Southern Rhodesia as a child. His wife, Ann Liptz, was born in Russia and came first to the Congo where her father had a hotel in Elisabethville. They arrived in Lusaka in 1932 and almost immediately opened a men's outfitters called Mendy's. They sold ready-made clothing to the less affluent, and mainly Afrikaans-speaking, members of the white population, and, later on, to the emerging African middle class. They later opened a shop selling women's clothing, called Kay's, and another which specialised in school uniforms.[74]

George 'Lippy' Lipschild arrived in Lusaka from Nkana, where he had been an accountant on the mine, in 1934. He was born in Cape Town and had first come to work at Broken Hill in 1922. He went on to work at Bwana Mkubwa mine and Nkana. He had a hard struggle in the 1930s to support himself and his family. He did accounts, wrote letters for people who were unable to write in English, ran a secretarial school and a stationery shop. He was, in his own somewhat eccentric and cantankerous way, a public-spirited person who founded a ratepayers' association in the late 1930s. This applied pressure on government for the democratisation of the Lusaka Management Board whose members were for many years nominated by the

Governor. He was determined to have as little as possible to do with either Judaism or Jewishness. His wife, May Davis, who was born in London and brought up in Cape Town in an observant family, saw herself as a member of the Jewish community, and was also active in many other causes.

Their daughter, Berjulie, remembers her father as a difficult man who kept her as a virtual prisoner in wartime Lusaka. She was not allowed to participate in the active social life in the town which was created by Lusaka's importance as a military transit point on the Great North Road. She is, however, grateful to him for the sound training which he gave her in book-keeping and business practice. She was glad to escape from Lusaka in 1946, but returned two years later for her marriage to Hubert Press, who was with his brother, Sydney, the promoter of Edgar's Stores, the South African retail clothing chain. Berjulie Press features under her own name as a minor, but significant, character in Lyndall Gordon's book, *Shared Lives*.[75]

Some Smaller Centres

Lusaka was originally just one of a score of sidings which were built at twenty-mile intervals along the Line of Rail between Livingstone and Ndola. The others included Zimba, Kalomo, Choma, Pemba, Monze, Magoye, Maza-buka, Kafue, Chisamba and Kapiri Mposhi. Some of these halts, like Tara and Batoka, attracted stores, but never became villages or townships. A few became small administrative and commercial centres, and have grown in the post-independence period into small towns. In theory, any one of them might have grown into a city. At one point Kalomo, which became a centre for the Barotseland and Congo cattle trades, seemed a likely candidate, but it never really took off.

There were Jewish traders at one time or another, as Jack Baitz recalls, at all the small centres along the Line of Rail, and at places at some distance from it, such as Namwala and Mumbwa. His own family was typical of those which stayed for a long time at a small centre which never attracted a Jewish community. His father, Pesach Baitz, a tailor from Lithuania, was in business as a shopkeeper and cattle dealer at Pemba and Nega Nega from the late 1920s until the late 1940s. His brothers-in-law, Max and Myer Klein, were traders at Pemba and Monze respectively. The Baitzes' daughter, Florrie, married George Hurwitz, who arrived from Latvia in 1921 at the age of twenty and was a trader at Chisamba, on the Line of Rail north of Lusaka. He also became a farmer and cattle dealer there, but lived latterly in Lusaka where he had a shop until the late 1950s. In Pemba, the Baitzes were neighbours of the Greek cattle traders, the Cavadia brothers, Kosta and Pangos, who had reached Northern Rhodesia in 1905. The main focus of the Pemba traders, whether Jewish or Greek, was on Namwala and Maala, the centres for the important Ila cattle trade.[76]

The small centre which, perhaps, came nearest to taking off in the 1930s, and to acquiring a Jewish community, was Mazabuka, which is about eighty miles south of Lusaka. It began to emerge as a significant centre in the late 1920s, when the government established a large agricultural research station there. It also became the site of the country's only white junior secondary school, the Robert Codrington School, and of the Jeanes School. It then attracted members of the related Illion, Iljon and Fischer families, who were all in business there for a while. Uri Illion started a branch of Elias Kopelowitz's firm there in 1927 which was taken over, first by his brother Lazar, who died in 1934, and then by Philip Fischer. Their cousins, the Iljons, who spelled their name differently in order to avoid, or rather to reduce, confusion, arrived in Mazabuka at the same time. Edward Kollenberg opened a branch of his firm there in 1927 for his son-in-law, Oscar Iljon, who had just arrived from Latvia.

The Kollenbergs' daughter, Johanna, had married Oscar Iljon in 1903. Her husband, who had rabbinical training, came from a prominent Jewish family in Sassmachen, and later settled at Wolmar. He was a successful, and relatively privileged, merchant, dealing in furs and skins, but was forced to retreat to St Petersburg in the face of the German invasion during the First World War. The outbreak of the Russian Revolution was a further blow to his fortunes, and compelled his return to Latvia which gained its independence at the end of the war. Oscar's son Benjamin (Benny) was the first member of the family to emigrate to Northern Rhodesia, arriving in 1925. Oscar followed him in 1927, and went immediately to Mazabuka. His wife, Johanna, and most of the rest of the family arrived in 1928. In addition to his rabbinical training, Oscar was also a *shochet*. His services as a ritual slaughterer were appreciated by Yao Muslims from Nyasaland. Oscar Iljon died in Mazabuka in his early fifties in 1934.

The business in Mazabuka was carried on and developed by Benny and his brother Nicholas (Nicky). Among their varied enterprises were cattle trading, road making and a hotel, the Mazabuka Arms. Benny became chairman of the village management board and, when giving evidence to the Bledisloe Commission in 1938, referred to various threats to the prosperity of Mazabuka, including the reduction of the staff of the Agricultural Research Station, and the move of the Jeanes School to Chalimbana. He expressed the fear 'that we shall meet the fate of the once prosperous centres such as Kalomo, Pemba, Monze etc., making a total desert between Livingstone and Lusaka'.[77] Benny Iljon helped to confirm his prophecy by moving to Livingstone in 1939, though he retained his interests in Mazabuka for some time. Nicky Iljon joined the Northern Rhodesia Regiment on the outbreak of war and did not return to the country until 1950. The career of their younger brother Eric (Ahron), who trained as a doctor, is discussed in a later chapter.[78]

Although Jewish traders achieved a dominant position in the trade of Barotseland, and on the Line of Rail, in the years before the Second World War, they never had things entirely their own way. There were always success-

ful traders, such as F. J. Clarke, who were not Jewish, and there were branches
at several centres on the Line of Rail of the African Lakes Corporation. A
branch of the southern-based agricultural equipment suppliers J. W. Tarry
was opened in Lusaka in 1929. Away from the Line of Rail, in the north and
east, which was traditionally supplied through Nyasaland, competition from
the African Lakes Corporation and other traders was always intense. While
Jewish traders, such as Deuss and the Beemers, had a brief presence in the
north and east of the country in the earlier years of the century, there were
large parts of the eastern half of the country in which there was little or no
Jewish presence. They were never able to compete for long with the African
Lakes Corporation which preserved its dominant position. It did, however,
in later years face increasingly intense competition from the networks of
stores which were established in the north by John Thom, R. N. P. Creed
and by Harold Booth, as well as from Asian traders, almost all Muslims, who
entered from Nyasaland where they were already strongly established.[79]

Conclusion

In considering the important role played by Jewish traders in the emergence
of towns in the few decades which separated the coming of the Line of Rail
from the Second World War, it is important to remember that these were
embryonic towns. John Smith's description of Livingstone, as he first saw it
in July 1913, gives something of the flavour of what was still not much more
than a village:

> Livingstone consists of one main street, Queensway, a dirt track with sand inches
> deep and a length of only about 200 yards. Another track, Mainway, running
> parallel, goes the seven miles, via Old Drift to the Falls. Again, by no stretch of
> the imagination could this be called a road. Deep ditches run down either side
> of Queensway to carry the stormwater from the rainy-season downpours. But
> now, when no rain has fallen for months, the air is thick with dust twenty-four
> hours a day, as the long spans of thirty or more oxen drag the solid-axled wagons
> past offices, stores, hotel and dwellings. At the same time, mule carts are driven
> at a less leisurely pace along the same single track adding to the confusion, dust
> and clatter.[80]

After the First World War, motor lorries and cars replaced ox wagons and
mule carts, and cinemas brought the white population into closer touch with
the outside world, but the commercial centre of Lusaka in the 1930s still
consisted of not much more than half a long street, or three complete
blocks. Livingstone, which had been deprived of the capital, and Broken Hill,
which was worst hit by the depression, both seemed to have outgrown
themselves, and had in the late 1930s the air of ghost towns. And yet, the
population of Lusaka grew rapidly from the mid-1930s and was given further
stimulus by the Second World War. The great demand for copper and other

minerals then brought back life to the whole of the Line of Rail from Livingstone to Ndola and beyond. As the great French historian Fernand Braudel has pointed out in another context, it is not the size of towns which is so important as their relationship with the surrounding countryside. They are like 'electric transformers. They increase tension, accelerate the rhythm of exchange and ceaselessly stir up men's lives.'[81] Each of the three towns which we have considered in detail was closely linked to an agricultural hinterland. Although seen as centres of white settlement, these towns always attracted four or five times as many black people. They were centres for the distribution of goods and credit, as well as for the purchase of produce, and were nodes of growth for a money economy. The town centres of Livingstone, of Lusaka, and of Kabwe (Broken Hill), still owe many of their architectural features – their shop fronts and their shop names – and their distinctive, and strangely attractive, urban characteristics, to their now largely forgotten, and often Jewish, builders.

CHAPTER 4

A Wandering Jew: Moss Dobkins's Story

It is difficult in a history such as this to get much real sense of the motives, the feelings, or the sense of identity of the people who, forced to emigrate from their homes in eastern Europe by economic, political and religious pressures, made their homes on the frontier of white settlement in southern Africa. Fortunately, one man of eastern European origin, though not birth, who arrived in Northern Rhodesia before the First World War, has left a fragment of autobiography. His name was Moss Dobkins. He is important in himself as the Jewish trader who lived longest in the country, and as a member of a family which has had the longest continuous connection with it, dating back to the arrival of his uncle, Chaim Hochstein, in 1905. His narrative is important because it provides some contemporary evidence of how it felt, and what it meant, to be an immigrant Jew in central Africa in the early years of the twentieth century. It is to his life story that we will now turn.

Moss Dobkins's autobiography consists of an account of his early life which he began to write in the 1970s when he was about eighty years old. It also includes his own transcription of a diary which he kept on a trek which he undertook in 1922 in search of work. He walked about 500 miles between the terminus of the railway west of Elisabethville in the Congo and the railhead of the Benguela railway which was then about 300 miles from the coast in Angola. This section of diary also contains flashbacks to his youth in England and early trading experiences in Northern Rhodesia. It is not always clear whether these recollections were written in 1922 or were added when he transcribed the diary in his old age. In spite of its fragmentary nature, Moss Dobkins's manuscript does provide a unique insight into the personal experience of one early Jewish settler in Northern Rhodesia. Dobkins was a typical Jewish immigrant of the time in that his origins lay in the Russian empire and he was a fluent speaker of Yiddish. He was untypical in that he had been born and brought up in London, and spoke, read and wrote English fluently. It was, perhaps, his bilingualism and his ability to move in the two worlds of the British and the eastern European which made him such an acute observer of the contemporary social scene.[1]

Origins

Moss was born in Whitechapel, London, on 14 May 1894. He was the son of Aaron Samuel Dobkins and Leah Levinson. His father was an immigrant from Vilna, where his paternal grandfather was a tailor who specialised in military uniforms. He did not know his father's family. They kept in touch through occasional visitors to London who brought messages and letters. His maternal grandparents, who lived with the family in London, also came from the Russian empire, but his mother was brought up in England. Her father was born in about 1835 and had served in the Russian army. He was a veteran of the Crimean War and the siege of Sebastopol. He was a powerfully-built old man who made a living in London by peddling tailor's scraps, off-cuts and ends of rolls. He would carry a 50-pound bag on his back, or hire a barrow by the day.

Moss's maternal grandmother, who was born in Finland, was in his own words the essential 'Yiddisher mama'. She was devoutly orthodox and clearly had a very strong influence on him. She ran a household in which there were eventually seven children and both parents went out to work. Camping in the bush in Angola he remembered his 'Boba', how she would sit up at night to see that he had a hot meal if he came in late, and would be up again early in the morning to light the fire. Moss often sat talking to her as a child. She told him of her own experience and taught him that he must be true to himself, 'lead a good life and a clean one'. When his grandfather died in 1919, Moss provided £100 to bring his mother, younger brothers and sisters, and his grandmother, out to central Africa. She was eighty when she reached Africa and died at Elisabethville.

Moss's father was a master tailor who ran a factory or workshop in the East End of London. At times he employed as many as thirty men and some girls. His employees were eastern European Jews, usually recent immigrants, on very low wages. In good times he supplied suits, and later women's dresses, to West End stores such as Harrod's. In spite of the number of his employees, his business was clearly precarious and vulnerable to the rise and fall of the trade cycle. On two occasions between 1900 and 1914 he was forced by depression to close his business and to emigrate.

Links with Africa

The family's first link with Africa was through Moss's maternal uncle, Abraham Levinson. He had travelled to South Africa before the Anglo-Boer War, in which he served. He was presumed to be lost until some time around 1903 or 1904. Moss provides a graphic, and typically breathless, description of his surprising return:

> Boba, there is a man in the passage with a box of fruit wants to see you.

Grandma came out of the kitchen (she was a small woman, wearing an apron, snub nose, and wearing a 'shatel' a plain wig, which was the custom among the Jewish Orthodox women), and after a few steps stopped, lifted up her hands and exclaimed 'Avronka, my kind' (Abraham my child) and hugged him – this was her son she had not seen for nearly twenty years nor heard from him for the last 10 to 15 years.

During his short stay in London, Uncle Abraham persuaded Moss's father and maternal uncle, Chaim Hochstein, who was living in the same house with his family, that they should leave for South Africa. As business was bad, they did not need much persuasion. Chaim Hochstein, after trading goods to markets with a horse and cart, had started a small greengrocer's shop, but was ready to close it. After paying the fares, there was not much money left, and life was hard for the families who were left behind. Hochstein found employment in Southern Rhodesia and by 1905 had, as we have seen, reached Kalomo. His wife and family joined him there in 1910. Moss's father did not find it easy to get established in South Africa. He did not have enough capital to set himself up in business as a tailor, so he found employment as a tailor, but the wages were not enough for him to send money home. Within a year he had returned to London and started another business in Aldgate.

London Life

It was in London that Moss's view of the world was formed. His sense of Jewish identity came from three sources: the home, institutions outside the home and from the street. In the home the dominant influence came from his grandparents. Judaism is a religion of the family and Moss had a very strong sense of family obligation. There are only a few references in his autobiographical fragment to institutionalised religion. If he attended synagogue or *shul* there is no reference to it. He does refer to his father hiring a *mohel* for the circumcision of his youngest brother, Len, in 1911. Moss attended state primary schools and was asked to leave the class during Scripture. He suspected that his fellow pupils were envious of this exclusion. He did not attend a *cheder* or Hebrew school, as he would have done in the Baltic provinces, but he did, for a time, have Hebrew classes once or twice a week. He acquired some knowledge of Judaism and a deep interest in religion.

The institution outside the home which had the greatest influence on him was the Jewish Boys' Brigade. This was established in 1895 and was modelled on its Christian counterpart. It was through his mother, who kept up with political, social and intellectual developments, that he joined the brigade. His grandmother, who had accompanied her husband as a camp follower through twenty years of military service, was opposed to his joining the brigade because of its military associations. For five years Moss attended weekly meetings of the brigade in the City, often cycling for an hour each way from his home in Southfields to attend, and returning home late at night. The highlight of the year was the summer camp at the seaside at Deal in Kent. Moss was filled with pride as several companies of the brigade, over 500 Jewish 'lads', marched with brass band playing through the City of London, and over the Thames to catch the train from Waterloo.

The education which Moss acquired in the streets of London was less positive and exposed him to the force of anti-Semitism. He noted that while the middle classes avoided contact with Jews, except in business, there was closer contact between Jews and gentiles among the lower classes. He was accustomed to being taunted in the streets with cries of 'Val shene! [vile? sheeny – an opprobrious epithet for Jew] Why don't you go back to your country?' When he left school he also found that anti-Semitism blocked many avenues of employment. After finding that he had no aptitude for his father's profession of tailoring, though he was good at drawing patterns, he tried to sign on as an apprentice engineer. It was made clear to him that as a Jew he was not welcome in this profession. He was offered, and accepted, a job as an office boy in an engineering shop. He also thought of accountancy as a career, but could not afford to pay the premiums necessary for entry to the profession.

Voyage to Africa

It is hardly surprising, therefore, that when his aunt, Becky Hochstein, wrote saying that they could give him work in Northern Rhodesia in the new store which they were opening at Livingstone, he jumped at the chance. He left England on the *Garth Castle* with a steerage class ticket costing £10.10.0. and a new suit costing £1.15.0. in August 1911. He was just seventeen years old and was not to see London again for forty-three years. His father closed his business for a second time soon afterwards and also sailed for Africa.

Most of the other passengers in steerage were Yiddish-speaking, and religious, central European Jews. The ship carried kosher food which was cooked by one of the passengers under the supervision of a rabbi who was also a passenger. Moss soon found that his bilingualism stood him in good stead. He was called upon to act as an interpreter for the ship's captain in a case which involved a gentile passenger who had allegedly pulled a gun on a Jew. Moss was proud of his knowledge of Yiddish which he saw as a beautiful and expressive language. It was also a language which he found very useful in business in central Africa in the early years of the century.

From Cape Town Moss took the train to Livingstone, travelling third class to Kimberley and second class from there to his destination. He collected £2.10.0. for the journey from a wholesale merchant in Bulawayo where one of his Hochstein cousins was already at school. Moss had no idea that Livingstone was close to the Victoria Falls and was astonished when the train passed close to them. He was met at the station by an African salesman from his uncle's shop who carried his suitcase. Moss showed solicitude for the man who had to walk on the hot sand without shoes or boots. He explained that the soles of his feet were hardened and that he was used to it.

Livingstone

In Livingstone Moss noted the government buildings and the administrator's house. There were, he recalled, two hotels or rather one hotel in two sections: the Livingstone and the North-Western. The Fairmount Hotel was still under construction. The largest shop was 'Mopani' Clarke's Zambezi Trading Company. There were a number of smaller Jewish shops, and there was the Susmans' butchery and bakery. His uncle's shop was in a large building, about ninety feet by thirty-five feet. The building was partitioned with living quarters for the family at the back. The kitchen was outside and hot water came from a device known as a Rhodesian boiler which he described as a forty-four-gallon drum in an oven. Moss's bedroom was the shop counter. Every night he took a few blankets from the shelves and put them back in the morning. He kept the sheets under the counter.

Livingstone was the port of entry and clearance for most goods entering the country. Many passengers and a large quantity of goods passed through on the way to the Congo. There were two mail and passenger trains a week, one up and one down, and a daily goods train. Many returning labour migrants also passed through on their way to Barotseland and the Tonga and Ila areas of what is now the Southern Province. There was a steady flow of tourists from the south for whom the hotels and curio sellers catered. It was also, of course, a centre for the cattle trade.

Soon after his arrival in Livingstone, Moss set off on the first of many trading expeditions into the bush. He travelled with a party of porters who carried black and white calico, and salt and sugar, as trade goods, as well as maize meal for provisions, pots, pans and blankets. They passed through Kalomo and into what Moss called the 'Mankoya country'.[2] Moss thought that the Nkoya people were hard workers. At that time they were producing large quantities of groundnuts for sale. He was badly sunburnt on this trip. After his return he had an attack of malaria and spent some time in hospital. As soon as he had learnt the business, he was sent by his uncle in 1913 to build and open a new store at Choma. He built the store from poles and dagga and was for a time his own manager.

The Outbreak of War

Soon after the outbreak of the First World War in August 1914, Moss joined the Northern Rhodesian Volunteer Force, Mobile Column, also known as the Northern Rhodesia Rifles.[3] This was raised by Major Boyd Cunninghame, with

Major Robert Gordon, the founder of the Lochinvar ranch, as his deputy, to assist in the defence of the country against the possibility of German invasion on the northern border. Moss joined up as a Grade A volunteer, indicating that he was prepared to serve anywhere in the world. He was not the only Jew in Northern Rhodesia to serve during the war. Marcus Grill's son-in-law, Joe Merber, was lost in action on the Western Front. David Kollenberg served in France and returned unscathed. Oscar Susman and Natie Grill served, as we have seen, in the East African campaign. The Northern Rhodesia Rifles were not a well-trained or disciplined fighting force. Moss spent the first few months of service in Livingstone, before moving on for several months each to Lusaka and Broken Hill. He was able to make good use of the training in drill which he had acquired in the Jewish Boys' Brigade, and was at one stage employed to drill other recruits. He took part in the regiment's famous march to the northern border at Abercorn (Mbala), and spent most of 1916 patrolling the Great North Road between Serenje and Mpika. It was near Abercorn at the end of 1915 that he saw one of the first motor cars to be brought into Northern Rhodesia. It was a Model T Ford belonging to Captain Duly, who had obtained the Ford agency for the Rhodesias. Motor transport was, however, a rarity. Moss spent most of his time supervising carriers who were conscripted for transport work. All the petrol for the ten cars which were in use on the Great North Road had to be brought in by carriers in four-gallon tins or 'Jerry' cans. Moss gives the impression that his carriers were well looked after, but there was a high mortality rate among them during the war as a result of overloading and starvation.

At the end of 1916, the Northern Rhodesia Rifles were disbanded, though its members remained in reserve. During 1917 Moss worked for the Beemer brothers at Mpika and later in their stores at Broken Hill, Bwana Mkubwa and Ndola which was just beginning to emerge as an administrative, commercial and mining centre. At the end of the year, after the closure of the Bwana Mkubwa mine, he decided to try his luck in the Congo. British influence in Katanga was very strong as Robert Williams's Tanganyika Concessions Company was the main employer, and much of the African mine labour came from Northern Rhodesia. The British presence was especially strong during the war when Katanga functioned as an extension of the Rhodesian economy. At this time there were many Jewish traders in the province who came from eastern Europe. After the war there was an influx of Sephardic Jews from the island of Rhodes who became the dominant group. There were 450 Jewish families in Katanga at the time of the independence of the Congo in 1960.

The Congo and Angola

Moss's father was already in Elisabethville. He had spent a short time at Livingstone in 1913 before moving on to the Congo. He tried to establish a tailoring business there, but soon found that there was no great call for

suits in a climate where most men wore shorts and shirts. He became the
manager of a hotel, but this was not a great success as he was reluctant to
stop credit to non-paying customers. Moss worked with his father for a
while, but was not happy in the hotel business; he did not approve of people
drinking into the early hours of the morning. Early in 1918 he was offered
a job as the manager of a butchery at Likasi (later known as Jadotville) near
Kambove. Its Jewish owner, a Mr Robinson, was about to return to
Johannesburg on his Harley Davidson motor cycle. Moss protested that he
knew nothing about the butchery business, but he was assured that he need
not worry about that. There were African butchers to cut up the meat and
make orders. Moss was said to be 'a reliable fellow', and all he would have
to do was to keep a count of the cattle slaughtered, and do the books. He
would be paid £20 a month, considerably more than he had been paid by the
Beemers. The job lasted for four months when the business was taken over
by the ubiquitous Barnett 'Bongola' Smith.

Moss worked for a while for a Mr Steinberg at Kamatanda near Likasi.
He was offered a half share in this business, which served a nearby mine,
for £500. He had saved almost all his earnings over the previous two years
as he had had free board and lodging – usually the shop counter – and no
living expenses, but he was not able to buy the business outright. He put his
savings down as a deposit, and agreed to pay the balance over twelve months.
He bought an iron shed from Paulings, the railway contractors, and put all
his profits over two years back into the business. A sudden devaluation of
the Belgian franc in 1920 threatened the sterling value of his stock, and he
was forced to run down the business in order to pay his suppliers and
extricate his capital. He eventually extracted £300 from the shop which
brought him £100 profit for over two years' hard work.

After working again for a while in his father's hotel, Moss set out in 1922
to look for work at Kambove. He found that the mine there had closed. His
brother Andrew suggested that he should join him in the dried fish trade
from the Congo side of the Pedicle on the Luapula river, where a man
known as 'Zanshen' was opening a store. He rejected this offer and chose
instead to set out, in company with a former Susman employee, George
Sterling, on a 500-mile walk with carriers to the diamond mines in Angola.[4]
It is not clear whether he ever reached the mines, but he did eventually reach
the Benguela railway and travelled the last 600 kilometres to the coast at
Lobito Bay by train. After most of two years at Lobito Bay, and a frustrating
year at Cape Town, he returned to Northern Rhodesia in 1925 and lived
there for another sixty years.

Religion and Philosophy

Moss's journal of his great trek across Africa sheds light on his views on a
variety of subjects, including the role of the Jews in central Africa, and what

being a Jew meant to him at this time. Moss befriended a number of Christian missionaries and enjoyed discussing religion with them. His uncle, Chaim Hochstein, was on good terms with the Paris missionaries at Livingstone. Moss himself had got to know the missionaries around Choma, and had provided prizes for children at mission schools. During the war he had established a close friendship with Malcolm Moffat, the Scottish missionary at Chitambo, near Serenje, whose aunt was David Livingstone's wife. In Angola he was befriended by George Hornby of the Christian Mission to Many Lands, who was based at Dilolo close to the boundaries of Northern Rhodesia and the Congo. Moss delighted in discussion of religious issues. He was surprised by what he saw as the missionaries' ignorance of the Old Testament, and their lack of awareness of what Christianity owed to Judaism. Some of them admitted that they had never known Jews, except as Yiddish-speaking traders, and were surprised that they could talk to him so freely.

Moss frequently engaged in conversation on religious matters with his African companions. He was fluent in a number of African languages, and was always very solicitous about the comfort of his carriers on trek. One or two of his employees from his Likasi shop insisted on accompanying him all the way from the Congo to Angola. A youth who was particularly devoted to him was known as 'Pickerneen' (picanin). Moss helped him to send money by postal order to his parents in Nyasaland. When asked by a group, including this young man, what church he belonged to, he replied: 'I do not belong to any church as I am not a Christian. I am a Hebrew and I belong to a Synagogue the same as Jesus for Jesus was born a Jew, was circumcised according to the law of the Jews, lived and prayed in the Temple as a Jew.'

Moss's writing is remarkably free of racism or paternalism. He recalled several meetings with King Lewanika of the Lozi with whom his uncle had been on good terms. His uncle had frequently had African visitors to the house and had provided them with food. Moss ate the same food as his carriers on trek though he ate his maize meal as soft porridge, and did not wait for it to harden into *nsima*. He noted that it was in 1922, when dining at Dilolo with the Hornbys and Mr Cardoso, a Portuguese trader with an African wife, that he first sat down at table for a meal with a black person. He described Mrs Cardoso as 'a very well-spoken woman'.

Of his own philosophy of life, Moss wrote, with his own inimitable style of punctuation, that he was:

> used to roughing it in town or the bush, accepting any job offered even for a meal, and doing it to the best of my ability – the main thing willingly – in my time I have worked as a shop assistant, went out into the villages trading – built African huts and stores of poles and *matepo* (which is just wet earth) also dried bricks made of the same material with a mould. Burnt bricks and built a shop and was a baker and used an anthill for an oven etc. and numerous other things – happy doing all – never thought about the future – main thought – not to owe – never to borrow – have some money to be able to send my grandfather and mother.

Of the Jewish diaspora, and the role of the Jews in central and southern
Africa, he noted that there were Jews in Africa before David Livingstone.
They were now scattered through South Africa, the Rhodesias and the Congo.
Most of them were small traders:

> opening a small store, or carrying bundles on their back, trekking from village
> to village or farm to farm – and then trading their goods for eggs which they
> sold to housewives – later when they managed to save a little money bought a
> donkey and cart and travelled further afield. That was the beginning of the
> large stores – but how many reached that stage … Hard work for all – mostly
> despised by the Gentiles.

Looking back to his early days in Africa from the 1970s he recalled:

> That was when Jews were living in ghettos and pogroms took place in all Jewish
> towns. The Jews were leaving for all parts of the world. So wherever one went
> in the wilds of most countries, America North and South, Australia, Africa, if
> you found a lonely European who was trying to live a quiet life, running a
> small farm, but mostly a small shop, you could be sure to find the Jew – after
> years some progressed – through hard work, saving all they could, if they were
> young to get married, help, perhaps, their parents to come to a quieter life.
> They were despised for their progress, worked like slaves.

Running through his account of his own experience, which was similar to
that of many of his contemporaries, are the themes of escape from persecution, the search for a peaceful life, hard work, the desire to reunite
divided families, and to create new ones. Some progressed and others did
not. For those who did succeed in creating a new life for themselves, there
was the nagging feeling that their success was resented. They felt that they
were despised for their single-minded dedication to the search for security.
This was something which tended to separate them from people who had
not shared, and could not fully appreciate, their experience.

Later Life

Moss did not write much about his later life. For this we have to rely mainly
on the reminiscences of members of his family. Moss ended his wandering
years in the mid-1920s when he returned from Angola via South Africa. By
January 1927 he had a general dealer's licence in the Broken Hill district,
where his uncle, Chaim Hochstein, was already established. Moss was apparently running a store at Kapiri Mposhi, at the junction of the Great North
Road and the Line of Rail. By the following year he had moved to the Ndola
district where the construction of the Copperbelt mines was getting under
way. He may then have been at Nchanga, but, when construction of the
mine there was suspended in 1931, he moved to Ndola. He was in partnership

there with his brother, Andrew, who moved north to the Congo in search of work at the low point of the depression, returning only when better times had returned to Northern Rhodesia.

After nearly forty years of bachelorhood, Moss married Fay Steinberg in the Masonic Hall, Ndola, on Christmas Eve, 1933. She was born in 1905 in Wynberg in the Cape to a Polish Jewish father and a Hungarian Jewish mother, but had lived most of her life in Gwelo (Gweru) where her father was a tailor.[5] Soon after his marriage, Moss started again at Nchanga where he acquired the lease of a concession store on mine property. It was not, however, until 1938 that he was able to give up the Ndola shop and to establish a permanent home at Nchanga. The elder son of the marriage, Walter, known as Wally, who was born at Ndola in 1937, remembers that in his youth life was difficult. The family lived in rooms behind the shop which was a corrugated-iron shed on a site which has now disappeared into the Nchanga opencast pit. Concession stores were not licences to print money. According to Arthur Kaplan, who knew him well, Moss was at one stage brought to the verge of bankruptcy when the Bulawayo wholesalers, acting as a cartel, presented all their bills on the same day. This was their response to his attempt to escape from their control by dealing with London agents. It was not until the early 1950s, Wally recalls, that the family seemed to become relatively prosperous.[6] Increased wages for African mineworkers, following the establishment of the African Mineworkers' Union, gave them more purchasing power, and may have increased the stores' turnover and profits. By this time Moss was running three shops, an African mine store, a European mine store, and a shop in the municipal township of Chingola which was not established until 1945. In 1954 he was able to afford to return to England on holiday, seeing London for the first time since 1911.

Freemasonry

A consuming passion of Moss Dobkins in his settled years was Freemasonry. The relationship between Jews and Freemasonry is a very complex one. Masonic symbolism is strongly influenced by Judaism and centres around the construction of Solomon's Temple in Jerusalem. God features as the great architect. Its symbolism has clearly been an attraction for some Jews, and there have been links between Jews and Freemasons in central Africa for many years. Over 100 Masons attended the laying of the foundation stone of the Bulawayo Synagogue in 1897.[7] In various places, including Gwelo in the 1920s, and Ndola, Luanshya and Mufulira on the Copperbelt in the 1930s and 1940s, Jews used Masonic halls for religious services. The mother lodge of Freemasonry in Northern Rhodesia was, and still is, 'The Scottish Lodge David Livingstone' at Livingstone. According to legend, Elias Kopelowitz's first attempts to join this lodge were rebuffed. Benny Iljon is said to have been the first Jew to have joined the Livingstone lodge. He did so by the simple expedient of joining in Bulawayo, where Jews were admitted, and presenting himself in Livingstone as a 'brother'.

According to Sir Roy Welensky, himself a Mason, a Scottish lodge in Broken Hill was closed down as a result of pressure from local members of the British Union of Fascists in the mid-1930s. There was, however, quite a strong strain of anti-Semitism within Freemasonry. It appears that the barriers to the admission of Jews, both in Lusaka and on the Copperbelt, were broken down only in the early years of the war. In Lusaka the secretary of the lodge, Brother B. Pollon, threatened to resign early in 1943 in protest at the admission of two Jews, Henrie Kollenberg and Jack Gerber, Lusaka's only plumber. Sam Osrin, manager of the Lusaka Hotel, was rejected at the same meeting. In a memorandum to the master of the lodge, Pollon said that he had been 'fighting this Jew business for the last three or four years and I'm tired of it':

> My candid opinion is that if any gentiles of any standing (such as Freemasonry requires) do think of enquiring they may be prevented by knowing so many Jews are in the Lodge. I am of the opinion that this steady infiltration of Jews will get them the Lodge eventually the same as they get most of the commercial business.[8]

It seems probable that there was less opposition to the admission of English Jews, such as the Dobkins, than there was to Jews of 'foreign' origin. Moss and his brothers were probably Masons by the early 1930s and remained very active in the movement. Acceptance by the Masons was for some Jews a certificate of respectability, and acceptance by the dominant British group within settler society. Other active Jewish Masons in Northern Rhodesia included Elias Kopelowitz, Benny Iljon, Nathan Schulman, David Shapiro, Harry Gersh, Wulfie Wulfsohn and Hanan Elkaim. Masonry remains a strong movement among business and professional people in Zambia today, and has latterly shown a surprising degree of adaptability and the capacity to absorb people of very different backgrounds.

Last Years

Moss worked steadily at his business in Chingola for most of forty years and spent the years of his retirement there. His son Wally remembers him as a rather remote and austere figure, who sent his son to boarding school in Cape Town at the age of seven, and hoped that he would grow up to be an observant Jew. Wally, on the other hand, felt the pressure of anti-Semitism in the streets of Chingola and at school in South Africa. His greatest wish was to assimilate. Moss recalled that he himself had had a very 'proper' upbringing. Wally recalls that his father would not permit loose talk. He frowned particularly on the racist talk which was so typical of white colonial society. He insisted that black people should be treated with respect.[9]

Moss died in 1984 at the age of ninety, having lived in Northern Rhodesia for most of his life, and for the greater part of the twentieth century. His widow Fay, who is now over ninety, still lives in Chingola. His brothers, Andrew and Len, were also in business on the Copperbelt. In the Congo Andrew married Sarah Rachel Liptz, a member of a large Bulawayo family. His wife's sisters included Annie Mendelsohn, the wife of Sam Mendelsohn of Lusaka, and Gertrude Osrin, wife of Sam Osrin, who was in business on the Copperbelt before moving to Lusaka. A number of the Dobkins's sisters also came to Northern Rhodesia. Florence (Flossie) married Julius Schlitner, an Austrian refugee who arrived in Northern Rhodesia in the late 1930s and built up a very large business on the Copperbelt. Another sister, Rose, married Nathan Gordon, one of Ndola's senior residents. He arrived there in 1911 and was one of the founders and leaders of the town's Hebrew Congregation. Moss's son Wally has spent much of his working life in Zambia and has made his own distinctive architectural contribution to the scene which will be considered in a later chapter. Moss and Fay Dobkins have, with a combined period of residence in Zambia of about 140 years, lived longer in the country than any other Jewish couple. Fay Dobkins has expressed a determination never to leave the country in which her husband and his father are buried.

CHAPTER 5

The Copperbelt: Boom, Bust and Recovery, 1924–39

In the course of the 1920s there were major changes in both the administration and the economy of Northern Rhodesia. The BSA Company's charter came to an end, and the government of the country was taken over in 1924 by the Colonial Office in London. For the first time Northern Rhodesia became the direct responsibility of the British government at Westminster and Whitehall. The head of the government locally was now a Governor appointed by the Colonial Secretary, and subordinate officials were no longer employees of a company, but members of the Colonial Service. The first Governor was Sir Herbert James Stanley, a product of Eton and Christchurch College, Oxford, who is said to have been a devout Anglican, but was of wholly Jewish descent. His father was Sigismund Sonnenthal, who changed his name to Stanley, and his mother was born Rose Meyer. Herbert Stanley had, while private secretary to the Governor General of South Africa, Lord Gladstone, attended a *seder* evening in Livingstone in 1912 at the home of Max and Jenny Shapiro.[1]

There was a worldwide economic depression following the end of the First World War. By the early 1920s there was the beginning of a recovery and there appeared to be bright prospects for copper. The electrification and plumbing of houses in the United States and western Europe, the spread of the telephone and, above all, the mass production of motor cars, created new markets for copper. At the same time, technological advances in the extraction of copper from sulphide ores began to make mineral deposits in Northern Rhodesia attractive to international mining interests.

Big Business

Before the BSA Company gave up its charter it began to take a greater interest than it previously had done in the potential mineral wealth of the country. In 1922 the country's major copper mine, Bwana Mkubwa, which had been worked intermittently since before the First World War, was reorganised. A new board of directors included Edmund Davis and Alfred

Chester Beatty, an American who had worked on behalf of the Guggenheims as a prospector on the Congo side of the Copperbelt. He had founded Selection Trust, a London-based mining investment company which was heavily involved in West African diamonds, in 1914. Another member of Bwana Mkubwa's new board was Ernest Oppenheimer who had founded the Anglo-American Corporation in 1917. He had been mayor of Kimberley, but had been compelled to leave the town during the First World War as a result of a wave of anti-German feeling which made no exception for German Jews. In the 1920s he was in the process of establishing the largest mining and industrial conglomerate in southern Africa, and was to take control of De Beer's a few years later. The BSA Company was represented on the new board by its shrewd, and tight-fisted, Scottish director, Dougal Malcolm.

In 1923 the BSA Company granted prospecting rights over an area of 50,000 square miles to Davis and Chester Beatty who set up the Rhodesia Congo Border Concessions Company. Once the enormous ore reserves of Nkana and Nchanga had been proved, they involved Oppenheimer in the development work. In the end, Oppenheimer's Anglo-American interests, working with Davis, became the dominant group on the Copperbelt, controlling about 60 per cent of mining activity, including the Nkana and Nchanga mines, as well as Bwana Mkubwa and Broken Hill. The development of the new mines in the late 1920s consumed large quantities of capital.

The details of the development of the two mining groups in Northern Rhodesia, Anglo-American and Rhodesian Selection Trust, are complex and hardly relevant to this story. Rhodesian Selection Trust, which was like Rhodesian Anglo-American, set up in 1927, eventually controlled about 40 per cent of Copperbelt mining production. Chester Beatty found that the capital required for the development of the Roan Antelope and Mufulira mines strained his company's resources. He sought American help, and brought in the American Metal Company which was controlled by the Hochschild family and had developed copper mining interests in the United States and South America.[2]

The Hochschilds were, like the Oppenheimers, German Jews from Frankfurt, though they had been in America for some time. Dr Otto Sussman, their mining expert, visited Northern Rhodesia on their behalf in 1927, and recommended that they should invest in the Copperbelt. By that year the reserves of underground sulphide ore at Roan Antelope were estimated at 40 million tons. American Metal (later American Metal Climax or Amax) was to become the dominant partner in Rhodesian Selection Trust with Chester Beatty's Selection Trust as a junior partner. By 1930 the Hochschilds had invested $15 million in the Northern Rhodesian mines. The support of American Metal was vital to the continued development of Roan and Mufulira after the onset of the great depression in 1929 ended the flow of investment funds from the open market. At one stage in 1931–32, the continued development of Roan was possible only because American Metal agreed to pay cash for copper ore as soon as it was loaded on to trucks at the Luanshya siding and not, as would usually have been the case, on delivery in London.[3]

The completion of the first of the major Copperbelt mines, Nkana for Anglo-American, and Roan Antelope for Rhodesian Selection Trust, coincided with the bottom of the depression and the lowest prices for copper. By 1931 prices had fallen to about five cents a pound from a high of twenty-four cents a pound in 1929. The Copperbelt, which had been experiencing a construction boom and high levels of employment, fell into very deep depression in 1932. It was assumed, though it was not always the case, that unemployed black workers would take care of themselves and return to their rural homes, but white unemployment and destitution was a concern of government.

Between 1931 and 1933 the white population of Northern Rhodesia fell from nearly 14,000 to 10,500. At the end of 1932 about one in ten of the white population was thought to be destitute. Roy Welensky, who came to work in Northern Rhodesia as a locomotive driver in 1933, recalled that white workers were leaving the country at the time on empty coal trucks, and were begging the engine drivers and firemen for food. Construction work at Mufulira and Nchanga was suspended. Nkana and Roan produced about 20,000 tons of copper each in 1932, but it was not until the later 1930s that they went into full-scale production. The Bwana Mkubwa mine closed in 1931 and did not reopen for many years.[4]

The Susmans and the Sussmans

Although Jewish entrepreneurs were heavily involved in the development of the Copperbelt, they represented international capital. The enormous investments which were taking place on the Copperbelt did, however, have significant repercussions for the Jewish businesses, both large and small, which were already established in Northern Rhodesia. The capital employed in the Susman brothers' business, which amounted to at least £100,000 in the later 1920s, equivalent to several million pounds in today's money, was small by comparison with the large sums which were being invested in the Copperbelt at that time. It was, however, capital which had been accumulated in Northern Rhodesia by people who had been resident in the country for most of thirty years. The Susmans were the local businessmen who were in the strongest position to benefit directly from the new mining activities. They did not, however, have the capital resources to do this on their own.

Ironically, they had from 1916 to 1918 owned two mineral claims which covered part of the Nkana mine. The claims were pegged by a prospector, H. C. Winnicott, in 1916. He was probably working for the Susmans whose names appear on the original deeds. An alternative suggestion is that they bought the claims from him for £100. Joey Susman maintained that no cash changed hands, the claims being acquired in exchange for a grand piano.

According to J. A. Bancroft, the geologist who surveyed the area for the Anglo-American Corporation in the late 1920s: 'Mr Susman did not think very highly of the property in dispute and offered to sell it to the Bwana Mkubwa Company if they reimbursed his out-of-pocket expenses, which he put at £100.' The offer was declined and the Susmans eventually sold the claims for that amount to William Lee in December 1918. Earlier in the year they had written off about £400 which they had spent on the 'Nkana prospects'. The claims changed hands several times for ever-increasing sums of money before Anglo-American began development work in 1927. They were sold as part of the Nkana Concession in 1924 by Messina Mines Limited for £60,000 and 500,000 shares in Bwana Mkubwa – a price which one of Messina's directors described as 'a mere bagatelle' in terms of their potential value. The Susmans had the bad luck to acquire these claims too soon. At the time of their brief ownership, the existence of the massive underground sulphide ore body was unknown, and it would have been unworkable if it had been known. This was not the Susmans' only venture into mining; they also put some money into the Rex Imperator mine – probably a small gold mine in the Mumbwa district.[5]

In 1928 the Susmans made their first move to take advantage of the construction boom on the Copperbelt which was just beginning to get under way. Elie Susman bought the Bwana Mkubwa Hotel from Harry Figov, and the Ndola bakery and butchery from Messrs Greenberg and Kriegler, who were brothers-in-law and partners. They were of Romanian Jewish origin, though they had connections with Manchester, and had been at Ndola since soon after the war. Elie Susman established a company, Northern Suppliers Ltd, to take over these properties, and sent his nephew, Maurice Gersh, up from Livingstone – he was twenty-two at the time – to take charge of the businesses for a while.[6]

Susman then recruited his old friend Willie Hepker to manage the hotel. Phyllis Lakofski-Hepker recalls her first visit to Bwana Mkubwa at Christmas in 1928. Her parents had worked hard to transform what had been a 'badly-run, ramshackle and dirty place into a clean beautifully run hotel'. There was a monthly dance at the hotel and people came from far and wide, thinking nothing of driving 200 miles to attend. The hotel guests were apparently

a friendly lot and at Christmas they really let their hair down. They had the habit of throwing gravel on to the roofs of houses to waken their sleeping friends and invited them to come and join in the fun. In the hotel they grabbed pots and pans and anything that could make a racket. In single file they sang and danced to the music, making my mother join in.[7]

These good times did not last, however. By the end of 1929 the depression was already looming, and Elie Susman found that Willie Hepker's refurbishment of the hotel had been too lavish. He attempted to dismiss Hepker who believed that he had been recruited as a partner, and not as an employee.

The High Court ruled in Hepker's favour and ordered the liquidation of the company, and the division of the remaining assets between the partners. The 'voluntary liquidation' of the company with Maurice Gersh as one of the liquidators, was gazetted in December 1929. This was a pyrrhic victory for Hepker as the repayment of loans to the Susmans absorbed most of the assets, and there was little left to distribute.[8]

This would appear to have been one of Elie Susman's few commercial failures, but it had the consequence of bringing new and stronger partners into the business. The Bwana Mkubwa and Ndola businesses were taken over by a new company, Northern Caterers Ltd, which was formed in 1930. The new company had a nominal capital of £100,000 and was, until after the war, the most highly capitalised company registered in Northern Rhodesia. The major shareholders were the Susman brothers, and members of an unrelated family of the same name, though spelt differently, the Sussmans. Philip Sussman was based in Kimberley and was a friend and horse-racing associate of Ernest Oppenheimer. The Susmans and the Sussmans were both involved in the Ngamiland cattle trade and knew each other well. Willie Sussman was a rancher in Southern Rhodesia, and was a business partner of Isadore Kollenberg who also took shares in the business. Two other Sussman brothers, Sam and George, also had small holdings, as did Harry Figov, who had been in business at Bwana Mkubwa since 1922. The Kimberley Sussmans had a rather larger holding than the Livingstone Susmans, but Elie Susman became a director of the new company. Northern Caterers established hotels, bottle-stores, bakeries and tearooms at Nkana, Luanshya, Nchanga and Mufulira, and also operated a mineral water factory. The bakeries were later hived off into a separate company, Northern Bakeries, the first makers of the still extant Supaloaf.[9]

Copperfields Cold Storage

In 1931 the same group of investors was involved in the establishment of Copperfields Cold Storage Ltd. This company acquired the meat contract for the Anglo-American Corporation's mines. The establishment of the company involved an agreement with Barnett 'Bongola' Smith for the division of the export market in cattle from Southern Rhodesia to the Congo and Northern Rhodesia. It was agreed that the new company would not compete with Bongola's company, Elakat, in the Congo, and his companies would not compete with it in Northern Rhodesia. Bongola handed over his interests in Northern Rhodesia, which may have included retail butchery outlets and farms, in exchange for a 25 per cent stake in the new company which was held by his Congo-Rhodesia Ranching Company.[10]

During the 1930s the overall management of both Northern Caterers and Copperfields Cold Storage was in the hands of Isadore Kollenberg. He remained on the boards of both companies for forty years, resigning only in

1970. Once the hotels and cold stores were constructed, and the business was running smoothly, he returned to his home in Bulawayo, but spent a large part of his time on the train between Bulawayo and the Copperbelt. He was assisted in the early 1930s by the Susmans' nephew, Maurice Gersh, and by Max Barnett. Gersh was responsible for Ndola, Luanshya and Bwana Mkubwa while Barnett took charge of Nkana, Nchanga and Mufulira. Max Barnett remained with Copperfields Cold Storage until 1947, but Maurice Gersh left the companies in the mid-1930s to join his brother Harry in the development of another company, Economy Stores Ltd, which was also established with the backing of the Susman brothers in 1931.[11]

Economy Stores

Maurice and Harry Gersh were among a group of remarkable young entre-preneurs who were attracted to the Copperbelt during the construction boom which was at its height from 1928 to 1930. They had, it will be recalled, reached South Africa with their mother and grandparents in 1913 and were educated in Cape Town. After completing a junior secondary school education at Cape Town's Normal College, Maurice Gersh arrived in Livingstone at the age of eighteen in 1924, and Harry came up in the following year. For a while they both worked for their Susman uncles. Maurice was based in the Livingstone office for a number of years and was at various times sent out to deal with problems in Barotseland, and to act as manager of the Leopard's Hill ranch. Harry soon branched out as a trader on his own account. After running a store at the Zambesi Saw Mills base at Mulobezi for a while, he moved north to the Copperbelt. He had a concession store at Nchanga in 1929, but moved to Nkana in 1931.

Economy Stores Ltd was set up, with the backing of the Susman brothers, to exploit the opportunities offered by the opening of concession stores which were situated on company property in the mine townships. Each concession usually involved two stores, one in the African mineworkers' compound, and one in the European mineworkers' residential area, though some of the early stores were divided into black and white sections. Although Ernest Oppenheimer on his first visit to the completed Nkana mine described the complex as a 'mining utopia', conditions for the storekeepers were primitive. Owners or managers usually lived at the back of their stores, which were little more than corrugated-iron sheds. The first of the Economy Stores' ventures was a concession at Nkana which Harry Gersh started in 1931. The company opened a concession store at Nchanga later in the decade. The Gersh brothers were remarkable entrepreneurs who had a vision which went beyond trading. They were, as we shall see, to play a major part in the development of the town of Kitwe, and in the development of secondary industry in Northern Rhodesia.[12]

Shim Lakofski

The Gersh brothers were not, however, the first Jewish traders to set up shop at Nkana which they reached after the end of the construction boom. The most successful of the early traders, though he stayed at Nkana for only five years, was Shim Lakofski. Over sixty years after he left the scene of his early triumphs, he is still alive and well and living in Geneva. His recorded reminiscences provide a more detailed and vivid picture of trading during the Copperbelt construction boom than can be found in any other source. They convey the atmosphere of a gold rush – seen by some as a 'second Rand' – when fortunes could be made or lost in a day.[13]

Simon, known as Shim, Lakofski was born in Vrededorp, Johannesburg, in 1905. His parents moved to Hillbrow when he was young. His father, Barney, was born in Lithuania and came to South Africa as a young man. He became a partner in several large butcheries in Johannesburg. Shim's mother, Rose Kirschner, was born at Libau in Latvia and also came to South Africa in her youth. His parents had achieved a fair degree of respectability, and Dr J. L. Landau, the Chief Rabbi, attended Shim's bar mitzvah in 1918. Shim was unusual among the early Jewish traders in Northern Rhodesia in that he was South African born and well educated. He matriculated at the Marist Brothers School, and spent a year at the University of Witwatersrand where he enrolled for a degree in commerce. He was bored with university and failed most of his first-year exams. Through his cousin, Isaac Osrin, who was a commercial traveller, he found, as we have already seen, a job in Isaac Rosen's store in Broken Hill in 1924.

Soon, however, he decided to branch out on his own. He persuaded Messrs Greenberg and Kriegler to lease him a shop in Ndola. He put in one of his friends, a 'greener', or new arrival, from the Baltic states, by the name of Wolpowitz, to run the business for a few months. When this proved successful, he left Broken Hill and moved to Ndola. He supplemented his earnings from the shop by running a transport business. This was very profitable at the time because branch lines to the new mines at Nkana and Luanshya were still under construction, and goods had to be trucked to them from the railhead at Ndola or Bwana Mkubwa.

Shim Lakofski was determined to get a concession, but he knew that at the age of twenty-three he would never be granted one. Concessions were given away by the mines to favoured individuals, but he realised that he would have to buy one. He was introduced to an elderly Scotsman who had been given a concession site at Nkana and agreed to buy it for £750 and a rental payment of £20 a month for three years. Shim had only £300, but he persuaded the local bank manager, another Scot called McGregor, to lend him £400. Both he and the bank manager were taking a gamble because the concession sites were not supposed to be transferred without the permission of the mine. He had to pose for a while as an employee of the original concessionaire.

At this time, in 1928–29, the construction of the mine had not yet begun. J. A. Bancroft had started in the previous year to carry out a series of test drillings which slowly revealed the extent of the Nkana ore body which he described to Sir Ernest Oppenheimer in 1929 as 'probably the largest copper mine in the world'. He later described Nkana as it was at this time as a 'snake park'. He had never seen so many puff adders, gaboon vipers and cobras, not to mention lions and leopards. The first drilling equipment had to be brought in on ox wagons which travelled at night to avoid tsetse flies.[14]

After the agreement had been signed, Shim went with his brother Max to see what he had bought. There was one store already established on a bush site, and it was evidently doing good business. Shim then agreed with a contractor to put up a wood and iron store measuring forty feet by thirty feet and costing £420. There would be a bedroom at the back. The store had to be built within two weeks, with a £5 a day penalty for any delay over that time. Shim gave a promise to pay within sixty days. Two weeks later the shop was built, and Shim and his brother transferred three truckloads of goods to it from the Ndola store, and ordered many more. He recruited a couple of African storemen and spent a day organising the shop.

That night he went to sleep in the shop on a camp bed. Fifty years later he could remember the events of the following day with apparently total recall. He was awakened at dawn by a crowd of people outside. He opened the door and asked them what they wanted. They said: 'We want to buy.' His reputation for running a 'chipisa', or discount store, had spread to Nkana from Ndola. He worked with his two assistants without breakfast or lunch and finally closed the shop at seven in the evening. His brother had arrived with another lorryload of goods and when they counted the day's take they had £212. He recalled that, among many other things, he had sold seven Singer sewing machines at £4 each, and six Raleigh bicycles at £5 each. On the second day they took £150 and he was able to pay off his bank loan on the third day.

Shim's business, known as the Nkana Trading Company, grew rapidly. In the first year he made a profit of £3,000 and in the second year £7,000. The frontage of the store grew from forty feet to 120 feet. There was a European and an African department and he soon had twenty European and fifty African employees. The store sold everything from needles to motor cars. He had acquired the much sought-after Ford agency at a time when the Model T Ford was still the standard motor vehicle. Maize grain was a staple of the business, and he had contracts to supply the Italian engineering company which was building the branch line to Nkana, as well as other contractors and the mine itself.

He employed a number of members of his own close and extended family in the business. These included his brothers Max and Izzy, his uncle, Alec Kirschner, who was only six months his senior, and several cousins including Max Rumor and Sam Osrin. The latter was one of a large family, several of whom worked in the Congo and Northern Rhodesia. A brother, Alec Osrin, was in business in Luanshya where he died in 1939, and another brother ran a hotel at Likasi in the Congo. Shim had a number of other Jewish employees, including Robert Longsberg, his accountant, and Harry Sossen, who was to become prominent in Livingstone. He also employed a number of Scots who had formerly worked for the African Lakes Corporation, and several Greeks.

Shim Lakofski established his business at Nkana in 1928–29 and got in on the ground floor in the construction boom. His years of rapid expansion and high profits were the years to 1931. He had built up the largest trading business on the Copperbelt before he reached his twenty-fifth birthday, but it was soon to be affected by the depression. In September 1931 Britain, and with it Northern Rhodesia, went off the gold standard while South Africa did not. Shim found that the value of his savings and his assets had been reduced by as much as 30 per cent. He realised that South Africa could not remain on gold indefinitely and that, when it did come off gold, the value of gold shares would rise. With the help of his cousin Barney Freedman, who was a stockbroker in Johannesburg, he put his savings of £5,000 into gold shares. South Africa did come off the gold standard. The shares rose and he recouped his earlier losses. By 1933, however, he found that his turnover and profits had halved. He decided that it was time to move on.

He looked for someone to buy his business and eventually sold it to a man called Appleby who had a store at the Kansanshi mine on the Congo border, and whose wife, Jill Bensusa, was a member of one of the Ladino families in the Congo. Appleby obtained financial backing from his London agents, Campbell Brothers, and bought the business. After a few years they took over the shop which they ran as Kitwe Stores. It became the first branch of a network which survived until recently as the ZCBC parastatal chain.

Meanwhile, Shim had moved to Johannesburg where he had several more successful business careers. In the late 1930s he branched out into property development. He put together syndicates which built some of the major buildings in Johannesburg's central business district. He was the patron of a number of remarkable architects who contributed to what the historian Clive Chipkin has called the 'Johannesburg style'. He also formed an alliance with Twentieth Century-Fox, in competition with the Schlesinger Organisation, and built cinemas in a number of southern African cities including Pretoria and Lourenço Marques. In 1961 he decided to leave South Africa. He moved first to London and then to Geneva where he has lived for over thirty years. In his early nineties he is still on line to London, New York and Johannesburg and continues to play the markets. He looks back on the ten years that he spent in Northern Rhodesia with nostalgia.[15]

At Bwana Mkubwa in December 1929 Shim met the woman whom he was to marry a year later. She was Phyllis Hepker, a remarkable young woman with an unusual upbringing. Her father, Willie Hepker, had been in partnership with Maurice Thal in a store at the Lonely mine near Selukwe in the early years of the century. He fell in love with a photograph of one of Maurice's sisters and urged him to bring her out to South Africa. The original object of his affections was unavailable, but another sister, Rebecca, made the journey. Willie met her at Cape Town docks, fell in love with her, and married her in 1903. Phyllis was their second child and was born at Selukwe in 1906.[16]

Phyllis was brought up at the Lonely mine and on an undeveloped farm – somewhat grandiloquently named Cowdray Park – near Bulawayo. She was educated by French-speaking governesses, spent three years at a convent school in Durban, and matriculated at the age of fifteen. Her account of her upbringing is reminiscent of Elspeth Huxley's *The Flame Trees of Thika* (based on her childhood in Kenya) with her family always hovering on the brink of financial ruin.[17] After leaving school, she spent seven years on remote small mines in the bush north of Selukwe, as her father struggled to save his farm, and to educate his children. She and her brothers staked a mine of their own – it was a 'rubble proposition' and produced £100 worth of gold. Her mother had been brought up by wealthy relatives in Riga, and had absorbed bourgeois values, but she was also adaptable, and was able to create a beautiful home with furniture made from dynamite boxes. She had no religious up-bringing, but passed on to Phyllis a strong sense of Jewishness. This was reinforced by accounts of the persecution of the Jews in Russia and by reading a book about the Spanish Inquisition. It was David Landau, of Bulawayo, a friend of her parents, who taught Phyllis at the age of five to say the *Shema* – 'Hear, O Israel, the Lord our God is One' – a prayer which she has said daily ever since.

Phyllis taught herself to type and to take shorthand and had also discovered that she had a talent for drawing. In 1928, when she was twenty-two, her uncle, Max Thal, agreed to pay the fees for her to begin an architecture course at the University of the Witwatersrand in Johannesburg. She very much enjoyed the course and completed two years of it, but at the end of 1929 she realised that she would not be able to continue with it. She felt that she must begin work to support her parents. She took a temporary job in Ndola with Metropolitan Vickers, and then moved to Border Engineering where she was paid £20 a month.

In the following year she met, fell in love with, and, overcoming initial parental disapproval, agreed to marry Shim Lakofski. She had rejected per-sistent proposals of marriage from her cousin, Abe Lowenthal who was in the process of establishing a cinema with his brother William at Ndola. A shadow was cast over the year by the death in a motor accident of her brother Albert, who had been running a concession store at Luanshya with Max Thal. Her parents were at the time living in a flat in Ndola where her father had a small agency business. Her brother Lionel was running a store

at Chambishi and another brother, Harold, was working for Anglo-American
as an industrial chemist on the construction of the leaching plant at Nkana.

Phyllis Hepker and Shim Lakofski were married at the Boma, or Magistrate's Court, in Ndola in December 1930. There was then no synagogue in
Ndola, but there was a recognised Jewish marriage officer – Mr Cohen, a
tailor. When Shim asked him to do the wedding, Cohen replied by asking
where he had his dress suit made. 'In Johannesburg,' Shim replied. 'Then go
and get married in Johannesburg,' was the response. Phyllis had an aunt,
Johanna, who was married to Herman Blumenthal, then one of the most
successful businessmen in Elisabethville, though soon to be ruined by the
depression.[18] It was arranged that they would have the religious service at the
newly completed, and as yet unfurnished, synagogue there. Elisabethville was
thought to be very attractive, and was much more highly developed at the
time than any town on the Northern Rhodesian Copperbelt. The religious
service was performed on 25 January 1931 by a shoemaker.

The honeymoon couple returned to Bulawayo from Cape Town early in
March. They were just in time to witness Phyllis's father's death there from
blackwater fever at the age of fifty-one. His favourite brother, Adolph, had
died a few weeks earlier from the same disease. The first child of the marriage,
Denise, was born at Nkana late in 1931. She left Northern Rhodesia with her
parents two years later. She was brought up in Johannesburg and studied
architecture at the University of Witwatersrand, completing the course which
her mother had begun.

Closed Townships

By the time that Shim Lakofski left Nkana at the end of 1933, there were
a number of concession stores at the mine. In addition to his own, which
was soon to become Kitwe Stores, there was the Gersh brothers' Economy
Stores, Sid Diamond's Standard Trading, which had also opened in 1931, and
a branch of the Kollenbergs' business which had been opened by Herman
Kollenberg. The African Lakes Corporation and the Rhodesian Copperfields
Trading Company were also represented. From about this time onwards there
was pressure from the government for the opening of a public township
which would not be on mine property.

The government did not, however, have the money to finance the building
of such a township. After negotiations in which Maurice Gersh played a
leading part, it was decided that the traders could be persuaded to finance
the development of a township in return for a long-term monopoly. This
was the origin of the distinction which arose on the Copperbelt between
open and closed townships. Traders at Nkana, who were not keen to move
off mine property, were persuaded to do so with the promise of twenty-year
leases during which no new shops would be opened to compete with the
original lessees. The government also undertook that for twenty years it

would not open any other new township within a ten-mile radius of the Nkana mine's smoke-stack.[19]

The Nkana traders were given first claim to sites in the new township of Kitwe, but had to pay a £2,000 premium for the privilege. Economy Stores, Kollenberg Brothers, Sid Diamond's Standard Trading and Kitwe Stores became, in competition with each other, the monopoly traders of Kitwe. These firms also had shops in the second-class trading area of Kitwe, and eventually acquired sites in the townships of Wusikili, Mindola and Chamboli as they were opened. Northern Caterers was also in at the beginning with a hotel, and the only bottle-store, bakery and tearoom in the first-class trading area. Copperfields Cold Storage eventually achieved a monopoly of butcheries in Kitwe, having the only outlets in each of the trading areas.

Asian Competition

It is clear that the exclusion of Asian traders from the main Kitwe shopping area was a major consideration in the establishment of the closed township. The management of the Rhokana Corporation was afraid that Asian traders might buy the plots which were allocated to the African Lakes Corporation and the Rhodesian Copperfields Trading Company, but not taken up by them. It was, therefore, decided that four general dealers were enough, and the original group were protected against Asian competition for over twenty years. Their shops were built side by side and were opened to the public late in 1937.[20]

Asian competition had first become an issue with the recovery from the depression in the mid-1930s. It was then that there was for the first time direct competition in the open townships of Luanshya and Ndola between Jewish and Asian traders. While in 1930 there was not a single Asian with a trading licence on the Copperbelt, ten years later there were over fifty Asian applicants for licences, and many of them were for more than one shop. Simon Zukas's father, who had recently arrived from Lithuania, bought his first business in Ndola from Moss Dobkins in 1938, but soon moved to Luanshya where he took over a tearoom from the Patel brothers. The family lived behind the shop, and the business was in direct competition with its Asian neighbours.[21] In 1938 it was estimated that the Asian population of Northern Rhodesia had tripled in the three years since 1935, and that there were now more than 500 Asians in the country. There were nineteen Asian store-owners in Ndola and nine in Luanshya. It was thought that African retail trade was being taken out of the hands of European shopkeepers. Asian traders in Ndola were themselves beginning to complain of 'over-trading'. In 1940 licensing boards were set up and this was recognised in the ordinance as a reason for refusing to grant licences.[22]

Sid Diamond

Shim Lakofski was the most successful of the traders to emerge out of the Nkana construction boom, but he left the country and continued his career elsewhere. Sid Diamond reached the Copperbelt as the construction boom was beginning, weathered the depression, and stayed to become the new town of Kitwe's most successful shopkeeper. He was born in London at the turn of the century to Polish Jewish parents. His father was a tailor in the East End of London, but died when Sid was eight. His elder brothers set up a successful silk business, but he left London in his teens and spent some time in South Africa. After working for his uncle, Egnatz Snapper, in Barotseland, he moved on to work for Harry Figov at Bwana Mkubwa. He then set up in opposition to Figov, but was forced by the mine closure to move with his corrugated-iron shed to Nchanga. When that mine also closed he moved to Nkana. He was unable to get either a concession or a licence there and was forced to go into partnership with Kennedy Harris, a member of the Legislative Council for the Ndola district who used his political influence to obtain them. He had only just managed to buy out Harris, and was short of funds, when he was faced in 1936 with the challenge of finding £2,000 for a site at the new township of Kitwe and £4,000 to build a new store there. He was on the point of abandoning the project and leaving the country when he received additional capital from his family in England.[23]

Sid Diamond's corrugated-iron shed was now retired, but provided the roof for what his widow, Molly, refers to as their first 'marital home' at Kitwe. Born Molly Hamilton in London to a Scots father and a Dutch mother, she was brought up in Bulawayo and reached Mufulira in 1934. She worked there for six months for a German hairdresser before moving to Nkana where she met her future husband. After a prolonged courtship, they were married in 1939. Although she was not Jewish, she played an active part in Jewish women's organisations, such as WIZO, and regarded herself as part of the Jewish community.

A Christmas brochure for Standard Trading in 1938 gives an indication of the extraordinary range of goods, including an impressive array of toys, which were available in a shop which had opened at the end of the previous year. Customers were assured that any goods in the shop could be supplied to relatives in Britain through the firm's London agents. According to legend, Sid did well in the early years of the war by cornering the market in khaki material. This could probably be explained by his direct access to London agents. He had originally been compelled to establish links with them because of his competitors' attempts to limit his access to Bulawayo suppliers. Molly Diamond emphasises how important ninety-day credit from these agents was to the success of the business. She also recalls the problems created by wartime price controls; she claims that on one occasion they had to change their prices three times in one day.[24]

The Gersh brothers and Sid Diamond were the most prominent Jewish businessmen in Nkana–Kitwe in the later 1930s. They provided work for a number of young Jewish immigrants who became shop assistants at a time when it was increasingly difficult for aliens to find employment on the mine. Among them were Sam Koslowsky (later known as Kelly) and Meir Rosenblatt who worked for Diamond, and Jacob Katz and Eli Lurie who worked for the Gersh brothers. They all remained in the country for a long time and prospered in different ways.[25]

Luanshya

Luanshya came into production at the same time as Nkana, and also remained open during the depression. It was never a closed township and was the only one of the original mine towns which did not have concession stores on mine property, though it did have first- and second-class trading areas. It attracted a number of Jewish traders, though none seems to have been as spectacularly successful as Shim Lakofski, the Gersh brothers or Sid Diamond. Phyllis Hepker-Lakofski's uncle, Max Thal, was among the first people to open a store at Luanshya, but his Luanshya Trading Company went bankrupt in 1931. He maintained that it was lack of capital rather than the depression which was the cause of his failure. This was his second bankruptcy: an earlier business venture in Southern Rhodesia had failed in 1921.[26]

Another early trader at Luanshya was Maurice Rosen who arrived in the township in 1930 and seems to have taken over Max Thal's failed business. He had emigrated from Scotland to Southern Rhodesia in 1914. He was a long-serving member of the Township Management Board. His son Philip was born in Scotland in 1912, served throughout the Second World War with the Northern Rhodesia Regiment, and was also a first-class rugby player.[27] He took over the business, following his father's death, not long after the war. Dennis Figov, whose family reached Luanshya in 1936, and set up in competition with the Rosens, recalls that the two families were on very close terms and enjoyed a harmonious trading relationship. He also recalls how they, and other Jewish shopkeepers on the Copperbelt, employed Scottish grocers, who had usually come out to work for Mandala. They brought with them specialised skills such as tea blending, coffee roasting and bacon curing. They were able to provide the kind of service to which British housewives were accustomed.[28]

Isaac Zlotnik had reached Luanshya by 1930. He was born in Poland but came to Northern Rhodesia in 1929 from Palestine. He seems to have spent some time at Wankie, and was originally in partnership with David Vilinksy or Wilensky, who is not to be confused with Roy Welensky's brother of the same name, who was a trade union leader at Wankie, and later moved to Broken Hill and Kitwe. Early in the war Zlotnik was one of the founders, with Julius Schlitner, a refugee from Austria who had worked for Abe

Lowenthal, and a German refugee, Alex Stiel, of the Northern Rhodesia Native Produce Company. This later grew, under Schlitner's ownership, into a substantial business: the Ndola Milling Company. Zlotnik and Schlitner had a brush with the authorities during the war when they were convicted of receiving a large consignment of razor blades which had been smuggled from the Congo. They received what appear to have been exemplary fines.[29]

Zlotnik was a wholesaler in Luanshya, and used the town as a base for the development, both during and after the war, of an extensive network of stores in the Luapula province. Colonial officials noted that, unusually for that time, he extended credit and gave discounts to emergent African traders in the area. He was one of the few Jewish traders who successfully developed a rural trading network in the eastern half of the country. During the war, he pioneered the bus service to Fort Rosebery (Mansa) and Kasama, and also transported goods for rural traders. He was involved in the fish business on the Luapula and Lake Mweru, where he kept a boat. He was also involved in the second-hand clothing business, then known as *kombo* and now known as *salaula*. A Zambian employee remembers him as a good businessman who was strict, and insisted on cleanliness in his employees, but who had a kindly streak. He gave instructions to his managers that children should not be apprehended for stealing sweets from his shops – provided that they ate them on the premises.[30]

The Minchuk brothers also reached Luanshya during the construction boom. Joseph Minchuk was born at Brest-Litovsk in Poland, and had worked in South America and Cuba before coming to Northern Rhodesia to work for Elias Kopelowitz in 1928. He came up to the Copperbelt in 1930, and had a shop in Ndola until 1933. By the following year he had two shops in the African trading area at Luanshya. His brother, Julius (Yudel) was in business in Mufulira. The brothers Sydney and Cyril Sussman, from Lithuania, arrived in the country in 1929–30, and also divided themselves between Luanshya and Mufulira. Sydney Sussman set up the Standard Butchery in Luanshya, and remained in business there for many years. Cyril Sussman worked at first in Luanshya, and then moved to Mufulira where he carried on a general dealer's business.[31]

Mufulira and Nchanga

Construction work at Mufulira and Nchanga had been suspended during the depression. Production only began at Mufulira in 1933 and at Nchanga in 1939, though construction work began again in 1937. Closed townships were opened at Mufulira in 1937 and at Chingola in 1945. Uri Illion was in business in Mufulira in 1930 at the height of the construction boom. He weathered the depression, and returned to the mine when construction began again. He was born in Libau in 1896, was in Berlin from 1919, and came to Northern Rhodesia in 1926. He worked for a year with his brother-in-law Elias

Kopelowitz in Livingstone and then moved to Mazabuka. Eric Iljon remembers him from his days in Mazabuka as a giant of a man, over six feet tall, well-built, and a gourmet. Uri's brother Eli worked with him in Mufulira, but died as a relatively young man in the 1940s. Eli's son, Mike, who was born in Mufulira, acquired fame in South Africa in the 1970s as the founder of Mike's Kitchen, the well-known Johannesburg, and now international, restaurant chain.[32]

There were not as many traders in the closed township of Mufulira as there were in Kitwe. Only two licences were granted for general dealers and four for African trade. Apart from Yudel Minchuk and Cyril Sussman, who have already been mentioned, A. J. (Jack) Mendelsohn, brother of Samuel Mendelsohn of Lusaka, was the most prominent Jewish trader in the town. He was manager there of the Rhodesia Copperfields Trading Company.[33] Until 1945, the traders of what was to become Chingola remained on mine property at Nchanga. The main traders there in the late 1930s, and during the war, were B. I. Menashe, Nahman Israel, Moss and Andrew Dobkins and Harry Dorsky, whose careers are dealt with elsewhere.

Ndola

Ndola, which had begun to emerge as an administrative and commercial centre in the years before the First World War, was favoured by government as the commercial and distributive centre of the Copperbelt and was given municipal status, together with Livingstone, in 1927. It was never a mine town, though it was close to Bwana Mkubwa, and has always had a rather different character from its neighbours. Apart from Nathan Gordon, and Messrs Greenberg and Kriegler, its most significant early Jewish residents were the Schulman brothers. They came from a rabbinical family in Britain and were acceptable spokesmen for the Copperbelt Jewish community in its dealings with government. Hyam Schulman was described in 1924 as a farmer and trader. By 1940 his letterhead proclaimed him to be the agent for the Beguela Railway, which had linked Ndola with the Atlantic Ocean in 1931–32. He became mayor of the town in 1937–39, and his wife was also a member of the Town Council. After his death in 1950, she carried on the agency business until her departure from the country in 1959. She retired to Cape Town, where she was still living in 1996. Her father, Max Port, was in Ndola for a decade from the late 1920s as the manager of a firm which was mainly engaged in the grain trade to the Congo mines.[34]

Hyam Shulman's brother, Nathan, was in business in the Ndola district in 1919, but went bankrupt in 1922 – a common experience for traders and farmers at that time. He and his wife were prominent members of Elisabethville's Jewish community in the 1920s and 1930s. He re-emerged in Kitwe at the end of the latter decade as a manager for Northern Caterers and was chairman of the company in the postwar years. He was also chairman of the

Associated Chambers of Commerce of Northern Rhodesia. He was the first
choice of the chambers of commerce to sit as their representative on the
Closed Townships Commission in 1948, but had to step down owing to ill
health. He was, in his spare time, a composer of music and had a daughter,
Sylvia Benater, who became a concert pianist. A son served in the RAF
during the war and later became a commercial airline pilot.[35]

Harry Figov, whose sister married Nathan Schulman, arrived in Northern
Rhodesia in 1920 and opened his Bwana Mkubwa Trading Company in 1922.
He had been born in London to Polish Jewish parents. His mud-brick and
thatched store, and hotel, at Bwana Mkubwa were the beginnings of a
business which survives until today, though it moved several times before
finding a permanent home at Luanshya. Harry came to Bwana Mkubwa from
Bulawayo, but also had relatives in the Congo. His wife was a member of the
Espinosa family, which was settled in the Congo; a brother-in-law, Jim Trout,
was also in the Congo before moving to Northern Rhodesia where he became
secretary of Border Motors at Ndola, and mayor of the town. The company
was owned by Harry Figov's close friend, Antoine (Tony) Attala, a Lebanese
Christian, who had the General Motors franchise for the Copperbelt.

Harry Figov was an enterprising man who supplemented the earnings
from his shop and hotel by pioneering in the late 1920s the first airmail
service to Bulawayo. He did so in partnership with an experienced wartime
pilot, but also learned to fly himself. He was the employer of a number of
young men who eventually prospered in Copperbelt trade, including Sid
Diamond. He sold his Bwana Mkubwa Hotel to Elie Susman in 1928, but his
initial attempts to establish himself in the new mining towns failed. Unable
to find the money to develop the first plot which he had obtained at
Luanshya, he was forced to sell to H. C. Werner, the butcher. When Bwana
Mkubwa closed for what appeared to be the last time in 1931, he moved to
Nkana where he set up a garage. It was after the return of prosperity to the
Copperbelt that he set up shop at Luanshya in 1936.[36]

The Figov family has now been associated with Luanshya for over sixty
years. Their shop, which originally included a garage and motor car showroom,
is the only Jewish retail outlet in the country to have remained in the
ownership and management of the same family from the 1930s until the
present. On Harry Figov's death in 1945, his brother-in-law, Harry Rayner,
who had come to the town as manager of the Luanshya Hotel, took over
the running of the business. Harry Rayner was also a member of the
Township Management Board and a leading member of the Jewish community. Another brother-in-law, A. Espinosa, was also then in business in the
town.

Important new arrivals in Ndola in the late 1920s included Abe Lowenthal
and his brothers. They came from Latvia, and were related to the Hepkers
and the Thals. Abe Lowenthal was born at Sabile, Latvia in 1904. He came
out to Southern Rhodesia in 1924 and was sent by his Hepker uncles to

manage a store at Dett in northern Matabeleland. He was once asked by a Scottish manager to help quell a riot by workers at the family's saw mills, and was advised to bring a gun. He thought that this was unwise, and received some credit for having faced and soothed the crowd without any threat of the use of force. He arrived at Ndola in 1926 and was followed by his brothers, William and Conrad.[37]

The Lowenthal brothers opened the Bijou cinema in Ndola in 1929. Abe had courted his cousin Phyllis Hepker, but was married in that year to Marlie Wulfsohn, who had recently reached South Africa from Latvia. After her death in 1933, he married her sister, Hessie. Their brother, Harry Wulfsohn, followed Marlie to Ndola in 1930. He was one of a number of young men who worked in the Bijou cinema in its very early days and was, as we shall see, to play an important part in the economic life of the country. Abe Lowenthal himself was, according to David Messerer, employed on the Mufulira mine in the late 1930s, and ran the recreation club there, while maintaining his interests in Ndola. His brothers moved to Southern Rhodesia in the later 1930s.[38]

Among the other early participants in the construction boom on the Copperbelt, who were based at Ndola, were the Glazer brothers. Sam Lieb Glazer arrived from Lithuania at the age of twenty-one in 1928, and set up Ndola Supply Stores with an initial capital of £100. His brother Bernard arrived in 1930. They were in partnership with one of the Sussmans, and their business went bankrupt in 1932. While, allegedly, undischarged bankrupts in Northern Rhodesia, they went on to achieve a measure of notoriety as the promoters of African City Investments, and as landlords in central Johannesburg. In 1955 the Federal Intelligence and Security Bureau, which estimated the value of their assets at £4 million, was concerned that their purchase from the Bechuanaland Exploration Company, with the backing of the Volkskas Bank, of large areas of land in the Tati and Tuli blocks, was a front for Afrikaner Nationalist expansion into the Bechuanaland Protectorate. They were also a problem to the colonial government there as the slum landlords of the Francistown location.[39]

The Rhodes Islanders

Another development in Ndola in the late 1930s was the opening by a group of Sephardic Jewish entrepreneurs of the country's first soap factory – one of the first examples of this kind of secondary industry in the country. The man behind this development was Ruben Amato who, with his brother Benny, was among the most controversial entrepreneurs to operate in southern Africa in the colonial period. His life story would make an exciting book in itself. He had arrived in the Congo from Rhodes Island at the age of sixteen in 1920, and laid the basis of a vast enterprise by selling cigarettes in the streets of Elisabethville (in modern Zambian parlance, by *mishanga* selling). He had, with his brothers, soon built up a business, Amato Frères, which dominated the trade of Katanga in vegetable oils and other commodities. By some accounts, the basis of their success was the position which they acquired as monopoly purchasers of crops, including palm oil and maize, which were grown by peasants under state compulsion in the Congo.[40]

They moved in the late 1930s into the Rhodesian and South African markets. Their firm, Union Congo Oil and Soap Industries, began the extraction of vegetable oils from maize, and created the market in South Africa for sunflower seed. They had originally worked as agents for Lever Brothers, but eventually became engaged in a price-cutting war with them, as well as with Premier Milling and Tiger Oats. They had taken on rather more than they could handle and their business empire collapsed in the late 1950s. They had also become involved, as we shall see, in textile manufacturing in competition with the Frame group. The Amatos' partners in the Ndola soap factory were Nic Capelouto and Joe Tarica, who were their original partners in the business which they had started at Kamina on the Kasai railway (the Chemin de Fer du Bas Kongo) in the mid-1920s, and B. I. Menashe.[41]

Boaz Israel Menashe was probably the only one of the Amatos' partners to live in Northern Rhodesia. He had spent nine years at Gwelo in Southern Rhodesia, where he maintained business interests in partnership with a relative, Isaac Benatar, and had reached Nchanga by 1930. He had a concession store there, but was forced to close it in 1933 at the low point of the depression. He returned to Nchanga a few years later after the recovery of copper prices and the reopening of the mine. He never married, but was known to live with an English woman, Miss Freeman, who was his accountant. His brother, Haim I. (known as Victor) Menashe, who was born in 1905, worked for him in the 1920s and early 1930s in Gwelo, Wankie and at Nchanga. He spent some time with his sister in the Congo at the low point of the depression, but returned to Nchanga in 1937. He continued to work for his brother until his own departure from the country in 1960. He is still alive and well and lives in Cape Town. Victor Menashe married Rebecca Alhadeff, a member of another prominent Rhodes Island family. Through the marriage of their sister to Nahman Israel, who moved from the Congo to Nchanga in 1939, the Menashe brothers formed the nucleus of Northern Rhodesia's small Sephardic community, which had its focal point after the war in the new town of Chingola.[42]

The Sephardic Jews were always a small minority within the Northern Rhodesian Jewish community, but they were well connected with the more important sections of their community in the Congo and Southern Rhodesia. They were initially regarded as inferior, and as something of an embarrassment, by many of the Ashkenazi Jews from the Baltic states, including the religious leader of that community, Moses Cohen.[43] They had close linguistic and cultural affinities with the Italian and Greek communities, even though they had been the victims of the anti-Semitic tendencies of both these groups in their birthplace. Most of the Rhodes islanders were able to speak French, Italian, Greek and English, as well as their native language, Ladino (a form of medieval Spanish). Victor Menashe says that he was encouraged to change his first name by gentile friends who used to tell him that, with his Latin accent and mannerisms, he was not a 'Hymie'.[44]

Italy's declaration of war on Britain in June 1940 had an impact on the Sephardic Jews in Northern Rhodesia. The Menashe brothers and Nahman Israel had all been born in the Turkish empire, but Rhodes was taken over in 1912 by Italy. All the Rhodes islanders in the country, with the exception of a few, such as B. I. Menashe, who had become naturalised British citizens, were regarded as Italians and as enemy aliens. Within days of Italy's entry into the war, about fifteen of them were interned in the Ndola Girls School, together with other Italian citizens. Those who were interned included the brothers, M. D. and V. G. Capelluto, Nissim Tarica, Nahman Israel, H. I. Menashe, M. Piha, C. Bardavid, who lived in Kitwe for many years, and members of the Hanon, Hazan, Berro and Caravaghia families.[45]

Among those who interceded with the Northern Rhodesian government on their behalf was Hyam Schulman, the leader of the Ndola Jewish community, and the former mayor of the town. After about two months the majority of the detainees were released on 25 August. Victor Menashe remembers that the letter from the Governor ordering their release reached them on Ndola railway station platform as they were about to board a train which would have taken them to internment camps in South Africa.[46] Among those who were not immediately released were the two Capelluto brothers and Nissim Tarica. A great injustice was undoubtedly done to these people. M. D. Capelluto, who was a carpenter on the Mufulira mine, was detained with his wife in an internment camp near Salisbury for the duration of the war on the basis of a single report that he had made anti-British remarks in 1938. Appeals from leaders of the Sephardic community in Southern Rhodesia, and from Roy Welensky, were of no avail. He was not finally released from internment until late in 1947 when he was given permanent residence in Southern Rhodesia.[47] His younger brother, who also worked on the mine, was judged to be guilty by association, and was detained for the duration of the war in internment camps in South Africa. His youth – he was only nineteen at the time of his internment – was held against him, as he was thought to have been educated during the fascist period. He suffered greatly as a Jew detained with anti-Semitic fascists, and had a nervous breakdown, but he was not released.[48]

Members of the Rhodes community were also interned in the Congo, but were rapidly released as it was found that the economy of Katanga could not function without them. The detention of one or more of the partners in the soap factory resulted in the dissolution of the partnership. The factory was taken over and run for many years by the Amatos' Rhodesia Congo Oil and Soap Industries. Their products in the post-war period included 'Rhoco' soap and 'Tarica' candles. B. I. Menashe became a director of the company and his association with the Amatos may be one explanation for what was seen at the time as his exceptional wealth.[49] The 4,000 Jews who remained on the island of Rhodes itself, including the majority of the members of the families which came to central Africa, were deported by the Italian authorities to Germany and almost all died at Auschwitz.[50]

The great majority of Jews on the Copperbelt were traders or shop assistants; there were very few Jews employed in the mines before the war. As the threat of war increased, there was pressure on the mining companies to reduce the number of aliens they employed in the interests of national security. A visiting Colonial Office minister, Lord Dufferin and Ava, expressed the fear that they might be involved in sabotage in the event of war. A survey at Nkana in 1938 reported that there were twenty-eight Germans and twenty Yugoslavs employed on the mine. Only one of the Germans, Hans Tuch, who was then employed as a skipman, appears to have been Jewish. Although there were a few Jews employed on other mines in the years before the war, government resistance to their employment began to break down only when recruitment for the army, from which recent immigrants were also excluded, made the shortage of skills intense.[51] It is to the pre-war debates on Jewish immigration that we will now turn.

CHAPTER 6

'Land of Milk and Honey': Settlement Schemes and Immigration Debates, 1934–39

Until the 1930s, almost all Jewish immigrants into Northern Rhodesia came from the former Russian empire. The First World War and the Russian Revolution produced dramatic changes in Europe. The Baltic states of Poland, Latvia, Lithuania, Estonia and Finland attained their independence. Jews, who had suffered persecution in the multi-ethnic Russian empire, now found that they were faced with hostility from nationalist governments within most of the new states. Jewish emigration from the Baltic states continued to western Europe, the United States, South America, Palestine and southern Africa. From 1933 Jews all over Europe were faced by a new threat, the rise of fascism and the coming to power of Hitler in Germany. Readers of his book, *Mein Kampf*, knew that he was deeply anti-Semitic and committed both to the 'racial purification' of Germany and to eastwards expansion. The Nuremburg Laws in 1935 deprived German Jews of citizenship, excluded them from the professions, and made it illegal for them to employ non-Jews. Concentration camps for critics of the regime, including many Jews, had already been opened.

The impact of institutional anti-Semitism was felt in South Africa before the coming to power of fascism in Germany. The Quota Act, which was passed in 1930, specifically restricted immigration from Poland, Lithuania, Latvia, Russia, Palestine and Greece. It made it virtually impossible for Jews from these countries, who did not have close relatives already in the country, to enter. The promoters of this legislation protested that they were not anti-Semitic and praised the Jewish contribution to the development of South Africa, but there was no doubt as to their real motives.[1] Germany was not originally one of the countries on the restricted list, as very few German Jews emigrated to South Africa before Hitler came to power. There was a dramatic increase in 1936 when over 2,500 German Jews entered the country, including over 500 who arrived in October on a single ship, the *Stuttgart*. The ship was chartered to enable refugees to enter the country before the implementation of new restrictions. This provoked demonstrations, and a further tightening of restrictions in February 1937 which slowed Jewish immigration from Germany to a trickle.[2]

The restrictions on Jewish immigration to South Africa had an impact on Northern Rhodesia. People in the south who had difficulty in getting visas for their relatives began to see Northern Rhodesia as a last resort. Its Immigration Ordinance of 1931 was similar to the South African Act of 1930, and required that potential immigrants should have £100 available to them on arrival, or have a guarantee of bona fide employment. There were, however, no restrictions on country of origin, and anyone with access to the necessary funds, or a job, was free to enter the country. The law in Northern Rhodesia was more liberal than in Southern Rhodesia where the authorities were very conscious of opposition to 'alien' immigration, and used their discretionary powers to limit entry.[3] There was, however, an immigration quota debate in the Northern Rhodesian Legislative Council in June 1938, and the government, which was always very sensitive to white settler opinion, responded by setting up a committee under the chairmanship of a legal officer to examine the question.[4]

The committee showed itself to be more concerned about the increased rate of Asian immigration than with the number of Jewish applicants. It had some surprisingly benign things to say about the refugees. It pointed out that stateless people from Europe 'are "Northern Rhodesians" in the real sense, in that they have little hope of ever residing elsewhere'. It commented on the high standard of craftsmanship displayed by some of the refugees and stated that 'no country in the stage of development of Northern Rhodesia could afford to turn away from its doors men of this type'.[5] It recommended a new immigration ordinance, but this was not promulgated until after the war.[6]

Settlement Schemes

The possibility of assisted Jewish refugee immigration to Northern Rhodesia was first raised by the Colonial Office with the Governor, Sir Hubert Young, in 1934. A list of potential German Jewish immigrants, mainly industrial chemists, was also provided, but no interest was shown. Mark Wischnitzer, the general secretary of the Hilfsverein, the German Jewish voluntary agency concerned with emigration and resettlement, paid a visit to Northern Rhodesia in June 1936 to investigate the prospects for employment for Jewish technicians on the mines. He saw the Governor, but was told that there were currently no openings for refugees. He was informed that the Nchanga mine would soon reopen and that this might provide employment opportunities. He said that he would visit the Anglo-American Corporation's office in London to discuss the possibility – apparently without result.[7]

During 1938 there was increasing pressure from the United States on Britain to do more about the refugee question. The Americans were the prime movers behind the calling of an inter-governmental conference on emigration and settlement which was held at Evian, Switzerland, in July 1938. As the date of the conference approached, the Colonial Secretary, Malcolm MacDonald, became increasingly anxious to show that the Colonial Office was able to offer the possibility of settlement for some refugees in its vast African dominions. When the retiring Governor of Northern Rhodesia, Sir Hubert Young, told a senior Colonial Office official, Cosmo Parkinson, over lunch that there might be a possibility of settling Jewish refugees in the remote Mwinilunga district of Northern Rhodesia, MacDonald seized at the chance.[8]

Young was persuaded to put his suggestion in writing. In doing so he provided the following testimonial to the Jewish community: 'The Jews are by no means unpopular in Northern Rhodesia and some of the Jewish traders are among the best educated and most public spirited of the community.'[9] MacDonald now put pressure on the acting Governor, William Logan, to come up with a positive statement on the subject which could be put to the imminent Evian conference. He consulted the Provincial Commissioner of the North-Western Province, H. F. Cartmel-Robinson, and the acting Director of Agriculture, William Allan, an outstanding agriculturalist. Neither of them was enthusiastic, though there was support from Ffoliott Fisher, a Plymouth Brethren missionary at Kalene Hill, who may have been the original source of the idea. Allan pointed out that the best land was in small patches, and was already in African occupation. He pointed, typically for the time, to the dangers of miscegenation and racial deterioration which would confront settlers who attempted to survive on a subsistence basis.[10]

The elected members of the Legislative Council unanimously rejected the proposal as put to them. Poor communications, distance from markets, lack of good soils and tsetse flies were all put forward as objections. They were, however, most concerned by the threat that any refugee settlers would be likely to abandon farming and compete on the labour market, or in trade, with already settled whites. At least three of the unofficial members were also implacably opposed to Jewish settlement on what were described as 'racial grounds'. Meanwhile Lord Winterton, a member of the British Cabinet, and a landowner in Northern Rhodesia, told the Evian conference that there were limited opportunities for agricultural settlement in east Africa.[11]

The leader of the unofficial members of the Legislative Council, Sir Leopold Moore, whose probable Jewish antecedents have already been suggested, brought the issue into the public arena with a speech at an agricultural show at Bindura in Southern Rhodesia at the end of July 1938. With typical sensationalism, he told his audience that it was planned to settle 500 Jewish families in a 'reserve' in the north west. He threatened his Southern Rhodesian audience that before long 'they would be over the Chirundu Bridge [into Southern Rhodesia], owning this farming country, running businesses and banks, and no one could live very long here'. Debates in the Assembly would be conducted in Yiddish, and Northern Rhodesia would become an 'annex of Palestine'.[12]

Moore's real target was the Colonial Office. In his view, it was trying to foist this scheme on Northern Rhodesia. It had not asked, and could not compel, Southern Rhodesia, which had settler self-government, to consider such a scheme. Northern Rhodesia's whites could, in his view, escape from Downing Street domination only by amalgamation with the south. Moore was an effective populist politician, and he did have a point. The British government was putting pressure on the Northern Rhodesian government to support schemes which were impractical, and the main objective was to relieve pressure on itself over its policies of restricting Jewish immigration to Palestine, and to Britain itself. Towards the end of the year, further pressure was put on the Colonial Office by the Foreign Office which provided various arguments as to the benefits for Britain of African settlement schemes. Most of these arguments related to satisfying the Americans, and reducing the pressure over Palestine.[13]

'Chirupula' Stephenson

Meanwhile, a number of other areas had been suggested as potential sites for settlement schemes. Perhaps the most practical of these came from J. E. 'Chirupula' Stephenson, a former member of the BSA Company's administration, and the founder of the town of Ndola. He retired to his house at Chiwefwe, near Mkushi, and subjected the colonial administration to a forty-year barrage of letters on a bewildering variety of subjects, including the injustices done by the colonial government to the Lamba and Lala peoples. Knowing that letters sent to Lusaka would be ignored, he chose to direct his proposal for a Jewish settlement in the Mkushi district to the Colonial Office through his friend Sir Herbert Stanley, the former Governor. Andrew Cohen, a rising star in the Colonial Office, forwarded it to Northern Rhodesia's new Governor, Sir John Maybin. As the suggested area included part of the present Mkushi farm block, one of Zambia's best commercial farming areas, it cannot be said to have been totally impractical, though his suggestion that 16,000 refugees could be settled was optimistic. Chirupula suggested that: 'Wild bees abound, and with cattle from Christian ranchers, judging from the success achieved by Jews at Tel Aviv, this suggested colony would soon be a land of milk and honey.'[14] Chirupula's scheme was not taken very seriously, but it was welcomed by Moses Cohen, the leading representative of the Jewish community in the region. Nothing came of his proposal, but Chirupula did provide a home at Chiwefwe for at least four German Jewish refugees in the early years of the war.[15]

Another former BSA Company official, Frank Melland, who had become a London-based Africa expert, also made a suggestion which was seized upon by the Colonial Office. In a memorandum which he sent to Major

Stern, a member of a committee on Jewish resettlement which was chaired by Anthony de Rothschild, he made the case for a settlement on the Muchinga escarpment north of Mpika. Colin Trapnell, the country's first and still most distinguished ecologist, told Stewart Gore-Browne that 'the scheme wants a much bigger and safer proposition than anything in Mpika district'.[16] Gore-Browne, who had built a mansion for himself north of Mpika, and was well aware of the difficulty of producing economic crops hundreds of miles from the Line of Rail, was equally sceptical. He told the Governor that, quite apart from any political considerations 'we should not hold out any hopes of Northern Rhodesia's providing a solution to the problem on a large scale'. He was in touch with Anthony de Rothschild and told him the same thing. De Rothschild agreed that Melland's suggestion might not be practicable, but pointed out that:

> any place which offers them a reasonable chance of making a living, even on a primitive standard and free from persecution, has to be considered, in view of the great difficulty of obtaining permission for them to enter countries which have already reached a high stage of development. There is also the expectation that these people, many of whom will be, perhaps, above the average of intelligence, will manage to do better than others in the past.[17]

There were other suggestions. Dr George Prentice, a retired Church of Scotland missionary living at Fort Jameson, suggested an area lying between the boundaries of Tanganyika, Nyasaland and Northern Rhodesia. This is the area known today as Uyombe which is noted for its remoteness, fertility and the industriousness of its people. The government itself was inclined to propose that some of the land in the Abercorn district, which was about to be taken back from the BSA Company, could be used for Jewish settlement. There were also rather more practical, but anonymous, suggestions for settlement on the Line of Rail in the Lusaka and Chisamba areas.[18]

After a certain amount of arm-twisting from Malcolm MacDonald, Sir John Maybin was able to persuade the majority of the unofficial members of the Legislative Council in September 1938 to accept a small-scale scheme with a first group of not more than thirty pioneers. He gave an assurance that this small scheme would not grow to more than 150 settlers. Even so, Moore and two others of this eight-member group were implacably opposed to the scheme. Kenya's agreement to a pilot scheme of thirty settlers had been triumphantly announced to the House of Commons in November 1938 by the Prime Minister, Neville Chamberlain, himself. MacDonald had made it clear that it would be impossible for him to explain to Parliament a refusal by Northern Rhodesia to accept a similar number of settlers. When further Foreign Office pressure was applied to the Colonial Office in the aftermath of *Krystallnacht*, MacDonald had to require that Northern Rhodesia accept a visit from a commission of inquiry which would be sent out by Anthony de Rothschild's group of voluntary organisations. The terms of reference of this commission would include the investigation of the possibility of large-scale settlement. MacDonald made it clear to the Governor that this was window-dressing, and that the commission was not expected to report in favour of large-scale settlement.[19]

Maybin had to work very hard to persuade the unofficials that they would have to accept the commission. They felt that they would be accused by their constituents of a breach of faith. MacDonald explained that the deterioration of the situation in Germany demanded a new look at the possibility of large-scale settlement in Africa. It was not only Moore and his diehards who protested at the Colonial Office's change of mind; Roy Welensky was reported to have said in February 1939 that he was flatly opposed to the commission and that 'a large number of the general public with whom he is in touch were opposed to the small scheme. They feel that the scheme won't succeed and that they [the Jewish settlers] will drift on to the labour market and compete at a lower rate of wages.'[20]

The majority of the unofficials was eventually persuaded to accept the commission, and the possibility that it might recommend large-scale settlement. Representatives of Welensky's Rhodesian Railway Workers Union protested at the threat of increased Jewish and 'alien' immigration. Another protester was the president of the white Northern Rhodesian Mineworkers Union which had been formed in 1937 in response to the strike of black workers on the mines in 1935. He was Victor Solomon Diamond, who was, as we have seen, a member of a Barotseland cattle-trading family, and was last heard of in 1930 when his Lusaka garage went bankrupt.[21] At a public meeting at Nkana, it was reported that resolutions were passed both against Jewish immigration into Northern Rhodesia, and for the provision of a Jewish National Home.[22]

In the end it was agreed that the commission representing the voluntary organisations under the chairmanship of Sir James Dunnett, who had retired from the Indian Civil Service, would visit the country, and that it would be accompanied by a locally appointed committee under the chairmanship of the Director of Agriculture, C. J. Lewin. Apart from Dunnett, the commission included Hector Croad, a retired Provincial Commissioner for the Northern Province, a Colonel Micholls (sic), who had been involved with the Kenyan settlement scheme, a representative of the Palestine Jewish Colonisation Association, and an agriculturalist serving in Uganda who had experience of Palestine. Stewart Gore-Browne was the most prominent member of the local committee.[23]

The commission and the committee travelled together and came, as was expected, to similar conclusions. The commission rejected Mwinilunga and Mpika, and concluded that there were limited possibilities for tobacco growers in Choma and Fort Jameson, for wheat growers in Chirupula's Mkushi district, for coffee growers in Abercorn, and for a few ranchers. It suggested that each family would require starting capital of about £1,400 if it was to produce a minimum cash income of £120. The report was clearly influenced by the fear that an unsuccessful settlement might add to the 'Poor White' class which existed among Afrikaner small-holders in the Lusaka district, half of whose children were said to be malnourished. It agreed with the view that Jewish settlers should have sufficient capital to allow them to merge with the white settler farming class.[24] When the commission's report was submitted to Anthony de Rothschild and his coordinating committee, they dismissed any possibility of pursuing settlement schemes in Northern Rhodesia on the grounds of expense. They also requested that the report should be suppressed. They were afraid that it might encourage other countries to increase their demands.[25]

A Jewish Critic

At least one intelligent Jewish observer thought that the commission was intended to come up with recommendations which would be unacceptable to its sponsors. Professor Herbert Frankel, and Dr Henry Sonnabend, both members of staff at the University of the Witwatersrand, Johannesburg, visited Lusaka in June 1939 to give evidence to the commission on behalf of the South African Jewish Board of Deputies. Frankel, who was in his mid-thirties at the time, was born in South Africa of German Jewish parentage, and was already South Africa's most distinguished economist. He had published in the previous year his classic book, *Capital Investment in Africa*, which was part of Lord Hailey's *African Survey*. He was a Zionist and had also provided the economic evidence which was presented to the Peel Commission on Palestine on behalf of the movement.[26]

Frankel had published a letter in *The Times* of London in December 1938 in which he deprecated the current enthusiasm for African settlement schemes as a way of coping with the exodus of refugees from Germany. He had pointed to the difficulty and expense of settlement in tropical as opposed to temperate areas and had said that much time and energy were being wasted on futile suggestions. He had no doubt that these schemes were being proposed as a diversion from the real issues of Germany's treatment of its Jewish population, which the policy of appeasement did not challenge, and from the Palestine question. There seems to be little doubt that the search for settlement sites in Africa was a part of the policy of appeasement, and implied a tacit acceptance of the right of the Nazi government to abuse, render stateless and drive out its Jewish population.[27]

In spite of his reservations or, perhaps, because of them, Frankel was prepared to take the time to give evidence to the commission. His colleague on the trip to Lusaka, Henry Sonnabend, was an equally interesting person. Born in Poland, he had been educated at the University of Padua where he studied demography and statistics. He was sent to Southern Rhodesia as part of a team of demographers which was commissioned by Mussolini to discover the secret of the allegedly superior virility and fertility of the African population. He chose to stay in Africa, and Frankel found him a job in the new Department of Sociology at the University of the Witwatersrand, where he did pioneering work on the social demography of the South African Jewish population. During the war he was involved in the education of Italian prisoners of war, and also served with the army on the Italian front, and with Tito's partisans in Yugoslavia. He was an enthusiastic Zionist and emigrated to Israel where he became mayor of Ashkalon.[28]

Secondary Industries

It may seem surprising that there was no apparent input into these discussions from Northern Rhodesia's own Jewish community. Although Isadore Kollenberg was involved in an abortive agricultural settlement scheme in Southern Rhodesia, it is fairly clear that Northern Rhodesia's Jewish community was as sceptical as almost everybody else in the country about the viability of such projects. It is also clear that they had rather different ideas. They saw a better prospect of employment for Jewish refugees in the development of secondary industries. This was an idea which had also been mentioned in the report of the Immigration Committee in the previous year. It had noted the existence of a factory producing 'Native' dresses in Lusaka, of a milling industry in the same town, a soap factory at Ndola, and of furniture factories at Mulobezi and Ndola. It had implied, as was in fact the case, that there was Jewish involvement in most, if not all, of these enterprises.[29]

The member of the Legislative Council who was most sympathetic to Jewish refugee immigration, and in closest touch with the Jewish community, was Captain 'Skipper' Campbell of Pemba. He had been a member of the Immigration Committee and was probably the source of the ideas about secondary industry which appeared in its report. He told the government in February 1939 that he had been in touch with leading members of the Jewish community in connection with a proposal for a large settlement of Jewish refugees, possibly as many as 50,000 families, who would be engaged in the development of secondary industries. He had presided over a meeting at Henrie Kollenberg's house where these ideas were discussed. They had themselves been in touch with leading Jews in Bulawayo and Johannesburg, and in Britain, on the issue.

He said that he was personally opposed to a large agricultural settlement, but he was in favour of a large settlement of people who would be engaged in secondary industries 'provided that there was sufficient capital to ensure that the settlement was not a failure'. The participants in such a settlement would, it was hoped, provide a market for local agricultural produce. The suggested projects included: the production of essential oils; the manufacture of citrus juice for bulk shipment to England; the production of cotton and wool blankets; the production of vegetable oils; and a shoe industry similar to the one which had recently been started by the Bata Shoe Company (a Czechoslovak business with Jewish links) in Bulawayo. It had also been suggested that metals which were produced in the territory might be manufactured there, and that spare parts for aeroplanes could be produced. He suggested that the Jewish community might be asked to draw up a memorandum on the development of secondary industries which could be submitted to the visiting commission. He was, however, told that this was impossible as the commission's terms of reference limited it to the consideration of agricultural settlement schemes.[30]

Campbell's 'pile of documents' on the subject does not appear to have survived. The suggested number of immigrants certainly seems to be exaggerated, but not all the suggestions for the development of secondary industries were impractical. The Bata Shoe Company opened branches in the country before the end of 1939.[31] Workers on the Copperbelt, mainly white women, were employed during the war in the manufacture of parts for tanks and bombs. Jewish entrepreneurs, including the Susmans and the Gershes, were to be closely involved in the development of secondary industries after the war. Suggestions for the employment of refugees in secondary industry were much more realistic than the fanciful and, in the end futile, schemes for agricultural settlement.

The main effect of these discussions was to give publicity to the fact that Northern Rhodesia was a possible destination for German Jewish refugees. While the discussions were going on, refugees from Nazi Germany did find their way to Northern Rhodesia in significant numbers on their own initiative, and through the ordinary immigration procedures. According to figures supplied by the South African Jewish Board of Deputies in 1946, a total of 230 German Jewish refugees reached Northern Rhodesia between the enactment of the South African Aliens' Act in 1937 and the outbreak of the Second World War in September 1939. This estimate seems to be on the low side, and takes no account of the refugees who arrived after the outbreak of war.[32] The Chief Immigration Officer estimated that 216 German Jewish refugees had entered the country in the course of 1939. Allowing for a number of refugees who had arrived earlier, and for a handful who entered during the early months of 1940, it seems likely that between 250 and 300 German Jewish refugees entered the country either before, or in the early months of, the war.[33]

Writing early in 1940, Henry Sonnabend estimated that there were 405 Jewish 'immigrants' in the country of whom forty were unemployed. This figure may have included some refugees from other parts of eastern Europe. At least sixty people arrived from the Baltic states at this time, and there was also a number of central European refugees who arrived from Palestine. It is difficult to be precise about figures because there does not appear to have been a comprehensive official list, and the figures which do exist were not always drawn up on the same basis. Some statistics counted only heads of families as immigrants, while others included wives and children.[34]

Superintendent Brodie

Northern Rhodesia's Chief Immigration Officer for much of this crucial time was Superintendent Norman Brodie, a Scots policeman who eventually became head of the Criminal Investigation Department, and acted for a time as Commissioner of the Northern Rhodesia Police. He was highly regarded by the Jewish community for his sympathy and cooperation on the refugee question. Maurice Gersh, who was involved with refugee settlement on the Copperbelt, described him as 'extremely helpful', and went so far as to say that no one was ever turned away.[35] Brodie certainly does seem to have interpreted the regulations in a humane and liberal way, especially with regard to the granting of visas to people who already had relatives in the country. It is also clear from the files that he responded very quickly to requests for visas. He was one of those unusual British officials who might qualify for the status of 'righteous gentile'. While the day-to-day administration of immigration policy was Brodie's responsibility, from the date of his appointment in February 1939, when he succeeded Chief Inspector William Totman in the job, the formulation of the policy rested with his superiors.

When applications from German Jews began to arrive in large numbers – there may have been as many as 900 – in November and December 1938, in the wake of *Krystallnacht*, Totman began to use his discretion to limit the numbers. In January 1939 the executive committee of the Legislative Council noted that it was possible that more German Jewish refugees might enter the country through the normal channels than would be allowed to enter through the small-scale agricultural settlement schemes which were then under consideration. The issuing of visas was suspended for a time and the Immigration Ordinance was amended to remove the suggestion that the country was bound to accept anyone with access to £100. In April 1939 Brodie reported that 152 visas had been issued to German Jews since 1 December 1938.[36] On 1 June 1939 the Legislative Council was told that visas issued to 100 German Jewish refugees, with fifty-eight dependants, were outstanding. Most of these visas had been issued before the change in the immigration regulations in February. The visas had been issued to people to enable them to leave Germany. It had not been possible to inform them of the change in regulations and it was felt that it would be unfair to impose the new conditions on people who had already left their homes. It was improbable that they would all arrive.[37]

In April 1939 twelve immigrants, with a probable nine dependants, had been allowed to enter Northern Rhodesia from Beira. They had originally been turned back by the Southern Rhodesian immigration authorities at Umtali (Muthare) who doubted the validity of their documents. They were living in pitiable conditions in Beira and were allowed to enter Northern Rhodesia on compassionate grounds. They were part of a group of forty families who were stranded in Beira and who narrowly avoided being returned to Germany. They were saved by the prompt action of J. M. Barnett, Beira's only Jewish resident. The remainder eventually found refuge in Uganda and Mauritius. Among those who reached Northern Rhodesia in this group was Dr Dublon and his family. He eventually joined the medical service and stayed in the country for many years. At this time Brodie reported that he intended in future to issue visas only to applicants who had secured jobs, or who had sufficient capital to start a business.[38]

The Immigration Debate

The question of immigration was debated by the Legislative Council for a second time in June 1939. A motion for the reduction of alien immigration was proposed by Colonel Arthur Stephenson. It was supported by all the speakers, including the more liberal members, Stewart Gore-Browne, Roy Welensky and Captain Campbell. Stephenson quoted from letters which, he claimed, showed that the Jewish refugees included old people, who would become a burden on the tax-payer, and young people who were prepared to work for nothing but board and lodging, and who would consequently depress wages. Welensky suggested that the government should publish monthly statistics on alien immigration in order to dispel some of the wild rumours which were circulating on the subject. He was, however, convinced that 'we have reached the point of saturation'. Cholmeley, a diehard opponent of Jewish immigration, expressed sympathy with the burden being borne by the existing Jewish community, and suggested that increased immigration would 'aggravate any feeling that the rest of the population may have against the Jews'. Campbell, who was sympathetic to Jewish immigration and was, as we have seen, in close touch with the Jewish community, also expressed concern about the burden which the refugees were imposing on it. He said:

> I can only say that I have been in touch with a lot of the Jews who came into this country years ago and without exception they have told me that it does not matter where the refugees come from. If large numbers are admitted they do not like the look of the future: that they will have to share whatever they have been making with a whole lot of others. They are not keen on them being admitted in large numbers. In fact I think that they would like to see it stopped until such time as the man who is already here is employed.[39]

There is other evidence that by the middle of 1939 the Jewish community was beginning to find the flow of refugees more than they could handle with their own resources. The actual number of refugees might not seem to be very large, but it is probable that their arrival had the effect of doubling the Jewish population of Northern Rhodesia within the space of a year. Harry

Susman, then in his early sixties, wrote on 29 April 1939 from Livingstone
to the Jewish Guild in Bulawayo:

> we don't know what to do, Livingstone is a small place with a Jewish community
> of eight families of whom four can give anything and four can give absolutely
> nothing. We are feeding three families already, and I myself have spent three to
> four hundred pounds in guarantees and money given to them. What can one
> man do for a community – it is heartbreaking.[40]

In the same month Brodie had received a report on Jewish immigration
from a police sergeant in Livingstone indicating that there was hostility to
Jewish immigration in the town. A number of local farmers and businessmen
had been approached to provide employment to refugees and had refused to
do so.[41]

The young Goodman 'Goody' Glasser, then secretary of the Refugee
Assistance Committee in Lusaka, whose other members included 'Tubby'
Wulfsohn and Sam Fischer, wrote on 25 April 1939 to the South African
Jewish Board of Deputies in Johannesburg:

> Our most urgent problem is that of accommodating refugees who, having
> procured visas to enter this country, find themselves stranded and destitute at
> the border. The Jewish public are already burdened to capacity supporting these
> people, and at the moment there is nowhere to place them, not even for food
> and lodging alone. People (men, women, children) stranded in our towns des-
> titute – and we are unable to find anything for them to do. There are many
> more on the way to this country, they have visas to enter the country, but
> nothing to do when they get here. The matter is urgent.

Writing from the Copperbelt in the same week, Maurice Gersh, who was
the chairman of the local assistance committee, told the chairman of the
Refugee Relief Sub-committee in Johannesburg that:

> the absorbative capacity of the Jewish merchants and private contractors has
> already been reached. The copper mines could solve the whole problem, but
> the policy is not to employ any aliens. Unless further facilities for employment
> can be created very shortly, the additional immigrants who have visas will
> constitute a very grave problem.[42]

The South African Jewish Board of Deputies responded very promptly to
these appeals. It immediately established the Council for Refugee Settlement
in Africa outside the Union to deal with such problems. The council set up
a Rhodesia sub-committee whose most active members were A. Mennell and
H. D. Landau, Herbert Frankel and Henry Sonnabend. Within a month
Frankel and Sonnabend were in Lusaka. They came, as we have seen, to give
evidence to the Dunnett Commission, an exercise which they regarded as
futile, but their journey was not in vain. They achieved a great deal by
helping the local Refugees Assistance Committee to cope with an influx

which had clearly overstretched its resources. From this time onwards, the financial burden of supporting the refugees was taken over by the South African organisations which had access to substantial funds.

The Refugee Farm

Writing from Johannesburg at the end of June 1939, Herbert Frankel explained to the government's Financial Secretary that he and Sonnabend had agreed to help the local committee by renting a farm where refugees could either be employed in agricultural work or be supported until they found other employment. They had also agreed to finance a boarding house in Lusaka. There were already twenty-five adults and five children on the farm. A further twenty refugees were expected to arrive within a few weeks. Fifteen people were being kept at the boarding house in Lusaka. By October he was able to report that there were thirty-five to forty people at the farm. Frankel's request for government help in agricultural training was rebuffed. It was not prepared to support what it regarded as an intensive settlement in a maize-growing area.[43]

The refugee farm was not an agricultural success, but it did serve its purpose as a holding camp and, as Goody Glasser recalled, it was a place where the refugees could be kept out of sight at a time when there was considerable settler hostility to their presence. Glasser was persuaded by Frankel to involve himself in the running of the farm which was at Lilayi, about seven miles south of Lusaka. Glasser recalled:

> There were tumbledown cottages on it, so we had them renovated, and cleaned the place up and made it liveable, and put in beds etc ... Some worked on the farm. We gave them some cows, chickens. We had to keep them. It was quite an exercise. They used to say: 'You've got a business. You're OK. What about us? We want a business like that too. We thought you'd have a business for us.'[44]

His recollections point to a fact which has been noted by many. German Jews were often highly assimilated members of the middle and professional classes. They were not well prepared for roughing it in Africa, although a few had been attending classes in agriculture in preparation for emigration to Palestine. Conditions at the Simonson boarding house, named after the German refugee couple who managed it, were not much better, with two families sharing a room. Many of the refugees left Germany after release from concentration camps into which they had been thrown at the time of *Krystallnacht* in November 1938. They were in a traumatised state. Settlement in Northern Rhodesia was never going to be easy for people who had, in many cases, to exchange a comfortable middle-class life for an initially penniless existence in totally unfamiliar surroundings. There was at the beginning, and there continued to be for some time, tension between the refugees and the existing Jewish population, almost all of whom were of Yiddish-speaking eastern European origin.[45]

One resident of the farm, who complained bitterly of misappropriation of funds supplied for German refugees by what he called 'Russian sharks', was later interned as an enemy alien in Livingstone. He had suggested that German anti-Semitism was the result of similar exploitation. Brodie described him after the war as 'most unpleasant and irrational'. He said that his Jewish origins were doubted by members of the Jewish community and that, if he was not a Nazi sympathiser, he was certainly a defeatist who was convinced of the invincibility of Nazi forces.[46]

Herbert Frankel did one more significant service for the Northern Rhodesian Jewish community. After his visit to Lusaka he was inspired to suggest that the farm needed a warden and the community a spiritual leader. He was able to inform the Northern Rhodesian government that he had been able 'to secure the services of a man of exceptionally high character and ability' who would be well able to perform both these roles. The man whom he had in mind was the Reverend Cantor Feivel Metzger, a Polish Jew who had spent most of his life in Germany and who had carried on his 'religious calling' in Dusseldorf. He was a fully qualified cantor and was, according to Frankel, a man of extensive rabbinical learning. He had worked for two years on contract with Hebrew congregations in Johannesburg, but was now stranded in Lourenço Marques on a visitor's permit. His wife and two children were still in Germany, but would be able to leave if he obtained the right of residence.[47] Frankel's appeal did not overstate Metzger's personal qualities, but may have exaggerated his rabbinical training and experience as a religious leader. According to his son Alf, he had been in business in Dusseldorf where he acted as a *baal tefilah*, or prayer leader, in a local synagogue, but received his training as a cantor in Johannesburg from Israel Alter, a close friend who was a famous cantor. Metzger, who saw himself as a loyal subject of the Emperor Franz Jozef, had previously made a living as a street trader in Vienna and had supported Alter during his course of training as a cantor there.[48]

After some delay the government agreed to allow Cantor Metzger to enter the country. He arrived at Livingstone on 22 August 1939 and was soon installed in Lusaka as warden of the farm settlement, secretary of the assistance committee, and spiritual leader of the whole community. His wife and two children were trapped with thousands of other non-German Jews in 'no man's land' between Germany and Poland on the outbreak of war. They were located by the International Red Cross and had a miraculous escape through Switzerland to Trieste. Travelling on Portuguese travel documents, which Metzger had secured through a Jewish contact in Lourenço Marques, they reached Beira on the *Gerusalemme* at the end of March 1940. Metzger himself was there to meet them. His contribution to the religious life of Lusaka is discussed in a later chapter.[49]

In December 1939 Henry Sonnabend visited Lusaka and met the Governor. By then he was able to report that he was engaged in a clearing-up operation. Few refugees were expected to arrive during the war. There were only twenty-five refugee heads of families who were unemployed. Ten of these were thought to be suitable for employment on the mines. He asked for government intervention to help secure a change of policy on refugee employment by the mining companies.[50]

Late Applications

A number of people continued to seek visas for relatives in Germany after the outbreak of war. In November 1939 Robert Simon, who had set up as a tailor in Lusaka, wrote asking for visas for his parents-in-law, who were in a concentration camp, and for his seventeen-year-old brother-in-law who, he hoped, could help him in his work. Brodie opposed the application. He felt that the Territory could not absorb any more refugees for some time: 'There is considerable anti-Semitic feeling among portions of the population; though latent it is none the less there.' He was concerned that the granting of the application might result in a flood of applications from people who were in South Africa and Southern Rhodesia on visitors' permits.[51] The issue generated numerous minutes and allowed one member of the Secretariat staff to voice typically anti-Semitic and racist sentiments. He wrote:

> It has often been stated that Jews are Jews first and citizens of the Territory in which they live afterwards. Here is a case in which a Jew establishes himself here and then attempts to get one of his relatives to join him and to increase his business. So it goes on; development of business being conducted on a basis of relationship and creed, all openings to Gentiles being denied. For this reason I should be inclined to refuse the application.[52]

This minute was written in February 1940 and shows no awareness at all of the predicament of German Jews. In the end a visa was granted for all three applicants, though it is doubtful if they were able to leave Germany. A clinching argument in favour of the application was in itself racist. Until Simon set up his business the only tailor in Lusaka had been an Asian. In March 1940 Northern Rhodesia adopted the official British position that no visas could be issued to German Jews still in Germany. In the following month, an application from Max Stammreich, who had started a 'Native' dress factory in Livingstone, for a visa for his brother in Berlin was rejected. An application in May from Cantor Metzger for his father, who was in Buchenwald, and for his mother, who was in Poland, was refused. He appealed on the grounds that as Poles they were not enemy aliens. Visas were finally granted in May 1941 by which time departure from Germany or Poland, let alone release from Buchenwald, must have been impossible.[53]

The Cyprus and 'Merra' Evacuees

In June 1941 the British government was faced with the problem of evacuating about 600 Jews, 500 Poles and 400 British citizens from the Mediterranean island of Cyprus which was threatened with invasion. The east African territories were all asked to help out. Northern Rhodesia's acting Governor offered to take 500 people in the first instance. His telegram contained, however, one significant reservation: 'Owing to strong local antipathy to Jewish refugees I should be glad if Poles and Britishers only were allowed here.'[54] By the middle of 1942, over 400 Poles, including an indeterminate number of Polish Jews, had arrived in the country from Cyprus, by way of Palestine, and were billeted in hotels, boarding houses and camps from Livingstone to Fort Jameson.[55]

Relations between gentile and Jewish Poles were not always good. In December 1941 relations between two such groups at a hotel in Mazabuka had become so strained that the matter was reported by one of the Jews to the Reverend I. Levine, the new minister of the Bulawayo Hebrew Congregation, who asked for an investigation. This revealed that there was, indeed, a small group of intensely anti-Semitic Poles at Mazabuka. It was, however, pointed out that this group seemed also to be on very bad terms with other non-Jewish Poles. Cantor Metzger thought that unemployment was the real cause of the problem. He told the Rhodesia Sub-committee of the Council for Refugee Settlement in Africa that the Polish group included 'a large number' of 'converted' Jews. The sub-committee took the view that they were not its responsibility.[56]

From the Copperbelt came a report on 'public opinion' of strained relations between Poles and German Jews. The Provincial Commissioner reported:

> There appears to be a certain amount of friction between the German Jewish refugees and the Polish evacuees. There is a feeling of resentment at the way in which the Polish evacuees have had everything done for them, whereas the Jewish refugees had to fend for themselves. This of course is entirely illogical and the two cases are in no way parallel, but the feeling is there and is being encouraged by other Jewish residents who are not refugees.[57]

Some resentment of the very different treatment of the pre-war refugees and wartime evacuees, as they were officially described, is understandable. This must have been compounded by the arrival in 1943 of a much larger group of Poles. The 'Merra' (Middle East Relief and Refugee Administration) group consisted of about 3,500 Poles who had made their way after the defeat of Poland through central Europe to Turkey and Persia. Camps were constructed for these evacuees at Lusaka, on what is today the site of the Lusaka suburb of Rhodes Park, at Bwana Mkubwa, and in Abercorn. There were also Jews among this larger group. A representative of the International

Red Cross, Gottfried Senn, who visited the camp in September 1943, paid special tribute to the welfare work done for the evacuees by the Lusaka Hebrew Congregation. He did not mention Cantor Metzger by name, but it appears from other sources that he was employed by the government to liaise with this large Polish population which suddenly appeared on the outskirts of Lusaka.[58]

Britain's willingness, in wartime, to provide space in Northern Rhodesia for thousands of Polish refugees, including a small proportion of Jews, demonstrates that much more could have been done for German refugees before the war. Wars do, of course, dissolve financial constraints. There can, however, be little doubt that the British government's handling of the refugee issue before the war, and its prevarication over agricultural settlements which we have earlier outlined, were the product of appeasement. Much more could have been done, though not necessarily in Northern Rhodesia, to save German and eastern European Jews from the shadow of the Holocaust.

CHAPTER 7

Escape from the Holocaust

For all those Jews who were able to leave Germany and eastern Europe in the years before the war, there were many more who could not do so. Almost all of the people who reached the safe haven of Northern Rhodesia left behind them fathers and mothers, brothers and sisters, uncles and aunts, or cousins, and, in a few cases, wives and children. It is only possible here to look at a few examples of escape from the Holocaust, and resettlement in Northern Rhodesia, but these accounts should help us to understand the often painful process of adjustment which refugees had to undergo. The experience of a few people must be taken as representative of many more.

It has already been suggested that German refugees differed from the earlier Jewish immigrants into Northern Rhodesia in a variety of ways. They did not come from the enclosed community of the *shtetl*, but were usually highly assimilated into the dominant culture. They spoke German rather than Yiddish, and had been educated within the normal school system rather than at separate Hebrew schools. Many of them were members of the middle and professional classes. They tended to be separated from Orthodox Judaism by several generations. Many of the men had served with distinction in the First World War as loyal Germans. They had been forcibly reminded of their Jewish identity by the rise of Nazism and anti-Semitism. There were, of course, others who were observant Jews, and some who were recent immigrants into Germany from eastern and central Europe.

The Caminers and Fraenkels

Horst and Hilda Caminer were typical of the upper middle-class refugees. Hilda Caminer's story is of particular interest because she was, until her death in July 1997, the last of the pre-war German refugees to live in Zambia, which had been her home for nearly sixty years and for two-thirds of her life. Hilda was born in Landsberg on the outskirts of Berlin. Her father, Gustav Herman, was the third generation of his family to own and manage a large business which specialised in the supply of animal foodstuffs. She was educated at the Lyceum for girls, and her ambition was to be a ballet dancer. At the age of eighteen, she married Horst Caminer, who came from a similarly affluent family. He was one of four brothers who had volunteered for service in the First World War, and had been awarded medals for gallantry. On his marriage, he joined his father-in-law's firm and became a partner. Both Gustav Herman and Horst Caminer were respected members of Berlin's commodity exchange. Both were among the 30–40,000 German Jews arrested on *Krystallnacht* in November 1938. This was the moment of truth for all those German Jews, like the Hermans and the Caminers, who had consoled themselves with the thought that Nazism was a passing phase – an unpleasant nightmare, but one which would come to an end.

After the usual knock on the door at four in the morning, Horst and Hilda were taken to an office in Berlin where men and women were separated. Horst was taken to Sachsenhausen concentration camp, and Hilda was allowed after some hours to return to her home which had been ransacked by the Gestapo. After ten days Hilda decided that she must try to secure Horst's release. She went alone, against the advice of his family, to the Gestapo headquarters where she claimed that her husband's arrest with a large quantity of cash had left her penniless. Hilda sensed that the man with whom she was dealing was more of a professional soldier than a Nazi. She gained the officer's sympathy by emphasising her husband's war record. She was able to produce proof of this and persuaded him to release Horst on condition that they both left Germany. At this stage the extermination of the Jews in its original sense of removal, rather than murder, was the main objective of Nazi policy.

Hilda had a cousin, Fritz Rosenberg, in Johannesburg. They immediately contacted him by telegram. On Christmas Day they received a reply which instructed them to approach the British Embassy in Berlin for a visa for Northern Rhodesia. Hilda recalled that this was the one occasion on which she cried and said: 'I'm not going there!' Horst and Hilda were among the hundreds of German Jews whose applications for entry reached Northern Rhodesia in the latter months of 1938. When the visa was issued they were able to get one-way passports, under the Jewish names of Israel and Sarah, which permitted them to leave Germany. In terms of the Nazi appropriation law, they were required to hand over all their jewellery and silverware which they packed in two suitcases. They were allowed to keep two silver spoons, forks and knives, and to leave the country with ten marks each.[1]

They set sail from Hamburg on a new German ship on 19 May 1939. Travelling on the same ship with them were friends of the family from Breslau: Hans and Margot Fraenkel. They were travelling with their twelve-year-old son, Peter. Hans Fraenkel had been until 1936 a senior civil servant in the Prussian administration and was a respected lawyer who used the title of doctor. As with the Caminers, it was *Krystallnacht* which was the moment of truth for the Fraenkels. Their search for a country of exile had produced visas for Northern Rhodesia, Swaziland and Peru, and the possibility of an

American visa for 1941. As with the Caminers, the African visas were obtained by relatives in South Africa.

The Fraenkels disembarked at Durban, while the Caminers changed ships and sailed round the coast to Beira. The two families met up again in Bulawayo, and entered Northern Rhodesia together in July 1939. The Fraenkels stayed for a while in Livingstone, where they were greeted by Elias Kopelowitz. They were accommodated at a boarding house which was being run for the assistance committee by a German Jewish family, Max Sommer and his wife and daughter, who had recently arrived from Aachen. Max Sommer had been released from Buchenwald. Their daughter, Laura, had started work as a nanny for the Kopelowitzes.

The Livingstone assistance committee did not encourage refugees to stay in the town which was still suffering from the transfer of the capital to Lusaka in 1935. A number of Jewish families did, however, settle there. They included the Aufochs and the Jacobys, who had come with more capital than was usual, and went into partnership in the ABC Bazaar, and Frieda Aufochs's parents, the Frieds, who also set up a shop next door. By December 1939 Max Stammreich, who had owned a large clothing factory in Berlin, had opened the Livingstone Dress Factory which was producing cheap clothing for the 'native' market. He invested most of £1,000 in the business, but it was not a success, and by the end of 1940 he had taken up a job with Macmurgas, the drapers. A number of unaccompanied teenagers reached Livingstone. They included Edmond Mayer, who arrived in 1939 at the age of sixteen, and worked for the Zambesi Saw Mills until 1950.[2]

After a short time, the Fraenkels were persuaded to move on to Lusaka where they shared a room with the Caminers at the Simonsons' boarding house. Horst Caminer went off to Broken Hill, where he took a three-month course in dry-cleaning from a recent Czechoslovak immigrant. On his return, he opened a dry-cleaning business, and took Hans Fraenkel in as a partner.[3] The partnership eventually broke up, but Margot Fraenkel had by then established her own dress shop – 'Margot's'.

Hilda Caminer took a job as a clerk at Shapiro's Milling Company, and supplemented her small wage by selling tickets in the evenings at Sam Fischer's cinema, while Horst worked as the projectionist. She remembered Fischer's kindness to the German Jewish refugees. He found small jobs for many of them and was an active member of the assistance committee. She later worked as a nanny, and in the Glassers' shop, until 1944 when she was appointed as a temporary clerk in the civil service. She served with the Public Works Department for seven years, and ended up in charge of the distribution of government furniture. After working for a while as a receptionist in her husband's dry-cleaning business, Capital Dry Cleaners, she set up her own dress shop, 'Milady's', in 1957. She sold imported dresses to customers who came from as far as the Copperbelt. The shop survived until very recently under Asian ownership and management. It was not until the early 1960s that

Horst and Hilda Caminer, who had no children, were able to afford to visit Europe. The Caminers were among the first of the German refugees to be naturalised. Hilda took pride in her British passport, and swore that she would never return to Germany. After Horst's death in 1977, she lived on in her house in Joseph Mwilwa Road, Lusaka, for another twenty years. She died in her early nineties, in July 1997, after nearly sixty years of exile in the country.[4]

The story of the Caminers and the Fraenkels is ultimately a tale of successful resettlement. But Hilda Caminer did not pretend that success came without struggle. She emphasised the difficulty of adjustment, though she gave credit to the British colonial government which made no serious difficulties for the German Jews on the outbreak of war, though they were required for a while to report to the police weekly and to get permission to travel within the country.

Things were easier for the younger generation. The Fraenkels' son, Peter, was a sensitive child who, according to Hilda, was top of the class after one term in the country. His first impressions of Northern Rhodesia shed an interesting light on the experience both of himself and his parents. He recalls that, unlike his parents, he left Germany without regret. He had been subjected to the full force of anti-Semitism at school, and was glad to leave the country. He saw departure for Africa as an adventure. He was not impressed by his first sight of Livingstone with its abandoned and derelict office buildings. Things were not much better in Lusaka, where his family lodged in the overcrowded and ill-equipped boarding house ironically named the Arcadia. He recalled that about 100 refugee families arrived in the country in 1939, and that twenty or thirty of them settled in Lusaka. He noted that at first there was nothing for them to do: 'They walked around the streets all day with their funny raincoats – special long coats designed for the tropics, and they stood out like a sore thumb.'

Peter's father played the violin and was offered a job playing in a small band at the Lusaka Hotel. He was supposed to be trained as a deputy manager at the hotel, but, as he was slightly deaf and spoke little English, the job lasted a week. There was tension between the old-timers and the new arrivals. The former thought that the latter were superior, while the newcomers felt excluded from the Refugees Assistance Committee. These tensions were overcome as the refugees set up their own committees, and then were integrated into the existing structures of the community. Peter noted how his father, who was almost totally without religion, and had never been to a synagogue, re-discovered Judaism in Lusaka under the influence of Cantor Metzger. He was very pleased when, as the tenth man, he could help to make up a *minyan*.[5]

The Wiesenbachers and the Rowelskys

Among the families who lodged with the Caminers and the Fraenkels at the Simonson boarding house were the Wiesenbachers. They had been in the textile business in Stuttgart, where they also owned urban property. They had made up their minds to leave Germany before *Krystallnacht*. Their daughter, Trude, who was sixteen and had just returned from finishing school in Switzerland at the time, has a very vivid memory of that night.

> We had just finished our evening meal when we heard shouting and screaming in the street. We ran to the window to see what was happening. People were running wildly. When we went outside we saw that the synagogue was in flames. I shall never forget the spectacle that met my eyes as I mingled with the crowd which collected in no time. The jeering and laughter as the synagogue roof caved in still rings in my ears ... The horrors of that night will never be erased from my memory.[6]

The family soon obtained 'dummy' visas for Costa Rica which enabled them to leave Germany for Switzerland. As the train left Germany, Trude swore that she would never return and she never has done. It was not until August 1939 that they were able to leave Switzerland for Northern Rhodesia, and they did so a few weeks before the outbreak of war. They would have liked to stay in South Africa, where they had relatives, but they were unable to do so and had to travel for three days northwards to Livingstone and Lusaka.

Trude noticed that Lusaka had a stimulating effect on her father. He was prepared to meet the challenge: 'He walked, looked and talked differently from the moment we arrived in Lusaka. Life would begin again.' For Trude the new life meant transition from a Swiss finishing school to employment for £3 a month with board and lodging in a little drapery shop run by Floretta Wulfsohn, the Scots Jewish wife of 'Tubby' Wulfsohn. Trude had to get used to living behind the shop in a home with an outside toilet, an outside kitchen, no electricity and no fridge. In the shop they sold buttons, ribbons, material and shoes. She once tried to tidy the place up but 'she [Floretta] didn't like it one bit and she put it all back the way it was'. In the evenings Trude took English classes.

Her life was transformed one day when the Wulfsohns' cousin, Harry, a rising star in Northern Rhodesia's commercial world, walked into the shop. Within a few months of her arrival in the country, Trude and Harry were married by Cantor Metzger in a room at the Grand Hotel. She recalls that there were anxious moments as they waited for the only *chupah*, or wedding canopy, in the country to arrive from Broken Hill. Trude's parents followed them to Livingstone where her father eventually worked in the textile section of the Susman Brothers and Wulfsohn business. Her brother, Freddy, spent part of his youth in Livingstone, but moved to Zimbabwe where he continues to run a successful clothing business. He is a former president of the Harare Hebrew Congregation.[7]

The marriage of Trude Wiesenbacher and Harry Wulfsohn was not the only one within the year which helped to bridge the gap between the old established eastern European Jews and the newly arrived Germans. In Living-stone, Laura Sommer married Harry Grill and then moved to Bulawayo. A few years later, in 1943, Sigrid Rowelsky married Sam Fischer who had been divorced from his first wife, Assia, some years previously.[8] Sigrid's father, Max Rowelsky, had arrived in Northern Rhodesia from East Prussia in July 1938. His wife and children remained for most of a year in Cape Town where Sigrid and her mother made dresses. The Rowelskys had left Germany with two electric sewing machines, two manual ones and their furniture. The immigration officer who handled Max's application for visas for his family was impressed by his ability. He noted that when he arrived in the country he could not speak a word of English. Less than a year later he was able to act as an interpreter. Sigrid and her mother had soon set up a dress shop in Lusaka – 'The Red Robe'. Sigrid's father, after working for a time as a barman in Sam Fischer's cinema, was eventually employed, like Hilda Caminer, in the Public Works Department.[9]

The Mohrers and Messerers

Some of the German Jewish refugees who reached Northern Rhodesia were themselves of mixed (that is to say, German and Lithuanian) descent. Helen Guttman was born in the city of Memel in East Prussia to a Lithuanian Jewish mother and a German Jewish father. After the First World War, Memel had been designated a free city, but it was soon taken over by Lithuania. The Nazis seized the town in 1938 in one of those aggressive acts which were ignored and condoned by the appeasement policy of the western powers. Both her parents could speak Yiddish, but German was their home language. After a year training as a beautician in England, Helen returned to Memel and, confronted by rising Lithuanian nationalism and anti-Semitism, joined the Herzliya Zionist Youth Movement. This was engaged in the training of young people in technical subjects in preparation for their emigration, legal or otherwise, to Palestine.

It was in Memel that she met Julius Mohrer. He had been born and brought up in Frankfurt where he had begun to study medicine. After the Nazis came to power, Jews were excluded from the medical schools and Julius, an enthusiastic Zionist, moved to Memel where he joined a kibbutz farm school and trained as a mechanic in preparation for emigration to Palestine. He was lucky enough to get a visa for Palestine, but turned it down when his kibbutz insisted that he should marry one of their members and emigrate with her. After his marriage to Helen Guttman in 1936, they began to plan for emigration to Africa. Through an uncle in Bulawayo they obtained visas for Southern Rhodesia, and arrived there in March 1937. Julius had heard that there was a shortage of hairdressers in Africa, and had undergone training before departure. He found that he was able to get a job in Bulawayo without difficulty. Once they were settled in Southern Rhodesia, they were able to get visas to bring out Helen's parents. They moved to Northern Rhodesia in February 1938 because they thought that it would be easier to get visas there for Julius's parents, and were able to do so. Julius had soon set himself up as Lusaka's only hairdresser. He was one of five Germans, not all Jews, who gave their profession as hairdresser when entering Northern Rhodesia in 1938.[10]

In November 1938 they heard from Julius's sister, Rose Messerer, that her husband David had been arrested on *Krystallnacht* and taken to a concentration camp. David, who came from a large orthodox community in Frankfurt, had studied maths and physics at the university there, and had been an instructor in a kibbutz training school near the town. He was arrested with sixty other members of the school and was taken to Buchenwald. He stayed there for six weeks, engaged in hard labour, until Rose was able to get a visa through the Mohrers for emigration to Northern Rhodesia. The Messerers were able to leave Germany and reach Mufulira within three months of David's arrest. They travelled on a new German ship, the *Watussi*. The crew were friendly and, surprisingly, the ship carried tinned kosher food. Rose Messerer remembered: 'We didn't look back. We had nothing to look back on. We were happy to be out of Germany. We were young. We could cope with the difficulties.' David remembered his amazement at the ease with which, as an electrician, he passed through the immigration formalities at Livingstone.[11]

When they reached Lusaka, David received two job offers from Mufulira by phone. The new town, in which they were to live for forty years, was being laid out and shops and offices were being built. David's first job was to work on the wiring of Barclay's Bank with the good wage of £35 a month. Rose remembered: 'We moved into a rondavel made of corrugated-iron with an open lean-to for a kitchen. No ablution facilities, but we were happy.' They were befriended by the Illion brothers who offered them the use of their house for washing. They soon moved to a house in the old town.[12]

The Mohrers and Messerers not only found a new home in Northern Rhodesia, but showed a lasting commitment to the Jewish community and to the country at large. Helen Mohrer was grateful for the home which the country gave to herself, her husband and their relatives. She recalled: 'Northern Rhodesia was very good to us, and as Northern Rhodesia grew, so we grew with the country.' The involvement of these two couples in the religious and social life of the Jewish community, in business and in local government is considered in later chapters.[13]

The Israels

The most dramatic last-minute escape from Germany to Northern Rhodesia involved the family of Solly Israel. A detailed account of their progress survives in their immigration file which, with many others, can still be found in the Zambia National Archives. (It must be the most exciting file in the collection and could be the basis for a novel.) Solly Israel described himself on the form which he filled in on his arrival in the country on 24 April 1939 as a farmer and cattle dealer. He gave his last address as Frankfurt. He had moved there with his family from Nassau, the town where he had been born in 1895 to an old-established orthodox family. His application for a Northern Rhodesian visa had been handled for him by Ben Baron, a Bulawayo solicitor, who processed a large number of these applications. Solly left Germany in March 1939 on his own. This was probably because he could not raise the £300 which might have been required for himself and his family.

On his arrival in the country he was found a job by 'Tubby' Wulfsohn on a farm near Mazabuka. His employer was a Mr Oertel, the manager of the Arnold Brothers farm at Simonga near Mazabuka. In June 1939 Nicky Iljon wrote to Norman Brodie, the Chief Immigration Officer, saying that Solly wished to bring in his wife and child. He could not raise the necessary money, but his employer was prepared to take on his wife to look after the poultry. Brodie agreed on condition that this was confirmed in writing. When the letter finally arrived in August, Brodie immediately instructed the British Consulate in Berlin to issue the visas. Before this could be done, however, the Second World War broke out in the early days of September.[14]

In a poignant letter, written on 20 September, Solly Israel wrote of Brodie's instruction to Berlin: 'so starts the war that it was too late.' He asked Brodie to issue similar instructions to the British consuls in Switzerland and Belgium in the hope that his wife and child could leave Germany with the help of relatives in those countries. Brodie said that he could not do that, but promised that, if the family could reach neutral soil, he would give instructions for the issue of visas. Three months later, in the first week of January 1940, Solly wrote to Brodie again to inform him that his wife and child had reached Geneva in Switzerland. Brodie immediately instructed the British Consul there to issue them with visas.[15]

Four months later, on 17 May 1940, Solly informed Brodie that he had 'pleasure to inform you that my wife Henny and daughter Ellen have left for this country'. They were passengers on an Italian ship, the *Gerusalemme*, which left Trieste on 9 May. The ship – the same one on which Cantor Metzger's family had travelled in March – was expected to arrive in Beira on 7 June. Brodie informed the British Consul in Beira that he had no objection to the Israels' entry into Northern Rhodesia.[16] The ship was the last carrying German Jewish refugees to reach Beira during the war. Henny and Ellen arrived at Livingstone on 5 June 1940, more than nine months after the outbreak of war.[17]

The bare bones of the story from the file can be supplemented by the recollections, recorded almost fifty years later, of Ellen Israel, or Cohen, as she had become on her marriage. The Northern Rhodesian visa helped, together with his Iron Cross, to extricate her father from Buchenwald. The guarantee was provided by the Transvaal-based cousin of a friend in Geneva. Permission to leave Germany was obtained after paying an intermediary to get clearance from the Gestapo office in Frankfurt. The struggle to get out of Germany used up her mother's *nashoma* – her soul. The worst part was the tension of crossing the German–Swiss border to Basle where her mother was subjected to a humiliating search. Even in Geneva her mother was in constant fear of the knock on the door.[18]

Ellen recalls the relief of seeing the ship in port: 'We got out by the skin of our teeth.' Passengers travelling to the ship from the Austrian side never arrived. At last on the festival of Pesach (Passover) they reached Beira. They arrived the day before Italy, which had been neutral, entered the war. Ellen believes that if they had arrived a day later, they would have been interned in Mozambique. After a night in Beira, where they were looked after by the indomitable J. M. Barnett, they took the train to Salisbury, Bulawayo and Livingstone, where they were met by Elias Kopelowitz with a bag of oranges. It was another night and a day before they reached Mazabuka where they were reunited with their husband and father. It was his birthday. 'When he saw us he was finished. We were all finished.'

They were reunited at the home of Herta Ilion, or Ficks. She must have fully understood their excitement. Born Herta Iljon in Latvia in 1908, she had herself been forced to move countries, or provinces, three times: from Riga to St Petersburg, from there back to Latvia, and from Latvia to Northern Rhodesia. She had married her cousin, Lazar Illion, but he had died in Mazabuka, probably of blackwater fever, soon afterwards. She had recently remarried. Her new husband, Zalmans Fichs (later known as Sam Ficks), was probably the last person to leave the Baltic states with a visa for Northern Rhodesia after the outbreak of war. His visa was issued by the British passport control officer in Riga, Latvia, on 17 November 1939 and, after travelling through Poland, Austria and Italy, he reached Northern Rhodesia in January 1940.[19] Kenneth Benton, the British passport officer who issued his visa, received a testimonial from the Jewish community of Riga for his services to it. He remained at his post until after the Russian invasion in June 1940, and eventually returned home after travelling around the world by way of the Trans-Siberian Railway, the Pacific, and the United States.

Solly Israel stayed on the farm until 1941. He supplemented his small wage by travelling to Broken Hill to officiate at religious services on high days and holy days. He then moved to Kitwe, where he managed a 'Native Eating House' in Mindola compound for Major Duncan-Little (known to some as 'Drunken-Little'). He eventually joined forces with Jacob Hamburger, one of three brothers who came from farming stock in Hanau, and who also arrived in 1939. They set up a chain of shops around Kitwe. Ellen married and moved south to Bulawayo in 1952. Her parents, who were relatively elderly when they left Germany, retired to the Cape and died there.[20]

There were, of course, many other German Jews who arrived in the years before the war, whose stories would be of interest. There was Max Hamburger, elder brother of Jacob. He was a shoemaker by profession and started work in Lusaka as a cobbler. He had a bicycle and rode around the town collecting, mending and returning shoes. After a while he had saved enough to set up a cycle shop in Lusaka which he ran for many years. He was admired for his hard work and his piety. He was the first of the German refugees to be elected in 1942 to the committee of the Lusaka Hebrew Congregation. His brothers also established cycle shops on the Copperbelt.[21] There were the Behrens brothers who started a successful electrical business which still bears their name. They were among the few German Jewish refugees who were allowed to work on the mines in the early years of the war at a time when official policy discouraged such employment.[22]

Another exception to this general rule, which even excluded from employment an experienced German Jewish coalminer, was Gert Rosenberg who arrived, with his parents, in Livingstone on 23 July 1939, and started work as a laboratory assistant at the Broken Hill mine four days later, at the age of eighteen. He was paid £10 a month and was able to support his parents, Siegfried and Hedwig Rosenberg, until they had established themselves in business in the town. His father had been the proprietor of a large shoe factory and shop at Witten in Westphalia, and had also been the president of the Hebrew Congregation there for many years. The Rosenbergs' elder daughter had left for South Africa in 1936, and was able to organise visas for Northern Rhodesia from there. While Gert worked in the mine laboratory, his father worked as a cobbler. Gert was also unusual in that he was the only German Jewish refugee who was allowed to join, at least for a while, the Northern Rhodesian Defence Force or Home Guard. When he later applied to join the army, his father received a personal visit from Roy Welensky, then Director of Manpower, who told him that there was no way that he would allow a youth, who had just escaped from the clutches of Hitler, to risk falling back into them. After Italy entered the war in June 1940, his father and two other German refugees were given a licence to run the canteen at a transit camp which was set up just north of Broken Hill for the convoys of South African troops who passed through daily on their way to the Abyssinian campaign. Later in the war, his father joined with the same two refugees, Hans Roetgen and Ernst Samter, to take over the Premier Bakery.[23]

Most established traders, including the larger firms, Werners, Copperfields Cold Storage and Northern Caterers, provided jobs for one or two refugees in each of the main centres. In Mufulira the Illions had already provided a job for Benno Simon who arrived from Cologne in 1938; he had tried to settle in South Africa and Southern Rhodesia without success. His family followed him and arrived in January 1939. He worked with the Illions for twenty years before setting up his own business. They also employed Julius Mohrer's father. The Sterns, the Rothschilds and the Goldschmidts were employed by Werners and Northern Caterers. In Chingola Sigismund Ettinger

worked for Moss Dobkins and 'George' Mandel worked for the Israels. He
had been separated from his wife by the war. They were reunited long after
the end of the war as a result of direct intervention by Roy Welensky with
Nikita Khrushchev. She was eventually allowed to leave the Soviet Union
where she had taken refuge.[24]

In Luanshya, Jimmy Silverberg, who on arrival could not speak a word of
English, worked at first as a storeman for Harry Figov. He later married
Annie Blumenthal, the owner of a very small shop which he helped her to
build up into a successful enterprise. She had arrived in the town in the early
1930s, and had been widowed soon afterwards. She was herself at the centre
of a small group of relatives on the Copperbelt, including her brothers-in-
law Akiva and Yonah Kapulsky, who ran a bakery in Ndola. They had other
brothers who started a well-known chain of coffee shops in Israel. Annie
Blumenthal's brother, Joseph Goldberg, with his wife and their twin sons,
Israel and Joseph, arrived separately from Lithuania not long before the
outbreak of war. He was able to get work on the mine, where he worked for
twenty years before setting up a jewellery shop in Kitwe in the late 1950s.
Among those who travelled with this family and arrived in 1939 was Sam
Esrachovitch, later known as Sam Esra, who became a prominent member
of the Kitwe Hebrew Congregation and set up a number of jewellery shops
in the Copperbelt towns.[25]

Eastern Europeans

The latter were among a number of Jews who arrived in Northern Rhodesia
from eastern Europe in the years before the war. They came from Lithuania,
Latvia and Poland and usually came to join members of their families who
were already settled. They were not refugees as they had not yet been rejected
by their countries and rendered stateless, but they were as much in need of
a place of refuge as the immigrants from Germany. Among the arrivals from
Poland before the war was Benjamin Szeftel who reached the country in
1937. He had been a star football player and had studied at a famous Hebrew
teachers' seminary in Vilna. Like the Mohrers and Messerers, Ben had originally
intended to emigrate to Palestine and had been a member of one of the
kibbutz training schools. He had tried South Africa and Southern Rhodesia,
but was compelled to move on to Northern Rhodesia. He worked at first for
Copperfields Cold Storage for a low wage. His father had been a butcher and
he was used to the work. He was very critical of what he saw as the
exploitation by the company of 'greeners', new arrivals, and after a clash with
the manager, Max Barnett, he left the company and was able to get a much
better paid job on the Mufulira mine.

At that time there was a small number of East European Jews working
on the mines. Ben was not alone in abandoning commercial employment for
the mines which, in the boom years before the war, were paying some white

workers £60 or more a month. With help from Sid Diamond and others, he was able to organise the emigration from Poland of his younger brother, Sam, who came to a job at Copperfields Cold Storage, and his own fiancée. But his mother and many other members of his family died in the Holocaust. After some years' work on the mines, Ben set up a transport business with two other recent immigrants, Meir Rosenblatt, from Lithuania, and Sam Kelly (Koslowsky) from Latvia, both of whom had started off as salesmen for Sid Diamond's Standard Trading Company, and became successful entrepreneurs. After the war Sam Kelly, who was also known as a remarkable philatelist, became the proprietor of a successful menswear business in Kitwe. Ben moved to Lusaka where, with his brother, he became involved in farming and the butchery business. The story of his competition there with Abe Galaun will be told in a later chapter.[26]

There was also a group of Lithuanian Jews who reached Northern Rhodesia in the years before the war by way of Palestine. They included Aryeh Zemack and his wife Rivka, a sister of the three Katz brothers, Jacob, Chaim and Max. Chaim Katz had also been in Palestine where he was taught the tiling trade by Aryeh. Zemack was a very resourceful person who, in partnership with various people, including the Katz brothers, was involved in the Rhodesian Lakes Trading Company which bought an ice plant and pioneered the frozen fish trade from the Luapula, and lakes Mweru and Bangweulu, in the early years of the war. They were also involved in the development of bus services on the Copperbelt, in a bakery, and in the development of a glass works on the Copperbelt. Zemack moved to Lusaka in the early 1950s where he ran the Hotel Victoria in Church Road, now the Fairview Hotel, and developed another glass business. Chaim Traub, with his wife Rachel, arrived from Palestine with Chaim Katz, and, after a short time in the Congo, joined his Kowalsky brothers-in-law in a running a furniture factory in Ndola.[27]

A handful of Polish Jews who arrived as members of the Cyprus group during the war also put down roots in Northern Rhodesia. They included Dr Grunfeld and Eric Hoffman who obtained jobs as accountants on the Copperbelt with Jewish businesses.[28] The best remembered of them in Lusaka was Abraham Bornstein who became a civil servant in the Audit Department and worked for the Bank of Zambia for many years until his death in 1983. He was one of those people who was tragically separated from his wife and child who remained in Cracow, and were never heard of again. He spent a great deal of time and energy, and travelled widely, in a vain attempt to trace them.[29]

The Outbreak of War

Although the Second World War was fought against fascism, anti-Semitism remained widespread among the white population in Northern Rhodesia. On the outbreak of war, German Jewish refugees were asked to report to the police regularly for a while, but only one person, whose Jewish origins and political opinions were suspect, was interned. Early in 1942 Cantor Metzger told the Council for Refugee Settlement in Johannesburg that 'the Government was very lenient towards refugees, but the general atmosphere amongst people in Rhodesia was anti-German, and they did not differentiate between Jews and non-Jews'.[30] In 1943 the Provincial Commissioner for the Copperbelt, Cartmel-Robinson, noted that Uri Illion of Mufulira had been attacked by an anti-Jewish Czech, and that a German Jew had his room wrecked by a group of 'drunken Europeans'. He commented that anti-Semitism 'was always apt to flare up'.[31] At the end of the war H. A. Watmore, Provincial Commissioner of the Central Province, reported of Lusaka that: 'The general public is showing some concern about the number of aliens who have taken up a very comfortable residence in Northern Rhodesia and feel that particularly those Jews of German, Continental and Levantine origin should be encouraged to return to their parent countries.'[32]

In the latter quotation it would appear that the prejudice may have been shared by the writer. It has to be remembered, however, that anti-Semitism was mild by comparison with the fundamental anti-black racism which permeated colonial society, and with which many Jews also identified. There was, in fact, a surprising amount of sympathy for fascism evident in the white population of Northern Rhodesia even at the height of the war, especially among Afrikaans-speaking people, some of whom supported the Ossewa Brandwag, an Afrikaner Nationalist organisation which was openly sympathetic with Nazi Germany. It was presumed that it was members of that organisation who raised a swastika on the flag pole of the Anglican Church in Broken Hill in September 1944.[33]

Although there were problems of adjustment, the arrival of the German Jewish refugees, and a number of other eastern European Jews, in the years before the outbreak of war had the effect of strengthening and diversifying the Northern Rhodesian Jewish community. Most of the new arrivals remained in the country after the war, and many became linked to the older-established families through marriage. Northern Rhodesia may not have made a very significant contribution in global terms to the accommodation of German Jewish refugees; in terms of its own ability to absorb refugees it was, however, more welcoming than either South Africa or Southern Rhodesia, and provided a home for a number of people who might not otherwise have been able to leave Germany.

CHAPTER 8

Bigger Business: from
the Depression to Independence,
1930–64

The main theme of this chapter is domestic capital formation and the development of an extensive network of companies in which the Susman brothers, and various partners, played a leading role. They shifted the main focus of their attention in the late 1920s and early 1930s from Barotseland, and Ngamiland, to the Copperbelt. Their involvement in Northern Caterers, Copperfields Cold Storage, and Economy Stores, represented significant new departures, though they were continuing a policy which they had begun earlier in the decade of taking minority shares in businesses which were run by other people.

By the onset of the depression, their long-standing partnership with 'Bongola' Smith in the Congo cattle trade was coming to an end as he no longer drew to any extent on their Ngamiland cattle sources, preferring to supply his markets from the south. He had merged his extensive interests in the Congo in a new company, the Brussels-based Compagnie d'Elevage et d'Alimentation du Katanga, known as 'Elakat', in 1925. This was effectively controlled by Belgian banking interests, Baron Henri Lambert and members of the Rothschild family. A subsidiary company, the Congo–Rhodesia Ranching Company, was set up in 1929. This took over Smith's farming interests in both Northern and Southern Rhodesia, and eventually owned 400,000 acres in Matabeleland, including the Susmans' Brunapeg ranch. It also had a stake in Copperfields Cold Storage. Smith moved south to Bulawayo in 1929, and transferred management of the Congo businesses to his son-in-law Abe Gelman, who remained in the Congo until 1937.[1]

The effects of the depression and the complex politics of the cattle trade were summarised by the Resident Commissioner of Bechuanaland, the notoriously outspoken, and frankly anti-Semitic, Colonel (later Sir) Charles Rey. After an exhilarating conversation with one of the Susmans, probably Elie, in Livingstone in November 1931, he noted that the real problem was that 'owing to the slump in the world price of copper, production has fallen off in the Congo and Northern Rhodesia, thousands of people have been

dismissed and the consumption of meat has fallen'. The future of cattle
exports depended on the outcome of talks between the major copper producers which were currently going on in New York.

> ... so does the price of copper in London and New York affect the sale of
> cattle in Bechuanaland! And there are other factors too: all the meat contracts
> in the Congo (the Union Minière, the railways, and the other big mines) are
> controlled by my villainous friend Mr Bongola Smith. His directors sit in
> Brussels – Mr Carton de Wiart, Count Lippens, ex-Governor of the Congo,
> one of the Rothschilds etc., and they in their turn control the Congo Govern-
> ment! A dirty game – and a network of intrigue covering Cape Town, Salisbury,
> Bulawayo, Livingstone, Elisabethville, Brussels and New York.[2]

The Susmans found themselves in an awkward position at this time as
they were both cattle producers in Northern Rhodesia and cattle exporters
from Bechuanaland. At the request of their good friend John Smith, the
Director of Agriculture, they had accumulated 5,000 cattle on the Bechuanaland side of the Zambezi between Kasane and Kachikau in 1931–32 in order
to supply the Congo market during a temporary closure of the Northern
Rhodesian border to the transit of live cattle from the south. The spread of
foot-and-mouth disease to Bechuanaland then resulted in these cattle being
temporarily stranded where they were. Furthermore, it was agreed by the
three governments in December 1932 that there would be a complete halt
for the duration of the depression to the movement of cattle between
Northern Rhodesia, Southern Rhodesia and Bechuanaland. Southern Rhodesia
was able to resume exports to the Congo, but Bechuanaland was prevented
from exporting to Northern Rhodesia.[3] This was intended to provide a
measure of protection to Northern Rhodesian cattle farmers. The Susmans
were allowed to import only 1,800 of their Bechuanaland cattle after direct
negotiations between the Governor of Northern Rhodesia, Sir Ronald Storrs,
and the Prime Minister of Southern Rhodesia, Godfrey Huggins, in December
1933. A special concession was made to them because of their 'straightforward
dealings' with government in the past, and because of the evidence that the
government had a 'moral obligation' to them. The concession to them also
had the approval of the Northern Rhodesian Farmers Association which
saw them as 'Northern Rhodesians with big Northern Rhodesian interests'
– an early recognition that they represented domestic capital. Elie Susman
had provided some evidence of his sense of a Northern Rhodesian national
identity when he had written to the Hilton Young Commission, a few years
earlier, opposing closer union with the south.[4]

Woolworths

It may have been the depression, and these accompanying frustrations, which
prompted Elie Susman, who was just over fifty, to 'retire' and move with his

family to Cape Town in 1931–32. The children had suffered from malaria in Livingstone, and in 1925 Bertha Susman had declined to give birth to her fourth and last child, David, there. Elie Susman retained a bungalow in Livingstone for some time, and kept a close eye on the Northern Rhodesian businesses. Harry Susman continued to live there until the end of the Second World War, and was responsible until then for day-to-day management.

While living in semi-retirement at Muizenburg, Elie renewed his friendship with Max Sonnenberg whom he had known in Francistown and Bulawayo at the turn of the century. Sonnenberg had inherited the Vryburg business of his uncle, C. Solomon, and, after a short career as a member of Parliament, had in 1929 taken over a large Cape Town department store. This became in 1931 the first branch of South Africa's Woolworths. It was not connected with F. W. Woolworth in Britain or America, but had pirated the name. It shared London agents with shops of the same name in Australia and New Zealand. In 1934 Sonnenberg asked Elie to open branches in Johannesburg, Pretoria and other towns on the Witwatersrand, and to become resident director of the company in the Transvaal. When Woolworths was floated as a public company in 1936, the Susman family subscribed rather more than 10 per cent of the equity. The Johannesburg branch opened late in the same year.[5]

Elie Susman did not leave Northern Rhodesia with the intention of starting a new business career in South Africa. He left the country at the low point of the depression, and at a time when it was impossible to withdraw capital from the family business. His new involvement in South Africa did not imply any reduction of interest in Northern Rhodesia, though he did say in 1933 that he was trying to close down the depressed Ngamiland side of the business. The investment in Woolworths was seen by the brothers as a joint venture, though Harry Susman was never involved in the management of the new company.[6]

Recovery from the Depression

With the recovery of copper prices in the later 1930s, the demand for beef in Northern Rhodesia soon outstripped local supplies. This did not, however, put an immediate end to the Susmans' problem of gaining access to the Copperbelt market for their Ngamiland cattle. At the same time, they were investigating the possibility of reviving the Barotseland cattle trade by driving cattle to the Zambesi Saw Mills railway at Mulobezi, and opening a chilling plant there. It was not until 1939 that controlled imports of Barotseland cattle to the Line of Rail were allowed. These cattle had to be slaughtered at a government abattoir at Katembora. Restrictions on the import of cattle from Ngamiland were lifted at about the same time.[7]

Following the outbreak of the Second World War, employment and production levels on the Copperbelt reached unprecedented heights. The

Anglo-American mines reckoned that they needed to provide a ration of five pounds of meat per man a week to maintain a contented labour force. Their workers had consumed about 500 tons of meat in 1936 and needed very much more in the early years of the war. At the end of 1941 Northern Rhodesia's Cattle Marketing and Control Board, which had been set up in 1937 to regulate prices and imports, estimated that Northern Rhodesia had consumed nearly 40,000 cattle during the year, about one-third of which was imported. Three-quarters of the local cattle came from 'Native' producers, mainly in the Ila and Tonga areas of the Southern Province, while the balance of 6,000 cattle came from settler farmers. Two-thirds of cattle imports were brought in 'on the hoof' from Bechuanaland, many of them from the Susmans' preserves in Ngamiland, while the balance was made up of chilled beef imports from Southern Rhodesia.[8]

Harry Wulfsohn

Apart from the big contractors, Copperfields Cold Storage and Werners, only two of the smaller cattle traders purchased more than 2,000 head locally in 1941. One was the Livestock Cooperative Society Butchery in Lusaka which was owned or managed by the veteran Scot, Sam Haslett. The other was Livingstone Cold Storage which was taken over in 1939 by Harry Wulfsohn. Born Hozias Vulfsohns in the village of Saldus, which lay midway between Riga, the capital of Latvia, and Libau, in 1911, Harry Wulfsohn was a generation younger than the Susman brothers, but his name was soon to be inseparably linked with theirs.

Harry Wulfsohn left Latvia, where his father had a small butchery business, in 1929 at the age of eighteen. He was the eldest son in a large family and had very little formal education. From his early teens, he had preferred cattle trading, fishing and gambling with the local farmers to school. According to his younger brother, Wulfie: 'Harry always had a knack of making money since his bar mitzvah.'[9] Their father, Isaac, was a tough disciplinarian and had academic ambitions for his eldest son, but their mother, Chaya, condoned Harry's truancy as he contributed the proceeds of his various ventures to the housekeeping budget. He was driven to leave Latvia by the usual reasons: ambition, the increasingly anti-Semitic direction of Latvian nationalism, and the depression. He travelled with his sister, Marlie, to South Africa where they had an aunt. Harry worked for a while in the bar of his aunt's hotel at Barkly East in the mountains close to the Transkei and Basutoland. When Marlie married Abe Lowenthal and moved to Northern Rhodesia, Harry followed her northwards. According to one witness who recalls his arrival in Ndola in 1930, he knew very little English. As a result of his swarthy appearance he acquired the nickname 'Gandhi'. He worked for a while in the cinema which Abe Lowenthal and his brothers had recently opened in Ndola.[10]

It is difficult to piece together Harry Wulfsohn's early movements or business activities, but, as the depression worsened, he moved south to Lusaka. He may have stayed there with his cousin, 'Tubby' Wulfsohn, who had recently returned after a long period in the Congo. According to family legend, Harry had one treasured possession: a gramophone. He is said to have pawned this to provide the capital for his first cattle trading venture in the Lusaka district, buying a cow for £1 and selling it for £1.10.0. He spent much of his time in the 'bush', established a close relationship with a local chief, and subsisted on *nsima* or maize porridge. According to another legend, he was given a first loan of £50 by a bank manager who was impressed by the audacity with which he sought a loan, though ignorant of the meaning of the term 'balance sheet'. He worked for a while for Greek traders at Namwala, probably the Cavadias, but by the mid-1930s he had, in partnership with Harry Dorsky, a young man from Lithuania, acquired a trading store at Tara Siding on the railway line near Choma in the Southern Province. This was, apart from a pole and dagga hut which he had earlier built for himself near Lusaka, his first home. It was the usual corrugated-iron shed where, as was traditional for young Jewish traders, he slept on the shop counter. It was the base from which he bought cattle and cereals in exchange for trade goods from peasant producers in the country around Namwala where he and his partner had subsidiary 'bush' stores. The Ila country was still at this time a frontier zone where lions were abundant. David Susman recalls that Harry lost many of the cattle in his first 'mob'. Through lack of experience, he had corralled them in a temporary thorn enclosure which was so well built that, when lions got in, the cattle could not escape and dreadful carnage ensued.[11]

It is some indication of Harry Wulfsohn's meteoric emergence as a businessman, and also of the opportunities that were presented to enterprising young men on the frontier, that he was able at the age of twenty-three, and after only a few years in the country, to negotiate in person with the Provincial Commissioner, T. F. Sandford, for the allocation of a store site at Namwala late in 1934. He then said that he and his partner had been encouraged by the Veterinary Department to set up in Namwala because of the shortage of beef in Lusaka, the new capital. The plot was eventually registered in 1937 in the name of the Northern Produce and Livestock Company in which he and Dorsky apparently had a controlling interest, though 'Tubby' Wulfsohn and Henrie Kollenberg may also have been involved. By this time they had employed L. S. Diamond, a veteran of the Barotseland cattle trade, as the manager of their store at Katengwa.[12] Wulfsohn and Dorsky were able to benefit in the mid-1930s from the temporary ban on cattle imports, and from the establishment of the Maize Marketing Board which was set up to protect settler farmers, but which had the unintended consequence of encouraging maize sales by peasant producers.[13] Harry was a compulsive dealer and acquired a nickname from the local people which translated as 'good bargainer'. He was also a gambler. On one occasion, he was able to meet a contract to supply grain to the railways only after winning a game of poker-dice, played with bags of grain as chips, with the prominent Greek trader Paul Zaloumis.[14]

The firm of Dorsky and Wulfsohn also operated on the Copperbelt. By the late 1930s, they had a large concession store at Nchanga, and another one at Mufulira. The partnership was, however, dissolved in 1939 after a disagreement over policy. Wulfsohn believed that the best prospects were in rural trade while Dorsky thought that the future lay on the Copperbelt. As a result of the dissolution of the business, Wulfsohn retained the Tara Siding store, and Dorsky remained at Nchanga. Harry Wulfsohn used the funds which were realised by the dissolution of the partnership to take over Pretorius's butchery in Livingstone. After the promise of a loan from a friend to finance the business fell through, his future was saved by a sub-stantial, and largely unsecured, loan from an Afrikaner farmer. It was still the case that adventurous capitalists, perhaps especially Jewish ones, could not rely on the banks for finance.[15]

Harry Wulfsohn's move to Livingstone coincided with his marriage to Trude Wiesenbacher who, as we have already seen, had arrived as a young refugee from Germany earlier in the year. Trude recalled her first impression of her future husband in an unpublished memoir:

> He was tall and slim, with a very dark complexion and beautiful black hair. His nose was on the biggish side. All round he made a handsome figure. But it was his dark brown eyes that were the most striking feature about him. They were kind and affectionate eyes, but at the same time keen and demanding – the eyes of a complicated personality. When I handed him the parcel of things he had bought, I noticed that he had the beautiful small hands of an artist, and that they were very neatly kept. These artistic hands of his contrasted with his person as a whole, somehow. For he gave the immediate impression of one who was physically alert and active – a man of the world as it were. And this world where I now found myself was much more concerned with commerce and farming than with art and culture. I concluded that, like so many others during those disturbed times, he had been driven here from more advanced areas of civilisation by the winds of adversity.[16]

She recalls that during the early months of their marriage her new husband rose at three in the morning to supervise the slaughter of two or three beasts. She was herself in the shop by seven and did the accounts. Harry was soon able to devote more of his time to cattle trading and to the supervision of the rural stores. It was his love of cattle trading which provided a bond with Harry Susman, his senior by thirty-five years. Harry Wulfsohn had earlier dealings with the Susmans, but it was following the move to Livingstone that they became close.[17]

Harry Susman became a father figure to the younger man, and funded Harry Wulfsohn's cattle-buying ventures. In 1941 Wulfsohn entered into his first formal joint venture with the Susman brothers. This involved the joint purchase of Kala ranch in the Kalomo district.[18] In the following year, the Susman Brothers' business, which had been run as a partnership for forty years, was incorporated in Northern Rhodesia as a public company with a nominal capital of £75,000. It is possible that it was launched at this time as a way of enabling Harry Wulfsohn to take a minority interest. Two years later, in 1944, his interests were merged with those of the Susmans in a new company which was later known as Susman Brothers and Wulfsohn Ltd.[19]

The new company took over Harry Wulfsohn's Livingstone butchery and the Tara Siding store, as well as the Barotseland stores of P. C. Nicolai, a trader who had been in the area since before the First World War and who had recently died. Harry Wulfsohn visited Barotseland with Harry Susman in 1945 to seek the approval of the Litunga, Imwiko, for the transfer of Nicolai's licences. An advantage of this takeover was the access which it gave to the export quotas held by Nicolai's London agents. This was important at a time when Northern Rhodesian traders were starved of imports from Britain because many of them bought from Southern Rhodesian agents. They tended to retain for local consumption British export quotas for commodities, such as textiles, which were related to Northern Rhodesia's pre-war levels of imports. The company also took control of an insolvent chain of stores in the Livingstone area.[20]

A second joint venture in which the Susmans and Harry Wulfsohn became involved in 1944 was the complete takeover of Werners, the second of the big Copperbelt meat companies. While Copperfields Cold Storage had the contract to supply meat to the Anglo-American Corporation's mines, H. C. Werner, who had been in the country for many years, had secured the meat contract for the Rhodesian Selection Trust's mines at Luanshya and Mufulira. He had died in 1933, but the business was carried on by his widow under the management of E. W. Dechow. In 1937 Werners was floated as a public company in Northern Rhodesia. The Susmans bought a minority share in the business soon afterwards, and Elie Susman became a director of the company. There was an increasing divergence from this time onwards between the interests of the Susmans and the Kollenbergs on the Copperbelt. With the takeover of Werners in 1944, the rupture was complete, and the Susmans were obliged to give up their stake in Copperfields Cold Storage because of a potential conflict of interest. Harry Wulfsohn became managing director of Werners in 1944 and his wife, Trude, also joined the board of the company.[21]

Maurice Rabb

For more than two years Harry Wulfsohn remained in sole executive control of the two companies. It soon became clear, probably even to himself, that he was better at doing deals and building a business than he was at running it. He was a brilliant entrepreneur, but he was impatient and he did not have a manager's eye for detail. With Harry Susman's retirement at the end of the war to a farm near Salisbury, there was no resident representative of the family in Northern Rhodesia, though Harry's son, Joey, did live in Livingstone for a while. The Susmans had complete trust in Harry Wulfsohn's commercial integrity, but they thought that he was inclined to be impetuous. Harry Wulfsohn himself suggested in 1946 that Elie Susman's son-in-law, Maurice Rabb, who was working as an executive in Woolworths, should come to Northern Rhodesia and take over the management of the trading business.[22]

Maurice Rabb was born in Doornfontein, Johannesburg, in 1910. His father, Joseph Rabinowitz, had emigrated from Popolan in Lithuania to South Africa in 1894 at the age of nineteen. He eventually became a director of Rand Cold Storage, a subsidiary of Imperial Cold Storage, and was also active in Jewish community organisations. Maurice was one of a large family and was brought up in a religious household. He had his early education at the Hebrew High School, and later transferred to Athlone High School. He studied medicine for one year at the University of the Witwatersrand, earning his fees by working as a petrol pump attendant at night, but then changed to commerce, which he could study part-time in the evenings while working during the day.[23]

Maurice was elected president of the Wits Students Union, and was from 1936 to 1937 the president of the National Union of South African Students (NUSAS), being only the third person to hold the post. He had been the leader of a NUSAS tour to Europe in 1934 during which he was introduced to Mussolini, though only after he had been searched for hidden weapons, and had paid a first visit to Palestine at that time. Among the younger members of the party was Helen Gavronsky, better known as Helen Suzman, who had been allowed by her father to travel on condition that Maurice was personally responsible for her welfare. In 1935 he joined the staff of Woolworths in the Transvaal where his boss was Elie Susman. After a long courtship, he married Elie's daughter, Peggy, in April 1939.

Maurice Rabb visited Northern Rhodesia for the first time with Elie Susman in 1944, and met Harry Wulfsohn on that occasion. When he was invited to move north in 1946, he eventually agreed with his wife that they would go for five years if they could get an acceptable offer which had to include a share in the equity of the two companies. After a visit to Livingstone in July 1946, he moved north in January 1947. He collected his wife and three young children, Tessa, John and Anne, from Johannesburg six months later. Among his first acts was the replacement of the bucket system of sewage disposal by the water-borne system in the house which he took over from Harry Susman. He also found that Livingstone had no reliable supply of fresh milk, and solved that problem by starting a dairy with Harry Wulfsohn at Maramba Farm. Livingstone was to be the Rabbs' home for nearly twenty-five years. The society into which they had moved was small, but highly stratified. One senior official's wife never greeted or spoke to Peggy Rabb during a stay of several years because Peggy, who was educated at St Paul's Girls' School in London, had inadvertently failed to return her visiting cards. The Rabbs' contribution to the public life of the town, and the country, will be considered in a later chapter.

The business expanded very rapidly in the late 1940s and early 1950s. Harry Wulfsohn was clearly the driving force behind this expansion, while Maurice Rabb provided the general management. In Rabb's view, there was a clear philosophy underlying the expansion of the business. He recalled:

> The policy was to take over or build stores in areas where the local people were producing items which we could purchase so as to do a two-way trade and generate purchasing power for our merchandise. We developed markets for grain, cattle, cattle-skins, beeswax, honey, wild animal skins, ivory, rhino-horn – in fact, anything which had a commercial value.

It was also their policy to provide good service and good quality at a good rate of profit. There seems to be little doubt that their stores did serve a dynamic role and were much sought after by local people, and by local authorities. They generated income for rural people, provided them with good quality commodities at fair prices, while producing a good profit for the shareholders. Much of this was, as we shall see, reinvested in Northern Rhodesia both in the expansion of the trading business, and in a variety of other activities which included farming and the development of secondary industry.

Among the first of the new acquisitions in 1948 was the Batoka Siding business of M. S. Pentopoulos, which controlled a network of stores in the remote Gwembe valley, and the trading network built up in and around Balovale in the North-Western Province by the Portuguese trader A. F. Serrano, known locally as 'Ndonyo'. A large warehouse was built at Balovale which supplied traders deep into Angola. Stores were also established along the Zambezi river between the Angolan border at Chavuma in the north and Mongu in the south. The major item of trade was cassava meal which was produced locally, or brought in from Angola, and exported southwards by barge.

It was only after Maurice Rabb joined the business that the name of the parent company was changed to Susman Brothers and Wulfsohn Limited. Harry Wulfsohn was conscious of the commercial value of the Susmans' name in Barotseland and was anxious to make use of it. The business was essentially a new enterprise which had only rather tenuous links with the Susmans' earlier Barotseland activities. In the next few years the company bought out many of the independent Barotseland trading firms, and extended its activities into the Mankoya, now Kaoma, district. The commercial dominance of the company was so complete that it used to be said by colonial officials that the national anthem of Barotseland was 'Susman Brothers and

Wulfsohn' sung to the tune of 'Land and Hope and Glory'.[24] The company
also bought stores in the smaller towns along the Line of Rail, and opened
stores on many of the farms which they acquired in the Southern Province.

In the mid-1950s, they extended their network of stores beyond their
original territory in the south and west of the country. The purchase of John
Thom's stores gave them an extensive network in the Luapula and Northern
Provinces which traded under the name of Chawama Stores. Thom's stores
had been the target of a successful nationalist boycott. Kenneth Kaunda
noted that the new owners were 'more amenable'. Thom's stores' main rival
in this area, the African Lakes Corporation, withdrew from Northern Rhodesia
in 1955. Susman Brothers also bought general trading stores on the Copperbelt
and opened shops in premises which were built for Werners in the second-
class trading areas. Their main experience was, however, with rural trade and
they found that the market on the Copperbelt was more sophisticated and
that competition was stiff.[25]

In the absence of detailed records and accounts, some idea of the nature
of the business on the ground can be found in the Mankoya District
Notebook. Between 1949 and 1955 the company opened fifteen stores in the
district under the names of both A. F. Serrano, or Ndonyo Stores, and
Susman Brothers and Wulfsohn. At Mankoya itself they had two European
managers, a store divided into a retail and a wholesale section, and a rice-
shelling mill. Goods were brought into the district by their subsidiary, the
Barotse Transport Company, and the outlying stores were supplied from
Mankoya by a lorry and a vanette. In 1955 their wholesale business, supplying
independent African retailers, was worth £900 a month. There was close
supervision and frequent stock-taking. Their only serious competitor in the
district was R. F. Sutherland, which had become a subsidiary of CBC Ltd,
with five stores. The directors of both companies visited the district every
few months and sometimes arrived in the same aircraft. The firm not only
sold a variety of commodities, but also bought rice and other foodstuffs, as
well as hides and beeswax. In 1959 it was reported that they had exported
from the district 761 hides and 3,000 pounds of beeswax.

By the time of independence in 1964, Susman Brothers and Wulfsohn
had about 120 trading stores spread over most of Zambia except for the
Eastern and Central Provinces. By that time they had built up a sophisticated
trading operation. Goods were supplied to their stores from large warehouses
at Livingstone. Goods were delivered to remote Barotseland stores by barge
and truck. Alex Freedman, Maurice Rabb's son-in-law, recalls that on one
occasion he travelled on the Zambezi river from Kazangula in a motorised
barge carrying a three-ton truck and two Land-Rovers. The barge stopped
periodically while the vehicles disappeared into the bush to deliver goods.
The company had been using aircraft for many years, and cash and accounts
were brought in to Livingstone from outlying stores by plane. Isa Teeger
recalls from her childhood the bags of money which had been flown in from

outlying stores being counted on the veranda of her uncle, Harry Wulfsohn's, house. Many of the stores were of a stock-pattern design – corrugated-iron sheds of twenty metres by thirty metres – though others were built of Kimberley brick. The majority of store managers were Zambian and accounting procedures had, as Tim Barnett recalls, been ingeniously simplified by Bobby Campbell, the group accountant. Goods were indented at sale price and this could be simply balanced against stock and cash.[26]

Max Barnett

The second string to the Susman and Wulfsohn bow was, of course, Werners. Harry Wulfsohn was managing director of the business from 1944 to 1948. He spent one week every month on the Copperbelt, but left the day-to-day management of the business to Eric Speck who had been the accountant under the previous management. Maurice Rabb found on his arrival in 1947 that the returns on the business were not satisfactory. In the course of 1947 he succeeded in persuading Max Barnett, the general manager of Copperfields Cold Storage, to switch his allegiance to Werners. He was induced to move with the offer of shares in both Werners and Susman Brothers and Wulfsohn.[27]

Max Barnett was born in South Africa in 1905 and reached the Copperbelt in 1931. He worked closely with Maurice Gersh in the establishment of Northern Caterers and Copperfields Cold Storage. He and his wife, whom he married in 1934, became highly respected members of the Copperbelt's colonial society. As Sylvia Emdin, she was born into a prominent Jewish family in Cape Town. Max Barnett was an enthusiastic horseman and was, with Frank Buch, the general manager of Mufulira mine, the promoter of the Mufulira Gymkhana Club, and later of the Kitwe Polo Club. The Barnetts' house, 'Tally-ho', is still a conspicuous landmark in Kitwe's Riverside suburb. Sylvia Barnett was active in social, communal and charitable work, and was in the early 1960s the proprietor of Kitwe's first, and probably only, antique shop.

Other members of their two families followed them to Northern Rhodesia. Max Barnett's brother, Isaac, who reached Northern Rhodesia in 1938, was a partner with his brother-in-law Herbert Bernstein in the agency of Bernstein and Barnett in Kitwe. Bernstein's brother Alex, who had served with the Northern Rhodesia Regiment in Burma during the war, was a first-class cricketer. He had the distinction in 1952 of captaining the first Northern Rhodesian national team to defeat Southern Rhodesia. He and his wife, Molly Martin, became the proprietors of the Monze Hotel.[28]

Sylvia Barnett's sister, Esther Emdin, married, in 1950, Jack Faerber, who was born in Latvia in 1907, joined an uncle in South Africa in 1924, and served in the Rhodesia Regiment during the Second World War. He worked with Susman Brothers and Wulfsohn in the early years of the business from 1946 to 1950, and was at that time a key lieutenant to Harry Wulfsohn. He found it difficult to work with his good friend and 'Jewish brother', and branched out on his own, buying a butchery in Monze from the Butts family, and running a number of stores in the Gwembe valley, which was then in the process of being opened up by road. Jack Faerber was not religious, but he was an intellectual and public-spirited. He was chairman of the Monze Village Management Board for ten years. Esther Faerber recalls that they only once saw a rabbi in Monze, but they used to celebrate Passover with the local Catholic priest, Father O'Riordan. The Faerbers retired to their house, 'Ndalumba', the chiTonga word for 'thank you', at Tokai, near Cape Town, where Jack Faerber died in 1995.[29]

Max Barnett succeeded rapidly in turning around the butchery business. In the early 1950s the company tried to take over from government the Livingstone Cold Storage depot which had been set up during the war as part of the programme for eradication of lung sickness and for the reopening of the Barotseland cattle trade, which had been completed in 1947. These negotiations fell through as the government was reluctant to grant the company sole control over the depot. New cold stores were, however, built at Lusaka and Kitwe. The company eventually had twenty-three butcheries on the Copperbelt as well as branches or subsidiaries in Livingstone, Lusaka and Mansa. Barnett was highly regarded by the Anglo-American Corporation whose meat supplies he had managed for many years. In the mid-1950s, it responded to public criticism of Copperfields Cold Storage's monopoly position as the only butcher in Kitwe and Chingola by inviting him to open Werners branches there. He was also encouraged to open butcheries in the second-class trading area, and in Kitwe's compounds.

As an inducement, Anglo-American gave Werners a share of their mine meat contracts. They pointed out at the time that these were of declining importance as Northern Rhodesia's mine labour moved in the mid-1950s away from partial payment in kind towards complete payment in cash. Wages were at this time greatly increased as a result of pressure from the newly organised African Mineworkers Union, but there was no commensurate increase in meat consumption. Given more disposable income, many people preferred to spend money on fish. There was a suggestion in the late 1950s that fish consumption was being encouraged by the African nationalist movement for political reasons, as fish retailing was generally in African hands.[30]

Max Barnett seems to have responded well to the butchery boycotts which were launched by the African National Congress in Lusaka in January 1954, and which were extended to the Copperbelt in the following month. The brunt of the boycott was borne by Abe Galaun in Lusaka, and his response is considered in another chapter. As a result of intervention by the DC in Mufulira, Max Barnett moved very quickly to defuse the issue on the Copperbelt by promising to put an immediate end to discriminatory sales practices, including divided shops and the sale of meat through hatches. Kenneth

Kaunda, Secretary-General of the African National Congress, wrote to the DC, Mufulira, on 19 February 1954:

> What you and Mr Bernard [Barnett] have done leaves one important impression on our minds and that is the presence in you of both commonsense and respect for the whole of mankind. You have helped to lay down one of the up to now lacking and yet necessary million foundation stones of the building of 'partnership' about which our Government has spoken so much and unfortunately done so little ... We have been accused of being anti-white and anti-government. The truth is that we are not, not in the slightest sense of the terms: all we are is ANTI-WRONG ... Let us hope that many other people will now brave the field and follow your example.[31]

There is no evidence that the targeting by African nationalists, either in Lusaka or on the Copperbelt, of Jewish-owned butcheries was the result of anti-Semitism on their part. The first butchery boycott was in fact mounted in Broken Hill in June 1953, and was aimed at Karl Heslop's butchery. This was the only significant butchery in the country which was not in Jewish ownership. It is, however, possible that the nationalists sought to exploit what they may have seen as the anti-Semitic attitudes of the colonial government and the white public. There is a suggestion that the latter, while not sympathetic to the traders, was critical of what it saw as the slow and weak reaction by government to Congress boycotts. The author of a Federal intelligence report on Northern Rhodesia, writing in the context of an apparently successful, and more general, African consumer boycott in Chingola in 1956, noted that:

> The Administration's approach to this question of boycotts is at variance with that of the traders. The Administration tends to take the view that those affected are mostly Indians and Jews, who have been exploiting their African customers for a long time, and therefore it may be a good thing to face them with a concerted sales resistance and bring down prices. This kind of trader is feeling the squeeze economically although the genuine European trade is not much affected ... Although there is very little sympathy for the Indians and Jews who are mostly affected, people are nevertheless critical of the Northern Rhodesian Government's alleged apathy in dealing with Congress.[32]

The rapid climb-down by the butchers on the Copperbelt in 1954, including Copperfields Cold Storage in Kitwe and Chingola, and Cyril Sussman's Standard Butchery in Ndola and Luanshya, took the ANC by surprise. There was an attempt in Luanshya to shift the focus of the boycott from discriminatory practices to the price of meat, but, as this was still controlled by the government, it soon became apparent that the butchers were the wrong target and the campaign dissolved in confusion. The boycotts, which were renewed in 1956 and 1961 in some places, may, however, have had a long-term impact on meat consumption. The cash flow from the township butcheries, which were run by a subsidiary company, the Northern Rhodesia Meat and Provision Company, was thought in the late 1950s to be inadequate, and these were diversified as outlets for general groceries and other provisions. Some of the butcheries were sub-divided and space was leased to Kaldis and Company, the Greek millers and grocers. Rhokana's general manager, O. B. Bennett, believed that protests by other traders at Werners' sub-division of its butcheries and entry into the grocery business were 'orchestrated' by the general manager of Copperfields Cold Storage, Len Pinshow.[33]

Len Pinshow

The relationship between Werners and Copperfields Cold Storage was a complex one. Max Barnett's successor as general manager of Copperfields Cold Storage was Len Pinshow who married Isadore Kollenberg's daughter, Nina, in 1945 and moved to Northern Rhodesia two years later. There was stiff competition between the two groups and there was a measure of commercial, if not personal, antagonism between the two chairmen, Isadore Kollenberg and Elie Susman on the one hand, and between the two general managers, Max Barnett and Len Pinshow, on the other hand. The relationship between Kollenberg and Pinshow was also uneasy. Pinshow, who takes some pride in his reputation as abrasive and as 'a bit of a stirrer', was determined that his promotion to the position of general manager should not be seen as a case of nepotism. He says that he was always determined that Kollenberg should be known as his father-in-law rather than that he should be known as Kollenberg's son-in-law.[34]

Len Pinshow was, and remains, one of the most interesting and controversial characters to emerge on the colonial Copperbelt. He was born in Johannesburg, where his father was a butcher, in 1916. He completed a degree in commerce at the University of the Witwatersrand and qualified as a chartered accountant before joining the army on the outbreak of the Second World War. Although willing to talk about his exploits in the butchery business, Pinshow is clearly most proud of his role as an organiser in the spheres of sport and politics (this is considered in another chapter). Something of the flavour of the man is provided by extracts from a 1965 profile written by Dick Hobson, editor of *Horizon* magazine:

> Len Pinshow is a man whose personality engenders positive epithets. He is dynamic and dominating (some would say domineering) and his organizing genius, allied to a ready appreciation of the value of public relations and sheer showmanship, ensures the success of any task he tackles. He is a go-getter who spares neither himself nor his associates in speedily reaching an objective by the shortest possible route ... He is breezy and bustling, a perfectionist who curtly rejects second-rate work and ideas. He knows what he wants and he invariably gets it through a combination of determination, cajolery, perseverance and sheer toughness. Tact, while employed on occasion, is not an important

part of the Pinshow armoury. He is adept at influencing people to support his chosen course of action, but he cares little about winning friends in the process.[35]

Pinshow clearly provided Barnett with stiff competition. He and Kollenberg had at first been alarmed at the granting to Werners by Anglo-American of a share in the mines meat contracts, but they were reassured by Sir Ernest Oppenheimer himself, who informed them that the contracts had in any case only another year to run. Pinshow maintains that Werners' moves into Kitwe and Chingola were unprofitable, and that he was able to undercut them by buying from the Cold Storage Board in Southern Rhodesia, which was looking for a way into the Copperbelt market. There is, however, other evidence that the business eventually suffered from Cold Storage Board competition, especially after it extended its operations to Northern Rhodesia in 1960.[36]

If there was stiff competition at the retailing end of the business, there was cooperation at the purchasing end. This was intended to keep down the cost to the butchers of cattle. There was a monopoly buying arrangement which functioned in the eastern Line of Rail region of Bechuanaland through the Northern Cattle Exporters Pool, which also involved Abe Gelman and Elakat. The cattle trade of Ngamiland was excluded from the pool and was dominated by the Susmans' Ngamiland Trading Company which supplied both Werners and Copperfields Cold Storage. There was, however, competition between the two groups for the purchase of cattle within Northern Rhodesia. Meat prices in the country were strongly influenced by the Federation of Meat Distributors which was effectively controlled by the two big groups, though a number of smaller butchers were also members. The Federation worked in cooperation with the Cattle Marketing and Control Board on which the Northern Rhodesian farmers and ranchers were also represented. This allocated import permits to the butchers. Permits were granted only to butchers who had agreed to support the local cattle industry at the 'Fair Indicated Prices for Cattle' which were published by the board. These arrangements were intended to benefit both the consumers and the Northern Rhodesian settler farmers by providing stable prices to both parties. Their influence on the sale of cattle by peasant producers in Northern Rhodesia is a matter of debate.[37]

Ranching and Farming

The most obvious practical demonstration of the cooperation between the two groups was the joint purchase and ownership of ranches. The main purpose of these purchases was to provide holding grounds for cattle imported from Bechuanaland. It was advantageous to hold these imported stock for sale between November and March when local supplies were difficult and meat prices were high. Ngamiland cattle were drought-resistant, and put on weight rapidly when provided with relatively lush pastures. The best known of these joint acquisitions was Lochinvar, a 105,000-acre ranch on the Kafue Flats, which was, at least for a time, the country's only quarantine ranch. A previous co-owner was Herbert Smith, father of Wilbur Smith, the successful popular novelist who acknowledges that his youth spent on the ranch was the inspiration for most of his books. Lochinvar was not ideal as a ranch as only a small proportion of the land was high enough to avoid annual flooding. There was also competition for grazing between cattle and game, including the vast herds of Kafue and Red lechwe which roamed the flats, and which increased greatly in numbers under the two companies' stewardship. There were in addition political problems caused by the ranch's position on a corridor for the movement of Ila-owned cattle to the Kafue river, and by the annual 'Chila' or ritual hunt and slaughter of lechwe by the Ila people. It was, however, a beautiful place and was kept up as a private game reserve for the friends and relatives of the proprietors of the two groups. Its visitors' book contains some unexpected entries from David Attenborough to Elspeth Huxley, as well as various Governors of Northern Rhodesia. It was bought by the government with the help of the World Wildlife Fund for use as a game reserve in 1965–66, and was declared a National Park in 1971. Other joint acquisitions by the two companies were Forsyth's estate at Zimba, and Heales and Nanga estates near Mazabuka which provided another 80,000 acres of ranching land. Len Pinshow points out that, as the butchers were also graziers, they were able to take their profits in both capacities. It seems, however, to have always been politically more acceptable for them to make their profits as ranchers.[38]

Susman Brothers and Wulfsohn also became heavily involved in agriculture on its own account. In addition to Kala ranch, the company bought in 1946 the Rietfontein ranch east of Lusaka which had been developed by Ben Woest, and was bought from his widow. In 1947 the firm took a half share in a company called Agricultural Enterprises which was set up with Geoffrey Beckett and Stuart Green to develop tobacco production on farms in the Choma district. Tobacco production did not prove very successful, but the company ended up owning two of the farms. Geoffrey Beckett was a farmer and rancher who had been elected as chairman of the Northern Rhodesian Livestock Co-operative Society in 1934. He was a nominated member of the Legislative Council in the post-war period and served as Member for Agriculture. Max Barnett was responsible for the development on behalf of Werners of two farming enterprises on the Copperbelt. These were the Chambishi dairy which supplied most of Kitwe's requirements for fresh milk and the Kamsuswa farm piggeries.[39]

For agricultural management, the company relied largely, as the Susmans had done for many years, on Scots and Afrikaners. The company's long-serving ranching and cattle manager was Robert Boyd, who had been 'bailiff' on the Duke of Westminster's estate near Mazabuka. The company's most successful mixed farming enterprise during the 1950s was the Rietfontein ranch which was managed from 1951 by Hermanus Cloete, the only white employee on the farm. In April 1956 the farm was credited with 'the finest commercial crop of maize standing in Northern Rhodesia'. It was expected to produce a then remarkable yield of twenty-five to thirty bags an acre on 400 acres, and a profit on the crop of £10,000. This success was attributed to high density planting and the heavy use of fertiliser. There was also favourable comment on the farm's herd of 2,300 Sussex Afrikander cattle and on the condition of the farm's thirty-five paddocks. The farm was then sending cattle to the butcher weighing 1,200 pounds at five years and aimed to produce this weight after four years. It may be recalled that in 1920 Elie Susman was buying cattle for slaughter with an average weight of 450 pounds.[40]

Northern Rhodesia Textiles

Some Jewish residents of Northern Rhodesia had in the late 1930s seen the development of secondary industry as a more realistic way of employing refugees than agricultural settlement. W. J. Busschau, a South African economist, was in 1945 commissioned by the government to investigate the possibilities for the development of secondary industry in Northern Rhodesia. He came to generally negative conclusions. In the following year, Susman Brothers and Wulfsohn were, however, to play the leading part in a major attempt to develop a new secondary industry in the country. The inspiration for this project came from Abe Gelman, son-in-law of 'Bongola' Smith. He had moved south in 1937 to become the first manager of the Rhodesia Cold Storage Commission, and had succeeded his father-in-law, who died in 1947, as the manager of the southern interests of Elakat. This had grown into an enormous enterprise, and continued to cooperate with the Susmans in the Ngamiland cattle trade. Gelman had the idea of setting up a blanket factory in competition with Philip Frame, one of South Africa's most successful, and controversial, Jewish entrepreneurs, who had opened a blanket factory in Bulawayo. Harry Wulfsohn became interested in the idea and it was agreed to set up the factory in Livingstone with the Susman Brothers and Wulfsohn trading network as the primary outlet. The first meeting of the board of the company was held in Livingstone in October 1946 under the chairmanship of Gelman.[41]

The founding directors of the company included Abe Gelman, Harry Wulfsohn, Maurice Gersh, Geoff Beckett and E. R. Raine, later founder of Raine Engineering. It was agreed that the Susman group of companies would be allowed to subscribe for one-third of the founding shares in an initial capitalisation of £60,000. Abe Gelman was also a substantial initial subscriber. Small shareholders included Paul Zaloumis, Harry Wulfsohn's gambling friend from Namwala, and H. H. Field, well known as the compound manager at

the Mufulira mine. Maurice Gersh played an active role in the early days of
the company, and Maurice Rabb took over Harry Wulfsohn's position on the
board in 1947. Rabb remained an active member of the board for over forty
years and was chairman from 1965 to 1974, succeeding Gelman and Geoff
Beckett. He clearly derived considerable satisfaction in his old age from the
contribution which he had made to the long-term success of the business in
the face of many difficulties.

In the course of 1947 a site for the new factory was found on the
Katembora road and a building – a disused aircraft hangar – was railed to
Livingstone from Gwelo. The factory was ready to begin production early in
1948 with nine looms which had been made in Bulawayo, but the outstanding
problem was to secure supplies of yarn and cotton warp. Consideration had
been given to spinning Northern Rhodesian cotton, but in the end yarn was
imported from India. Abe Gelman sought to involve Ruben Amato, a friend
from his days in the Congo, who had entered the textile business in South
Africa. Provision was made for him to take a one-third share in the business,
but in the end he failed either to pay for his shares or to provide yarn, and
the additional shares were taken up by Susman Brothers and Wulfsohn which
eventually owned 75 per cent of the business. In spite of these difficulties,
production began late in 1948, though it was not until 1951, when Maurice
Rabb paid a visit to Prato, the blanket capital of Italy, and the traditional
supplier of 'shoddy' blankets to the African market, that the company was
able to acquire a reliable source of the right kind of yarn.

The viability of Northern Rhodesia Textiles depended on the small margin
of protection which was provided by tariffs against Southern Rhodesian
competition. The establishment of the Federation of Rhodesia and Nyasaland
in 1953 removed that protection. Plans which had been made to increase the
number of looms from nine to twenty-seven, and the production of blankets
from about 5,000 to 15,000 a week, had to be abandoned. The company
survived the Federal period because the Frame group priced its cheaper
blankets just above the Northern Rhodesian product, and the bulky nature
of blankets provided them with a degree of natural protection through the
cost of transport. The end of the Federation created new opportunities
which will be discussed below.[42]

Zambesi Saw Mills

Another major diversification of Susman Brothers and Wulfsohn was the
takeover from the Southern Rhodesian government in 1948 of Zambesi Saw
Mills. This business, whose origins are outlined elsewhere, employed up to
4,000 people in the extraction of Rhodesian teak from forests on the eastern
side of the Zambezi river within Barotseland. It had been developed by
Messrs Tongue and Knight in cooperation with Rhodesia Railways as the
major source of railway sleepers in the region. The company had used

1. ABOVE. The wedding of Harry Susman and Annie Grill, Livingstone, July 1910.

2. BELOW. The Susman family at Memel, East Prussia, 1913. From left: Joseph Susman, Annie Susman, Harry Susman, Taube Susmanovitch, unidentified maid, Harry Gersh, Behr Susmanovitch, Harry Gersh, Dora Gersh.

3. ABOVE. Lusaka's first shop. Glasser's store in Cairo Road, *circa* 1920. Note the corrugated iron construction of the shop and of the house on the left which was the scene of the first meetings of Lusaka's Hebrew Congregation.

4. BELOW. The Kollenberg family outside their house in 13th Avenue Bulawayo in 1903. From left: Isadore, Herman, David, Johanna (later Iljon), Edward, Gertrude (the baby held in the arms of a black boy), Glicka, Henrie.

5. ABOVE. Harry Wulfsohn with colleagues at his Namwala store, *circa* 1937.

6. BELOW. Imwiko, the Litunga (Paramount Chief or King) of Barotseland, at his palace at Lealui with Harry Wulfsohn (left) and Harry Susman (right), 1945.

7. ABOVE. The Synagogue, Mufulira, 1947.

8. BELOW. Elias (standing to left) and Henne (seated to left) Kopelowitz with members of their family, including their daughter, Minda, son-in-law, John Schlesinger, and grandchildren, Livingstone, *circa* 1950.

9. ABOVE. Leading members of the management of the Susman group of companies at the first meeting of the board of directors of Rhodesian `mercantile Holdings, Salisbury, 1956. From left: A.D. Weskob (Ngamiland Trading Company), Geoffrey Beckett, Nathan Zelter, Harry Robinson, David Susman, Elie Susman, Harry Wulfsohn, Maurice Rabb, S. Emdin, Benny Gelfand, W.E. Warriner.

10. BELOW. The first Jewish mayoral service held in Northern Rhodesia, Kitwe, 1955. From left: Rabbi Maurice Konviser, Reevee Gersh, Maurice Gersh, first mayor of Kitwe, Mrs Pichankik, and Ha5rry Pichanick, mayor of Salisbury.

11. ABOVE. Jack Fischer in his robes as first mayor of the City of Lusaka, 1961.

12. BELOW. Simon Zukas is welcomed by crowds of wellwishers on his return to Lusaka after eleven years in exile in London, Feburary 1964.

13. ABOVE. Dennis and
Maureen Figov outside their
shop in Luanshya in 1989. The
shop was built by Harry Figov
in 1936.

14. RIGHT. Hanan Elkaim, of
Ndola, receiving the Order of
Distinguished Service (First
Division) from President
Kaunda at State House, Lusaka,
1990.

15. ABOVE. The Sefer Torahs of the Lusaka Synagogue including one donated by the Mendelsohn family in memory of Sam Memdelsohn.

16. BELOW. History of the Jews in Zambia Project committee, Lusaka, August 1997. From left: Dr. Michael Bush, Hugh Macmillan (in attendance), Michael Galaun, Malcolm Gee, Simon Zukas.

obsolete rails and antique locomotives and rolling stock, and built a 120-mile private railway – once said to be the longest private line in the world – to a railhead some distance beyond its main saw mills at Mulobezi. The Susman brothers had acted as agents and transport contractors for the company and had also, in the mid-1930s, supplied the saw mills from their own timber concession in the Chobe district of Bechuanaland. When the Southern Rhodesian government nationalised the railways in 1947, it decided to sell the controlling interest in the saw mills which it then acquired. Harry Wulfsohn had the idea that Susman Brothers and Wulfsohn should take over the company.[43]

Maurice Rabb's explanation for this move is that Elie Susman had joined the minority shareholders in the original company, Messrs Tongue and Knight, in a substantial, but problematical, investment in a Mozambican timber project. Harry Wulfsohn had the idea that the takeover of Zambesi Saw Mills would allow for the merging of the Northern Rhodesian and Mozambican businesses and enable Elie Susman to rescue his investment. Edwin Wulfsohn has another, and a more personal, explanation. He believes that his father had been humiliated over a meat contract by the Zambesi Saw Mills manager and that the takeover was undertaken as a way of getting his own back. Edwin Wulfsohn thinks that the investment, though initially profitable, was not in the long run worthwhile.[44] Rabb's explanation seems plausible, though Edwin Wulfsohn's explanation does point to the fact of anti-Semitism as a pressure which may explain the over-achieving drive of Jewish entrepreneurs such as Harry Wulfsohn. His widow, Trude Robins, recalls that, when she protested on one occasion that he was driving himself too hard, and urged him to slow down, he had replied: 'Money isn't my main objective, Trude. I want stability and I want recognition. That is the least I am entitled to if I am to live my life in the wilds of Africa. Without it I feel I'll sooner or later go to pieces.'[45]

Whatever his motives, Harry Wulfsohn succeeded in pushing the deal to a conclusion. He was called with Maurice Rabb to see the Governor, Sir John Waddington, and outlined the scheme to him. On hearing that Elie Susman was a backer of the scheme, Waddington gave his approval. Tongue and Knight agreed to come in on the scheme and the Mozambican company, with its saw mill at Beira, was included in it. A controlling interest in the new company was held by Susman Brothers and Wulfsohn and the Gershes' Economy Stores, while Abe Gelman also had a stake.

The new company was able to increase its prices to Rhodesia Railways, and the market for sleepers was extended to South Africa. As a by-product of the sleeper business, battens were produced for parquet flooring, and were also exported to South Africa. The company's furniture factory in Livingstone was the major supplier of office furniture to the Northern Rhodesian government. This business soon fell foul, however, of the Federation of Rhodesia and Nyasaland which was run largely in the interests of Southern Rhodesia. Government purchasing was centralised in Salisbury, and

in 1955 the Federal government excluded *mukwa*, Northern Rhodesia's indigenous hardwood, from its specifications. This was a serious blow to the
company which was eventually forced to close its factory and sell most of
its machinery to South Africa.

The Mozambican side of the project did not work out as planned. Distance
and Portuguese bureaucracy made operations difficult and large loans were
made to the subsidiary without much hope of recovery. Harry Wulfsohn
eventually agreed to buy the enterprise, and the debt, for a small sum. He
worked with Portuguese partners and eventually made a substantial profit on
the deal. He went on, with another partner, to develop separate timber
interests in South Africa, including vast tracts of forest in the eastern
Transvaal between Ermelo and the Swaziland border.[46]

The Gersh Brothers

While Harry Wulfsohn pursued his own interests in Mozambique and South
Africa, there was one branch of the Susman family enterprises in which he
had no part. This was the diverse group of businesses built up on the
Copperbelt by Maurice and Harry Gersh. Maurice Gersh was an extremely
astute businessman who pursued his own vision on the Copperbelt. Although
he did acquire some agricultural assets, the focus of his enterprises was in
urban areas and on the development of secondary industry and services.[47]
The core of the Gersh brothers' network was Economy Stores which had
both department and concession stores in Kitwe and Chingola. Stores were
later started in other Copperbelt towns and in the surrounding rural areas.
The first diversifications of the business were into mineral waters, garages
and cinemas. These were launched after the Second World War as separate
companies. Central African Motors (known as CAMS), which was launched
in 1946, acquired the important Volkswagen and Land-Rover franchises.
Northern Theatres, which built Kitwe's first cinema, the Astra, was floated
in the same year. An African cinema was opened by the company in Kitwe's
Bauchi Township in 1954.

Cinema segregation remained a fact of life until the early 1960s. The
Astra cinema café was the scene of a major racial incident on 1 April 1957
when Harry Nkumbula and Kenneth Kaunda, President and Secretary-
General of the African National Congress, who had been told that they
could buy sandwiches there, made the mistake of entering the café instead
of waiting to be served outside. Nkumbula, who objected to being told by
a seventeen-year-old girl that 'boys' were not served, became involved in
what Kaunda described as 'an *apartheid* type of brawl' with other patrons. He
was also, allegedly, beaten up by the police who had told him, for good
measure, that he should not 'call a white lady a girl'. Their supporters among
Kitwe's mineworkers threatened retaliatory violence, and the cinema was put
under police guard.[48]

Rhodesia Bottling, which later became Copperbelt Bottling, was launched in 1949 and acquired the increasingly lucrative Coca-Cola franchise for Northern Rhodesia. Its long-serving manager was Jack Price, a prominent member of Kitwe's Jewish community. Among its activities was the leasing of refrigerators to the emerging class of African café and tearoom proprietors who would otherwise have had difficulty in getting credit. Maurice Gersh had a commercial pilot's licence and the brothers acquired in 1946 a minority stake in Thatcher Hobson Airways, the country's first commercial airline, which was later incorporated into Central African Airways.

African Commercial Holdings was established as an umbrella company for the majority of these assets, excluding the stores, in 1949. The Gersh brothers owned about half the ordinary shares in this company, while the Susman brothers subscribed for rather more than a quarter of the shares, and also had separate holdings in many of its subsidiaries. In an unusual development, a minority of ordinary shares and the majority of the loan stock were subscribed by the subsidiaries of a British company, Cable and Wireless Ltd. This was the only example of direct foreign investment in any of the companies associated with the Susman group. It is not clear why Cable and Wireless decided to make this investment at this time. They may have been attracted by the opportunity to back enterprises which were, directly or indirectly, associated with the prosperity of the copper industry with which their primary business had a natural affinity.

In 1952 African Commercial Holdings was the largest single backer of Raine Engineering which became one of the largest engineering businesses on the Copperbelt. In 1962 the company was, through a subsidiary, and in association with Leyland, the promoter of the Land-Rover assembly plant at Ndola, the first motor assembly plant in the country. As we have seen, the Gersh brothers also had minority interests through Economy Stores in Northern Rhodesia Textiles and Zambesi Saw Mills. They had property interests in Kitwe, as well as a farm near Luanshya, and acquired the Kaleya estate at Mazabuka. Maurice Gersh was also involved with Lion Tile Ltd, and became a director of the Northern Rhodesian Industrial Development Corporation, the predecessor of Indeco.

Southward Expansion

Between 1953 and 1963 these businesses operated within the Federation of Rhodesia and Nyasaland which provided a regional free trade area. The Federation was run, as we have already seen in some instances, largely in the interests of Southern Rhodesia. Revenues derived from the taxation of the copper mining companies were largely channelled to the provision of services to the settler population, and to the development of secondary industry in the south. Similar developments in Northern Rhodesia were continued in the face of stiff competition from, and discrimination in favour of, Southern

Rhodesian companies. Against this trend, the Susman and Wulfsohn group was able to extend its operations into Southern Rhodesia, and to take over a number of companies in that country.

The southwards move in the focus of expansion began in 1954 when Harry Wulfsohn left Livingstone and moved with his family to Johannesburg. This was as a consequence of a serious row between the partners which involved tensions between the major figures in the directorate, Elie Susman, Harry Wulfsohn, Maurice Rabb and Max Barnett. Serious consideration was given at this time to the possibility of dismantling the companies and distributing their assets. David Susman joined the board of the companies as a young man in the early 1950s, and recalls stormy board meetings which came close to physical violence with 'Max Barnett chasing Harry around the desk with a stick, or Harry banging his fist on the table and walking out of the meeting, or my father saying "that's the end of it".' These tensions arose primarily from the juxtaposition in one business of some strong-willed and forceful personalities, including two quite exceptionally talented and successful entrepreneurs: Elie Susman and Harry Wulfsohn. There was also tension between Harry Wulfsohn – the impetuous risk-taker – and Maurice Rabb – the cautious and fastidious manager. In David Susman's view, Maurice Rabb was the 'ham in the sandwich', caught in the middle between Elie Susman and Harry Wulfsohn.[49]

The Susmans were not alone in finding Harry Wulfsohn difficult to work with. There is, however, general agreement as to his exceptional talents. David Susman describes him as 'an aggressive and very intelligent trader who drove the business very strongly after the war'. The few of his dictated memoranda which survive from the mid-1960s demonstrate unusual powers of analysis and a fluency in English which was remarkable for a man with little formal education who had begun to learn the language in his late teens. Towards the end of his life he earned a standing ovation for a lecture which he delivered to the Institute of Directors in London.[50]

It is not clear whether the rupture occurred over any specific issue. There may have been tension over the Mozambican timber investment, but, in Edwin Wulfsohn's view, another factor was his father's feeling that Northern Rhodesia was too small an arena for his talents, and was limiting his commercial horizons. After a cooling-off period of a year, there was a reconciliation between the partners. Harry Wulfsohn returned to active participation in the management of the companies, but he did not return to Livingstone. He moved to Salisbury, and the headquarters of Susman Brothers and Wulfsohn soon followed him, though Maurice Rabb continued as general manager in Livingstone. From this time onwards David Susman used his undoubted diplomatic skills to try and bring order to meetings, and to ensure that these stuck to an agenda and avoided personal issues.[51]

A consequence of Harry Wulfsohn's move to Salisbury was the formation of a new alliance with Harry Robinson. He was a member of a prominent

Southern Rhodesian family of Lithuanian Jewish origin. He had become associated with the Susman family through his marriage to Harry Susman's daughter, Ella. Susman Brothers and Wulfsohn formed a new subsidiary, Rhodesian Mercantile Holdings, in 1956. The new company took control through subsidiaries of the Northern Rhodesian stores network, the Ngami-land Trading Company in Bechuanaland, which took over Riley's Hotel and store in Maun at this time, and Harry Robinson's Southern Rhodesian wholesaling business and stores.[52]

Both Robinson and his lieutenant, Nathan Zelter, a Romanian-born radical intellectual, and a brilliant salesman, who had been travelling to Northern Rhodesia for Robinson and Schwartz since the late 1930s, joined the boards of the new companies. Zelter later claimed credit for suggesting the central-isation of the group's buying and accountancy services in Salisbury.[53] They later bought another network of rural stores in Southern Rhodesia, African Stores Limited, from the BSA Company, whose directors had very little interest in trade. Maurice Rabb recalled that their chairman, Sir Ellis Robins (later Lord Robins), fell asleep during the meeting at which the purchase of the group was concluded. It was found that these stores were difficult to run, and they were eventually sold to their managers.[54] According to David Susman, the majority of the directors were used to the relatively liberal colonial administrations of Northern Rhodesia and Bechuanaland, and were never really at home in the politically harsher environment of Southern Rhodesia.[55] The move into the south was to cause serious problems for the group after the end of Federation and Southern Rhodesia's unilateral declara-tion of independence (UDI).

Woolworths and Marks and Spencers

In 1951 the Susman brothers donated a clock and tower to the new Rhodes–Livingstone Museum in Livingstone to commemorate the fiftieth anniversary of their first arrival in the country. Harry Susman, who had earlier retired from the business, died at Muizenburg in January 1952. In his will he left £5,000 to the Livingstone Children's Holiday Fund and a substantial sum to the Paris mission.[56] Elie Susman continued to visit Northern Rhodesia for meetings at least twice a year until his death in January 1958. They had both lived through a period of dramatic change, and had contributed substantially to the economic and commercial development of the region. In the last twenty years or so of his life, Elie Susman had devoted much of his time and energy to the development of Woolworths in South Africa, but he had continued to maintain and to expand his interests in the north. He had lost none of his commitment to the scene of his earliest trading adventures.

For some time before his father's death, David Susman had been involved both in the development of Woolworths and of the Northern Rhodesian companies. He had spent the first six or seven years of his life in Livingstone.

Although his family moved to Cape Town, and then Johannesburg, while he was a child he continued to be a regular visitor to Northern Rhodesia. He recalls a holiday spent with his father's old friend and partner Robert Sutherland, at his farm at Katembora near Livingstone. The Scots frugality of diet on the farm caused some anguish to a growing boy. He also recalls shooting his first leopard with an Irish hunter, Paddy Drake, on the Leopard's Hill ranch at the age of twelve in 1937. David was educated at Kingswood School in Grahamstown, and went on from there to study commerce at the University of the Witwatersrand. His period at university was interrupted by war service. He joined the Natal Carbineers in 1943 and served in the Italian campaign. He returned to university after the war, and was then one of a number of young men with Zionist sympathies who volunteered to fight in Israel's War of Independence in 1948. He was wounded in action and invalided out of the army. He returned to South Africa for an operation, but he then went back to Israel and served for over a year in the Foreign Ministry of the new state.[57]

Before he left for Palestine, as it then was, in 1948, he had met his future wife, Ann Laski, who was visiting South Africa with her uncle, Simon Marks, chairman of Marks and Spencers, the British chain-store group. In the period of post-war austerity and foreign exchange shortages, it was important for British businesses to generate exports as their allocation of foreign exchange for imports was linked to their export performance. Simon Marks was introduced to Max Sonnenberg and his son Richard, who was playing an increasingly important role in the management of Woolworths. It was agreed to establish a partnership between Marks and Spencers and Woolworths which would involve new investment, and the modernisation and upgrading of what was still an old-fashioned and downmarket business.

David Susman and Ann Laski were married in London in 1949, and spent the first year or so of their married life in Israel. They then returned to London where David joined Marks and Spencers as an executive. He had been working in London for over two years when Richard Sonnenberg invited him to become general manager of Woolworths in South Africa, and to apply the knowledge which he had acquired in London to the modernisation of the company. David and Ann Susman's marriage was an affair of the heart, but it did add a personal dimension to the close and continuing ties which were established between Marks and Spencers and Woolworths. It also linked the Susman family, and its Northern Rhodesian businesses, to some of the leading members of Britain's Jewish and Zionist communities. Three of Ann Susman's uncles, Simon Marks, Israel Sieff, both later members of the House of Lords, and Harry Sacher, were not only the promoters of one of Britain's most successful trading enterprises, but were also, in alliance with Chaim Weizmann, major contributors to the Zionist movement, and to the establishment of the state of Israel.

David Susman became general manager of Woolworths in 1953 and served in that capacity, or as managing director, until 1981 when he became chairman of the new company, Wooltru Ltd, which was formed after the merger of Woolworths with Truworths. During this time he had the primary responsibility, under the overall command of Richard Sonnenberg, for the expansion of the business, and the introduction of Marks and Spencers' standards of management, quality control and staff welfare. David Susman remained chairman of the company until 1993 and still retains an office in Cape Town as president of the company. In 1962 he was invited by Simon Marks to join the board of Marks and Spencers in London. On his retirement from the board in 1993, he was the longest-serving director. He modestly describes himself as primarily a manager, though 'perhaps a bit of an entrepreneur'.

Throughout this time, David Susman continued to serve as a director of his family's Northern Rhodesian, and later Zambian, companies. In 1963, for instance, he was on the board of well over a dozen of these enterprises, and he has maintained his involvement through Zambezi Ranching and Cropping and Trans Zambezi Industries until the present time. These companies undoubtedly benefited from his knowledge of the most advanced management practices, and his association with some of the most dynamic and progressive business enterprises in Britain and South Africa.

By the time of the independence of Zambia in 1964, the Susman, Wulfsohn, and Gersh, group of companies was the largest non-mining conglomeration of business interests in the country. These extended from rural trade and butcheries through agriculture to urban trade and secondary industry. There was no comparable group of business interests in the country. It had been built up almost entirely on the basis of local and regional trade, and with a minimum of foreign investment, or assistance from outside. These interests represented the most successful example in the country of domestic capital formation and enterprise.

CHAPTER 9

The Climax of the Community,
1945–70

The rise of Nazism, and the Second World War, stimulated self-consciousness and heightened awareness of Jewishness among people of Jewish descent. The involvement of many of the younger generation of Northern Rhodesian Jewry in the war also gave an added sense of legitimacy and respectability to the community. It was more difficult, though not impossible, for other members of settler society to be openly anti-Semitic when they knew that many Jews were serving in the armed forces both within and outside the country. Some, such as Max Barnett, Moss Dobkins, Goody Glasser, Raymond Radunski and David Gerber, were among those who served in the Northern Rhodesian Defence Force or Home Guard. Many others, like the four sons of Maurice Thal, and Basil Herbstein, from Broken Hill, Morris Goldstein from Kitwe, Len Mow, Philip Rosen and Simon Zukas from Luanshya, Max Tow, who was severely wounded in Egypt, and Oscar Susman, the younger, from Livingstone, Nicky Iljon from Mazabuka, Jack and Lewis Baitz from Pemba, and Jack Fischer from Lusaka, all served either in Africa or overseas. Women were also recruited. Ann Fischer was among the first recruits from Northern Rhodesia to the Women's Auxiliary Air Force (the WAAF). A number of these people returned to Northern Rhodesia after the war and were active in business, industry, local government and in the Jewish community. There was some tension in the post-war years between the men who had gone to the war and those who had remained. The returnees felt that it was unfair that they had to start again in business from scratch, while the people who stayed in the country during the war had got ahead of them. There were, of course, many men who were not allowed to join up because they were recent immigrants or 'enemy aliens'.

The Northern Rhodesian Copperbelt made an enormous contribution to the allied war effort. One and a half million tons of copper were produced. Although a post-war depression, as had followed the end of the First World War, had been confidently predicted, the post-war period was one of rapid growth in the economy, and in the settler population. As Wally Dobkins and Aviva Ron recall, it was not until the early 1950s that their rather typical

Jewish families seemed to be at all prosperous, and able to afford new cars and overseas holidays.[1] It was also in these years that electricity, refrigerators, running water and piped sewage became available for the whole of the white population, and the Northern Rhodesian towns with their newly tarred roads began to lose their 'frontier' look. It was in the same period that the more prosperous shopkeepers began to move out from rooms behind their shops in town centres into newly built houses in leafy suburbs such as Fairview in Lusaka, and Riverside in Kitwe. The mid-1950s marked the numerical high point of the Jewish community, as well as the peak of prosperity and self-confidence for the settlers as a whole, though even then the rise of African nationalism and commercial boycotts were beginning to pose a threat to an apparently secure and prosperous way of life. For most of the Jewish population, with their background as economic or political refugees, this was a way of life which they had only just attained after years of relative deprivation, self-sacrifice and hard work. Although the Jewish community was small, there were class divisions within it. There were always tensions between the better-off, who saw themselves as leaders of the community, and the less prosperous members.

Demography

It is not easy to get an accurate picture of the size of the Jewish community in Zambia at any time. Census estimates are almost bound to be unreliable because of the difficulty of deciding who is, and who is not, a Jew. A religious definition would tend to exclude people with no strong religious convictions. There appear to have been about seventy Jews recorded in the first census in 1911. Moses Cohen, who was interested in statistics, but who would have taken a conservative religious view, estimated the population in 1921 as 110 and in 1928 as about 200. There must have been a substantial increase during the construction boom on the Copperbelt which peaked in 1931, and a subsequent decline during the depression. The population recovered in the mid-1930s, and was probably about 300 before being doubled by the influx of refugees from Germany and the Baltic states at the end of the decade. According to Rybko, who may have been quoting the 1946 census, there were 612 Jews in the country in 1947.[2] By the date of the next census in 1951, the number had increased to about 780, while in 1954 it was estimated at between 1,000 and 1,200. It is unlikely that the latter figure was ever exceeded.[3]

In spite of this apparently rapid growth in the years after the war, the proportion of Jews in the white population as a whole had steadily declined. This was probably never higher than in Livingstone in 1911 where it made up about 15 per cent of the total. At that time Jews were estimated at 46 per 1,000, or less than 5 per cent of a settler population in the country as a whole of 1,500.[4] By 1951 the proportion of Jews had fallen to 21 per thousand, or just over 2 per cent in a total of just over 37,000. By the end of the decade it had fallen further to little more than 1 per cent of a population which had doubled.

A remarkable feature of the white population of Zambia throughout the colonial period was its rapid rate of turnover. Rates of re-emigration were often as high, and sometimes higher, than rates of immigration. In the period 1931–46, for instance, the 27,000 immigrants were more or less evenly matched by emigrants. Even in the boom years, 1946–51, when there were over 26,000 immigrants, there were also 14,000 emigrants, including 3,000 Polish refugees. The white population is thought to have reached a peak of about 76,000 in 1960, but in the preceding three years a total immigration of about 15,000 people was approximately matched by emigration. Emigrants in 1958, which saw the onset of a sharp depression, had exceeded immigrants by 3,300. The population grew only because of a relatively high rate of natural increase – about 2 per cent – in what was, by European standards, a young and fertile population.[5]

Although the Jewish community certainly did not double itself, as the general settler population did, in the years between 1951 and 1960, and was probably no more than 1,000 in the latter year, it was less volatile than the white population as a whole. The majority of Jews was still engaged in trade, and traders tended to put down deeper roots than the bulk of the white population which consisted mainly of miners and other artisans, many of whom came 'up north' from South Africa for short periods of work for high wages. There was some emigration of German Jews in the years after the war, as a number of them left a country in which they had been virtually imprisoned by South Africa's refusal to allow them visitors' visas, let alone residence permits, but there was a remarkable continuity and stability in the Jewish population. The leadership of the community was fairly stable from the 1940s until the 1960s. There were, of course, a number of new immigrants during this period, some of whom put down roots and stayed for long periods. The majority of newcomers came from South Africa and Britain. They tended not to identify so closely with the country as had the people who had arrived earlier in the century.[6]

Although the Jews were relatively well rooted in the country, there were a number of factors which discouraged the development of a permanently settled and self-perpetuating community. In common with other members of the settler population, Jews often sent their children away for primary, and almost always for secondary, education in the south. Children, often as young as seven, left home for school, embarking on four-day train journeys to places as far away as Cape Town. In the early days they might only return, as Wally Dobkins did, for holidays once a year, or they might stay away for years, as Berjulie Press did, seeing her parents only when they went south for annual holidays at the Cape. Parents were concerned to get their children the best possible education, and were also influenced until after the Second

World War by the belief that Northern Rhodesia was not a healthy place for children.

An additional motive for many Jewish parents, as in the case of the Dobkins, was the desire that their children should have a good religious education. According to David Messerer, parents only realised that they had made a mistake when their children protested in later years that they had been deprived of a normal family life.[7] As a consequence of this practice, only a minority of the younger generation returned to live and work in the country. A few returned to take over family businesses, and there were also some who came back to practise their professions – at least for a while. It was only latterly that a few families, such as the Galauns, kept their children in the country for the whole of their school education. Even they had to send their sons to Southern Rhodesia and South Africa for university education. The parents tended in their old age to follow their children to their country of residence, and to retire elsewhere.

A decline in the Jewish population had probably begun in some places, such as Livingstone and Broken Hill, before the end of the 1950s. This reflected the relative stagnation of the economies of these towns. The Congo crisis of 1960 may have contributed to insecurity in some sections of the Jewish population, but rapid decline began only in the years immediately before and after independence. The Jewish population fell by two-thirds from about 1,000 to 300 in the later 1960s. This decline coincided with fairly buoyant economic conditions, but was encouraged by restrictions on trade licences for non-citizens, the tightening of exchange controls, and the difficulties of communication with the south, all of which affected traders more seriously than professional people. By the end of the 1970s, the Jewish population must have fallen below 100 for the first time since before the First World War.

There were a number of ways in which the involvement of Jews in the urban economy of Northern Rhodesia in the post-war period differed from the pre-war situation. As a result of Asian competition, Jewish traders were almost completely excluded from African retail trade except in the 'closed townships' of Kitwe, Mufulira and Chingola. Although there was still a large number of Jewish shopkeepers, the majority of them ran more specialised shops which mainly catered for the growing European market in the major towns. There was, for instance, an extraordinary proliferation of jewellery shops in Lusaka and on the Copperbelt. The butchery and bakery businesses continued to be dominated by the large Jewish-owned companies, but there was also a number of smaller Jewish bakeries. A new development was the increased involvement of Jewish entrepreneurs in light industry, such as milling, printing, furniture manufacture, metal fabrication, foundries and engineering.

Livingstone

The best starting point for a survey of the community as it was in the years after the war is Wolf Rybko's account of his visit in 1947. He took an interest not only in the history of the community, but also in its demographic and sociological features. He provided a comprehensive list of the occupations of the Jewish population of his first port of call, Livingstone, in 1947.

> There are twelve shopkeepers, two book-keepers, seven shop assistants, one hotel assistant, one taxi-dealer, one civil servant, one brickmaker, one plywood manufacturer, one basket manufacturer, one cattle and butchery dealer, one company director, one curio dealer, one furniture dealer, one agent, one poultry farmer, two furriers, one upholsterer, one wholesale merchant, one fitter, one butcher, two tanners and one trader.[8]

The activities of the three largest businesses in the town – Zambesi Saw Mills, Susman Brothers and Wulfsohn, and Northern Rhodesia Textiles – have already been described. Their resident directors, Harry Wulfsohn and Maurice Rabb, were among the most conspicuous businessmen in the town. While Livingstone was their base of operations, their activities were on a regional scale. The major businessman in the town itself was Harry Sossen, who, as we have seen, had married Bella Grill in 1935. He was born at Telz in Lithuania in 1908 and travelled with his parents to South Africa as a small child. He worked for Gordon's store at Wankie from 1924 to 1930, where he became a friend of the young Roy Welensky, and, after a short time on the Copperbelt, settled in Livingstone in 1931. He had been attracted north of the Zambezi by visits to the Victoria Falls where parties of Jewish youth from Bulawayo and Salisbury congregated for annual camping holidays at Easter. He eventually took over the PSA shop and the Capitol Theatre from other members of the Grill family. He acquired the General Motors franchise and established Sossy's Motors in Mainway in 1944. A much larger showroom and workshop for Chevrolet and Vauxhall cars, as well as Massey-Harris tractors, was opened in Jameson Road in 1956. In his speech at the opening of this complex he indicated his confidence that Livingstone would remain, as it has done, a major halt on the Great North Road. Most heavy truck traffic from the south still by-passes Zimbabwe and enters Zambia from Botswana. Although the main focus of his activities was Livingstone, he did open branches in the 1950s at Choma and Kalomo on the Line of Rail, as well as in Victoria Falls township, and Wankie, in Southern Rhodesia.[9]

For many years his wife Bella ran the drapery section of their shop, the PSA, which grew into a large department store in Stanley House, Mainway, a handsome building previously occupied by Barclay's Bank. The Sossens were a musical family and were well known in the 1940s and early 1950s for their jazz band, Sossy's, which played on Saturday evenings at the Victoria

Falls Hotel on the south side of the Zambezi. Harry played the violin while Bella played the piano. She is especially remembered as the organiser of fund-raising concerts during and after the war. As the representatives of the Schlesinger Organisation, they entertained in the 1950s a number of visiting celebrities in the world of film, including Danny Kaye, Laurence Harvey (both Yiddish-speaking) and Alfred Hitchcock. Their house, aptly named 'Melodie', was an important social centre for Livingstone's settler population.[10]

The great majority of the Jewish population was, however, still employed in much smaller businesses, and was engaged in retail trade and the provision of services. A few, like Max and Jenny Shapiro, had remained in the town for over fifty years – they died and were buried there in the early 1960s. Elias Kopelowitz, the wholesaler, also lived in the town for over fifty years, dying, as did his wife, Henne, in 1968. They were, at the time of their deaths, not only the senior members of the Jewish community, but were also among the town's most senior and respected citizens. In the post-war period, he extended his interests into secondary industry when he became the main backer of the foundry which was set up by his relatives, Harry and Max Tow, in 1946. They had arrived from Lithuania as young men in the late 1930s. Harry worked in the foundry at the Broken Hill mine during the Second World War and became a skilled moulder. There is some dispute as to whether their first products were three-legged cooking pots, which Elias is said to have ordered for the rural trade, or manhole covers for Livingstone municipality, but they built up a successful business, and began to supply the mines with drill bits. The Tow Brothers Iron Works was one of the largest employers in the town in the mid-1950s. They then moved their headquarters to Kitwe, although they retained a branch in Livingstone under the management of Lazar Judelman. They sold their Copperbelt business to the Anglo-American Corporation at independence. It has since been both nationalised and privatised, and survives under the name of Scaw Ltd.

A number of the refugees from Germany who had arrived in the town immediately before the war remained in business there after it ended. They included the Aufochs and the Jacobys who ran the ABC Bazaar. Kurt Aufochs eventually took over a number of other shops, but his business ultimately failed, and he returned to Germany with his wife, Ilse. Heinz Behrens, who married Cilla Scher, Elias Kopelowitz's niece, was also in business in the town. Among the younger generation was John Schlesinger who married Minda Kopelowitz. He was an active member of the Jewish community, but died tragically in 1956. The Kopelowitzes' only son, David, also died at the age of nineteen while a student at the University of Cape Town in 1952. Another youthful newcomer was Wulfie Wulfsohn. He was the brother of Harry Wulfsohn, and had arrived in the country from Latvia in 1939 at the age of eighteen. After a short time working in his brother's butchery, he moved on to the Copperbelt where he worked as a skipman at Mufulira mine. He returned to Livingstone in 1942 and worked for Zambesi Saw

Mills. For some time after the war, he was in charge of the hides and skins department of Susman Brothers and Wulfsohn.[11]

Among the more remarkable post-war arrivals in the town were the Radunskis and the Slutzkins. Raymond Radunski had reached the Copperbelt from Vilna, then in Poland, in 1930. He had opened a cycle shop in Mufulira in 1936, but worked on the mine as a blaster later in the decade and during the war. Following his marriage in 1946 to Paddy Kleinman, who came from South Africa, he moved to Livingstone. They set up a small factory to make basketwork containers and cane furniture, and traded under the name of 'Milaka' – a Lozi word meaning reeds. Among those who worked for him as an accounts clerk was Ilute Yeta, who eventually became, and still is, the Litunga Yeta IV of the Lozi. As the demand for cane products declined, the business was converted in the mid-1960s to the production of steel furniture. Raymond and Paddy Radunski were liberal in politics and were among the handful of settlers who joined the United National Independence Party (UNIP) before independence. Following Raymond Radunski's death in the late 1960s, the business was carried on until 1971 by his son, Saul. The latter left Livingstone to pursue his studies, and lived in Australia for many years. His mother, Paddy, had left Livingstone in the early 1970s and moved to Lusaka. She moved to Australia in the late 1980s. Saul Radunski retained an interest in Zambia and has recently returned with his family to live and work in the country.[12]

Alex Slutzkin arrived in Livingstone from South Africa in 1950. He was originally employed by Erica Critchley, the daughter of F. J. 'Mopani' Clarke, as the manager of the old-established Zambezi Trading Company. He eventually took over the company which, after a period of expansion, later became insolvent. Alex Slutzkin had, perhaps, devoted too much of his time and energy to public work. He became mayor of Livingstone in 1958–59. He died as a result of a motor accident in 1970. His widow, Riva, has lived and worked in Lusaka since soon after her husband's death. She remembers Livingstone's lively social life, but thinks that the Jewish community was rather inward-looking and divided into factions: the older settlers, the German refugees, and the South African newcomers.[13]

Other new arrivals in the town, though not in the country, were the Iljon brothers. Benny Iljon moved to Livingstone in 1939 from Mazabuka. Nicky Iljon had moved to Southern Rhodesia after the war, but returned to Livingstone in 1950 with his wife, Helga Sonnabend, who had arrived in Southern Rhodesia from Germany in 1939. She was the niece of Dr Henry Sonnabend who has already featured in this story. Nicky Iljon set up his own business which dealt originally in motor cycles and car accessories, but eventually became a hardware business. Helga's great interest in life was music. She ran the Music Circle in Livingstone and was for many years chairperson of the Northern Rhodesia Music Association. She organised concerts in the Victoria Hall which was often filled to capacity by a crowd which had come to hear visiting classical soloists who extended their tours of South Africa to include engagements in the north. Nicky and Helga Iljon left for England in the early 1970s. The Iljons' sister, Herta Ficks, had also moved to Livingstone where her husband, Sam, ran a clothing store under the name of Fix Outfitters.[14]

During the Federal period, Livingstone, which was always partially dependent on tourism for its prosperity, suffered a number of setbacks to its development. These included the down-grading of the airport, which was replaced by Salisbury as the region's premier international airport, and the departure of the Rhodesian Air Force. The Jewish community had begun a slow decline by 1956 when it was reported that a number of families had left the town, and that several were expected to follow them. Among the first to move in the early 1950s was the formidable Gertie Merber who left for Bulawayo where she remained until her death in 1979 at the age of ninety. Her furniture factory was taken over and run successfully for a while by Alec and Esther Beau. Esther Rubenstein, as she was before her marriage, had worked at Kohler's garage for some years. Max and Harry Tow moved to Kitwe in 1954, and the Wulfsohns left for South Africa in the same year.

The disintegration of the community began, however, only with independence. Among the last to leave were the Sossens in 1969. Bella Sossen had by then lived in the town for sixty years and was to die a year later. They were encouraged to leave by the difficulty of retaining experienced staff. The Rabbs left in 1971 and were followed by the Iljons and Radunskis a year or two later. Livingstone's last Jewish resident was Meyer Flax, who had never been an active member of the Jewish community, and had become a recluse. He continued to live without electric light, and surrounded by cats, behind his colonial-style shop until shortly before his death in 1979. The shop – an Aladdin's cave of antique treasures – occupied a prime corner site on Mainway, where there is now a bank. His enthusiasm for the Soviet Union, which had attracted the attention of the police in the early 1930s, had been replaced, Ian McKillop recalled, by a tendency to blame all the ills of the modern world on Stalin.[15]

Mazabuka

Further north along the Line of Rail there were, as we have seen, a number of Jewish families settled in the smaller towns, including the Baitz and Klein families in Pemba and, from 1950 onwards, the Faerbers in Monze. The most successful of this group of traders was Philip Fischer at Mazabuka. He was born in Libau, Latvia, in 1905 and reached Northern Rhodesia in 1926, following his half-brothers, Sam and Lazar. He worked at Bwana Mkubwa, and at Luanshya during the construction boom, and also in Lusaka, where he formed a lasting partnership with George Hurwitz. In Mazabuka he worked from the mid-1930s as a manager for Elias Kopelowitz and then took over the business from him. In a fine example of endogamy, which was so typical of the central African Jewish communities, he was not only related to 'Old Man Kop', as he called him, but also married Ann Kopelowitz of Cape Town, the daughter of another Elias Kopelowitz, a cousin of the first. Following the death in 1963 of his first wife, Ann, he married Paula, the posthumous daughter of Paul Kopelowitz, and the former wife of Benny Iljon.[16]

Philip Fischer's son, Stanley, was born in Mazabuka in 1943 and lived there until 1956. He has provided a graphic description of a typical small town store in a commercial farming area as it was in the post-war years:

> When I was growing up in Mazabuka, the large sign above the entrance said 'P. Fischer General Merchant' and general the shop was, like an American country store. Aside from the standard retail store, selling among things I remember, clothing, candy, soft-drinks, pocket knives, golf-balls, cloth, hardware, and no doubt many other products, the business included a maize mill, a gasoline pump or two, a tailor, and possibly other services. My father would order anything his customers wanted (I remember orders for both a tractor and a rugby ball), with the products usually coming from Bulawayo by train.

Stanley Fischer's mother worked, as was the case in so many Jewish families, in the business as the accountant. According to one opinion, she was responsible for her husband's commercial success, as it was only after his marriage in 1943 that the business took off. Much of the business was done with farmers on seasonal credit. Stanley recalls his father asking farmers, many of whom were Afrikaans-speaking, as they came into the shop: 'Hoe gaan die oes?' (How goes the harvest?). He notes that the question was not disinterested as his father's prosperity was closely tied to that of his farming customers – in an area which is known for unreliable rains.

Stanley has also provided a revealing description of the material quality of life in his early childhood in the 1940s, a description which would fit the lives of many Jewish and settler families in the towns and villages of Northern Rhodesia at the time:

> When I was born, my parents lived in a house behind the store. There was no running water. Rainwater was collected in big storage tanks at the side of the house, probably via runoff from the roof. We kept water to drink in a canvas bag that cooled through evaporation, suspended in a tree outside the back door. Water had to be boiled for drinking. There was a bath, filled by water that ran in from a heated 44 gallon petrol drum outside, and the rainwater tank. There was an evaporation type cooler chest, but we later bought a kerosene-powered refrigerator. In that house we used hurricane lamps for lighting, and batteries to power the radio. We also had a wind-up gramophone.

There was, of course, no Jewish community in the village. The only other Jews to live there in the 1940s and 1950s were two government doctors, Dr Dublon, who, with his family, had been among the group of German Jewish refugees who were stranded at Beira in 1939, and Eric Iljon, whose career is outlined elsewhere. The Fischers did not keep a kosher home, but they did go to Lusaka, and occasionally to Livingstone, for the High Days and Holy Days. Stanley Fischer did not get a Jewish education in Mazabuka, but his father taught him the Hebrew alphabet before he left for school in Cape Town at the age of eleven. It was there that he began the study of Judaism and was prepared for his bar mitzvah. He has a vivid recollection of seeing his father 'one morning standing at a window, facing out, "laying *tefillin*", i.e. putting on phylacteries, wearing a *tallit* (prayer shawl) and saying the morning prayers – I guess now that may have been his mother's *yahrzeit*, the anniversary of his mother's death.'

Stanley Fischer recalls that in Mazabuka in his childhood: 'Racism was rife, there was no social mixing, and the school was of course segregated. I remember once organizing a cricket game with some African children, and being reprimanded by a passerby. Nor was there any social mixing between the Indians and the whites.' He also, however, points to the paradox that 'although we did not interact socially with Africans, we talked to them a lot, and inevitably knew a lot about their lives and about them'. As was the case with most Jewish families, especially those engaged in retail trade, they were in constant contact with a large number of domestic servants, employees and customers, and discussed the issues of the day with them.

The Fischer family business prospered and expanded in the 1950s, first taking over neighbouring premises and then moving to a new site. Stanley Fischer feels that his father would have been happy to stay in Mazabuka, but his mother wanted to move to a town with a Jewish community. She had been asked by her mother in Cape Town before her marriage whether she really wanted to 'live in the jungle'. His father was fortunate to be able to sell the business in 1956 to CBC Ltd. The family then moved to Bulawayo, and it was there that Stanley became involved with the Zionist youth group, Habonim. He then acquired an interest in Israel which he has maintained ever since. His remarkable career will be considered in a later chapter.

Lusaka

Wolf Rybko provided the following catalogue of the activities of the Jews in Lusaka in 1947:

> There are twelve Jewish shopkeepers who serve the European trade, one jeweller, one tailor, one shoemaker, one hairdresser, one doctor, one solicitor, one dry-cleaner, one cinema operator, two electricians, two plumbers, one radio engineer, one dressmaker, two farmers, one brickfield owner, one miller, one book-keeper, one cinema owner and five government officials.[17]

The Jews were still mainly involved in retail trade and the provision of services, but Asian traders had largely succeeded in excluding them from African trade which was confined, at least in theory, to the town's second-class trading area. It was only in the later 1940s and early 1950s that Asians were allowed to open shops in the central business district on Stanley Road, now Freedom Way. It was not until the end of the latter decade that they were able to penetrate Cairo Road.

While the last of the Kollenbergs, Henrie, left Lusaka in 1947, two of the oldest-established Jewish families, the Glassers and the Fischers, remained in the town after the war. Frieda Glasser remained the doyenne of the community until her death in 1958 after nearly fifty years in the town. She is buried in the Jewish section of the Old Cemetery in Rhodes Park. After the departure of her son, Louis, at the end of the war, her younger son started his own shop under his own name, Goodman's, in 1945. He worked with his wife to build up a successful department store catering mainly for the European market. He ran it until 1965 when he closed the business. His name is perpetuated in Goodman House in Cairo Road, a shop and office building, which he put up on the site of the store. He was a prominent member of the business community, and was chairman of the Lusaka Chamber of Commerce for twenty-one years. He retired to Cape Town in 1970 where he still lives in a house with a fine view of the Atlantic Ocean – as different a setting as can be imagined from Lusaka where he was born, and spent the first fifty-six years of his life.[18]

Sam Fischer was the doyen of the community until his death in 1957. He continued to serve on the Lusaka Township Management Board until a few years before his death. His main business ventures remained his cinema and properties in the town, though he had made an ill-fated venture into gold mining with the purchase, just before the war, of the small Jessie mine which is about 150 miles north-east of Lusaka. He had been forced to abandon this during the war because of the difficulties of obtaining supplies, not to mention the danger of lions in the area. Writing to Roy Welensky in 1953, he described his involvement in raising £1,000 for the celebration of the coronation of Queen Elizabeth II in that year. There had been free showings of the film 'A Queen is Crowned' in his cinema for 2–3,000 school children, both black and white. For this, and many other public services, dating back to his work on the Distressed British Subjects committee during the depression, and including his work for the reception of German Jewish refugees, and the provision of free entertainment to British troops during the war, he was awarded the MBE in 1956. He was already terminally ill, and the Governor, Sir Arthur Benson, made the unusual gesture of coming to his house to bestow the honour. He died at Sea Point, Cape Town, in February 1957.[19]

Sam Fischer's nephew, Jack Fischer, who had been educated in Lusaka and South Africa, returned to the town in 1946 after six years' service in the Northern Rhodesia Regiment in Abyssinia, Madagascar and Burma. He has provided a fascinating account of his experiences as an officer, and the experiences of thousands of black troops, during the Japanese withdrawal

from the Arakan between December 1944 and August 1945. He rarely saw
the enemy, and his unit took few prisoners, but he endured some of the
worst conditions experienced by allied troops anywhere during the war,
including a cholera outbreak which killed many of his troops. He is one of
those survivors of the war in Burma who feels that his life may well have
been saved by the use of atomic weapons at Hiroshima and Nagasaki.

On his return to Lusaka, he did not simply move into his uncle's business
but developed his own interests. He played an important role as a pioneer
in the development of light industry in the town. He became a master
printer, and took over the Commercial Press in 1949. He was also involved
in the supply of office equipment and the manufacture of steel furniture, as
well as in a company which assembled truck bodies. He was a member of
the Lusaka Town Council for six years from 1956, and served as mayor in
1960–61. The town's elevation to the status of city was announced by Queen
Elizabeth, the Queen Mother, on her visit to Lusaka in 1960 – a highlight
of his period in office – and he became the first mayor of the city of
Lusaka. He married his uncle's widow, Sigrid, in 1958. She not only served
as lady mayoress, but continued to run a successful dress shop, the Red
Robe, until their departure from the town in 1966. The engineering business
was taken over at that time by Sigrid's brother, Hans Rowelsky, who ran it
until his death in 1974.[20]

Some other old-timers survived the war and remained in business after it,
though, in some cases, it was not for long. 'Tubby' Wulfsohn, who had been
so active in the refugee reception committee, and is described by Alf Metzger
as a 'lovely man', was involved in a succession of partnerships, but seems to
have been unable to establish a stable business. He died tragically in 1949
after the failure of a scheme for the importation of prefabricated housing.
His daughter, Frieda, worked on the Copperbelt as a nurse, until she went
on *aliyah* to Israel in the mid-1960s.[21]

David Shapiro left Lusaka soon after the war and moved to Salisbury, but
he retained a controlling interest in his milling company. In the early 1950s,
Harry Wulfsohn helped his younger brother, Wulfie, to become a partner in
Shapiro's Milling which was greatly expanded at this time. This was necessary
to meet the demand for what was then a new and more refined type of
maize meal: 'roller' meal. The mill, in which Shaya Donin, a Sephardic Jew
from Southern Rhodesia, became a partner, also began to produce sorghum
malt for the brewing of opaque beer for the African market. Wulfie Wulfsohn
was, with his wife, Millicent Dombie, whom he married in 1950, an active
supporter of UNIP in the years immediately before and after independence.
The Wulfsohns left the country following the sale of Shapiro's Mill to the
National Milling Company in 1970, and now live in London.[22]

Many of the shops serving European customers, to which Rybko referred,
were new, and were owned by the German Jewish refugees who arrived
before the war. They included the Rowelskys, the Mohrers, the Caminers, the

Fraenkels and the Hamburgers, though both Hans Rowelsky and Hilda
Caminer may have been included in 1947 in the list of civil servants. There
are probably few residents of Lusaka today who know that the various
branches of Rovell Fashions, now in Lebanese ownership, owe their name to
the Rowelskys. Horst Caminer brought in new equipment for his dry-cleaning
business after the war, and, in the mid-1950s, his wife Hilda started her own
dress shop, 'Milady's', which she ran until the early 1970s. The Mohrers
expanded their hairdressing salon and started to sell jewellery, watches, and
mainly classical gramophone records. Solly Heilbronn ran Solly's Bakery.
Among post-war arrivals was Heinz Guttman who had spent the war in
Kenya, and married Jack Fischer's sister, Ann. A toy and furniture shop
bearing their name survives in Cha Cha Cha Road. There were, however,
also a number of shops catering for the European market which were run
by people who had arrived in the 1930s. The Mendelsohns continued to run
their clothes shops, Mendy's and Kay's, until the untimely death of Sam in
1956. Their son, Moggy, remained in the town until the mid-1960s as the
proprietor of 'Moggy's Milk Bar', and a bookmaker's shop. The Hurwitzes
and the Gerbers also remained in business in the town. Jackie Gerber's
monopoly position as the town's only plumber was ended in the early 1950s
by the arrival of a second Jewish plumber, Ephraim Grill.[23]

George 'Lippy' Lipschild's stationery and artists' materials shop prospered
in the post-war years, and the family moved into a house, 'May Villa', in
Fairview. He had acquired a number of agencies including one for Imperial
Typewriters. He remained in business in Lusaka until the mid-1970s, and was
probably the last Jewish shopkeeper in Lusaka to attend personally to his
customers. His wife, May, was awarded the MBE in 1958 for her services to
the British Empire Ex-Servicemen's League and the Girl Guides. The Lips-
childs' only son, Barnett, known as 'Sonny', had been killed in action in the
Korean War. In his last years in Lusaka, Lipschild was noted both for the
fabulous extent of his stock, and for his apparent reluctance to part with it.
He achieved everlasting, but involuntary, fame as a consequence of events
which followed the sale of what President Kaunda described – a little
ambiguously – as his 'antique' shop in 1975. He sold the shop, and undeveloped plots adjacent to it, to Solar Investments who immediately resold
them for a substantial profit to the Development Bank of Zambia. This
provoked Kaunda's 'Watershed Speech' in which he announced the abolition
of freehold property rights, and prohibited the practice of estate agency. An
interview with Kaunda, in which Lipschild sought, and received, permission
to externalise funds for his retirement, may have drawn attention to the
apparently excessive profits which had been made by the resale of the
properties.[24]

The electricians Joe and Fritz Behrens were, perhaps, the most successful
of the German refugees who remained in Lusaka. They built up a large
electrical equipment and service business which continues to operate under

their name. They also became involved in the cinema business, and built the Twentieth Century cinema in central Lusaka. It was in competition with the Fischers' Carlton cinema which continued to be supplied by the Schlesinger Organisation.

Other important newcomers to the town in the post-war years included Abe Galaun and the Szeftel brothers whose battle for dominance in the butchery business is discussed in another chapter, as is the nationalist campaign to end the segregation of shops in the mid-1950s. This was not an issue for the smaller and more specialised shops which were usually prepared to accept African patronage – their main criterion for admission being their customers' ability to pay. Jewish businesses continued to dominate the central business district of Lusaka until shortly before independence. By that time, however, Asian competition had become more intense. There are a number of shops in the town today which still bear the names of their original Jewish owners, but they are all now in Asian, or Lebanese, ownership.

In Broken Hill, the Hochstein girls and Myer Brin were the main survivors from the pre-war period. Most of the other Jewish businesses in the town, where there was strong Asian competition, were in the hands of refugees from Germany. Siegfried Rosenberg died in 1961, and the Premier Bakery, and grocery, was carried on by his son Gert, who had resigned from his job as senior metallurgist at the Chingola mine in 1955. He continued to run the business with his wife, Marianne von Geldern, a German Jewish refugee who had moved with her family to Chile as a child, until shortly before their departure from Zambia in 1966. His last service to the country was as the supervisor of petrol rationing in Broken Hill during the crisis which followed Southern Rhodesia's UDI. They moved first to Chile, and now live in the Canary Islands. Other traders included H. Jablonski, from East Prussia, who ran a hardware shop, and Josef and Bertie Rotter, who came from Vienna, and, after the war, took over the Jacobsons' store which they ran for many years. She had been a concert pianist with the Vienna Symphony Orchestra, and had organised fund-raising concerts in the town during the war.[25]

The Copperbelt

Wolf Rybko, visiting the Copperbelt towns in 1947, noted that there was quite a marked difference between Ndola and Luanshya on the one hand and Kitwe, Mufulira and Chingola on the other hand. Ndola was the first town in the Rhodesias which he had visited in which there was not a single Jewish 'general dealer'. In Luanshya he was told by Joseph Minchuk that, as a consequence of Asian competition, Jewish traders had been forced out of 'Native' trade. The 'closed township' system delayed for about twenty years the penetration of Asian traders into the other centres. Jewish traders and companies were the major, though not the only, beneficiaries of a system which was intended to protect European business in general.

There were complaints during the war that Copperfields Cold Storage and Northern Caterers had abused their monopoly position in Chingola which did not formally become a closed township until 1945. In December 1942 the District Commissioner conflated the two companies and noted that:

> members of the public are no better disposed towards the two Copperfields Cold Storage enterprises here, the bakery and butchery. The general feeling is that these monopolies do not cater for the public sufficiently as there is no opposition and that they will welcome the time when they can place their trade elsewhere. This is the type of reaction which is bound to occur when monopolies exist.[26]

By the later 1940s, there was increasing pressure for the opening of the 'closed townships', especially Kitwe. This came from, among others, Roy Welensky and spokesmen for the white Northern Rhodesian Mineworkers Union. They wished to open a cooperative society department store in the town, but found their way blocked by the 'closed township' regulations. The government appointed a commission of inquiry into the matter in 1948 on which Maurice Gersh, who was hardly disinterested, represented the Associated Chambers of Commerce. The commission recommended the maintenance of the system, arguing that the government was bound by its earlier promises and that existing legislation allowed for the opening of new businesses if the need could be shown. It recommended the opening of a number of specialised retail outlets in Kitwe, as well as a cooperative department store, and a third garage. Maurice Gersh dissented from the latter proposal.[27]

In evidence to the commission, Mrs Sarah Taylor Zaremba, secretary of the Copperbelt Co-operative Society, attacked the stranglehold which a few companies had over the trade of Kitwe. Northern Caterers, Copperfields Cold Storage, Economy Stores and Kitwe Stores all came in for criticism. She maintained that these traders had not only achieved a monopoly position, but had also bent the rules to suit themselves by selling commodities which were not covered by their licences. She alleged that Economy Stores was selling Hudson motor cars on a general dealer's licence – a practice which was apparently permitted. Frank Maybank, the communist trade unionist, also gave evidence to the commission and is likely to have been equally critical, but his evidence does not seem to have survived.[28]

There does not appear to have been an anti-Semitic element in these criticisms of trade monopolies. In practice Jewish traders benefited from the stronger prejudices which were harboured by many settlers against Asian businesses. This point was rather well made by Doris Lessing in *Going Home*: 'And of course there is anti-semitism; or a complicated anti-anti-semitism, thus: Jews are all right; the Indians are the Jews of Africa.' It was argued by some people at this time that the boycott of Asian businesses by African consumers in Luanshya, which had been prolonged for three months in

1947, had been justified on the grounds that prices in the Kitwe shops were lower. This was taken as evidence that the monopoly position of traders in the 'closed' townships did not have the effect of putting up prices. It was not until the late 1950s, not long before independence, that Asian traders began to penetrate the 'closed townships' of Mufulira, Chingola and Kitwe. In October 1959 the *Northern News* carried a report with the sensational headline: 'White traders believe Asians will take over NR – another East Africa?' It reported that over twenty shops in Mufulira had been acquired by Asian businessmen since the beginning of the year. These included four shops in the town's main street, twelve out of eighteen shops in the second-class trading area, and five shops in the African township's business area. The report claimed that there was over-trading in Luanshya as a result of a less spectacular growth of Asian business in the previous five years. There were seven Asian shops in Kitwe's second-class trading area, and efforts were being made to penetrate the city centre. Negotiations were under way for the purchase of a Chingola department store. European traders were said to be surprised at the prices paid. There was a suggestion that the purchases were being financed by cheap loans from a Bombay finance house. The Dotsons, who did research in the early 1960s on the Asian communities in central Africa, believed that some Asian businessmen were paying more for Jewish businesses than they were worth in order to acquire their licences. Maurice Rabb noted that Susman Brothers and Wulfsohn sold some shops on the Copperbelt to Asian businessmen at this time. He said that they would otherwise have found it difficult to acquire trading sites. There was also in the mid-1950s a marked increase in the number of trading licences which were being given for shops in the 'compounds' to a newly emerging class of African traders.[29]

Kitwe

Kitwe was the largest town in the country until independence. In the immediate post-war years its population, both black and white, was twice that of Lusaka, which was also smaller in terms of population than Mufulira and Luanshya. As in other places, the stable core of the Jewish population on the Copperbelt was provided by people who established businesses and put down roots. In Kitwe the same group of traders continued to provide the nucleus · of the population until the 1960s. The most influential of them were the Gersh brothers, whose varied activities are dealt with elsewhere. Maurice Gersh served as mayor of Kitwe, 1954–56. His wife, Reevee Melamed, was born in Lithuania and came as a child with her mother and eight siblings to Johannesburg in 1919. Her brother, Max Melamed, also lived for a while in Kitwe in the 1950s. One of her nephews is Dan Jacobson, the writer, whose book *The Electronic Elephant* describes a nostalgic journey from Kimberley along the Line of Rail through the northern Cape and Botswana to

Livingstone, and shows a special interest in the disappearance of the small
Jewish communities of the region. Most recently, he has published *Heshel's
Kingdom* which tells the story of the Melamed family and their fortunate
escape, through timely emigration, from the Holocaust. Among the Gershes'
employees was Eli Lurie who arrived in the town in 1935, and worked for
Economy Stores for over twenty years, before starting his own business in
the late 1950s. Morris Goldstein, who set up a mineral water factory and a
garage, was also a former employee.[30]

David Kollenberg, with his wife Joan, had moved to the town in 1938,
and remained there until his death in the early 1960s. He formed a partnership
with Teddy Herr, who had arrived on the Copperbelt from Lithuania in 1927
and died in Kitwe in 1968. Their joint enterprises operated under the name
of Kolherr. Teddy and Shirley Herr's daughter, Deirdre, married Nathan
'Gus' Leibowitz, an accountant, who arrived in the town in 1961, built up his
own mining supplies business, and has lived there ever since. The Kollenberg
family was also represented between 1947 and 1969 by Len Pinshow with his
wife Nina, daughter of Isadore Kollenberg. Pinshow, as we have seen,
managed the Copperfields Cold Storage business throughout this period and
was six times chairman of the Kitwe Chamber of Commerce. The Tow
brothers, who set up their foundry in Kitwe in 1954, were also connected to
the Kollenbergs through the marriage of Max Tow to Doreen, daughter of
Henrie Kollenberg.[31] Nathan Schulman lived in Kitwe in the post-war years
as general manager of Northern Caterers, a firm in which the Kollenbergs
had a large share, and was succeeded by Len Pinshow. Max and Sylvia Barnett
were closely associated with Kitwe, as were related members of the Barnett
and Bernstein families, but they also spent some of the post-war period in
Mufulira.

The doyen of Kitwe's Jewish community was, until his death in 1960,
Sidney Diamond. According to Len Pinshow, Diamond did not attend
religious services after his marriage, but was never found wanting as a member
of the Chevra Kadisha, which provided vigils at funerals. He and Pinshow
took the midnight shift. In the post-war years, Diamond took over some of
the shops of his neighbours and competitors and built up what Dennis
Figov describes as the best department store in central Africa. The secrets
of his success seem to have included his single-minded dedication to, and
affable cigar-smoking presence in, the shop. He was apparently trying to sell
his business, which included eight shops catering for the African market in
the second-class trading area and in the compounds, in the year before his
death for over £1 million. His personal achievement as a trader was the
more remarkable because, unlike his main competitors, he did not have the
backing of an extended family in the region, or of multi-national interests.
He eventually outdid all his rivals in Kitwe as a shopkeeper, though he did
not have the vision which took the Gershes into a wide variety of other
activities.

Arthur Kaplan, a post-war representative of the South African and Southern Rhodesian clothing manufacturers, recalls that Diamond was, as a buyer, 'huge'. He was, by the 1950s, big enough to be able to dictate his own terms to the Bulawayo wholesalers and agents. He recalls that Diamond was the best customer in southern Africa for South Africa's leading manufacturer of women's slacks. He was a shrewd trader, but a hard man with whom to do business. Standard Trading, which began to decline after his death, was scheduled for takeover in the Mulungushi reforms of 1968, and became part of the ZCBC group. His widow, Molly, has continued to live in Kitwe which has now been her home for over sixty years. Their daughter, Maxine, worked for the company in the mid-1960s as a buyer, but moved with her husband to Greece and later Bulgaria, where they have run clothing factories. Their son, Maurice, lives at Siavonga, and has been involved in the Lake Kariba fisheries and the restaurant business.[32]

Luanshya

Isaac Zlotnik, Sydney Sussman and Joseph Minchuk, whose earlier careers have been outlined, continued in business in the town in the post-war years, as did the Rosens, the Figovs and the Rayners. The latter were among the most public-spirited of the Jewish business people on the Copperbelt. Maurice Rosen and his son, Philip, Harry Figov and his son, Dennis, and Harry Rayner were all actively involved in local government. When Harry Figov died in 1945, Harry Rayner took charge of the business until 1957 when Dennis returned to the town after completing a commerce degree at the University of Cape Town, and training as an accountant. He continued to run a general store and grocery until the mid-1970s, but dropped out of retail trade because of the problems caused by price controls and foreign exchange shortages. He had been able to subsidise his trading business from the profits of his activities as an estate agent, but, when dealing in property was prohibited in 1975, it was no longer possible for him to do this. His main business since then has been as Zambia's best-known auctioneer – an activity which he took over from Harry Rayner. His shop, which now serves as an auctioneer's showroom, is the only one in Zambia which has been in the ownership of the same Jewish family since it was built in the 1930s.

Dennis Figov, with his wife Maureen, has shown extraordinary dedication to the public life of a town in which his family have now lived for over sixty years. It is a town which has suffered, along with the rest of the Copperbelt, severely from the economic decline which began in the early 1970s. He was mayor of the town for two years in 1963 and 1964, the last year of Federation and the first of independence, and served for many years as chairman of the Chamber of Commerce. He was in the 1960s an active member of UNIP, and served as branch treasurer of the party. He was, however, critical of UNIP's dismantling of the old structures of municipal government, and of the decision to end the sale of electricity by the municipalities. This had been a major independent source of revenue for the Copperbelt towns. He has also been an active member of Rotary International, and has, with his wife, served on innumerable local committees, dealing with all aspects of the life of the town.[33]

Chingola

The most successful of the Chingola traders was B. I. Menashe, whose B. I. Stores became the town's largest department store. He was for many years the chairman of the town's Chamber of Commerce and represented the business community as a witness to the Closed Township Commission in 1948. He had apparently led resistance on the part of the Nchanga traders to the move to Chingola. In 1954 he had, in addition to his department store, two African trading stores in Chingola's government and mine townships. He was alarmed by events in the Congo in 1960 which adversely affected the Sephardic community of which he was a prominent member. He later told Sir Roy Welensky that he had transferred £165,000 to Salisbury at that time. According to his brother, Victor Menashe, who left the town in 1960, speculation on the Johannesburg and Salisbury stock exchanges had added to his wealth which may also have been increased by his links with the Amato brothers. He was a long-serving director of their company, Rhodesia Congo Oil and Soap Industries.[34]

Menashe's brother-in-law, Nahman Israel, also remained in business in the town. Only one of his four sons chose to live and work in the country. Albert Israel, who had, as a young man, served in Israel's War of Liberation in 1948, was a founder of Associated Printers. He was an active member of the Jewish community, and was also a member of Chingola's municipal council. He moved to Kitwe in 1965, and stayed there until his death in the early 1990s. The Dobkins brothers, Moss and Andrew, and Harry Dorsky, who remained in the town until his death in 1969, continued to provide the stable core of an otherwise rather unstable Jewish community. They were joined in 1956 by David and Doreen Marcus, who remained for ten years. She was the daughter of Henry Herbstein, formerly of the Congo and Broken Hill. He spent the last years of his life in Chingola and is buried in the Kitwe cemetery.[35]

The majority of Jews on the Copperbelt in the post-war years were employed on the mines and as shop assistants. These people tended, however, to be transient and seldom stayed for more than a few years. Rybko collected statistics for the number of Jews employed on the mines in 1947. There were surprising differences between the various mines. At Nkana there were thought to be about thirty Jewish employees, a marked increase since the pre-war period. At Luanshya there were only eight. At Mufulira there were seven underground miners, and thirteen surface workers, but at Nchanga there was only one Jewish mine employee. Most of the Jews who were working on the mines at that time were young men from eastern Europe and Germany. Many of them had arrived in the country as refugees in the years before the war. Whether they started work on the Copperbelt as miners or as shop assistants, there was a tendency for those who stayed for any length of time to open their own businesses. Lazar Benigson, for instance, who had first come to work in Livingstone, Broken Hill and Luanshya in the 1930s, returned to work on the Nkana mine in 1948 after a period in the south, and set up 'compound' stores which he ran with his brother until his departure in the early 1970s.[36]

Mufulira

In Mufulira, Uri Illion had held a farewell party when he sold his shop, which became MacClellands, in 1947 and went to Johannesburg. He must have returned soon afterwards and remained in business in the town. He continued to be an active member of the town council and of the Hebrew Congregation for many years. Julius (Yudel) Minchuk and Cyril Sussman helped to provide the commercial core of a community which was somewhat exceptional in that long-term mine employees were also a stabilising factor. Frank Buch, who came from Lainsburg in the Karoo and was a graduate of the University of Cape Town, had joined Rhodesian Selection Trust as a mine chemist at Luanshya in 1933 and rose very rapidly to become general manager of the Mufulira mine soon after the war. He ended a remarkable career as deputy general manager of Rhodesian Selection Trust. It may or not have been coincidental that there were a number of other Jewish professionals who remained with the mine for a long time. Barry Epstein ran the water purification plant for many years, and later became a partner with Albert Israel in Associated Printers. He was politically active, and was close to Simon Kapwepwe. Samuel Surdut, who arrived from Lithuania with his wife, Fanny, late in 1939, was an operator at the smelter for many years. Harry Favish, who was also of Lithuanian origin, worked underground. His wife was, unusually for the time, from a Sephardic family. There were a number of Sephardic families, including the Nahmans, who may have been from Egypt, and the Israels, who lived in Mufulira in the post-war years.[37]

David Messerer, whose contribution to the religious life of the community, and to local government, is described elsewhere, built up over many years a large electrical engineering business which reached its peak after independence, when he undertook contracts for the electrification of secondary schools and other developments all over the country. He was also involved in the electrification of the township at the new Chibuluma mine, and of the housing at the Kariba North Bank hydro-electric project. At one stage he had over 250 employees. He was joined in the town in 1955 by his brother Alex and his wife Fanny, who stayed for over fifteen years. By the 1970s his

business faced difficulties as a result of regulations for the award of government contracts which discriminated against non-Zambian businesses, but he
remained in the town until 1981, when he was the last of the Jewish
community to leave.[38]

Ndola

Although Ndola grew quite rapidly after the war as an administrative, commercial and industrial centre, it always took second place to Kitwe in terms
of size and population. As the social anthropologist A. L. Epstein discovered
in the mid-1950s, it differed quite markedly in character from the other
Copperbelt centres as it had never been a mine or company town.[39] After
the death of Hyam Schulman in 1950, the most prominent member of
Ndola's Jewish community was Abe Lowenthal. He was a public-spirited
person who was on the town council for a number of years and whose name
is commemorated by the Lowenthal Theatre, which still survives, and by a
street. He was concerned about proper housing for Ndola's African population, and fought hard for the electrification of the town's 'compounds'. He
was not conventionally religious, but he was very knowledgeable about
Judaism, including such arcane subjects as the Kabbala, and passed on to his
children a strong sense of their Jewish identity. He was not politically
outspoken, but was essentially liberal in matters of race. He objected strongly,
as his daughter Isa Teeger remembers, to the manifestations of racism which
were so prevalent in colonial society. His second wife, Hessie, was very
active in Jewish communal organisations, especially in the Women's International Zionist Organisation (WIZO). Abe Lowenthal died at the early age
of fifty-six in 1960. His son Mark returned to the town as a young doctor
a few months later and lived there until 1974.[40]

The second major figure in the Jewish community in Ndola in the post-
war period was Hanan Elkaim who succeeded Abe Lowenthal as the informal
leader of the community. He came from Palestine, a member of a Sephardic
family which had moved from Fez, Morocco, to Gaza in the 1850s. They
had, with other members of the small Jewish community of the town, been
forced to abandon their home in 1929 during communal riots. Hanan was
fifteen years old at the time and had vivid memories of his family's escape
from Gaza. He came out to Africa in 1938 in order to help to support his
family in Palestine. He was drawn to central Africa by a relative, Ephraim
Cohen from Jerusalem, who was a chemist in Bulawayo for many years.
Hanan's first job in the country was as a supervisor on the building of the
Kitwe–Ndola road. He lived for a while in Mufulira, spent a year or so in
the Congo, building the airport at Elisabethville, and settled in Ndola at the
end of the war. He eventually took over the contracting business for which
he worked. He was not only one of the country's most enthusiastic Zionists,
but also played an important role in the building of Ndola's synagogue. He

was an ecumenically-minded man and was generous in the building and road-making work which he did for the Christian churches, especially Ndola's Catholic church of which he was an honorary member. He also had close contacts with the Hindu, Muslim and Bahai communities. He was both a Mason and a Rotarian, and his philanthropic work was recognised when, not long before his death in 1991, he was made a member of the Order of Distinguished Service (First Division) by President Kaunda. His nephew, Avner Elkaim, came from Israel and spent some time on the Copperbelt in the mid-1950s before moving to Bulawayo where he became prominent in the textile industry. He married Ronnie Furmanowsky, daughter of Joe Furmanowsky, formerly of Livingstone.[41]

When Marta Paynter arrived in 1945, there were, she recalls, a number of German refugee families in the town, but they do not seem to have been well integrated into the Jewish community at that time. A meeting which was held for Rabbi Konviser in 1946 was attended by only twenty-two people, and Rybko identified less than a dozen heads of families. There was a significant increase in the Jewish population in the mid-1950s when it was reported that a dozen families had recently arrived, and that there was a regular attendance at the *shul* of about forty-five people. Prominent members of the Jewish community in Ndola included Nathan Gordon, who continued to run a cycle shop, and Julius Schlitner (later known as Slater), who came from Austria and worked at first for Abe Lowenthal. He built up a substantial business – the Ndola Milling Company – in the years after the war. Both he and Nathan Gordon were married to sisters of Len Dobkins who was also in business in the town. Jacob and Zena Katz were important figures in the Hebrew Congregation throughout the post-war period, and were eventually joined there by Jacob's two brothers, Max and Chaim. The careers of two prominent women doctors, Manya Damie and Sylvia Lehrer, are discussed in a later chapter.[42]

Decline

There were a number of shocks before independence which may have contributed to the beginning of a decline in the Jewish population of Northern Rhodesia as a whole. An economic downturn, which began in 1958 and lasted until 1963, may have unsettled some people. The Congo crisis of 1960 may also have had a disturbing influence, especially on the small community in Chingola which had the closest links with the Sephardic Jews who were so dominant in the economic life of Elisabethville. The Hebrew community halls in both Ndola and Kitwe were made available to accommodate the refugees who passed through on their way to Salisbury at that time. Only a minority of the refugees were, however, Jewish, and David Messerer does not think that the crisis had much impact on the morale of the Northern Rhodesian community as a whole. The Cha Cha Cha campaign of 1961 may also have had an impact, but the imposition of exchange controls by the Federal government two years before independence may have been a more disturbing factor, especially for people who had been forced to leave Germany in the 1930s with a single suitcase.[43]

Although there was a strong liberal element within the Jewish community, including a surprisingly large number of people, such as the Wulfsohns, Iljons, Radunskis and Figovs, who were sympathetic to the African nationalist movement and gave moral and financial help to it, the majority of Jews were no different in their political and racial attitudes from the bulk of the settler population. They did not look forward to a future under black majority rule. Departures began before independence, and accelerated in the years immediately after it. Among the reasons which were commonly given for departure was fear about the quality of education. This had become a more serious concern as most parents during the Federal period kept their children in the country for primary education.

The late 1960s were a boom time with unprecedentedly high copper prices, a great increase in the purchasing power of the black population, and a great deal of government expenditure on development projects. At the same time, however, life was made difficult for businessmen by the effects of UDI in Southern Rhodesia, the disruption of established lines of supply, and by fuel shortages. A few Bulawayo-based Jewish businessmen with Zambian links, such as Alan Feigenbaum and Avner Elkaim, as well as Victor Cohen, who was to become so prominent in the Zimbabwe textile industry and to take over the Frame group's share in Zambia Textiles, bucked the trend. They set up clothing factories in Livingstone at this time in order to avoid the new customs barriers which were established after the end of Federation.[44] But the majority of Jewish businessmen had left Zambia with their families before the Mulungushi Reforms of 1968–69 which restricted businesses owned by non-citizens to the former first-class trading areas of the main towns. There were only a few Jewish businessmen, such as Teddy Herr, the Benigsons and Harry Dorsky, who continued in the late 1960s to have shops in the compounds and second-class trading areas, and who were, therefore, affected by these measures.[45]

It was not difficult for those who wished to remain to obtain Zambian citizenship, but the majority of Jewish businessmen chose not to do so. Almost invariably, whether in Livingstone, Lusaka or on the Copperbelt, the Jewish-owned businesses which were not taken over by parastatal companies were bought by Asian traders. Lewis Gann, followed by the Dotsons, had already identified in the 1960s an ethnic succession in which the same shop might pass from Scots to Jewish to Asian and, finally, to Zambian ownership.[46] In the Luapula province, for instance, many of Isaac Zlotnik's stores, some of which may have been founded by the African Lakes Corporation, were taken over before independence by the Patel brothers, who were based, as Zlotnik had been, in Luanshya. They still own his former Fort Rosebery shop, now known as the House of Mansa, but have sold some other shops to Zambian traders.[47] It would be interesting to investigate further – though there is not space to do so here – the role of Jews, as well as Scots, Greeks and Asians, in training Zambian entrepreneurs, many of whom either worked for such traders, or are the children of men who worked for them as shop assistants, *capitãos* and store managers. The Galauns, who not only stayed on but expanded their business interests in the years following independence, are an exception to the general rule. It is to their story that we will now turn.

CHAPTER 10

The Galaun Story

Abe Galaun is today the doyen of Zambia's small Jewish community. He has been the dominant figure in the community since independence, and is unusual in that he built up his business in the years when most other Jews were leaving the country. The roots of Abe's success lie, as with the Susmans, in Barotseland, but it was in and around Lusaka that he became the essential butcher and grazier, benefiting from the rapid growth of the population of the city in the years after independence.[1]

Abe was born in the *shtetl* of Vorne, near Riteve, in Lithuania, then part of the Russian empire, in July 1913. He was the fifth of ten children. Among his ancestors were farmers and rabbinical scholars. His father was a butcher, and accompanying him on cattle-buying expeditions was part of Abe's childhood experience. His father was not, however, a successful businessman, and was supported latterly by remittances from his children in South Africa. Three of Abe's elder brothers and a daughter emigrated to South Africa between 1926 and the mid-1930s. One of his brothers became the promoter of a property development north of Johannesburg: Vorne Valley. Abe's elder siblings emigrated to South Africa because the United States was effectively closed to them by the quota system. They were attracted to South Africa because they already had cousins in the country.

According to Abe, there were three main reasons why Jews chose to leave Lithuania. These were military conscription, anti-Semitism and poverty. Abe chose to do his military service, but left as soon as he had completed it. He did not, he says, hate Lithuania. He was concerned to bring about progressive change in the country and was a member of the communist underground movement. He disapproved of business, had no intention of becoming a businessman, and has always thought of himself as a socialist. He left the country for South Africa in December 1938 because, as he says: 'I could feel Hitler approaching. I was one of the lucky ones.' Hitler took his first bite out of Lithuania three months later when he seized the town of Memel. Abe felt the pain of leaving his home and his parents. When he reached Cape Town, he heard the news of his father's death. It was, as it transpired, a fortunate death. Abe's mother and his youngest sister were murdered in the Holocaust. Another sister joined the partisans, survived the war, and emigrated to Palestine soon afterwards.

Abe himself had originally wanted to go to Palestine. He had spent a year at a Zionist agricultural training school, but the restrictions on Jewish immigration made it impossible for him to enter Palestine legally. In South Africa he was also faced by the quota system, and was allowed to stay for only six weeks with his family in Johannesburg. His brothers then remembered that they had a relative, Max Taube, who had been in Livingstone since before the First World War. He had started out as a plumber, and eventually ran a hardware store. It was through him that Abe obtained a visa for Northern Rhodesia which he entered on 28 February 1939 with, so he says, £2 in his pocket. People in South Africa were sorry for him as he left for the north which they saw as a graveyard. Abe's first impression of Livingstone was that it was 'like a little dorp'.

Abe's first eighteen months in the country were to be the most frustrating of his life. Livingstone was in a depressed state, and he could not find a job there. While looking around on the Copperbelt for something to do, he met Chaim Katz who had recently arrived from Palestine. Chaim suggested that he should collect scrap metal on the Copperbelt for sale to the foundry at Luanshya's Roan Antelope mine.[2] He went on to Lusaka and Livingstone looking for 'any old iron'. He paid £5 a ton and had it sent up to Luanshya on the train. He collected thirty tons of scrap and made a profit of about £80. He had soon collected all that he could, and was back to unemployment. It was not until the middle of 1940 that he got his first real break.

Barotseland

Abe was offered a job as a store manager in Barotseland by Jehiel (also known as Michael) Jacobs. Popularly known by his Lozi name, 'Chipisa', Jacobs had, as we have seen, reached Livingstone before the First World War. He had a farm at Sinda near Livingstone, but his main business was as a wholesaler supplying African hawkers. He also ran stores in Barotseland through his company, the Barotseland Trading Company, which had its headquarters at Mongu. Jacobs had a house in Livingstone, but had no social contact with Livingstone's Jewish community, perhaps because of his relationships with African women. Abe can now recall meeting him on only one occasion when he was appointed to the job. He sent in monthly reports on the business from Mongu, but had no further contact with him. Abe travelled from Livingstone to Mongu via Lusaka as there was still no road between Livingstone and Mongu, and a road from Lusaka to Mongu had only recently been opened. Most European travellers still used river transport.

Mongu was to be Abe's home until the end of the war. On taking up his appointment, he knew very little English. He was accompanied for the first few months by Jacobs's chief clerk, Nelson Nalumango, who acted as his interpreter and helped him to write his reports. Nalumango was related to the Lozi royal family, was a founder of the Livingstone Welfare Association, and a prominent member of the emerging African educated elite. A few years later he was nominated by the colonial government as one of the first African members of the Legislative Council.

An important part of Jacobs's business was the recruitment of labour for railway and road work in Southern Rhodesia. Abe was paid from £30 to £40 a month as a store manager, but also got 7s. 6d. per head for all labour recruited. In a good month he could recruit two or three hundred workers. He employed runners who had to be licensed and wore a badge of office. They brought in labour from as far afield as the Kalabo and Balovale districts, and from beyond the boundary with Angola. Abe was himself responsible for the recruits' provisions and safety on the three-week walk to Livingstone. After a while he acquired another job as agent for the small five-seater plane which began weekly flights to Mongu before the end of the war. He recalls that he was paid £5 a flight and received a 10 per cent commission on ticket sales.

After a year or so at Mongu, Abe began to invest the profits of his various business activities in cattle which he bought from villagers and grazed on the Zambezi flood plain. From 1939 onwards there was a slow recovery in the Barotseland cattle trade as controlled exports were allowed to the government abattoir at Katembora. After eighteen months of purchases, he had accumulated about 200 cattle, and made a good profit on his first sale. This encouraged him to pursue the business further. He reckons that by the time he left Mongu at the end of the war, and went down to Cape Town, he had accumulated £2,500 and 'felt like a millionaire'.

Abe's life in Mongu was not single-mindedly devoted to the accumulation of wealth. He remembers his time there for his very active social life. He maintains that he has never in the ensuing fifty years made as much use of his dinner-jacket as he did then. Mongu was a provincial centre with a European population of about thirty families. Abe was one of seven bachelors, and was soon an active member of this small social network. He feels that his rural upbringing, and his ability to ride a horse, made a good impression on this snobbish circle. At home he had ridden a horse in the winter to get from one place to another, but it was easy to convince a British audience that anyone who could ride a horse well must come from an aristocratic background. Abe was soon captain of the tennis team and a member of the chess circle. His interest in chess endeared him to the Provincial Commissioner, Gordon Read, who became a good friend.

Abe combined this social activity with his socialist beliefs. He established a discussion club at which he gave talks on democracy and promoted friendship with the Soviet Union, Britain's wartime ally. There cannot have been many radicals in Mongu in the early 1940s, but there was at least one. Abe became friendly with Max Gluckman, with whom he shared an interest in the Soviet Union and a Lithuanian Jewish background. Abe remained in touch with Gluckman until his death in 1975, and with his widow, Mary, until her death in the early 1990s.

Abe had lost his faith at the age of fourteen, but he enjoyed the company of missionaries, both Catholic and Protestant. His house became known as a missionaries' rest house. His social circle was not confined to settler society. He was on good terms with the Litunga, Yeta III, who featured earlier in this story as Prince Litia, an early trading partner of the Susmans. King Yeta had suffered a stroke and was partially paralysed, but he frequently sent his car over to collect Abe with whom he enjoyed drinking sherry. He was also friendly with the traditional Prime Minister of the Lozi nation, the Ngambela Wina, and his two young sons, Arthur and Sikota, who were both to play an important part in the struggle for independence, and in post-independence politics. He also recalls the intelligence and local knowledge of Francis Suu, a clerk in the colonial administration who was later a leader of the 'traditionalist' party, the Barotse National Party. Abe became, like many other Jewish traders, a tolerable speaker of siLozi – a skill which he was to find useful in later years in Lusaka, where it eased relationships with some leading political personalities.

Lusaka Cold Storage

As the war ended, Abe moved to Lusaka. After a visit to South Africa in 1945, he married Vera Harris, whom he met through his brothers in Johannesburg. The newly married couple rented a house from George Hurwitz in which electricity had just been installed, but the toilets were outside. There were still no street lights in the town, and the fuel used for cooking was wood and charcoal. The town was still liable to annual floods, and the stream which runs down the centre of Cairo Road had not yet been covered.

Abe had invested some of the proceeds of his Mongu ventures in buying out 'Tubby' Wulfsohn's share in a Lusaka butchery. He then found himself in partnership with E. W. Dechow, who had been the general manager of Werners butcheries until the previous year. Dechow was a heavy drinker and Abe saw his capital rapidly eroding. The partnership was gazetted in August, and dissolved in October, 1945.[3] Dechow then handed over his share in the business in settlement of a debt, and Abe became the sole owner of the Lusaka Butchery with its main branch in Cairo Road, and another in the second-class trading area. He soon found that he had ventured into a business in which competition was fierce. In Lusaka itself the main opposition came from the veteran Sam Haslett, a Scotsman who had acquired fame as a cattle trader and auctioneer in Northern Rhodesia before the First World War. Haslett eventually agreed to merge his business with Abe's, but he insisted that his manager should become a partner in the combined firm. Haslett had rejected Abe's original offer of commercial cooperation, but was persuaded to change his mind when he lost an important government contract to him. Haslett found it particularly galling that, after forty years in the country, he should lose the contract to a younger man when they had both tendered for the same price – six pence and three farthings a pound. Abe attributed his success to the contacts that he had made, and the reputation for honest business which he had acquired, during his years in Barotseland. The new firm, Lusaka Cold Storage Ltd, was registered in January 1946, and continues to occupy Haslett's site on Cairo Road until the present day.[4]

The opposition now came from the big meat firms, especially Werners. The battle here was not over markets, as Abe could not threaten their mine contracts or their Copperbelt retail business, but over sources of supply. When Abe undertook to buy 300 head of cattle from a sympathetic Afrikaner farmer, who usually sold to Werners, Max Barnett, Werners' new manager, was not amused. The farmer was warned that Abe did not have £3,000 in ready money with which to pay. When the farmer demanded cash down, Abe told him that he would be back in two hours with the money. He managed to persuade a bank manager to give him an immediate and unsecured loan of £4,000. Northern Rhodesian banks were not in the habit of gambling, but Abe's powers of persuasion were unusual. He later discovered that this vital loan had caused the bank manager a great deal of trouble with his head office.

This coup secured his position as Lusaka's major butcher, but it did not end his problems with Werners. According to Abe, Max Barnett indicated that they intended to take him over, or to freeze him out of business. They reckoned that they could do this in two weeks by cutting off his sources of supply. In the end a more or less amicable arrangement was worked out. Werners bought out Abe's partner, and secured a majority interest in the firm, though the voting shares were evenly split and Abe stayed on as manager. The company became in effect a subsidiary of Werners. As Abe says, they became partners in his business, but he was not a partner in theirs. It proved to be a successful, if sometimes stormy, partnership which lasted for over twenty years, and was not finally unscrambled until the early 1970s.[5]

Lusaka Cold Storage did not, however, have things all its own way in Lusaka. New competition was provided by the Szeftel brothers, Ben and Sam, who arrived from the Copperbelt, bought a large farm from Henrie Kollenberg, and opened a competitive butchery – the Lusaka Meat Market – in the second-class trading area in 1948. The Szeftel brothers had arrived from Poland shortly before the outbreak of war. Their father had been, like Abe's, a butcher and they had been brought up in the business. Ben and Sam had worked for Copperfields Cold Storage, then under Max Barnett's management, on their arrival in the country. It was not an experience which Ben had enjoyed. He felt that newcomers, 'greeners', were exploited by the large companies.[6]

Both sides agree that the Szeftel brothers provided Lusaka Cold Storage with stiff competition. Initially Ben concentrated on the butcheries, which were in Lusaka's second-class trading area, while Sam concentrated on the farm and on cattle buying. At one stage, they were slaughtering as many as 500–600 cattle a month and had many government contracts. There was, however, a disagreement between the brothers, and in 1951 their partnership was dissolved. Ben took over the butchery, but the farm was sold. Sam left for Southern Rhodesia, while Gutel Szeftel, a cousin, opened up in competition with Ben, and with Abe Galaun. Ben later bought a farm on the Great East Road at Chalimbana which is still being worked by his son, Leslie, today. His elder son, Morris, studied in Cape Town and Manchester, and at the University of Zambia. He is currently a member of the Politics Department at Leeds University. He and his wife, Carolyn Baylies, have written extensively on the political economy of Zambia.

African Nationalism

Abe Galaun has never been a stranger to controversy. He became the major protagonist in a clash with the emerging African nationalist movement over racially discriminatory trading practices which resulted in the first victory of the nationalist movement. In January 1954 the Lusaka butcheries became the target of a mass boycott by African consumers. The boycott, which was launched by the African National Congress, had a deeper political objective than the change of sales practices at Lusaka Cold Storage, and other butcheries. The ANC, which had been frustrated in its efforts to prevent Northern Rhodesia's incorporation into the Federation of Rhodesia and Nyasaland in the previous year, chose the Lusaka butcheries as a target in a campaign which was timed to coincide with a visit to the country by the British Colonial Secretary, Oliver Lyttelton. The boycott was intended to demonstrate the strength of popular feeling against the Federation.[7]

African customers in Lusaka were generally, though not always, excluded from the shops in Cairo Road, and even from some shops in the second-class trading area. In some places they were allowed to enter the shop but were served at counters which were partitioned between Europeans and Africans. In many cases, they were allowed to buy from shops only through 'pigeon-holes', or hatches at the back of the shops. Complaints against these discriminatory practices were not new. Ten years previously, at a time of wartime shortages, African consumers had complained that the major Cairo Road shops refused to sell to them – even through hatches – scarce commodities such as rice and sugar. These were not available in the Asian shops in the second-class trading area, and were sold to Africans in the Cairo Road shops only if they carried notes from Europeans to say that the commodities were required for their own use.[8]

Complaints against the butcheries in 1954 were not confined to the emotive issue of the 'pigeon-holes'. Kenneth Kaunda, Secretary-General of the

African National Congress, in a statement made after the boycott in Lusaka had been in force for seven weeks, referred to a number of other issues. These included the division of shops into African and European sections; the preference which was given to Europeans where they were served at the same counter as Africans; the practice of wrapping meat for African customers without allowing them to inspect it; and the use of what were claimed to be unhygienic wooden cutting blocks. There were also complaints about the poor quality of meat sold to Africans. It was during this struggle that Kenneth Kaunda became, and remained, a vegetarian. He still does not eat red meat.[9]

The boycott was enforced by pickets who were organised by Lewis Changufu, later Minister of Home Affairs. Women were very actively involved in the protest movement.[10] The boycott was sufficiently successful to force the temporary closure of the Lusaka Cold Storage outlet in the second-class area. Abe initially rejected demands for the closure of one and the reorganisation of another of his shops, and refused to meet with representatives of the ANC. Three weeks later he was quoted as taking a less belligerent approach. He then said that the 'pigeon-holes' were not meant for the sale of meat, but for the despatch of European orders by messengers, and that Africans were welcome to enter his two upmarket butcheries. He said: 'We are here purely for commercial purposes and don't discriminate between customers.'[11]

After the boycott had been in force for seven weeks, Abe complained that the problem could have been solved at the beginning if he had given way to Congress demands. In resisting these demands he had acted on the advice of the Lusaka Chamber of Commerce and of the government. He felt that they had failed to back him up in a stand which they had encouraged. A few days later, the Chamber of Commerce agreed to give way to Congress demands. In concessions which did not only relate to butcheries, but to all shops, their spokesmen, Goody Glasser and Richard Sampson, agreed that the hatch system should be phased out and that there should be no sectional service. They also condemned the sale of poor quality meat and said that preference for European customers should be avoided, prices should be displayed, and cases of short weight should be reported.[12]

At a meeting under the chairmanship of Harry Franklin, a nominated member of the Legislative Council, and attended by Galaun and Ben Szeftel, by Glasser and Sampson, and by members of the African Urban Advisory Council, whose leading representative was Safeli Chileshe, it was agreed that sales in all Lusaka shops should in future be on 'a first come, first served' basis. It was agreed that the butchery boycott, which had lasted for nearly two months in Lusaka, and which had resulted in the imprisonment of a number of people on charges relating to illegal picketing, would end on 1 March 1954. Although it is not certain that all the changes promised were immediately implemented, these concessions did represent a first victory for direct action by the ANC. The decision of the Lusaka Chamber of Commerce, as well as the Copperbelt butchers, to give way to the pressure of the boycott was an indication of the growing importance of African purchasing power.[13]

In his old age Abe Galaun puts a slightly different gloss on these events. He maintains that he was always fully conscious of the political importance of the confrontation. He sees it as a landmark in the nationalist struggle for independence and is proud of his own role. He recalls that he had approached the Chief Secretary, A. T. Williams, at the beginning of the boycott, and had asked him to intervene in what was clearly a political conflict. Williams refused to do so, arguing that the issue was economic and not political. The colonial government, which was always sensitive to settler opinion, was unwilling at this stage to take a stand against discriminatory policies which were deeply entrenched. Abe clearly feels that he was caught between settler prejudice and nationalist demands, with a government which chose to sit on the fence. He recalls behind-the-scenes negotiations which, unknown to the contemporary newspapers, ended the boycott. Harry Nkumbula, the President of the ANC, who was reported at one stage in the confrontation to be seeking to raise capital to open an African butchery, came to see him at his house at ten o'clock at night. Abe made him an offer: 'I'll open the doors to all if you call off the boycott.' Nkumbula accepted the offer and it was, he says, this private agreement which underpinned the public negotiations between the Chamber of Commerce and the Urban African Advisory Council. He recalls that there was a rush of black customers into the shops in the first few days of March, but that the excitement soon died down. It was not until much later, in 1960, that the colonial government legislated to end racial discrimination in all public places.

Independence

Abe's role in this crisis was clearly a learning experience for him. He does not conceal his support for the Federation, his friendship with Sir Roy Welensky, nor his active involvement with the United Federal Party. His own early experience of confrontation with African nationalism did not, however, lead him to react against it. Abe Galaun and Kenneth Kaunda were ranged on opposite sides as spokesmen in this crisis, but they were later to develop a harmonious relationship. With the impending collapse of the Federation, and the approach of independence in the early 1960s, Abe was one of the few Jewish shopkeepers who did not sell up and leave the country. He was determined to stay on, and was equally determined to establish his own commercial independence.

Harry Wulfsohn, Harry Robinson and Max Barnett drove a very hard bargain. It was agreed in 1961 that Abe Galaun should buy them out at the rate of £2,000 a month. When he was later unable to meet the payments and went to Salisbury to ask for more time, they showed him no mercy. While he had acquired effective control at that time, it was not until the early 1970s that he was able to gain sole control of Lusaka Cold Storage. Abe and Vera Galaun are, with their son Michael, who has been actively involved in the business since the 1970s and took control of the major enterprises in 1988, unique among Jewish business people in that they not only remained in retail trade after independence, but greatly expanded their business in the post-independence period. The butchery business in Lusaka grew with the dramatic expansion of the population from not much more than 100,000 people at independence to well over one million by the mid-1990s. Suburban butcheries at Woodlands and in Roma had been set up before independence. The Galauns had also diversified into bottle stores and furniture manufacture. Another early diversification was the Palace cinema in the second-class trading area which was the first unsegregated cinema in the town. In the last few years Mike Galaun has set up a chain of combined butcheries and groceries, Jemmy's, which has provided competition in an area which was dominated from the 1970s by Greek traders.

Following his retirement from the major butchery and farming businesses in the late 1980s, Abe launched himself into a variety of new businesses centred on the Grand Hotel in Cairo Road. The building, which dates from the 1920s, encloses an attractive grass quadrangle which has become Abe's domain. The Grand enterprises include a furniture shop, a pharmacy, an insurance broker's business, a travel agency and, perhaps surprisingly, a butchery. Vera has also resisted retirement. She can still be found at work on most days at the Lusaka Cold Storage offices at the other end of Cairo Road.

Farming

In the early 1950s Abe began to extend his activities, as had the Susmans earlier, from the butchery business into farming. There is, perhaps, a natural tendency for butchers to become involved in the production process. There may also be a tendency for traders to put surplus cash into the development of fixed assets. Abe bought a farm on the Great East Road in 1951 and entered into a partnership with an Afrikaans-speaking farmer to develop it. The farm consisted of 3,000 acres of virgin land, and was part of a 200,000-acre block which was sub-divided by the colonial government and allocated on ninety-nine-year leases to people who were prepared to invest a minimum of £3,000. Abe recalls that it took them a day with a compass to find the farm. They had to bring in labour from the Eastern Province to work it. Clearing the bush with a caterpillar tractor, and sinking boreholes, was arduous work. In their first year they grew tobacco on forty acres. As the work of clearing continued, they were able to grow tobacco on 200 acres as well as 1,000 acres of maize. The remainder of the land was used for cattle. This was to be the first of about eight farms, including five in the Ngwerere and International Airport areas, which were to make Abe a major figure in the commercial farming world. The farms, though scattered, extend over about 25,000 acres. The bronze sculpture of a bull, designed by the late Henry Tayali, is a conspicuous landmark at the entrance to Galaunia Farms on the airport road.

It is in the agricultural sphere that Abe and Michael Galaun have made their most remarkable contribution to the economic development of Zambia. They have had as many as 14,000 cattle on their various farms. They have regularly slaughtered 1,000 head of cattle a month to supply their own retail outlets and the many competing butcheries which had been established in Lusaka by the 1980s. They have also been major purchasers of cattle from Zambezi Ranching and Cropping and from what was until recently the Anglo-American Corporation's ranch at Chisamba. A key area in which they invested heavily from the early 1980s was milk and cheese production. They brought in Israeli dairy experts and cheese technologists who played an important part in the redevelopment of this sector. Residents of Lusaka, and of Zambia as a whole, in the late 1970s will recall that there was at that time no edible local cheese, and that the quality of milk produced by the Dairy Produce Board, which had a monopoly, was not high. The pre-independence dairy industry had been forced into decline, and eventual collapse, by price controls. Diamondale cheese and milk – the brand name derives from the name of a farm which previously belonged to A. B. Diamond – have been a welcome addition to the market.

The Galauns' other agricultural activities included the development of horticultural exports, such as sweetcorn and baby marrows for the London market, in the later 1980s. These were profitable for a while and were encouraged by foreign exchange incentives, but have suffered in recent years from unreasonable freight rates and, in the days before the collapse of Zambia Airways, unpredictable flight schedules. The relaxation of exchange controls has also removed some of the incentives which had been attached to agricultural exports. Other areas in which the Galauns have been active include the production and processing of soya beans, both for export and local consumption, through a subsidiary company, Soy Nutrients. They have also been involved in the revival of tobacco production, an area in which Abe was interested from the beginning of his farming days in the early 1950s, when the value of Northern Rhodesia's tobacco exports was second only to copper.

A more sensational development in recent years has been coffee production which was pioneered at Kasama in the Northern Province, but has spread into the Lusaka, Central and Southern provinces. High coffee prices in the last few years, and the high quality of Zambian coffee which is now highly prized on the world market, have helped the Galauns' farming interests to come through the difficult years of drought which affected Zambian agriculture in the early 1990s, and forced many commercial farmers to the verge of bankruptcy. Their farms have produced as much as 300 tons of coffee a year, selling for up to $4,000 a ton.

Community and Social Work

Abe Galaun is a man of unusual energy and has always liked to involve himself in social and community work. Soon after his arrival in Lusaka, he became involved with the affairs of the synagogue, arranging for the re-laying of the floor. It was not, however, until the 1960s that he became chairman of the Lusaka Hebrew Congregation, a position which he held for twenty years. He found on arrival that Lusaka's Jewish establishment of Kollenbergs, Shapiros and Fischers was firmly entrenched. Abe acknowledges that he only rediscovered his religion after his marriage out of respect for his wife Vera's orthodox beliefs. They sought to bring up their children in a traditional, if not orthodox, way.

Their elder son, Jack, was educated in Lusaka, and at the University College of Rhodesia and Nyasaland in Salisbury. He completed a degree in economics and moved to London. After a period of employment as an accountant, he set up his own silk screen business. He has shared his father's interest in community work and has been the honorary secretary of the Commonwealth Jewish Council. Michael Galaun was also educated in Lusaka, completing the sixth form at Kabulonga Boys' School. He recalls that twice a week there was *cheder* (Hebrew school). He attended these classes until his bar mitzvah. He went on from school in Lusaka to the University of Cape Town where he did a degree in commerce before returning to join his father in the business.

Abe Galaun has been known to call himself a Zionist socialist. His commitment to Zionism, and the idea of the Jews as a nation, goes back to his Lithuanian days. In the years before the numerical decline of the Zambian Jewish community in the mid-1960s, Abe was active in the movement, and was a major fund-raiser for Israel. He admits to the use of high pressure tactics to extract what he thought were suitable contributions. He claims that on one occasion he tore up an inadequate cheque from one of the most wealthy members of the community. He played a leading part in the establish-ment of the Council for Zambia Jewry which is described elsewhere. One of his greatest coups was to use his influence with President Kaunda in 1979–80, long after the severing of diplomatic relations between Zambia and Israel in 1973, to arrange for the transfer of nearly K200,000 from the Zambian Jewish community's resources to Israel. This was at a time when exchange controls were tight and the Kwacha was still worth significantly more than a dollar.

Abe was for many years an active member of the Lusaka Chamber of Commerce and of ZINCOM, the predecessor of ZACCI, the Zambia

Association of Chambers of Commerce and Industry. He was a member of the committee which raised funds for the building of the Lusaka Playhouse, and was chairman of the fund-raising committee for the building of the University of Zambia. He has also been an active participant in Rotary International and is a former National Governor. He has recently been involved as chairman in the organisation of a new Zambia Charitable Trust which is intended to raise funds for medical and social purposes. Outside Zambia he has been an active member of the Royal Agricultural Society of the Commonwealth and of the Commonwealth Jewish Council.

Whether as butcher, farmer, entrepreneur, or as community and business leader, Abe Galaun has been an innovative and creative person. He has never been a man to suffer fools gladly, and he is not without his critics. None of them, however, can deny his energy or his staying power. He has not only refused to retire, but continues to take new initiatives in both the commercial and the charitable spheres. Lusaka Cold Storage is now more than fifty years old. He is no longer involved in the day-to-day running of this business, but has seen it through the extraordinary political, social and economic changes which have transformed Lusaka and Zambia not once, but many times, in the last half century. He has not been a passive observer of these events, but has been an active participant who has helped to mould them. Abe, Vera and Michael Galaun have shown a remarkable degree of adaptability, and resourcefulness, and an exceptional long-term commitment to Zambia.

CHAPTER 11

Bigger Business Continued:
Independence and After

There is no reason to believe that the managers of the Susman group of companies viewed independence with foreboding. In the view of David Susman they did, however, suffer something of a 'quantum shock', comparable with the shock experienced by the Afrikaner establishment after the South African elections of 1994. They were used to doing business in an environment in which they knew the decision-makers. They met them regularly, drank and played golf with them. They knew whom to phone to sort out a problem, and had more or less instant access. Three of the leaders of the group, Harry Wulfsohn, Max Barnett and Maurice Gersh were each recipients of the OBE, which served as a seal of approval on the part of both the Federal and the colonial governments. Maurice Rabb had, perhaps surprisingly, not been honoured in this way, but was himself part of the outgoing political establishment. After independence they were no longer on first-name terms with the people in government, and were no longer certain that they knew the rules of the game. They were, however, willing to adapt and they certainly did not think in terms of immediate disinvestment. They continued to expand their trading network, and to consolidate their agricultural holdings for some years after independence.

Stores

The Susman Brothers and Wulfsohn trading business was not initially threatened by commercial decline in the years after independence and continued to open new stores. These included stores at the new Maamba Collieries township, and at the Nakambala Sugar estate, which were opened in response to requests from government. Southern Rhodesia's Unilateral Declaration of Independence in November 1965 did, however, present the company with political problems. Harry Wulfsohn in Salisbury found himself, and the headquarters of the business, on the wrong side of the border between independent Africa and the settler-ruled south. Nathan Zelter had apparently failed to convince his fellow directors that the headquarters of the company should be transferred back to Lusaka following the dissolution of the Federation of Rhodesia and Nyasaland in 1963. He left Southern Rhodesia himself at this time and moved to Lusaka where he ran his own textile business in partnership with Dinesh Patel for a number of years.[1]

Harry Wulfsohn may have been a little slow to realise the political need to move the headquarters of the company to Zambia and to Zambianise the management. Early in 1967 he acknowledged in an internal memorandum that he had changed his position on these issues. He now recommended the strengthening of the expatriate management at Livingstone and the establishment of a 'shadow' accounting office. This was in anticipation of the possibility that accounting and other administrative services could no longer be provided from Salisbury. The strengthening of the centre was to allow for closer supervision of the outlying stores. Their management should be broken up into smaller groups which, in his view, would better suit Zambian managers. He cited the Mankoya and Balovale Groups which had continued to run 'relatively smoothly under Zambian management'.[2]

In April 1968 President Kaunda announced the Mulungushi Reforms. Their declared objective was to take control of the economy into Zambian hands. This move came at a time when the economy was booming as a result of almost unprecedentedly high copper prices which resulted from the demand created by the Vietnam War. It was in line with the avowedly 'socialist' policies which were then espoused by UNIP, the party in government. The proprietors of twenty-six companies were 'invited' to offer 51 per cent of their shares for sale to the government operating through the Industrial Development Corporation (Indeco) which was headed by Andrew Sardanis, a young Greek Cypriot trader, and ally of Kaunda, whose main trading interests were in Chingola, and in the North-Western Province. He had been in competition there, in a relatively small way, with Susman Brothers and Wulfsohn's subsidiary, A. F. Serrano. The majority of the companies scheduled for takeover were the Zambian branches of multi-national companies. The nationalisation of the copper mining companies was announced in Kaunda's Matero speech in the following year.[3]

Zambesi Saw Mills was the only company in the Susman group which was scheduled for nationalisation. Kaunda justified this takeover in his Mulungushi speech by saying that the company was a major employer in Barotseland, and that its directors had been threatening for a long time to close it down.[4] Few tears were shed over the nationalisation of this company which was valued at about £200,000. Its timber resources represented wasting assets, and the markets for railway sleepers and parquet flooring were increasingly difficult. It had never been very profitable and it had little or no potential for growth. In Edwin Wulfsohn's view, it had taken up more of the time and energy of management than it was worth. The company had, however, acquired some assets in Britain and South Africa which could not be taken over.[5]

While the rationale for the choice of companies for nationalisation is not clear, it is surprising that Susman Brothers and Wulfsohn, Zambia Textiles, and the Gersh brothers' African Commercial Holdings were not listed. The big butchery companies, Werners and Copperfields Cold Storage, also escaped nationalisation. The Susman group's main trading rival, CBC Ltd, had offered itself for partial takeover before the Mulungushi speech, and was to form the main parastatal holding company for retail stores, together with Andrew Sardanis's own Mwaiseni Stores. Although Susman Brothers and Wulfsohn was not listed, there were other aspects of the Mulungushi reforms which threatened its continued existence. In a measure which was aimed mainly at Asian traders, it was announced that only Zambian citizens, or Zambian-owned companies, would be allowed to hold trading licences in rural areas. Bank overdraft facilities for non-Zambian businesses were also to be severely restricted. A Zambian business was deemed to be a business in which the majority of the shareholding was held by Zambian citizens.[6]

Susman Brothers and Wulfsohn's response to this crisis was to set up a new company in which all their Zambian store managers became shareholders. The parent company would continue to provide finance and administration until such time as the managers were able to pay for the purchase of the stores out of profits. This scheme had to be abandoned when the licensing authorities at Balovale challenged the arrangement and licences were refused. Susman Brothers and Wulfsohn then had no option but to ask the government to take over 51 per cent of the company.[7]

It was in the middle of this crisis that Harry Wulfsohn died in Salisbury in August 1968 at the age of fifty-seven. In the view of his son Edwin, it was the stress caused by this crisis which led to his death. He had already had to face a situation in which the company's main source of income was in one country and its overdrafts were in another. The two were separated by exchange controls and mandatory sanctions. He now faced a serious threat to the continued existence of a business to which he had devoted the better part of his life.

Edwin Wulfsohn was working at the time for the Chase Manhattan Bank in New York. He had been born in Livingstone in 1942, and had lived there until 1954. He finished school in Salisbury, and did his first degree at the University of Cape Town where he studied economics. He was one of many students who came under the political influence there of Jack Simons, who features elsewhere in this book. Edwin was not drawn towards Marxism, but he was influenced by Simons's radical analysis of colonialism and racism. After completing an MBA degree at Columbia University, he had registered for a doctorate at New York University. The sudden and unexpected death of his father put an end to any plans for further academic work. The directors of Susman Brothers and Wulfsohn asked him to return to Zambia to take over the management of Werners, and the Chambishi and Kamsuswa farms, which were all making losses at the time. On his return to the country, he was also faced by the crisis over the trading licences for the stores group. He became involved, with Maurice Rabb, in the negotiations for the takeover of the trading business.

The negotiations with Andrew Sardanis were difficult. Edwin recalls that, when he asked for the value of the buildings to be taken into account, Sardanis literally threw the book at him. The relevant act specified valuation at book value with no allowance for goodwill. Maurice Rabb pointed out that it had been the company's policy to write down the value of the stores to £1 in their first year. It was unreasonable that the government should buy 123 stores for £123. A compromise was eventually worked out, but Edwin Wulfsohn reckons that the stores were taken over at a price which was equivalent to nine months' earnings. It was agreed that the government would pay for its shares over four years, and that Maurice Rabb would remain as managing director for that period. The government was eventually persuaded to buy the balance of the shares over ten years.[8] This marked the end, at least for the duration, of the Susman group's involvement with retail trade in Zambia. Susman Brothers and Wulfsohn survived as the holding company for the group's shares in Zambia Textiles. In his Matero speech in 1969, President Kaunda praised the directors for their good sense in asking to be taken over, and contrasted their behaviour with that of Solanki Brothers, an east African trading group, which had resisted takeover.[9]

The group's interests in Rhodesia and Botswana were not affected by the Zambian takeover. It proved difficult, however, to run the Ngamiland business from Salisbury, and the stores were sold to their managers. Funds from Botswana were used to take over the group's London agents, E. Stenham Ltd, and T. A. Crombie and Company. These companies, together with a British timber company which had been bought in connection with the Zambesi Saw Mills business, provided Edwin Wulfsohn with a base from which he was able over the next two decades to develop a successful financial services business.[10]

The passing of the Susman Brothers and Wulfsohn's stores was a matter of regret to many in the rural areas, especially in Barotseland. The government's banning of recruitment by WENELA (the Witwatersrand Native Labour Association) for the South African gold mines in 1966 had reduced employment opportunities, and was also a bone of contention. When the government gained control of the management, it did not, in Maurice Rabb's view, manage the stores on commercial lines. It was clear to him that they would be run at a loss, and would not provide the good service and value, with good profits, which they had done previously. The decline of incomes in the rural areas in Zambia in the 1970s and 1980s was part of a general economic decline which began with the oil price rise and collapse of copper prices in 1973. The disintegration, however, of old-established rural trading networks was certainly a contributing factor. In the mid-1980s it was clear to anyone visiting the Western Province, formerly Barotseland, that there had been an almost total collapse in rural trade. Villagers often had to travel great distances to obtain the most basic commodities, and they complained of the lack of opportunity to sell their produce, especially cattle. In places where there had been a Susman Brothers and Wulfsohn store, there was often no store at all. Where parastatal stores survived, they were poorly managed and irregularly supplied. It was not unusual for a store to receive a truckload of a single commodity, such as salt, but to have no other stock. The decline of rural markets was a factor which contributed to the exodus of people from these areas to the towns.

Butcheries

There were aspects of the business which had begun to experience quite radical change before independence, and where contraction had been a fact of life for some time. The nature of the butchery business had been transformed from the mid-1950s with the end of the big meat contracts which had been the mainstay of Werners, and Copperfields Cold Storage, since their establishment in the 1930s. Werners had responded to this change by an expansion of its retailing network into areas such as Kitwe and Chingola which had been the preserve of its main rival. Changes in the pattern of food consumption had, however, compelled it to branch out into general trade, and then to sub-let parts of its butchery outlets. From 1962 onwards, it had leased its Copperbelt butcheries to Eric Speck for a period of five years, and had become a rentier company. It had also parted with some of its cold stores to the Federal Cold Storage Board which had moved into Northern Rhodesia in 1960. Max Barnett, who had been ill for some time, died in 1966. His death marked the end of an era for the butchery business in which he had been a prime mover for over thirty years.[11]

In 1967 the lease of the butcheries to Eric Speck was renewed for a period of three years, but Werners took a 50 per cent share in his business. With the application of price controls to meat in January 1968, the butcheries almost all became loss-making and Werners resumed complete control. Edwin Wulfsohn took over the management of Werners, and the two Copperbelt farms, and succeeded over a period of two years in restoring them to profitability. He then negotiated for the lease of seventeen butcheries to the Cold Storage Board for a period of five years. When it eventually became apparent that the Cold Storage Board was not prepared to buy the butcheries, they were sold to individual buyers. Meanwhile the Livingstone butchery had been sold to Dennis Zaloumis and, in Lusaka, the company had sold its remaining interest in Lusaka Cold Storage to Abe Galaun. The company's Chambishi dairy and Kamsuswa piggeries were also sold in the mid-1970s.

By that time, Werners had ceased to exist as a butchery business, and its remaining assets were farms. Its name was changed to Concorde Agricultural Development Ltd in 1979, and it then became the ultimate holding company for the group's agricultural interests which were concentrated in Zambezi

Ranching and Cropping Ltd. Werners' rival, Copperfields Cold Storage, appears to have faded out of the butchery business at about the same time, and for the same reasons. Both Copperfields Cold Storage and Northern Caterers remained in existence as property-owning companies, and were transferred to Zambian ownership in the late 1980s. Len Pinshow had left Kitwe in 1969, and started a new career for himself in financial services in Botswana.[12]

Farms

The ownership of land was a potentially explosive political issue in the years before and after independence. In April 1965 the Susman group sought to defuse this issue, and proposed to the Ministry of Agriculture a joint venture in a 'national cattle ranching project'. They indicated that they were the owners, with associates, of 244,000 acres of ranching land in seven blocks situated between Lusaka and Livingstone. Their ranches were stocked with about 20,000 cattle of which nearly 6,000 were breeding cows. They anticipated that Zambia's expanding economy would 'bring about sharply rising living standards and a growing internal demand for beef'. There was a potential for the export of beef from the projected new Livingstone Cold Storage, and abattoir, and also for the development of ranching in the Northern Province along the line of the proposed rail link with Tanzania. They proposed that the government should take a 50 per cent share in a new ranching company, and provide loans at reasonable rates of interest for the expansion of the business.[13]

It is not clear what the government's response, if any, to these proposals was, though similar proposals were apparently still on the table five years later. In October 1966 the Lochinvar ranch, which was the most politically contentious of the group's properties, was sold to the government as a game reserve for a relatively small sum. Part of the Nanga ranch on the Kafue, which was also jointly owned with Copperfields Cold Storage, had been used for the Kafue Polder Pilot Project. This was an experiment in irrigation on the Kafue Flats which was the brainchild of Sir Ronald Prain, chairman of Rhodesian Selection Trust, and had been financed by that company. Part of this property was handed over to the government as an experimental station, and the balance of the ranch was later sold to it. At the same time that it was handing over large areas of land in the Southern Province to the government, the Susman group was consolidating its land holdings in the Choma district. They eventually owned about ten farms in a block in this district which extended over 80,000 acres. In 1967 they consolidated their land holdings in the Mazabuka district by the purchase from departing settlers of several developed farms, including Kangila and Sikolozia, extending over a further 20,000 acres.[14]

In the same year they negotiated with Maurice Gersh to take over the

Kaleya Estates near Mazabuka. All the farming interests of the group were then consolidated into a single company, Zambezi Ranching and Cropping Ltd, in which Susman Brothers and Wulfsohn owned a 75 per cent stake, and the Gersh brothers' African Commercial Holdings owned 25 per cent. Maurice Gersh was the first chairman of the new company, while Jack Tuffin became general manager with the Gershes' talented former manager, Chris Lowe, as his deputy. As a result of these adjustments, the overall extent of the land holdings of the group remained much the same as they had been at independence, but the quality and carrying capacity of the ranches and farms was considerably improved. By 1973 Zambezi Ranching was running 24,000 cattle on its farms, and also had 4,000 acres under maize.[15]

It was at about that time that Maurice Gersh completed the sale of African Commercial Holdings to Tiny Rowland's Lonrho, which had begun to build up assets in Zambia in the 1960s with the acquisition of Heinrich's Chibuku Breweries. Maurice and Reevee Gersh left Kitwe in 1971 and retired to Cape Town. They have since moved to the United States where they live in Massachusetts near their daughter, Kate Quinlan. Their son, Bernard, was a Rhodes Scholar at Oxford and was until recently a professor of cardiology at the Mayo Clinic in Minnesota. Many of the Gershes' companies, including Central African Motors and Copperbelt Bottling, have continued to flourish under Lonrho's ownership. According to Neil Molver, it was the Coca-Cola business which was the great attraction for Lonrho which saw it as a 'cash cow'. The acquisition of African Commercial Holdings gave Lonrho a 25 per cent share in Zambezi Ranching and Cropping. After a few years it became obvious that it was difficult for Susman Brothers and Wulfsohn to have such a large multi-national company as a minor shareholder in its subsidiary.[16]

It was no longer possible to hand back the Kaleya Estate to Lonrho in return for its shares. The estate was adjacent to the Nakambala Sugar Estate, which was developed by Tate and Lyle, and the Zambia Sugar Company, and it had been compulsorily purchased for the establishment of a small-holders scheme which was funded by the Commonwealth Development Corporation. Zambezi Ranching and Cropping had declined to become involved in sugar production because of the risks involved in producing a crop for which there would be only one buyer. Lonrho was a highly politicised company, and Tiny Rowland was not prepared to sell his stake in Zambezi Ranching and Cropping. He did not wish to be seen to be reducing his involvement in agriculture in Zambia at a time when he was under political pressure to increase it. Nor was he prepared to offer much for the takeover of the whole company. Among those involved in the protracted negotiations over these issues in 1976–77 was Vernon Mwaanga, Zambia's former Foreign Minister, who was then working as an executive for Lonrho. He was shown around the farms by Jack Tuffin, and clearly saw a marked contrast between his conservative and Lonrho's more 'aggressive and dynamic' styles of management. At one stage in the negotiations, Edwin Wulfsohn threatened, not entirely in jest, to deliver Lonrho's share of the assets in cattle – about 6,000 of them – to their headquarters in Lusaka's Cairo Road. In the end Zambezi Ranching handed over its most highly developed farm, Rietfontein, and a 25 per cent share of the cattle on all its farms, in exchange for Lonrho's shares.[17]

Zambia Textiles

Northern Rhodesia Textiles, which became Zambia Textiles at independence, was unaffected by the moves towards nationalisation, and was the piece of the Susman and Wulfsohn jigsaw which came through the post-independence period with least disturbance. With the end of the Federation in sight, Maurice Rabb approached the government of Northern Rhodesia in 1963 with a request for protection against Southern Rhodesian competition. He promised in return that the company would increase both production and employment. His request was granted, and what he called the 'extreme competition' from the south was, at least temporarily, eliminated. Philip Frame's Consolidated Textiles company responded to these moves by making plans to establish a factory within the boundaries of Zambia. Rabb flew to Durban and explained to Frame that the market in the country was limited, that there was not room for two blanket manufacturers, and that the Susman group had the advantage of owning its own retail outlets. Frame wanted to take a controlling interest in Zambia Textiles, but in the end it was agreed that he would buy half of the Susman group's stake, and that the two groups would share control through a new company, Livingstone Industrial Holdings. It was also agreed that the company would buy its yarn from Frame for a ten-year period, and that he would provide know-how for the updating of the plant and diversification of production.

The agreement to buy yarn from the south was rendered null and void by the effects of UDI. By 1968 Zambia Textiles had re-established its supply lines from Italy. Production continued to expand, and in 1981 a spinning plant was established; it was opened by President Kaunda. At first yarn was spun from textile waste, but by 1985 the company was able to meet half its requirements through the spinning of Zambian-grown cotton. By the end of the decade only foreign exchange shortages, which made the importation of machinery difficult, prevented the company from supplying the blanket requirements of Zambia without the import of raw materials. The company appears to have withstood, though with difficulty, the gale of liberalisation and tariff reductions which in the mid-1990s threatened to sweep away much of Zambia's manufacturing industry. Zambia Textiles had by then proved itself to be not only one of the first, but also one of the most durable, of the country's manufacturing enterprises.[18]

Trans Zambezi Industries (TZI)

Edwin Wulfsohn, who has been responsible for the supervision of the Susman group's interests in Zambia since the premature death of his father in 1968, looked upon Zambia's experiment with what he calls 'state socialism' as a phase that would pass. Exchange controls made it impossible for substantial investments in Zambia to be liquidated. From the early 1970s onwards, the policy of the group was to concentrate its investments in land and cattle and to strengthen this base by the reinvestment of profits. For over twenty years the group owned and developed assets in Zambia, but it did not derive income from them.[19]

By the early 1990s Zambezi Ranching and Cropping controlled about 230,000 acres of land and 23,000 cattle held in eleven farming blocks between Livingstone and Mazabuka. In 1975 freehold tenure had been abolished and all land was held on a long lease from the state. Land itself was deemed to have no value, though it was possible to sell improvements on it. The main asset of Zambezi Ranching and Cropping was not the land, but the 23,000 cattle which it supported. Zambian beef was of high quality and only veterinary regulations prevented its export to the international market. The company was also involved in the production of some maize, soya beans, vegetables and coffee, and prided itself on the high level of Zambianisation of its farm management. This had been made possible by the establishment of its own residential college. The conservation of water was also a priority and the company employed a permanent dam construction unit.[20]

Simon Zukas, whose political career is outlined elsewhere, had become a director of Zambezi Ranching and Cropping in 1986. He succeeded Jack Tuffin as chairman in the following year. He had become an advocate of economic liberalisation – a process which began in Zambia rather tentatively, under pressure from the World Bank and the International Monetary Fund, in the late 1980s. It was against this background of political and economic liberalisation that Edwin Wulfsohn decided, in conjunction with Hillary Duckworth, a London-based merchant banker, who had also been brought up in Zambia and Zimbabwe, to launch an investment company which would specialise in what were now called the 'emerging markets' of Southern Africa. The new company was set up in August 1993 and was named Trans Zambezi Industries(TZI). It had its headquarters in Harare, and was primarily listed on the Luxembourg stock exchange. Since 1997 it has also been quoted on the Lusaka stock exchange. The policy of the company was to take control of established businesses at a price which would be low in relation to the value of their assets and earnings. Edwin Wulfsohn became chairman of the new company and its chief executive was Hillary Duckworth. Its directors included David Susman and, as his alternate, John Rabb, his nephew. He is the son of Maurice and Peggy Rabb and grew up in Livingstone. After doing a degree in agriculture at the University of Natal, he worked briefly at Werners' Chambishi farm near Kitwe. He is currently the head of the properties division, and a director, of Wooltru Ltd. A Zambian director of the company is David Phiri, former chairman of Roan Consolidated Mines and Governor of the Bank of Zambia.[21]

The new company's first acquisition was an 82.5 per cent stake in Zambezi Ranching and Cropping whose assets had been valued in September 1991 at about $11 million and which had made an average profit in the previous four years of about $500,000. The purchase was negotiated by Hillary Duckworth from Concorde Investments Ltd which represented the Susman, Wulfsohn and Rabb family trusts. TZI took control of the company through a transaction in which no money changed hands. The first issue of $3 million of TZI shares was allocated to Concorde in exchange for its holding in Zambezi Ranching and Cropping. The price indirectly paid represented about 25 per cent of the company's asset value and about six times its recent average earnings, which had been exceptionally low in 1992 as a result of drought. Following this initial acquisition, the company succeeded in raising $30 million from sources such as Morgan Stanley, J. P. Morgan, the Rockefeller Foundation, and the Yale and Harvard University Foundations, for further investment in the region. As a result of this injection of capital, and the raising of a similar amount in 1996, the share of the founding families in the business was diluted, though they remain well represented on the boards of both TZI and Zambezi Ranching and Cropping.

At the time of the takeover, the company was selling about 5,000 head of cattle a year to the Chibote Meat Corporation's abattoir. The company had substantial Kwacha debts which were liquidated at a time of high interest rates by an injection of $1 million of capital in 1994 from the new parent company. Drought conditions forced some stock reduction during the year, and in the following year the company's cattle sales were adversely affected by the repercussions of the collapse of Andrew Sardanis's Meridien Bank on the Chibote group of companies. The changing fortunes of the Sardanis and Susman groups of companies provide an interesting example of the cyclical nature of Zambian history.[22]

Zambezi Ranching and Cropping now sought to safeguard its beef market in the country by moving 'downstream', in the jargon of economists, from beef production to the butchery business. It did this in 1996 by taking a 50 per cent share in Zambeef. This was a new butchery business which had secured the important new retail outlets provided by the arrival on the Zambian scene of the South African firm Shoprite Checkers. As part of the Zambian privatisation process, and the unravelling of the nationalisation of the late 1960s, Shoprite had bought supermarkets in Lusaka and on the Copperbelt from the ZCBC and Mwaiseni parastatal companies. One of the promoters of Zambeef, Carl Irwin, is the son of Oliver Irwin, who was not only a close friend and business associate of Len Pinshow, but also negotiated with Edwin Wulfsohn, on behalf of the Cold Storage Board, for the lease of the Werners butcheries on the Copperbelt in 1970. Oliver Irwin became the senior partner in Coopers and Lybrandt, the chartered accountants, and started his own Kyundu ranch, and butcheries, in Lusaka in the 1980s.[23]

Zambezi Ranching and Cropping further extended its involvement in the cattle and beef industries in 1996 by the purchase of Len Burton's Chisamba abattoir, which was transferred to Zambeef, and of the Anglo-American Corporation's Chisamba ranch. The latter purchase added over 50,000 acres of land and 7,000 cattle to the company's holdings which now came close to 300,000 acres and 35,000 cattle. The acquisition of the Chisamba ranch provides some insurance for the company against the droughts which have recently prevailed in the Southern Province. It also spreads the risk to beef supplies which might result from an outbreak of cattle disease on either side of the Kafue river. In that year it also purchased Lonrho's agricultural interests. This involved the reacquisition of the Rietfontein Estate which had, until the mid-1970s, been the group's most highly developed property, and the acquisition of Kalangwa Estates at Chisamba. Following $5 million of new investment, the old Lonrho and Anglo farms in Chisamba were developed to provide vegetables for export through Agriflora, also a subsidiary of TZI. This company has built a modern packing shed at Lusaka International Airport and is Zambia's largest exporter of horticultural produce. According to its chief executive Hillary Duckworth, TZI has invested $15 million in Zambian agriculture since 1993, and is now by far the largest foreign investor in this sector of the economy.

TZI's other major investment in Zambia has been in the financial services sector through the purchase from the liquidators of the Meridien Bank of Madison Insurance. An earlier suggestion that it might take over the other surviving remnant of the Susman group, Zambia Textiles, seems to have been dropped. It has, however, taken over the remnants of the group's Zimbabwean interests through the acquisition of Mercantile Holdings which has, in cooperation with a subsidiary of Wooltru, developed the Metro Megacentres in Harare and Bulawayo. It has plans to open a third centre in Lusaka. Other investments in the region have included the purchase of Chloride, the manufacturer of motor car batteries, which has branches in Zimbabwe, Zambia and Malawi. Its largest single investment has been in the forestry and paper industry in Zimbabwe.[24]

Conclusion

TZI, Zambezi Ranching and Cropping, and Zambia Textiles, were in the late 1990s the remaining parts of an enterprise which began when Elie and Harry Susman crossed the Zambezi river from Bechuanaland in April 1901 on what they described as 'the Barotseland trading expedition'. Their business survived many crises. Zambia's independence need not in itself have been a crisis, and was not initially seen as one, but Southern Rhodesia's UDI created a political climate in which hostility towards foreign investment seemed almost natural. The Susman group was not really foreign, and was not a primary target of the moves towards nationalisation which followed soon afterwards. The stores business was a more or less accidental victim of this process. There was little awareness at the time of how easy it was to destroy, but how difficult it would be to re-create, the networks of rural trade which had been built up over many decades in areas such as Barotseland and the North-Western Province.

It would be wrong to suggest that hard-headed businessmen such as Edwin Wulfsohn, David Susman or Hillary Duckworth, make decisions based on sentiment. Members of the Susman, Wulfsohn and Rabb families have, however, shown a high degree of affection for, and commitment to, the country in which they spent many of their formative years. It was this commitment which encouraged them to take a long view of the country's future, and to ride out the storm of nationalisation in the late 1960s, and of economic depression, and mismanagement of the economy, in the 1970s and 1980s. Their patience has now paid off, and they have been able to use their Zambian interests as the basis for the development of a new regional enterprise whose slogan is: 'Business knows no boundaries.'

The emphasis on regional development harks back to the colonial period when the Susmans were able to extend their interests from their base in Livingstone to Bechuanaland, the Congo, Southern Rhodesia, Angola, Mozambique and South Africa. There is, however, a fundamental difference. A main characteristic of the Susman group of enterprises in the colonial period was that it used capital which was largely accumulated from the profits of local production and trade. In the new post-colonial dispensation in which the watchword, for the moment anyway, is globalisation, they have used their international links to bring in substantial amounts of new foreign capital which is desperately needed for the reconstruction of the Zambian economy. This capital will, no doubt, expect to be rewarded with profits, but it is clearly necessary to enable the country to exploit its own natural and human resources for its own benefit, and for the benefit of the region as a whole.

CHAPTER 12

Religion

As with all world religions, there are various forms of Judaism and it is difficult to make generalisations about it. It is probably true to say that Judaism is, by comparison with most forms of Christianity, a religion of the family in which observance of the law, and of ritual, is as important as belief. Most Jews in Northern Rhodesia belonged to the Ashkenazi branch of Judaism, though there were major differences within that group as to degrees of orthodoxy. Many Jews described themselves as 'traditional' which implied a selective, rather than a strict, adherence to orthodox norms. There was always a minority of Sephardic Jews whose customs differed from those of the Ashkenazi. There were also British and, latterly, German, and South African Jews, whose traditions also differed in some ways from those of most of the earlier settlers. The number of observant Jews in any one place was generally small, and they were compelled to sink their differences if they were to have any communal religious life. It is also necessary to bear in mind, when discussing this topic, the fundamental paradox that while Jews are defined in terms of religion, not all Jews are religious, and a minority is actively hostile to religion.

It is always easier to write the history of religious organisation than that of religious belief. The central institution of organised Judaism is the *minyan* – the quorum of ten males over the age of thirteen required before a full service can be held. It is clearly the intention, or function, of this institution to compel Jewish men to come together for prayer in groups larger than the family. In the small towns of Northern Rhodesia it was always difficult to gather a *minyan*. Goody Glasser, David Susman and Aviva Ron all remember that they were required as small children to run around the town seeking to persuade often reluctant males to come together on Friday evenings. They also remember the excuses that were offered. Goody Glasser recalls that a bottle of whisky on the *stoep* of his parents' house served as an encouragement. The date of the first *minyan* is remembered for several towns (Lusaka in 1910 or Ndola in 1923) as well as the fact that men had to come in from far away to make this possible. The willingness of marginal Jews, such as Roy Welensky or Hans Fraenkel, to help make up a *minyan* is also remembered, as is the way in which disagreements among members of a community could on occasion, as in Broken Hill in the mid-1930s, make the formation of a *minyan* impossible. It was on the High Days and Holy Days, Rosh Hashanah, the New Year, and Yom Kippur, the Day of Atonement, that the need to form a *minyan* was felt most strongly.

In the early days on the frontier, the small number of Jewish men who could ever gather in one place made formal religious observance virtually impossible. There were, however, a number of men on the frontier who attempted to maintain orthodoxy. These included A. B. Diamond, who played an important part in the formation of Hebrew Congregations in Bulawayo and Elisabethville, Behr Susmanovitch, who refused in Southern Rhodesia to work on the Sabbath and eventually qualified as a rabbi in Palestine, and Marcus Grill, who had some rabbinical training and served for many years as *baal tefilah*, or leader of prayers, in Livingstone. There were, however, many other Jewish men of strictly orthodox upbringing in the 'Old Country' who found that the impossibility of keeping kosher (observing the dietary rules) or of keeping the Sabbath, which were such an essential part of orthodoxy, led them to abandon any attempt at religious observance. An old settler in Luanshya explained this tendency to Wolf Rybko in 1947 as follows:

> He had come out to Rhodesia while still very young, and he went to work on a lonely railway station far from any Jews. There was no possibility of obtaining kosher meat, and he soon got into the habit of working on the Sabbath and of eating *trayffa*. He became so ashamed of himself that he eventually refrained from praying and practising Judaism in any way at all, so as to avoid what seemed to him hypocrisy.[1]

Judaism is a religion of the family and women play a very important, though often an invisible, part in it. The absence of women and children in the early days on the frontier meant that an important dimension of religious life, the family *seder*, or Sabbath evening meal and prayers, was missing. It was only with the arrival of Jewish women and the formation of families, which went together with the development of modern towns along the Line of Rail, that there was any attempt at organised religious activity. Women such as Faiga Grill, her daughter, Annie Susman, and Henne Kopelowitz in Livingstone, and Frieda Glasser and Fanny Aberman in Lusaka, played a central part in the development of Hebrew Congregations. We have already noticed Frieda Glasser's attempts to observe the dietary laws in Lusaka, helped by the arrival of her brother, Chaim Bloch, a *shochet*, but it was generally impossible for Jews in Northern Rhodesia to observe the rules of *kasruth*. Jewish butchers catered for a predominantly gentile market and did not find it profitable to supply kosher meat. It required an exceptional effort on the part of Harry and Gertie Gersh, including the purchase of new utensils, to provide kosher meals for the visiting Chief Rabbi of the Commonwealth, Israel Brodie, in 1950. 'Moggy' Mendelsohn recalls that his family also entertained Brodie, and was only able to do things properly for him because their grandmother was still alive: 'She knew exactly what to do.' Isa Teeger recalls that her family in Ndola would have been unable to afford, even if it had been possible in the 1930s and 1940s, the expense of a kosher diet. Observance of the Sabbath was also difficult in a country in which Sunday was the official day of rest. Jewish shops in Livingstone and Lusaka did close on the High Days and Holy Days, but they were normally open on Saturday mornings.[2]

Livingstone

It was in Livingstone that there was, as we have seen, for the first time a Jewish community in Northern Rhodesia. Harry Susman's wedding to Annie Grill in 1910 was in itself a milestone in the development of the community. The Reverend Moses Cohen's visit was the first by a Jewish religious leader to the town and provided the stimulus for the organisation of the Hebrew Congregation. Among those who are said to have attended the first meeting of the Jewish community in 1910 were the Susman brothers, Marcus Grill, the Levitz brothers, the Peimer brothers, Max Shapiro, David Wersock, M. Jacobson, J. Rubin and Messrs Bloch, Barnett and Kiehl. A number of these people had been, or still were, Barotseland traders.[3]

Moss Dobkins recalled that, soon after his arrival in 1911, the Jewish New Year was celebrated in a room in an unfinished hotel. He noted that the service was conducted by laymen as was to be the case for most of the remainder of his seventy-three years' stay in the country. Elias Kopelowitz recalled that when he reached Livingstone in 1913 there was already a Jewish library. According to Harry Susman's account, Christian missionaries may have helped to set up this library. The congregation had a *Sefer Torah* which was kept in a cigarette carton. A *minyan* was held at the home of Harry and Annie Susman, and the *chazonim*, or cantors, were Marcus Grill and Israel, 'Der Alter', Levin.[4]

The Livingstone Hebrew Congregation was formally established in 1910, and a plot for a synagogue was acquired soon afterwards, but it was not then used. The plot became the site of the present St Andrew's Church. It is probable that the pre-war depression, and the war itself, delayed construction. Further stimulus to the development of the congregation was given by the arrival of Elias Kopelowitz's wife, Henne Illion, who came from a rabbinical family in Latvia, and had reached Livingstone by 1925. From then onwards, she played a very active part in Jewish community life. She was one of the few Jewish women able to maintain a kosher home.

Elie Susman, then president of the Hebrew Congregation, laid the foundation stone of the synagogue, the first in Northern Rhodesia, or in central Africa north of the Zambezi, on the 20th day of the month of Tammuz in the year 5688 according to the Jewish calendar. The *shul*, which eventually had a hall, *cheder* (school room) and rabbi's house attached, was completed within a few months and was officially opened, in the absence of the Governor, by the Chief Secretary, the Hon. H. A. Northcote, on 11 September 1928. It was consecrated by the Reverends M. I. Cohen and A. Weinberg of Bulawayo. In his address at the consecration service, during which the *Sefer Torah* was carried around the *shul* by the committee and deposited in the Ark, Cohen spoke of the role of the synagogue in the years since the destruction of the Temple. He expressed the view that 'the future of Africa depended not on scientific technique, but on the character of its inhabitants, and the Synagogue should make a significant contribution to that development'. At an evening meeting at Harry Susman's house, he talked about the history of Jewish settlement in southern Africa, and stressed the role of the Livingstone congregation in keeping open the road to the north for Jewish settlement in central Africa. He noted that the consecration of the synagogue had made an impression 'in the history of the Jews of Rhodesia and especially of Northern Rhodesia', and expressed the hope that 'the centres in the Far North will follow suit'. The building was optimistically designed to seat 200. It was noted that as the *shul* was a single-storey building with no gallery, men and women would sit on opposite sides of the aisle. Max Taube and Marcus Grill were acknowledged as having played a major part in the organisation of the building work. It was estimated that the synagogue complex when complete would have cost £2,000 – a substantial sum at that time.[5]

The Livingstone Hebrew Congregation was the first to be organised in Northern Rhodesia, and was for many years the largest. A rabbi, the Reverend Maurice Diamond, who was also a *shochet*, was appointed soon after the consecration, and was still there at the time of the Weizmanns' visit in 1932. He was the first rabbi to serve in Northern Rhodesia, and was succeeded by Rabbi Lessing, who stayed until 1939, Rabbi Kramer who served through the war, and Rabbi Bach, who served for a short time after the war. The longest serving, and the last, minister of the congregation was almost certainly Rabbi Szlapak who, with his wife and daughter, had survived incarceration in a Nazi concentration camp in Poland, and reached Livingstone soon after the war. He remained in the town until the mid-1950s. He was sent by the congregation to Johannesburg to train as a *shochet* and was licensed by the Beth Din.[6]

When Wolf Rybko visited Livingstone in 1947, he found a community of just over 100 souls. It is unlikely that this number was ever exceeded. The president of the congregation at the time was Elias Kopelowitz, with Max Shapiro as vice-president, and Harry Wasserson as treasurer. Kopelowitz's predecessors as president were Elie Susman, Marcus Grill, H. D. Sher, Max Taube and Harry Susman. His successor was Maurice Rabb. Many people who grew up in Livingstone in the 1940s and 1950s remember the active religious and social life of the congregation in those years. A decline seems to have begun in the late 1950s, and by the late 1960s communal religious life was no longer possible.[7]

Lusaka

According to Henrie Kollenberg, a *minyan* was first gathered at Lusaka from as far away as Broken Hill for Rosh Hashanah in 1910. A *Sefer Torah* was obtained for the community by Edward Kollenberg in 1914. For many years the Glassers' home was the religious centre of the small Jewish community, which met there regularly on Friday evenings, though Sam Fischer's cinema was also used for larger gatherings. It was the influx of German Jewish refugees, and especially the arrival of one remarkable man, Cantor Feivel Metzger, which provided the catalyst for the formal organisation of the congregation and the building of a synagogue.[8]

Cantor Metzger, whose recruitment and arrival in Lusaka has already been described, was the most remarkable Jewish religious leader to serve in Northern Rhodesia, and he did so at a critical time. His services were valued by both German and central European Jews and were appreciated by the wider settler community. He was also respected by the government, which not only employed him as the official censor of letters written in German, Yiddish and Hebrew, and as a liaison officer with the Polish refugees in Lusaka, but also allowed him to make the first radio broadcast by a Jewish religious leader. In his address on the occasion of Chanukah in December 1942 he compared the contemporary struggle for freedom with the earlier struggles of the Maccabees and emphasised the role being played by Jews in the armed forces. He quoted General Smuts's observation that: 'In the years that follow the war it will surely be remembered that, whoever else faltered or failed, the Jews have played their part by the side of the Allies.'[9]

There can be no doubt that Metzger was the inspiration behind the building of the Lusaka synagogue. Its foundation stone was laid by Henrie Kollenberg, then president of the congregation, on 20 July 1941. 'Moggy' Mendelsohn remembered the laying of the stone and how 'we put a few coins in a tin and put it behind the stone and buried it'. Little is known about the actual construction or furnishing of the *shul* which was completed in the course of 1942.[10] Although records may one day be found, it is impossible at the moment to say who the architect was. Goody Glasser recalls, however, that there was heated debate as to whether it should be built east or west of the railway line. (Mrs Mendelsohn was not amused by his compromise suggestion that it should be built astride the line!) The decision to build to the west of the line in central Lusaka is understandable, as many members of the Jewish community still lived behind their shops, but the synagogue is the only substantial religious building in the city centre. The main Anglican, Methodist and Catholic churches, the Hindu temple and the mosque were built in the new parts of the town to the east of the railway. It is probable that David Shapiro, who may have donated the bricks, and Jack Gerber, the plumber, played an important part in its construction. Sam Fischer, Henrie Kollenberg, Sam Osrin, 'Tubby' Wulfsohn, Ivie Shapiro and Sam Mendelsohn were also leading members of the congregation at this time. Sigrid Fischer recalls that she was the secretary of the building committee.[11]

The completion of this fine building in the darkest days of the war was an intensely symbolic act which may well have been intended not only as a gesture of defiance of Nazism and anti-Semitism, but also to bring together the two halves of the Jewish community. In a report on the year 1942, David Shapiro praised Metzger's 'outstanding devotion to duty' and commented on the way in which regular services on the Sabbath and on all festivals, as well as various social functions, had helped 'to unify the congregation and promote Jewish social life in Lusaka'. According to Alf Metzger, his father was the gentlest of men who would not normally kill a fly, but he received a special licence as a poultry *shochet*. He clearly had a strong sense of drama, and Alf recalls the amazed response of the congregation when his father appeared as Haman, who planned the murder of the Jews, in his blood-stained *shochet*'s cloak at the celebration of Purim. Metzger, though never a rabbi, was the ideal minister who was able to combine the roles of pastor and representative of the Jewish community to society at large. He remained in Lusaka for most of the war, but moved in August 1944 to Durban, South Africa, where he served a much larger congregation for most of twenty-five years. He died in Israel in 1969.[12]

The synagogue was not consecrated until 8 March 1946 on the occasion of the first visit to the country by Rabbi Konviser of Salisbury. He may have felt at home in Lusaka as two of his wife's cousins, Annie and Gertrude Liptz, were married to leading members of the congregation, Sam Mendelsohn and Sam Osrin. The service was conducted by Max Rowelsky and Konviser gave an address. All members of the congregation attended this service, as well as a meeting on the following day which was chaired by Sam Osrin. There had been no minister there since the departure of Cantor Metzger in 1944, but the congregation had appointed a new rabbi, Dr Poswell, a Lithuanian scholar of distinction, and a concentration camp survivor. He was then in a displaced persons camp in Italy, but was expected to arrive shortly. He stayed in Lusaka for about four years, and was succeeded in 1950 by Rabbi Sidney Clayman, who came from a congregation in Finsbury Park in London.[13]

Morris Szeftel, a leading member of Lusaka's Jewish youth in the 1950s, held Clayman, who served the congregation throughout the decade, in high regard both for his pastoral and spiritual qualities. In his view, Clayman, who was a modest and simple man, though with a powerful voice, was good at dealing with young people and succeeded in retaining their interest and loyalty to the faith. He was unmarried and lived with his sister in the rabbi's house which was built on the plot next to the synagogue. According to one source, his sister was a kindly soul who would invite the gardener in for coffee and cake on hot days – a practice which was probably frowned upon by the more conservative members of the community. Clayman served the congregation throughout the 1950s, its heyday, when it may have consisted of as many as seventy families or 200 souls. It was during his time in office that the community hall, which matches the synagogue in appearance and size, was completed in 1951.

Although he was clearly an excellent pastor, Clayman was not temperamentally suited to the public relations role which Metzger had performed so well. Abe Galaun was one of those who felt that the community needed a presentable leader who would project a good image and be able to hold his own on public occasions with other religious dignitaries. He felt that the government wanted a representative of the community with which it could deal. He was not alone in thinking that Clayman was unable to fill this role. Some people felt that he would not make a suitable chaplain to Jack Fischer on his anticipated election as mayor of Lusaka in 1960. The question of Clayman's replacement was one which divided the community. His supporters included Ben Szeftel and Maurice Diamond, a prominent local lawyer who became Northern Rhodesia's first Queen's Counsel in 1957. Morris Szeftel recalls a furious debate on this issue. In the end Clayman left, but the division within the community remained.[14]

None of Clayman's two or three successors stayed long, or fulfilled the role which was intended for them. One was compelled to leave in a hurry after being involved in extramarital relationships. The fact that these involved black women only added to the scandal in the eyes of the congregation. From soon after independence in 1964, there was no permanent rabbi and the congregation reverted to lay ministry. Among those who played an active part in the congregation at this time was Moritz Prins, who was chairman for some time during the 1960s. Reuben Moss, who arrived from Salisbury in 1963 to represent Benny Gelfand's accountancy firm, was also an active member of the congregation until his departure in 1969.[15]

With the exodus of the majority of the settler population in the mid-1960s, the era of the 'expatriates' began. Among those who played an active part in the life of the congregation in the mid-1960s was Mort Teicher, who came from Yeshiva University in New York to work at the Oppenheimer School of Social Work, a precursor of the University of Zambia. Among those who came as expatriates, but stayed for a long time, was Michael Bush, who came first to Siavonga in 1972. He was to become an important member of the Jewish community, serving as Abe Galaun often did, as *baal tefilah*. The burgeoning diplomatic community also provided the congregation with temporary recruits, including some from the Israeli Embassy. After independence, and until the Yom Kippur War of 1973 which resulted in Zambia breaking off diplomatic relations with Israel, there was a considerable influx of Israelis, some of whom became active members of the congregation. A number of them worked for a large Israeli construction company and some were involved with the Gwembe Valley Development Project. From that time until the restoration of diplomatic relations between the two countries after the Zambian elections of 1991, the only representation of Israel was through Amiran, the agricultural implement suppliers. Some of their managers were also active members of the Jewish community.[16]

Dvora Rankow was an Israeli woman who arrived in Lusaka with her South African husband, Tuvia, in the early 1960s, and stayed for thirty years. She was brought up on a pioneer Zionist settlement in Palestine and, as a sixteen-year-old-girl, served in the Haganah underground movement in Israel's War of Independence. She opened her Lusaka International Nursery School, one of the first non-racial nursery schools in the town, in a church in Woodlands in January 1964, but this was soon transferred to the Hebrew Congregation's community hall. Among the school's early pupils were some of the children of President Kenneth Kaunda. For twenty years after the synagogue ceased to be used on a regular basis in the early 1970s, her nursery school's 200 pupils brought life and purpose to the building. The parents and children were both aware that they were using religious premises, and the school observed the Jewish High Days and Holy Days.[17]

Broken Hill

It appears that it was only in the 1920s and 1930s that there was a very active Hebrew Congregation in Broken Hill. We have seen that Maurice Thal, who was president until his departure in 1935, was an intellectual who took a deep interest in Jewish religion and history. We have also noted elsewhere his frustration on his departure at the inability of the community to form a *minyan* at Rosh Hashanah. Rybko, who visited the town as a Zionist emissary in 1928, remembered an optimistic community which was on the point of building a synagogue. The Hochstein family, who had arrived in the early 1920s, had a *Sefer Torah* which was kept in an Ark in their home and served as the religious focus of the community. The Jacobsons, Rosens, Thals, Feigenbaums and Herbsteins provided the nucleus at this time of a community of about forty souls, including a number of bachelors who worked as shop assistants or on the mine. There were usually enough men in the town to form a *minyan*, and services were held at the homes of leaders of the community. When Rybko returned to the town in 1947, he found a smaller and a rather depressed community, and noted that 'time seemed to be moving backwards'. Leon Kuritzky, who came from Vilna and had trained as a lawyer at the Sorbonne in Paris, arrived as a refugee before the war and organised a Jewish library in 1942, but this closed due to a lack of interest. Rabbi Konviser did not include the town on his itinerary in 1946, and in 1952 it was reported that the community had declined to accept the offer of a visit by Rabbi Clayman. Gert Rosenberg, who arrived with his parents from Germany in 1939 and stayed for most of the next thirty years, recalls, however, that there continued to be some organised religious life. Services were not held weekly, but were held on the High Days and Holy Days, and on other special occasions, at the home of the increasingly elderly Hochstein 'girls'. During the war, Solly Israel sometimes came from Mazabuka or Kitwe to conduct services, as did Cantor Metzger from Lusaka. Harry Tow, who worked on the mine during the war, was also able to act as a *baal tefilah*. After the war ministers were sometimes brought in from the south to conduct services on the High Days and Holy Days.[18]

The Copperbelt

While a *minyan* was gathered for the first time at Ndola in 1923, and brought together eight men from the town and two from Bwana Mkubwa, it was not until the beginning of the construction boom that congregations began to be formed on the Copperbelt. A *minyan* was regularly formed at Ndola from 1926 onwards, and the congregation, which was led by Hyam Schulman, had acquired a *Sefer Torah* before 1930. In that year Harry Gersh formed the first *minyan* at Nchanga, and used to make the long return journey to Ndola to borrow the *Torah*. Services were held in that year in an unoccupied shop belonging to Sam Osrin. After Harry Gersh had moved to Nkana, he asked his grandparents, the Susmanovitches, to arrange for the writing of a *Torah* in Palestine. Soon after his marriage in 1933 to Gertie Baron, they travelled to Palestine to collect the finished work which had been done by the family scribe, Rabbi Moshe Epstein, in Jerusalem. They were surprised to be given the *Torah* as separate sheets of parchment which they carried back to Africa in a suitcase. They had the sheets stitched together into a scroll in Bulawayo, and also had a portable Ark made, for which Gertie Gersh embroidered a mantle. For a number of years they held services in their homes at Nkana and Kitwe. They found that the *Torah* was in great demand in the neighbouring towns 'for services, bar mitzvahs, weddings and other *simchas*'. Among these events was the *bris* (circumcision) of their son Errol, which was performed by Rabbi Weinberg of Bulawayo in 1936. Twenty years later they discovered, after the appointment of a rabbi in Kitwe, that the *Torah* was incomplete. By that time the congregation, of which Maurice Gersh was the long-serving president, had been given another by 'Ma' Davis, mother-in-law of Jack Price. She presented it in memory of her son, Norman Davis, who had been killed during the war.

Harry Gersh has left an account of religious life as it was in Kitwe in the late 1930s and early 1940s:

> I took over the unofficial role of *chazan* and *shamos*, and Jacob Katz the post of reader and *chazan*. We also had a good stand-by in Mr Lurie and Mr Solly Israel. Civil marriages were conducted by ourselves with the *ktubah* and translation read. As we had no rabbi in those days we relied solely on our *shulchan aruch* [a compendium of religious practice] to guide us spiritually, and we endeavoured to carry on our Jewish way of life to the best of our ability.[19]

As was the case in Lusaka, it was the war, and the influx of refugees which preceded its outbreak, which provided the stimulus for the creation of more tangible religious institutions on the Copperbelt. Synagogues were completed in Kitwe, Ndola and Mufulira in the year or so following its end. Rabbi Konviser of Salisbury made his first visit to Northern Rhodesia in March 1946 and has left a report of his impressions of the religious and communal life in the country at that time. Taken together with the account provided, and already frequently quoted, by Wolf Rybko of his visit in 1947, it is possible to create a fairly comprehensive picture of the Copperbelt community as it was in the years immediately after the end of the war.

Rabbi Konviser's Visit

Konviser inspected the recently completed, but unfurnished, synagogue at Kitwe-Nkana, and the Mufulira synagogue, which was nearing completion. He noted that the Nkana synagogue was a fine building, with communal hall attached, in a prominent position at the entrance of the town. The synagogue at Mufulira was a dual-purpose building which could also serve as a community hall. It had been designed by the mine architect and was, according to David Messerer, financed by more or less equal contributions from members of the congregation. When it was furnished, there were double doors to the Ark and a fine *bimah*. In Ndola, Konviser was able to inspect the plans for a further dual-purpose synagogue and community hall. Building, which was undertaken almost single-handedly by Hanan Elkaim in the face of some opposition from Hyam Schulman, was about to begin, and was completed in the following year.[20]

Konviser returned to the Copperbelt in July 1946 to consecrate the two completed synagogues at Kitwe-Nkana and Mufulira. The first of these services was conducted on 19 July which was the Sabbath. The second service at Mufulira was held two days later on 21 July which was a Sunday. The Governor, and the leaders of the Christian churches were invited, though in each place the government was represented on the day by the senior local official, the District Commissioner, and the churches were represented by a few members of the local clergy. The services in both places were almost identical. The minister, followed by the president of the Congregation and other officers, brought the Scrolls of the Law to the doors of the Synagogue and recited: 'Open unto me the gates of righteousness; I will enter them, and praise the Lord'. Three circuits of the *Almemar* were performed during which the 'Ma Tovu', and Psalms 24 and 30, were chanted. Prayers of consecration were offered as well as prayers for the Governor and the royal family. In both places the service was ended with the singing of the 'Hatikvah', the Zionist, and later Israel's, national anthem.

Konviser's addresses in both places reflected the shadow of the Holocaust. In Kitwe he spoke of 'the necessity of restoring the equilibrium of the

Jewish people by creating new centres of Jewish religious life, since the vandalism of the enemy has destroyed the more ancient synagogues of Europe'. In Mufulira he noted that 'our need of this House of God is even greater today than it has ever been before if we are to assume responsibility in self-reconstruction and in the rehabilitation of a decimated Jewry'.

The officers of the congregation in Kitwe were Maurice Gersh, M. Cypin, Nathan Schulman and Hans Tuch, with Eli Lurie and David Kollenberg as members of the committee. The officers in Mufulira were Uri Illion, A. J. Mendelsohn and David Messerer. Mrs Israel Schatz, whose Lithuanian husband had arrived from Germany before the war and ran a 'Native Eating House', was also an active member of the community at that time. Their son, Harry, was a secondary school teacher in Ndola in the 1950s. Konviser took the opportunity of the same visit to consecrate the Jewish burial grounds at Kitwe and Ndola which were already in use.[21]

Both Konviser and Rybko concluded that Mufulira was the best organised of the Copperbelt communities. This seems to have been due to cooperation between the 'old guard' settlers, represented by Uri Illion, and the 'newcomers', led by an energetic couple, David and Rose Messerer. It may also have reflected the fact that in Mufulira, by contrast with other centres on the Copperbelt, the majority of the Jewish community was not engaged in trade, but was employed on the mine. A common employer seems to have contributed to a more homogeneous society. There were, however, still some tensions within the community. Wolf Rybko's account of the history of the community and the building of the synagogue prompted an angry response from a reader who, in a letter to the *Zionist Record*, complained that the 'newcomers' and Uri Illion had been given too much prominence in the article. It was true that Illion was 'the living soul of the Mufulira Hebrew Congregation'. Credit should, however, also have been given to the past president, Jack Mendelsohn, who had been in the town for fourteen years and had collected £250 for the synagogue building in addition to his own substantial contribution; to Joseph Israel, who had been there for seventeen years; to Cyril Sussman and to Uri Illion's brother, Eli, who had served as *chazan* until his untimely death (he was succeeded in this role by Harry Favish). David Messerer recalls that many Jewish functions, including an annual dance in the hall, were also attended by gentiles, and that in the 1950s it was the Mufulira congregation which was most active in organising social events for the entire Copperbelt community. These included regular picnics on the Kafue to celebrate Purim.[22]

Although Konviser appears to have had a successful meeting at Luanshya attended by twenty people, including a number of young men 'originally from Lithuania or mid-Europe', Rybko formed the impression a year later that the religious and social life of the community of sixty souls, including twenty children, was at a low ebb. The Zionist society, of which Joseph Minchuk was president and Harry Rayner vice-president, was the only functioning communal institution. He learned from Minchuk that the Jewish population had in recent years been an unusually transient one. People tended to stay for a few years, make a little money, and then move on to the larger centres. A synagogue was built in Luanshya in 1953 and was dedicated to the memory of three founders of the community, Harry Figov, Maurice Rosen and H. P. Sussman, a younger brother of Cyril and Sidney Sussman, who had died as a young man. The mining company provided the plot, together with free electricity and water, and, as was its practice with all religious buildings, it also laid out the garden. The synagogues in Ndola and Luanshya were apparently never consecrated.[23]

Konviser did not visit Chingola which always had the smallest Hebrew congregation on the Copperbelt. It was the only one of the major Copperbelt towns in which no synagogue was built, though a plot was at one stage obtained and plans drawn up. Rybko noted in 1947 that the community, in which there seem never to have been more than fifteen families, consisted mainly of young couples with young children. He formed a favourable impression both of its religious life and of the Zionist enthusiasm of its women: 'There is neither a reverend nor a *shochet*, but the Jews are good traditional Jews, and have a *minyan* and a Hebrew school, where Mr Mottel Katz, a shop assistant, is voluntarily teaching the local Jewish children Hebrew. Every *Yom Tov* is celebrated by both parents and children in the proper manner.'[24]

The leaders of the community were members of the Dobkins, Dorsky, and Israel families who had all been settled in the town since the late 1930s. Services were held in the homes of the leading members of the community. In later years 'George' Mandel acted as the *baal tefilah* of the congregation which also received occasional visits from the Kitwe rabbi when there was one. In the late 1950s and 1960s, David and Doreen Marcus also played an active part in the congregation.[25]

Religious Education

The main objectives of Rabbi Konviser's two-week visit to Northern Rhodesia in March 1946, on which he was accompanied by a senior Lusaka resident, David Shapiro, were to make contact with the leaders of the community as a whole, to encourage the separate communities both to join the Council for Rhodesian Jewry, and to send delegates to a conference on Jewish education which was due to take place in Salisbury in the following month. In his report Konviser adopted a rather superior tone in relation to what he called the 'older towns ... and mushroom villages' of Northern Rhodesia, which he compared rather unfavourably with the larger centres of Salisbury and Bulawayo. He observed that:

The great difficulties that confront these organised Communities are certainly far greater than those confronting us in the larger centres of Jewish life. They

are far removed from the spiritual currents of Judaism and yet, I was proud to
see how each one is called upon to maintain, alone and unaided, the Jewish
Consciousness and the Jewish life in his Congregation.

Konviser, who did not endear himself to the Copperbelt communities at
this time, expressed concern at what he saw as the alarming rate of 'intermarriage', by which he meant marriage out of the faith, which was prevalent
on the Copperbelt. In his view there was a clear relationship between this
and the lack of religious education. In so far as Judaism is not a religion
which seeks converts, and is a religion in which entry by birth is the norm,
Konviser's preoccupation, and that of several other visitors, with rates of
'intermarriage' is, perhaps, understandable. He noted that:

> Intermarriage has been rather prevalent in the Copperbelt ... perhaps possibly
> due to their being divorced from Jewish life and the necessary Jewish back-
> ground. This 'straying' is more probably due to the apathetic ignorance of the
> fundamental values of Judaism, and for this, there is only one solution that
> goes to the root of the evil ... that is Education ... the only guarantee for the
> survival of Judaism and Jewry in these isolated Communities.[26]

These strictures seem a little harsh on a Copperbelt community which
was in the process of building three synagogues and which sought assistance
from the Council for Rhodesian Jewry for the recruitment of a travelling
minister/teacher. Aviva Ron points out that many Jewish men, such as the
Katz brothers, Sam Esra and Yonah Kapulsky, remained bachelors for many
years because of the impossibility of finding Jewish wives in the country,
and the difficulty of finding wives on occasional short visits to South Africa.
Her own father, Hanan Elkaim, was given two weeks by his employer,
Chisholm Jack, to find a wife. He met her mother, Yona, on the train between
Bulawayo and Salisbury, and was married within a week.

At various meetings there was discussion of the need for Jewish education
at all levels: for children, adolescents and adults. There was also talk of the
need for a Hebrew correspondence course and of the possibility of exercising
the right of entry into government schools by Jewish laymen and women.
Jewish education for children was already being provided at this time not
only in Livingstone and Lusaka where there were usually ministers, but also
in Mufulira where David and Rose Messerer, Mr Levisohn, a government
school teacher, Barry Epstein, a Polish refugee employed for many years at
the mine's water purification works, and Rica Israel were all actively involved.
Sam Esra was conducting Hebrew classes for children in Kitwe and Max
'Mottel' Katz was doing the same in Chingola.[27]

Konviser was very conscious of the fact that in some centres there was
a division in the community between the early settlers and the refugee element
or, as they preferred to call themselves, 'the newcomers'. The situation of
the Jewish refugees in Northern Rhodesia was very good and they had no

fear of repatriation: 'The great majority are well settled in commerce or have good positions in the various mines of the Copperbelt. They certainly have gained much materially, but in a good many cases have still not become fully integrated in the general life of the community.'[28] He was told in both Ndola and Kitwe that the majority of the refugees had stayed away from his meetings, fearing that he had come on yet another fund-raising campaign. This was not, however, the case in Lusaka, Luanshya or in Mufulira, where the meetings were attended by German and Polish 'newcomers'.

Konviser recommended the establishment of a Copperbelt regional committee to coordinate the activities of the five congregations. This was established in 1949, following a further visit from a representative of the Council for Rhodesian Jewry, and grew into the United Hebrew Congregation of the Copperbelt. The efforts of the Copperbelt community to recruit a rabbi did not, however, bear immediate fruit. There was, according to Rybko, some difference of opinion in Kitwe as to the role which a minister should play: 'Some members of the community wish to have a rabbi to attend to Jewish spiritual needs. They want him to be their instructor and teacher, to provide guidance for themselves and their children. Other people feel, however, that the reverend should serve mainly as a decoration and representative for the outside world.'[29]

There seems to be an echo of these debates which, as we have seen, were to recur some years later in Lusaka, in a short story, 'The Reverend', which Wolf Rybko wrote in Yiddish in about 1950. Rybko was born in Poland in 1896 and settled in South Africa in 1927. He was the only contemporary Jewish intellectual to take an interest in the history, demography and religious experience of the Jewish community in Northern Rhodesia. His accounts of his second visit to the country in 1947, which were published in the *Zionist Record*, have been an important source for this book. He was fascinated by the communities on the frontier, but was also shocked by what he saw as their lapses from strict orthodoxy, by their failure to observe the Sabbath or the dietary laws, and by their tendencies towards assimilation and materialism.[30]

His story is set in the fictional town of Chilimanzi, 'a very active and prosperous mining area', which seems to combine elements from Lusaka and a Copperbelt town. It provides an entertaining account of the experience of a fictional rabbi who, having survived the Holocaust in Poland and having been through the 'Seven Gates of Hell', is recruited from his place of refuge in Italy after the war to be the first rabbi of a central African congregation. He is a deeply religious man, educated at the great Polish rabbinical school of Radin, but he soon falls out with his congregation when he decides to chide them for their laxity.

Aviva Ron rejects this kind of criticism, and the suggestion that the Jews of the Copperbelt built synagogues, or sought rabbis, as status symbols. She feels that her parents' generation built synagogues because 'they were proud Jews and wanted a place to worship'. Neither Konviser nor Rybko appreciated 'how close to Judaism and Jewish life many of us were – without kosher meat'.[31]

Renewed efforts were made to recruit a minister for the Copperbelt following the visit to Northern Rhodesia in 1950 of the Chief Rabbi, and a substantial salary of £1,500 was offered. It was not, however, until 1955 that a Rabbi Kibel was appointed. He could not cope with the burden of ministering to such a widely scattered flock and stayed only for a short while. He was succeeded by the Reverends Wolfson and Cantor who each stayed at Kitwe for a few years. In the absence of a resident rabbi, the Sephardic rabbi from Elisabethville, Maurice Levi, or the Lusaka rabbi, Sidney Clayman, sometimes visited for special events like bar mitzvahs. In later years ministers were sometimes brought from further afield at considerable expense to perform on the High Days and Holy Days, but in general lay ministry remained the norm for most of the Copperbelt congregations until the later 1960s or early 1970s when communal religious life became impossible.[32]

Regional Organisation

One of the intentions of Rabbi Konviser's visit was to persuade the congregations in the north to affiliate with the recently formed Council of Rhodesian Jewry, which eventually became the Rhodesian Board of Jewish Deputies. It is clear from his report that none of them had yet done so, although David Shapiro, who was in the process of moving from Lusaka to Salisbury, had become a vice-chairman of the council. It seems that in the later 1940s the Northern Rhodesian congregations did join the council. In the Federal period it was natural that the congregations should be part of this wider regional organisation. During this time a number of people, including Julius Mohrer, David Messerer and later 'Val' Magnus and Abe Galaun, played an active part in the meetings of the Rhodesian Board of Deputies. The involvement of the Jews of Northern Rhodesia in an organisation which had its centre of gravity in the south, where the community was ten times as large, meant, however, that no national institutions were established in the north until after independence.

During the 1950s the general secretary of the Rhodesian Board of Deputies, M. Wagner, made fairly regular visits to Northern Rhodesia and wrote reports on the progress of the community. As had been the case with Rabbi Konviser, in 1946 his major concern was with religious education and what he saw as the 'danger of mixed marriages'. In 1956 he recorded estimates for the rate of 'intermarriage' for the three largest congregations, presumably Lusaka, Kitwe and Livingstone, and for two of the smaller centres, which suggested that about 15 per cent of these marriages involved one partner who was not Jewish. This rate was only slightly higher than in Southern Rhodesia where it was estimated at 12 per cent. These rates were probably low by international standards, but he noted that there had been a 'deterioration' in the previous two years. He felt that this tendency could only be checked through the appointment of minister/teachers. There were at that time ministers only in Lusaka and Livingstone.[33]

The existence of a regional body was threatened by the break-up of the Federation and the independence of Zambia. According to Barry Kosmin it was largely through the advocacy of 'Val' Magnus that a new supra-body, the Central African Jewish Board of Deputies, was established in 1964. This was intended to provide for continued cooperation between the Jewish communities in the two countries. Such cooperation was, however, made very difficult by Rhodesian UDI in November 1965 and by subsequent restrictions on movement. In June 1969 the Central African Board was dissolved and a separate Council for Zambian Jewry was established. A Zambian Zionist Council was set up at the same time. There was some irony in the fact that national Jewish organisations were being established in Zambia at a time when the Jewish community, which was always small, had declined by two-thirds, and numbered not many more than 300 souls.[34]

The first, and possibly the last, major meeting of the Zambian Jewish community as a whole was held in Kitwe in December 1970. This was a joint meeting of the Council for Zambian Jewry, the Zambian Zionist Council and the Zambian Women's Zionist Council, and was presided over by Abe Galaun, who was by that time chairman of two of these organisations. Vera Galaun chaired the women's organisation. The conference, which was organised by David Messerer of Mufulira and Mr S. Fisher, chairman of the Kitwe Hebrew Congregation, was attended by thirty-four delegates from Kitwe, Ndola, Chingola, Mufulira, Luanshya and Lusaka. The Israeli ambassador to Zambia, Mr M. Dagan, and his wife were also present. The group photograph provided a roll call of the senior members of Zambian Jewry and most of the names of those present are familiar. Moss Dobkins, with almost sixty years in the country, was there with his wife, Fay, and was the senior person present, but Julius Minchuk of Mufulira, Dennis Figov of Luanshya, Mr and Mrs H. Bernstein, and Mrs Price, of Kitwe, and Mr and Mrs Jacob Katz of Ndola, were among those who had been in the country since the 1930s. Among those who had arrived in the 1950s and 1960s were the Leibowitz brothers from Kitwe, Dr Sylvia Lehrer from Ndola, and Moritz Prins, then chairman of the Lusaka Congregation.[35]

There had been no representative at this meeting from Livingstone. Maurice Rabb, the last president of the congregation and the last surviving male member of the committee, closed the *shul* before his departure from the town at the end of 1971 and sent the *Sefer Torah*s to Lusaka. The foundation stones were removed and deposited at the Livingstone Museum. The premises were offered to the government as a school, but the offer was declined. They were then sold to the Seventh Day Adventist Church on condition that the hall would be used as a church and the *shul* as a hall. Maurice Rabb regretted that this condition was not in the end met.[36]

When Harry Gersh donated the *Torah* which he had brought from Jerusalem to Kitwe to the Old Synagogue in Cape Town in 1972, he reported that there were then only three Jewish families in Kitwe and that the *shul* was closed. Dennis Figov recalls that it was the departure of Israeli workers from the Kafubu settlement scheme, following the Yom Kippur War in 1973, which marked the end of communal religious life in Luanshya and that the *shul* there was sold soon afterwards. It was at about the same time that it became impossible to gather a *minyan* in Mufulira or Ndola. David Messerer recalls that Hanan Elkaim, in the last years before his death in 1991, used to go alone to pray at the *shul* in Ndola which he had himself built forty years previously. Elkaim's daughter, Aviva, recalls that he would read the *Torah* portion for the day, and then listen to the singing of the Seventh Day Adventists who used the communal hall on Saturdays – the Baptists used it on Sundays.

The Ndola and Mufulira *shuls* were in the 1990s the last to be sold. In 1994 a number of *Sefer Torah*s from the Zambian congregations were sent to Israel by the Council for Zambia Jewry for distribution to new congregations in that country. It is today only in Lusaka that there is a *shul* where a *minyan* can sometimes be gathered and the most holy of Jewish prayers, the kaddish, can be said. Michael Bush and Michael Galaun, and other leaders of the community, are determined that the Lusaka *shul* should be kept open not only as a reminder of the past, but also in the expectation that there may be a revival in the size of the Jewish community. The reopening of diplomatic relations with Israel, and the arrival of a small number of new Jewish immigrants from the former Soviet Union, as well as a small but steady flow of religious Jewish expatriates, make this a not unreasonable expectation.[37]

Further hope for the future has been provided by the recent establishment of the African Jewish Congress which is intended to improve communications between the dispersed Jewish communities of sub-Saharan Africa, and the appointment of Rabbi Moshe Silberhaft as its spiritual leader. Prompted by Cecilia Krasner, formerly of Livingstone, and Joyce Barnett, whose grandfather, Uri Rabinowitz, was buried in the old Jewish cemetery close to what is now Independence Avenue in Lusaka in 1917, he has made several visits to the country since 1996. He has taken a special interest, in cooperation with Michael Galaun and the Council for Zambia Jewry, in the preservation of the country's Jewish cemeteries. The Council has made its own contribution to the regional work of the congress by a donation for the restoration of the synagogue in Maputo, Mozambique.[38]

Conclusion

It is difficult to draw any conclusions as to the relationship between Judaism and Jewishness in the Northern Rhodesian, or Zambian, context. For many, though not all, Jews there was a close relationship between Judaism and

Zionism. It is almost impossible to tap into the private religious beliefs of individuals. The closest thing to a spiritual diary which is available to us is in the writings of Maurice Thal who lived and worked in Broken Hill in the 1920s and 1930s and was, as we have seen, a victim of anti-Semitism and fascism. In lengthy diary entries, and in a letter to his son which he wrote on 6 February 1936, he touched on themes which may have been the inspiration of many of his contemporaries:

> If we now seek rest in Zion it is not for conquest. We wish to take up the thread of the development of our spiritual and national life interrupted two thousand years ago by our unjust and forcible ejection. We have never ceased protesting. In our daily prayers we laid claim to it, by virtue of the covenant of God with Abraham. We have never admitted the justice or right of conquest of Zion from us. We have had faith in the prophecy of our prophets of the return of our people to Zion. Once more, we lay claim to live in our land, the free life of a free people, in obedience to the Laws of Moses and the Covenant of Abraham. We believe that by being allowed to lead our life in our own way, we shall be able to work out a plan beneficial to the whole world.[39]

In spite of the criticisms of Rabbi Konviser, and the fictional critique of Wolf Rybko, what seems most remarkable is the extent to which the Jews on the frontier in Northern Rhodesia were able to maintain a measure of religious observance and of belief largely through lay ministry. The writings of Maurice Thal demonstrate that there were on the frontier Jews with deep religious convictions. These were based on wide reading and were expressed with eloquence and power. Although he came from a rabbinical family, Maurice Thal was a shopkeeper. David Messerer, an electrical engineer, is proud that, through the efforts of the lay members of the Mufulira community in the sphere of religious education, few children were 'lost to the faith'.[40] It is also a tribute to the Jewish religious ethic that the Jews as a group were, and still are, widely respected for honest dealings in business, for their public service to the wider community, and for their charitable work.

CHAPTER 13

Politics

Zionism

The memory of persecution, and the fear of its revival, were strong among the Jews from the Russian empire who reached Southern Africa in the early decades of this century. From the 1930s to the 1960s, Jews from the two Rhodesias made larger financial contributions to the Zionist movement, in proportion to their numbers, than any other community. Zionism appealed most strongly to people of eastern European origin, but it also acquired enthusiastic supporters in the German and Sephardic sections of the population. Zionist organisational structures were much the same in the two Rhodesias and in South Africa. The history of the movement in the region as a whole has been dealt with in two excellent books by Gideon Shimoni and Barry Kosmin. Here, therefore, it is necessary only to point to some of the special characteristics of Zionism in Northern Rhodesia.[1]

There were some surprising links between Palestine and Northern Rhodesia. These were to be found in the experience of officials who espoused the cause of Zionism, or served in both countries, and in the immigration to Northern Rhodesia of a number of people, such as the Gershes, David Shapiro, the Pinhassoviths, Hanan Elkaim, Isaac Zlotnik and the Zemacks, who were either born in Palestine, or had spent a period of time there. Sir Harry Johnston, the first Commissioner for British Central Africa, who was based in Nyasaland from 1891 to 1896, and held a watching brief over the BSA Company's claims north of the Zambezi, moved on to Uganda as Governor. He was at first sceptical about plans for the settlement of Jews in east Africa, but became an ardent supporter of Zionism under the influence of the British writer Israel Zangwill. The so-called Uganda scheme, which referred to the area of Kenya later known as the White Highlands, was first mooted by the Colonial Secretary, Joseph Chamberlain, in 1903. The proposal split the Zionist movement and contributed to the premature death of its founder, Theodor Herzl, in the following year. The report which finally killed the idea was written in 1905 by Major H. St A. Gibbons, who was an early traveller and settler in Northern Rhodesia. His two-volume book, *Africa from South to North through Marotseland*, which was published in 1904, is a major source of information on the state of the western half of the country at the turn of the century. Gibbons bought a farm in the Lusaka district from the BSA Company, and was a leader of the settler community until his death in action in France during the First World War.[2]

Israel Zangwill became the founder and leader of the Jewish Territorial Organisation which continued to look for possible areas of Jewish settlement outside the Middle East for many years. Among the British backers of his movement were a number of Manchester businessmen, including Nathan Laski. The Reverend M. I. Cohen of Bulawayo was also a supporter of Zangwill's movement, and was an advocate of Angola as a suitable area of settlement. It is probable that his information about Angola, which was investigated by the organisation, came from the Barotseland trader A. B. Diamond. The Jewish Territorial Organisation approached the BSA Company, probably before 1911, with a request for land within its territories. The company apparently suggested that there might be possibilities in North-Eastern Rhodesia. Nothing came of this suggestion which referred to the part of the country in which there was always a minimum of Jewish commercial activity. Cohen saw his Bulawayo Hebrew Congregation as having a special role in relation to Jewish settlement in the north. He had a great vision: 'The next generation will reveal an epic still more wonderful, when the South African Jewish community stretching from the Cape to the distant interior will meet the expanding Jewish communities of North Africa in their advance to the South, and the foundation will be laid of the great African Jewry of the future.'[3]

Zionism was the first nationalist movement to have an active presence in Northern Rhodesia. The first Zionist organisation in the country, the Livingstone Herzl Zionist Society, was established early in 1912. Michael Levitz, a Barotseland trader, and M. Aukstolker, a plumber, are said to have been the prime movers in its inauguration, but Elie Susman was elected as the first president, with O. Zwick as vice-president, Harry Susman as treasurer, and M. Peimer as secretary. It is possible that the existence of a Zionist movement in the country may have had some influence on the development of African nationalism. Nelson Nalumango, one of the founders of the African Welfare Society movement in the 1930s, and of the Northern Rhodesian African National Congress in 1949, worked for Jewish traders, including the Jacobs brothers and Abe Galaun, and had close contacts with Livingstone's Jewish community.[4]

Zionism in Northern Rhodesia always tended to follow the Weizmann line of accommodation with British imperialism. At its first public concert, which was held at Marcus Grill's house in Livingstone in 1912, he insisted that 'God Save the King' should be sung together with the 'Hatikvah' and 'Dort wo die Seder'. At Chanukah in the same year, a meeting was held at Harry Susman's new 'premises' which were decorated with both Zionist flags and Union Jacks. A choir of a dozen boys and girls, all dressed in blue and white, and carrying Zionist flags, sang 'Ma Tovu'. There was, however, some controversy over the question of flags. A few years later, H. D. Sher objected so strongly to the children marching into a service behind the *Sefer Torah* at the *Hakofes*, carrying Union Jacks, that he snatched a flag from his daughter's hand and walked out of the *minyan*. He said: 'You are a Jewish child and you have your own flag.' A few days later he gave her a small blue-and-white Zionist flag which, she told Wolf Rybko in 1947, she still treasured. Helene Sher had by then been a member of the committee of the Livingstone Herzl Zionist Society for most of twenty years.[5]

Most of the Jews who were prominent in the religious life of the community in Northern Rhodesia were also active in the Zionist movement. This provided the major source of political and intellectual stimulation to people who were often relatively well educated, but who were cut off from the mainstream of intellectual life. In the early years the community had to rely on lectures from its own enthusiastic members, such as Joseph Finkelstein of Lealui, later of Sesheke. On 1 May 1920, the Sabbath, all the Jewish shops in Livingstone and Lusaka were closed in celebration of the granting of the mandate over Palestine to Britain by the League of Nations. It was reported that even Saul Jacobs, a legendary character, and the last of the *smous*, or itinerant Jewish traders, who lived on a wagon and traded in grain between Lusaka, Chisamba and Mumbwa, delayed his departure in order to attend the service. Substantial sums were raised in both towns for the Zionist cause.

The death of Oscar Susman, the younger brother of Elie and Harry, a few weeks earlier had been a serious blow to southern African Zionism. He had lived in Palestine with his parents for five years before coming to Africa, and had attended a Yeshiva school in Jerusalem. He had suffered badly from blackwater fever during the East African Campaign. This may have encouraged him to leave Northern Rhodesia, but he died after a short illness in London in March 1920, while waiting for a visa to re-enter Palestine. While the idea of *aliyah*, of 'going up' to Israel, was not then a major feature of southern African Zionism, as it was to become after the Second World War, he had decided to settle permanently in Palestine, and to invest in the territory. While in London he had been introduced by Mark Abrahams, the leading South African Zionist, to Chaim Weizmann and Nahum Sokolow, the leaders of the World Zionist Organisation. They had apparently been 'delighted to meet such a fine specimen of South African Jewry, ready to give his life to the great national cause'. He had himself been impressed by them, and had written to 'a Rhodesian friend': 'The prospects for Zionism are very good ... There seems to be unity of work and thought among our leaders and all they require now is our financial support. We have, or shall have, the right settlers, and also the leaders. The sooner our masses know that they will have our strong financial support the better.'

Oscar Susman was a young man of considerable wealth. His share of the capital employed in the family business had grown to over £10,000 at the time of his death. He noted that the development of Palestine would depend on small-scale farming and that 'this means hard work and a very simple life to which South Africans are not habituated'. On the other hand, southern African Jews 'might do well there in commerce, and for that conditions are very favourable'.

In a tribute, the Reverend M. I. Cohen wrote:

He came here ten years ago from a Jerusalem Yeshiva. He soon mastered the English language and became a practical man of affairs, a real pioneer of Barotseland. Life to him in the Zambezi valley was but a means to an end. He dreamt ever of the time when he should be able to return to Palestine, and help to build up our land. He was a most ardent Zionist and the movement in Rhodesia owes much to his support. When the war broke out he felt it was his duty as a Jew to go to the front. His kit bag did not lack a prayerbook, and [in] all he did and suffered he strove to uphold the honour of our name ... A most promising life has been tragically cut short. Oscar Susman died on national service. We mourn his loss, and honour and cherish his memory.[6]

A succession of notable Zionist leaders and intellectuals visited Northern Rhodesia from the mid-1920s onwards. Many of them came on fund-raising tours of southern Africa, and included the Victoria Falls on their itineraries. The majority of them penetrated no further than Livingstone, but for men like Maurice Gersh, who was secretary of the Livingstone society in the late 1920s, these visits were memorable events. Zionist leaders were the only internationally renowned politicians and intellectuals, of any nationality or persuasion, to visit Northern Rhodesia between the two world wars. The first of the Zionist emissaries to visit Livingstone was Dr Alexander Goldstein in 1924. He was followed by Rabbi Zlotnik in 1925 and Nahum Sokolow, chairman of the Zionist Executive, in 1926. He returned as president of the World Zionist Organisation in 1934. Colonel Kisch, the head of the Zionist Executive in Palestine, came in 1928. About £400 was raised in Livingstone on this occasion. Elias Kopelowitz gave a personal donation of over £50 which would be a very large sum today. The Shapiro, Wasserson and Grill families also made large contributions.[7]

Wolf Rybko, the Zionist propagandist and fund-raiser, made his first visit to the country in August and September of the same year. He was the first emissary to travel north of Livingstone, calling at Lusaka, Broken Hill and Ndola. He continued along the Line of Rail into the Congo and held meetings at Elisabethville and Likasi. Although he did not write his own account of this journey, as he was to do on his return visit in 1947, reports of his meetings and fund-raising activities were published in the *Zionist Record*, and shed some light on the relative strengths of the Jewish communities in Northern Rhodesia and the Congo. At Broken Hill a meeting was held at short notice at the Jacobsons' house. It was attended by twenty-five people, including the young shopkeepers Shim Lakofski and his friend David

Pinhassovith, who donated £15 and £10 respectively. A total of £262 was subscribed in the town, where Meyer Jacobson was by far the largest contributor. Lusaka produced £242, almost half of which was donated by members of the Kollenberg family, but only £80 was raised in Ndola where the development of the Copperbelt was only just beginning. By contrast, Rybko was able to raise £900 in the Congo, the bulk of which came from Elisabethville, which was the only place north of Livingstone where there was an organised Zionist Society. It is noticeable that the contributions of the Sephardic section of the population, which was already in the majority in the Congo, were small. A contribution of about £5 from Messrs Amato, Capelouto and Tarica of Kamina would seem to indicate either that they were only just beginning their spectacular business careers, or that they had little interest in Zionism. The fact that Rybko addressed the meetings in Yiddish may not, of course, have encouraged the Ladino-speaking section of the community. It is also noticeable that there was a high degree of overlap between the Northern Rhodesian and Congolese Jewish communities. The leading member of the Zionist Society in Elisabethville was Mrs Nathan Schulman, who had previously lived in Northern Rhodesia, and was to return there with her husband in the late 1930s. Members of the Wulfsohn, Glasstone, Herbstein, Gelman, Marcus, Wasserson and Osrin families, who attended the meetings in Elisabethville, lived at different times in both countries. Among the largest donations was that of the Blumenthal brothers who also had family links with Northern Rhodesia.[8]

Maurice Gersh recalled visits in the 1920s from Menachem Ussishkin and Dr Olsvanger, but the dates of their visits are uncertain. Schmaryahu Levin, regarded as the most brilliant of Zionist lecturers, came in 1933. Professor Selig Brodetsky, a distinguished mathematician, came in 1936 to launch the *Keren Heyesod* (Foundation Fund) campaign. From 1922 onwards, there were biennial campaigns to raise money for this fund. The large individual contributions which were made by people in southern Africa were facilitated by the stop order system which was introduced at this time. This allowed for contributions to be paid in instalments over twenty months.

The most memorable visit was that of Chaim Weizmann, the charismatic leader of the Zionist movement, in March 1932. He had been compelled to step down as president of the World Zionist Organisation in the previous year as a result of the Passfield Memorandum which indicated a reduced British commitment to the creation of a Jewish state in Palestine. The leaders of the reception committee were Max Taube, president of the Hebrew Congregation, the Rev. Maurice Diamond, minister of the Congregation, and Lewis Hochstein, president of the Herzl Society. A reception was held at Harry Susman's house and nearly £400 was raised. This was a remarkable amount of money to raise at the bottom of the depression. Bertha Wasserson, who was nine years old at the time, presented a bouquet to Mrs Vera Weizmann. This was an honour which Bertha vividly recalled many years later.[9]

The outbreak of the Second World War provided fresh stimulus to both religious and secular communal organisations. It also brought fresh blood to the community. Two related German Jewish couples, David and Rose Messerer in Mufulira, and Julius and Helen Mohrer in Lusaka, were to be particularly active in the Zionist movement for many years. The establishment of effective Zionist committees in Lusaka and on the Copperbelt seems to date from early in the war, and especially to the visit of a group of Zionist emissaries, Dr Alexander Goldstein, Rabbi Z. Schwartz and S. Hirschmann, in August 1942. Moses Cohen had noted as early as 1929 that Zionism had done more than anything else, though aided by the prevalence of anti-Semitism, to foster 'an intensive Jewish spirit' in the region. Small communities, which could not always agree on religious issues, were generally united in their support for Zionism. Rybko, on his second visit to the country in 1947, found that Zionism was well organised in all the main centres, including the new towns of the Copperbelt. In some places, such as Luanshya, the Zionist Society seemed to be better organised than the Hebrew Congregation. Moses Cohen had also noticed that it was in the Zionist movement, and other communal welfare organisations, that women first took a prominent part in Jewish public life. There is a general consensus that the most active of the Zionist organisations from the 1940s to the 1960s was the women's organisation, WIZO. From the early years of the war, this was well organised in the major centres and held weekly meetings and sales. There were regular visits by women speakers from the south, including Mrs Rachel Baron from Bulawayo. It was in the 1950s that the Zionist youth organisation, the Habonim, was most active in the country. Aviva Ron recalls that they received visits from *shlichim* (emissaries) and young people from South Africa, and that camps were held at Ndola and Mufulira.[10]

The recognition by the United Nations of the independence of the state of Israel in May 1949 was a major turning point in the history of the Zionist movement. Elias Kopelowitz, then leader of the community in Livingstone, held a reception at his home to celebrate the event. H. Oza, an Asian businessman in the town, recalls that this was the first occasion on which he, or any other member of the Asian community, received a formal invitation to a Jewish community event. The stream of Zionist dignitaries to the country did not end with the achievement of the state of Israel. Over the next twenty years, prominent Israeli visitors included Moshe Sharett, Israel's first Foreign Minister, and second Prime Minister, Menachim Begin in 1953, General Moshe Dayan in 1957, and Golda Meir, as Foreign Minister, on the occasion of Zambia's independence in 1964. Zionist intellectual visitors included Sir Isaiah Berlin, a distinguished Oxford academic. The visits of Begin and Meir caused some controversy. The great majority of Zionists in the country were moderates who had little or no sympathy with the right-wing 'Revisionists' and the 'terrorist' Begin. Golda Meir caused some offence by refusing to meet the Jewish community in Livingstone, though she was warmly welcomed by the Jewish community at Ndola airport. She was anxious to win the support of members of the Afro-Asian bloc in the United Nations, and appears to have thought that it would be undiplomatic to be too closely identified with a section of white settler society.[11]

For some time after independence, Israeli development workers were actively engaged in agricultural cooperative schemes, based on the *moshavim*, on the Copperbelt. President Kaunda was so impressed with the progress of the Kafubu Block near Luanshya that in 1969 he asked Israel to draw up a plan for development in the Western Province, formerly Barotseland. Apart from the building of an abattoir at Mongu, the proposed projects there had not made much progress before the Arab–Israeli War of 1973, after which Zambia broke off diplomatic relation with Israel. According to Dennis Figov, the government vainly hoped that Israeli experts would stay on after the break in relations. The presence of Israeli workers provided a boost to the depleted numbers of the Ndola and Luanshya Hebrew Congregations, and also encouraged people to think of going on *aliyah* to Israel.

As the size of the Jewish community dwindled, the majority of emigrants left for South Africa, Britain and the United States, but a significant minority made their way to Israel. A number of young people, who had been influenced by their membership of Habonim, emigrated to Israel from 1960 onwards. They included, among many others, Cecilia Kopelowitz and her sister, Minda Schlesinger, from Livingstone, Aviva Elkaim Ron from Ndola, Renée Dobkins Wide from Chingola, the Goldberg twins from Luanshya, and Belle Zemack from Lusaka. Aviva Ron has had a distinguished career in the Israeli Ministry of Health and has recently worked for the World Health Organisation, and for the International Labour Organisation in South East Asia as an expert on social insurance. Some of the German Jewish refugees who had been active Zionists, such as the Mohrers, and Alex and Fanny Messerer, also left for Israel. Their only son, Ron, a helicopter pilot, was killed in action in Lebanon in 1984, as was a son of Dvora Rankow. In 1997 David Messerer was planning to leave South Africa to join one of his daughters in Israel. Among those who emigrated after a relatively short time in Zambia were Dr Harold Slomowitz, with his wife Zoe and four daughters, who were in Ndola during the 1960s.[12]

Local Government

There was always some tension between the support of Jews in Northern Rhodesia for an independent Jewish state, and their desire for assimilation into colonial society. At the level of local government, members of the Jewish community made a remarkable and quite disproportionate contribution to public life. Dr Monica Fisher, a senior surviving member of Northern Rhodesia's colonial establishment, recalls that contribution, and believes that the Jews were, on the whole, 'altruistic and good for the country'.[13] It was often the case that the same people who were active in Jewish communal and Zionist organisations were also active in public life. Obvious examples would include Sam Fischer, Maurice Gersh and Maurice Rabb, who all combined prominent positions in local government with communal leadership. It would appear that most of them saw their involvement in local government as a public rather than as a political service. This view reflected the situation in the early days when members of village and township management boards were not elected but were nominated by the colonial government.

Jews were involved at one time or another in the government of almost all the major towns, and many of the smaller ones, in Northern Rhodesia. The first Jewish mayor in the country was Hyam Schulman, who held that position in Ndola from 1937 to 1939. The contribution of Maurice Gersh to the development of Kitwe has already been outlined. The contribution of Sam Fischer and his nephew, Jack, to the development of Lusaka was also considerable. Maurice Rabb was twice mayor of Livingstone in 1951–52 and 1956–57, and Alex Slutzkin held that post in 1958–59. Maurice Rosen and Harry Rayner served as chairman of the township management board in Luanshya while Rayner's nephew, Dennis Figov, was twice mayor of the town. In Mufulira, Uri Illion and David Messerer both served for a number of years on the township management board and Town Council. Messerer was deputy mayor for a while until pressure of business compelled him to retire from local government. In the smaller towns along the Line of Rail, Benny Iljon and Philip Fischer both served as chairman of the Mazabuka management board while Jack Faerber held the same position at Monze for many years.

The most public-spirited of all these people was, perhaps, Maurice Rabb. A list of all the public and voluntary posts which he held in Livingstone and in the country at large would run to several pages, and he also made substantial donations to local charities. These included donations for the building of the Hillcrest High School hall and for the Natural History wing of the Livingstone Museum. He was also responsible for the establishment of an Agricultural Education Fund for Barotseland in 1961 to commemorate the sixtieth anniversary of the Susmans' arrival. His wife Peggy was equally active. She was not only elected as Federal president of WIZO, and national president of the Union of Jewish Women, but was also for three years president of the Women's Institutes of the Federation. She served for over ten years on the Northern Rhodesian Education Advisory Board, which was primarily concerned with the promotion of African education, and was for eight years a member of the Federal Education Advisory Board. She resigned from that position in August 1962 in protest at the continued policy of segregating European, 'Coloured' and Asian education within the Federation. She was also a member for sixteen years, 1955–71, of the Victoria Falls Trust.[14]

National Politics

Maurice Rabb was one of only two active members of the Jewish community to move from local government into national politics. In 1958 he was invited by the United Federal Party to stand in the elections for the Northern Rhodesian Legislative Council for the Livingstone seat, and was elected unopposed. He remained a member of the Legislative Council until 1962. He was chairman of the Public Accounts Committee and was party spokesman on financial matters. He also attended the Lancaster House constitutional talks in London in 1960. He stood for a national, as opposed to an African or European, seat in 1962. He obtained the largest number of votes in a constituency which included Barotseland, but he did not win a seat as an insufficient number of people voted on the lower roll to satisfy the complex terms of the 'slide-rule' constitution. Although he was tipped by the press in 1962 as the shadow Minister of Finance, he had become increasingly disillusioned with the Federation. He felt that the policy of 'partnership' had continued to subordinate Africans and that the Federation was run in the interests of Southern Rhodesia. He referred in a speech to the Federal cow which grazed on lush pastures in Northern Rhodesia, but was milked in the south. He was also critical of the failure of the British government to put back into Northern Rhodesia money which came from the taxation of the mining companies.[15]

One other prominent member of the Jewish community was elected to Northern Rhodesia's Legislative Council as a member of the United Federal Party in 1963. Shmuel, known as 'Val', Magnus was born in Russia, but moved to England as a small child. He had both rabbinical and legal training, and moved to Northern Rhodesia to work as a lawyer in Kitwe in 1958. He played an active role in the Jewish community, and was instrumental in the formation in 1959 of the United Hebrew Congregation of the Copperbelt. He also became a vice-president of the Rhodesian Jewish Board of Deputies, which became the Central African Board on the break-up of the Federation. He had been an active member of the Liberal Party in Britain, and served as an elected member of the Legislative Council, the Legislative Assembly and the National Assembly in Northern Rhodesia. He was, together with Len Pinshow, on the liberal wing of the United Federal Party. He left Parliament in 1968 when he was invited by President Kaunda to become a judge, and left the country in 1971. He was strictly orthodox, and was cut off after UDI from his supply of kosher meat which came from Bulawayo. He claimed that the question of his diet was discussed by the Cabinet which declined to make an exception to sanctions on his behalf. He was subsequently reduced to a diet of fish.[16]

Although he was never a member of Parliament, Len Pinshow was also actively involved in Federal politics. He had had an interest in politics from the age of thirteen when he helped in the office of Sir Patrick Duncan during a famous election contest in the Yeoville constituency in 1929. He joined the South African army at the beginning of the war and attained the rank of staff sergeant, but his military career was cut short in 1942 when he was sent home from Egypt after trying to organise an international Parliament for allied troops of all nations and races. After the war, he was a member of the Springbok Legion – a radical ex-servicemen's organisation. He is proud of his roles as Northern Rhodesia's most energetic sports promoter, and as a political organiser. He clearly sees close links between sport and politics. He was in 1948 one of the founders, with Gervase Clay, of the Northern Rhodesian (later Zambian) Amateur Athletics Association, which he ran for six years. He was also a founder of the Olympic and Commonwealth Games Association, and of the Kitwe Playing Fields Association. His greatest organisational triumph was, however, the Festival of Sport which was held in 1953 at Kitwe as part of the Rhodes centenary celebrations. This had more participants than the Empire Games which were held at Vancouver in the following year and made a profit of £6,000.

Although the festival had been a whites-only event, he was in 1959 awarded the MBE for his contribution to the development of non-racial sport in the Federation. He had been campaigning on the issue since 1956 and had taken on the whole Federal sports establishment, Roy Welensky and most of the United Federal Party, when he insisted that the young Northern Rhodesian runner, Yotham Muleya, should be allowed to run against the Olympic medallists Gordon Pirie and Murray Halberg in a three-mile race in Salisbury – an event which Muleya won. In 1961 Pinshow resigned from all his sports commitments, but proceeded almost immediately to found the first branch of Lions International which survives in Zambia as a popular service organisation.

He was president of the important Kitwe branch of the United Federal Party and had the support of Val Magnus, and of many Asian members, in pressing for legislation to prohibit racial discrimination in public places, and for the opening of public schools to people of all races. He acted as public relations adviser to the party, but quit 'when it became clear that they were only prepared to pay lip-service to the policy of partnership'. Although he was once close to him, he thinks that Welensky was too cautious, and seems to have fallen out with him and his party in 1961, the year of the Cha Cha Cha campaign. He joined UNIP before independence and, with his friend Oliver Irwin, a young chartered accountant, gave Kaunda advice on party organisation.[17]

Roy Welensky

There were three other people of Jewish descent – all three had Lithuanian fathers – who were to play important roles in the political history of Northern Rhodesia and Zambia. They were Roy Welensky, Simon Zukas and Aaron Milner. Between them they ensured that there was a son of Lithuanian Jewry in almost every government of Northern Rhodesia, the Federation, or Zambia for nearly sixty years. One of them was associated with settler rule and white supremacy, while two were identified with the African nationalist movement.

Roy Welensky was born in Salisbury in 1907, the thirteenth and youngest child of Michael and Leah Welensky. His father, who was then about sixty, came from a village near Vilna, and had left the Russian empire before 1870. He began a long and varied career as a pedlar, moved to Sweden to avoid conscription, and went on from there to Prussia and the United States. After saloon-keeping and fur-trading in the Midwest, and oil prospecting in Texas, he moved on again to South Africa in 1881. He arrived in Kimberley too late for the diamond rush, but went on to make and lose a small fortune as an ostrich feather trader. It was at this time that he met and married a young Afrikaner girl, Aletta Ferreira, at Willowmore, a small town to the east of Oudtshoorn. She became a convert to Judaism and changed her first name to Leah. The family soon moved to Southern Rhodesia where Michael served in the Afrikander Corps in the suppression of the Ndebele Rebellion of 1896, and was the first president of the Gwelo Hebrew Congregation. At the time of Roy's birth, his parents were running a boarding house and bar in Pioneer Street, Salisbury. When Roy's mother died in 1918, his father was an old man, and earned a little money by acting as a *wocher*, a Watcher for the Dead, for the Salisbury Hebrew Congregation. Roy recalled that he attended *shul* with his father, who had then become very 'frum', or pious, on Friday evenings and, like many other Jewish boys, he had to run around to find a *minyan*.[18]

After an interrupted primary school education, Roy started work as a shop assistant at the age of fourteen. He worked in Glendale and Salisbury before joining the railways in 1924. An elder brother, Ben, was also employed on the railways, while the eldest brother, Dave, was working for the Wankie Colliery Company. All three brothers became involved with the Rhodesia Railway Workers Union which recruited members at Wankie Colliery in the late 1920s, and all three were victimised for their involvement in a strike there in 1929. Roy was sent in 1933 to Broken Hill which was extremely depressed at the time and regarded as a punishment posting. His promotion from shunter to mainline engine-driver was delayed until the late 1930s. He had married Liz Henderson, an Afrikaans-speaking girl with a Scottish name, in 1928, and they had two children at the time of their move north of the Zambezi.[19]

Broken Hill was to be Roy Welensky's home for twenty years, and his power base throughout a career in trade unionism and politics which lasted for thirty years. There is little doubt that it was the pressure of anti-Semitism which drove him to become politically involved in Broken Hill. Like many Jews in Germany in the 1930s, he had little consciousness of his Jewish identity until this was thrust upon him by fascists. He had little formal Jewish education, though an important element in his upbringing was reading through the whole Bible, both Old and New Testaments, twice with his father. He had little knowledge of the liturgy of Judaism, though his father had insisted that he say kaddish on his mother's death, and he was, by some accounts, prepared on occasion to help make up a *minyan*.[20]

There was a small, but active, group of members of Oswald Mosley's British Union of Fascists in Broken Hill in the mid-1930s. Roy Welensky was anathema to them both as 'that fat Jew-boy' and as a Mason. After he had found his locomotive placarded with anti-Semitic slogans, he retaliated at first with his fists. As the former heavy-weight boxing champion of Southern Rhodesia, he was well able to defend himself, but he then decided on a more positive line of action. He took over and organised the almost defunct Broken Hill branch of the Rhodesia Railway Workers Union. His small house at 24 Central Avenue became the unofficial headquarters of the union and resembled a doctor's surgery. He and his members soon found that he had remarkable forensic and negotiating skills. His friend, Isaac Benatar, a Sephardic Jew from Rhodes, noted that 'Fascism gave Roy his first political consciousness'. Welensky himself told one of his biographers, Garry Allighan:

> It was to some extent to combat the advance of Fascism in our little locality that I intensified my trade-union activities. It did not take me long before I decided to give the Fascists a real go for their money. There was, first, their struggle for strength and control of the union and I won that by an overwhelming majority. Opposition inside the union from the Fascist element then began to fade away ... I decided that the best thing to do was to ignore the anti-Semitic side and organise the trade union movement because I was convinced that one of the best bulwarks against the advance of Fascism was the British system of trade unionism. I knew that if Fascism were able to get a firm grip, it would be the death-knell of the trade union movement because the trade unions stand for freedom of opinion and action.[21]

For Welensky in Broken Hill in the 1930s the major 'race question' was between Jews and gentiles, and not between whites and Africans. There was at the time only a minority of black employees on the railways, and there was none on the footplate. When he was asked by John Freeman in a famous 'Face to Face' interview on British television in 1960 about his knowledge of black people, he replied that he had, as a child, swum with them 'bare-arsed' in the Makabusi river in Salisbury. This was, no doubt, true, but he had little direct contact with black people in the course of his work. It proved to be a fatal limitation that he was unable, in spite of considerable intelligence, eloquence and charm, and a course in self-education which took in the works of Karl Marx, William Morris and John Stuart Mill, to move much beyond the realm of white labour politics.[22]

By 1935 Welensky had become so well established in Broken Hill that he was able to deliver the railway vote to the Legislative Council candidate of his choice, Stewart Gore-Browne, a mildly eccentric and wealthy upper middle-class Englishman with Fabian socialist sympathies, and a partly Jewish wife, Lorna Goldman. Three years later, Welensky replaced Gore-Browne as the member for the Northern District while the latter continued in the Legislative Council as a nominated representative of African interests.[23] Gore-Browne was, as we have seen, one of the members of the local committee set up to investigate the possibilities for Jewish agricultural settlement in Northern Rhodesia. Many years later Welensky gave Sarah Gertrude Millin, the then elderly South African Jewish novelist who was writing a book on white Africans, his recollections of the debate on Jewish immigration. He then claimed that, at a secret meeting of the Legislative Council which he attended soon after his election in 1938, the unofficial members were split five to four on the issue of an immigration quota, and that it was 'my vote that allowed the refugees to come into Northern Rhodesia'. In a curious passage which must refer to Sir Leopold Moore, and another unidentifiable member of the council, he recalled that among the four unofficial members who voted against the motion were

> two members who were in fact Jews. Neither of them acknowledged the fact, though both of them were aware that I knew their backgrounds. Naturally I never said anything, but I did alter my attitude towards them, quietly, and I often have tried to work out the mentality behind their action ... This happened nearly thirty years ago, but I have often tried to understand the motives for their attitude – I still don't.[24]

Although Jewishness may have been imposed upon him, Welensky was certainly not inclined to conceal or deny it. The contemporary prevalence of anti-Semitism in the settler community did not prevent him from emerging as the most effective spokesman first for Northern Rhodesia's settlers, and then for the settlers of central Africa as a whole. It is, of course, often the case that people of marginal identity emerge as leaders. They have to work harder than others to overcome their apparent handicap, and, in the process, make themselves indispensable. As Welensky told the London *Jewish Chronicle* in 1958: 'I am one of those people who never deny their Jewish origins: it has certainly not prevented me from becoming Prime Minister.'[25] Although he was singled out for attack as 'the Polish Jew' by the Nazi overseas broadcasting service, 'Zeesen', in 1942, following his appointment as a member of the government as Director of Manpower in the previous year, there is no evidence that anti-Semitism was a political problem for him after the war.[26] It is interesting to note, however, that when the African nationalist leader Harry Nkumbula chose to launch an ethnic attack on him in the context of the imposition of Federation, he did not attack him as a Jew, but as a 'Pole of humble education'. Nkumbula appears to have realised that it was more damaging at that time to associate him with Northern Rhodesia's former camp-based Polish refugee population than with its more prosperous Jewish community.[27] Welensky did, however, become the target of anti-Semitic attacks when he attempted to enter Southern Rhodesian politics in 1964, the

year after the collapse of the Federation, and the year before Southern
Rhodesia's Unilateral Declaration of Independence.[28]

There is some irony in the fact that a labour leader who had entered
politics as a determined opponent of fascism should have become the main
target of African nationalist attacks in the years before Zambian independence.
There were two main issues which separated him irrevocably from African
nationalist opinion. These were his position as a white labour leader – he
established the Northern Rhodesia Labour Party in 1941 – and his consistent
support for the amalgamation of Northern and Southern Rhodesia. He was
initially opposed to African unionisation, but he was impressed by the African
railway workers' organisation of a successful strike in 1945. In the following
year, he indicated that he was opposed to the proliferation of 'mushroom'
unions, but favoured legislation for the recognition of a small number of
African trade unions, beginning with a mineworkers union. His own union
feared the substitution of African workers for white workers at a lower level
of wages. It demanded the protection of European interests, and could not
agree to the idea of equal pay without 'some formula which will give social
security'. In practice the railways remained an area of protected white employment throughout the colonial period. In so far as the Rhodesia Railway
Workers Union remained Welensky's political power base, he was effectively
opposed to 'African advancement'.[29]

As the Rhodesia Railway Workers Union operated on both sides of the
Zambezi, it is hardly surprising that Welensky was a keen supporter of
the amalgamation of the two Rhodesias. He took control, with a partner, in
1941 of the Copperbelt newspaper *The Northern News*, and used it to campaign
for amalgamation. Two years later, he introduced a motion in the Legislative
Council calling for amalgamation which received the support of the majority
of the elected members. He played an important part, as leader of the
unofficial members of the Legislative Council, in the negotiations with
Britain's Labour government between 1948 and 1951 on the question of
'closer union' in central Africa. His role as a trade unionist, and his social
democratic credentials, eased relations with British Labour Party ministers.
The key negotiator in the Colonial Office was Andrew Cohen, who began
to see a Federation of Rhodesia and Nyasaland, in which the Colonial Office
would retain control of 'Native' affairs in the two northern territories, as an
island of racial 'partnership' between rising African nationalism in west Africa
and the threat of Afrikaner nationalism in South Africa. Welensky now
moderated his own amalgamationist views and decided to accept the compromise of Federation with its slogan of 'partnership'.[30]

As a Northern Rhodesian settler leader, Welensky had also been involved
in two campaigns which emphasised the separate identity and interests of the
territory. The first of these campaigns for so-called 'Responsible Government', meaning settler self-government along Southern Rhodesian lines, was
unsuccessful as the Colonial Office remained committed to the idea that the

Zambezi was to be the northern boundary of untrammelled settler power. The second was the campaign against the BSA Company's right to levy a mineral royalty on copper produced in Northern Rhodesia. In 1938 the Colonial Office had ruled that the validity of the company's mineral claims could not be challenged and the post-war Labour government rejected the suggestion, favoured by Welensky and Gore-Browne, of nationalisation. Welensky, however, threatened in 1948 to introduce a motion for a royalties tax. The company agreed in the following year to hand over 20 per cent of its royalties to the Northern Rhodesian government immediately, and to hand over its mineral rights in 1986. Welensky received some credit for this deal although, as a 50 per cent tax on the royalties was a possibility, the company had the last laugh. It continued to draw enormous royalties from Northern Rhodesia until independence and put very little back into the country.[31]

The Federation of Rhodesia and Nyasaland was established in 1953 by Britain's new Conservative government. It was imposed on Northern Rhodesia and Nyasaland in spite of the opposition of the most vocal representatives of African opinion, and the reservations of many colonial civil servants. The opposition of Africans in Southern Rhodesia was more muted, and there were conservative whites in the south who distrusted the association with the black north. Welensky became Minister of Transport and Communications in 1953 and Prime Minister on the retirement of Godfrey Huggins, Lord Malvern, three years later. He then became the main target of growing African nationalist attacks which resulted in 1963 in the dissolution of the Federation and the independence of Northern Rhodesia and Nyasaland.

Welensky was primarily a Northern Rhodesian politician and had no political base in the south. Early in the history of the Federation he was faced with a decision which tested both his loyalty to Northern Rhodesia and the loyalty of his constituents to himself. At the time of the establishment of the Federation, Huggins had given assurances to Northern Rhodesian representatives, including the Governor, that the Kafue river hydro-electric project in Northern Rhodesia would be given priority over the larger and more expensive Kariba project. Early in 1955, Huggins announced that the government intended to renege on that assurance and proceed with the Kariba scheme. It was seen as a prestige project which would create the largest man-made lake in the world. This would inundate parts of Northern and Southern Rhodesia and provide a potent symbol of Federal unity. The decision to go ahead with the Kariba project provoked a storm of protest in Northern Rhodesia among both the black and white sections of the population. Welensky addressed stormy meetings of white people in Lusaka, and on the Copperbelt, in which he defended the government's decision. By doing so he may be said to have betrayed the interests of his Northern Rhodesian constituents, but he ensured his own succession as Prime Minister in the following year.[32]

One of those who attended these meetings was Peter Fraenkel who also

met Welensky socially in Lusaka at this time. He was intensely aware of
Welensky's chameleon-like qualities. With liberal Jewish friends he would say,
'We Jews know about the suppressed aspirations of a people', but with white
workers on the Copperbelt, he would pander to their racist views. According
to Lewis Gann, there was a joke at the time which alleged that he attended
the Synagogue on Saturdays and the Dutch Reformed Church on Sundays:
'two-faced as usual'. Fraenkel did not think that he was 'a conscious, calcu-
lating hypocrite. I started to understand when I observed that he could not
face a hostile meeting.' During the Kariba crisis he noticed that this

> big, aggressive bull of a man almost broke down under the onslaught of a
> hostile crowd. His chief quality as a politician was not his strength at all, but
> his sensitivity and intuition. He sensed what people thought, believed, wanted
> to hear and he adjusted himself with great skill. It was not hypocrisy, but an
> emotional necessity. His sad youth in the hostile slums had left its scars.[33]

While individual Jews were major contributors to the funds of the United
Federal Party, some major Jewish businesses, such as Susman Brothers and
Wulfsohn, did not on principle make contributions to political parties. David
Susman recalls that he sought to persuade Welensky when he became Prime
Minister that he should use his overwhelming majority to sweep away all
forms of racial discrimination. Welensky was not prepared to be persuaded
and took no action. Susman recalls that, when they met many years later,
Welensky attributed the failure of the Federation to British machinations
rather than to his own failure to grasp the nettle.[34]

While Welensky had for many years been seen as the devil incarnate by
African nationalist politicians, his reputation underwent a revival after Ian
Smith's Unilateral Declaration of Independence. Welensky's fundamental
loyalty to the British Commonwealth, despite what he saw as betrayal by
Harold Macmillan and Iain Macleod, made him a bitter opponent of Smith
and UDI. This improved his standing in the eyes of Zambian politicians to
whom he now appeared as a relatively benign figure. He was invited by
President Kaunda to visit Zambia in 1974, the tenth anniversary year of
independence, and to take part in the celebrations. He was not able to come
for the celebrations, but his visit in January 1975 was a success. On his
return to England, where he then lived, he gave a talk about his visit to the
Royal Commonwealth Society in London. He was apparently most impressed
by what he saw as the emergence from invisibility of Zambian women. He
was surprised to find that they were now not only driving cars, but were
occupying responsible administrative and managerial positions.[35]

Simon Zukas

Simon Zukas's first involvement in central African politics came while he was
at the University of Cape Town through the Rhodesia Study Club which was

formed by radical students from the Rhodesias with the encouragement of Jack Simons. Its newsletter was first published in October 1948 by Zukas, Harry Chimowitz, a civil engineering graduate, Robert James Chikerema, a law student, and John Shoniwa. Harry Chimowitz was born in Gatooma, Southern Rhodesia, where his Lithuanian-born father was a butcher. Chikerema, who was deported from South Africa before he completed his degree and was to become a leader of the Zimbabwe African People's Union (ZAPU), and Shoniwa were also from Southern Rhodesia. The newsletter was produced regularly until February 1950 and was circulated clandestinely in Northern Rhodesia by Best Kofie in Ndola. The first issue contained a warning that the British government would soon give way to settler demands for amalgamation. The newsletter had sufficient impact for Roy Welensky to launch a lengthy attack on it in the Legislative Council late in 1949.[36]

Simon Zukas was born in Lithuania in 1925. His grandfather had been in South Africa in the early years of the century, but had returned home. With the rise of fascism and the threat of war in Europe, his father, Chaim, set off for South Africa in 1937. He was unable to settle in South Africa and moved on to Northern Rhodesia. In the following year he sent for his wife and three sons, of whom Simon was the eldest. They lived at first in Ndola and then in Luanshya. In Lithuania Simon had been a member of the socialist Zionist youth movement, the Hachaluc Hazoir, and had become politically precocious in the highly charged atmosphere of the country. His family background was orthodox, and his first rebellion was over his bar mitzvah. He had begun preparation for this in Lithuania, but when he reached Northern Rhodesia he refused to go ahead with the ceremony. He had, he says, by then become a free thinker. In his first years in Northern Rhodesia he was faced with the problems of learning a new language and adjusting to a totally different society. For a while he suppressed his political radicalism and concentrated on the process of adaptation. It was not then possible, even for white children, to complete their secondary education in the country, and after a few years he was sent to boarding school at Milton High School in Bulawayo. Among his contemporaries there were Peter Fraenkel and Alan Feigenbaum. When he left school in 1943, his application to join the army resulted in his only meeting with Roy Welensky. In his official capacity as Director of Manpower, Welensky sought to dissuade Simon from military service and to encourage him to take up his Beit Scholarship to study civil engineering, arguing that engineers would be in demand after the war. Simon was not persuaded and joined the Northern Rhodesia Regiment. He was sent to east Africa where he served as an non-commissioned officer. After the end of the war in 1945, but before his demobilisation, he served with the King's African Rifles in Uganda in action against the Bataka movement which had been involved in the assassination of the *Katikiro*, or Prime Minister, of Buganda. This experience of colonialism in action rekindled his political radicalism which was to be developed at the University of Cape Town where he studied civil engineering between 1948 and 1950. Under the influence of people such as Jack Simons, and a young contemporary, Lionel Forman, he became a Marxist, though he did not join the then legal Communist Party of South Africa.[37]

Simon Zukas graduated in 1950 and started work early in the following year in the engineer's department of the Ndola Municipality. On his arrival in Ndola he found that there was a political discussion club already in existence. It had been formed in the previous year through the inspiration of another young Jewish intellectual, Arnold L. (Bill) Epstein, who was doing research on the Urban Native Courts system.[38] (Epstein's contribution in the field of social anthropology will be considered in a later chapter.) The discussion club brought Zukas into contact with a number of the best educated and most radical young men on the Copperbelt. They included Bridger Katenga, a welfare officer from Nyasaland, Justin Chimba, a clerk in the Mines Department, and Reuben Kamanga. While Katenga eventually became Malawi's ambassador to Ethiopia, Chimba and Kamanga were to become ministers in Zambia's first post-independence government. Simon was also in contact with Godwin Mbikusita-Lewanika, first president of the recently formed Northern Rhodesian African National Congress, but found that he was not responsive to the suggestion that the congress should prepare to mobilise mass resistance to the Federal proposals. He suspected that Lewanika was under the control of the government.

On the day that the Federation White Paper was published, 13 June 1951, Zukas met Bridger Katenga who agreed to call an emergency meeting of the discussion club in the Welfare Hall. The meeting set up the Ndola Federal Proposals Examination Group with Justin Chimba as chairman and Zukas as secretary. The study group met almost every evening for two weeks in a classroom in the 'Location' on the Ndola–Bwana Mkubwa Road. Among the twenty or so people who regularly attended were Nephas Tembo, Thomas Mtine, who both later became prominent in different fields, Abnor Kazunga, then a member of the Ndola Urban Advisory Council and of the African Provincial Council, and Israel Kasomo, a Tribal Elder who represented Chief Tafuna of Mbala. Zukas has provided an account of the procedure of the group:

> Every paragraph in the White Paper was read out in English and then discussed at length. The Secretary would read out his summary on each point and this would be agreed or amended. Discussions usually lasted till midnight. The object of this rather drawn-out process was to prepare a cadre of people whose understanding of the issues would be such that they would not easily be hood-winked or intimidated by District Commissioners. In this it succeeded: not only would most of this group be able to handle well the arguments against Federation, they would also be prepared to make considerable personal sacrifices in *mobilising* Mass Action against it.[39]

The group reported back to a public meeting in the Welfare Hall on 5 July at which the Ndola Anti-Federation Action Committee was formed. Their cyclostyled report was published under the names of Justin Chimba and Simon Zukas as 'The Case Against the Federal Proposals' on 20 August. Although this document was the collective work of a group, Zukas had clearly played a key role in its drafting. Calling as it did for universal adult suffrage and an end to all forms of racial discrimination, it was the most radical document which had yet been produced by the African nationalist movement in Northern Rhodesia. Its main purpose was to refute the argument which it described as 'the Malan bogey': the suggestion that Federation was necessary to prevent the northward spread of Afrikaner nationalism and apartheid. It suggested, on the contrary, that Federation was aimed at 'halting African advancement in the Northern territories'. It argued that 'Federation on a basis of truly democratic principles might merit consideration by the people', but rejected proposals which would hand Northern Rhodesia over to settler domination. It concluded that:

> The proposed Federation would be in the interest of only a minority of the people of Central Africa; it would place the African workers at the 'tender' mercies of their employers; it would stifle the growth of the Northern Rhodesian trade union movement; it would result in the alienation of African Trust land; it would result in a policy of segregation not integration of the races; it would close the constitutional door to African political advancement in the Northern territories; it would be a complete denial of democracy. We have no hesitation in completely rejecting such a federation. The proposals do not form a basis for discussion.[40]

It called upon the people to:

> Study and understand the dangers in the Proposals. Condemn the Proposals in strong terms; give a definite NO! But do not leave it at that. Back your answer with organisation; organise opposition to the implementation of the Proposals. Federation will be inevitable only if the African people do not rise to the occasion of self preservation. The Africans of the Cape Province failed to oppose the Act of Union in 1910, hence their plight since. We must not repeat their mistake.[41]

The Ndola Anti-Federation Action Committee acted as a radical influence within the still moderate Northern Rhodesian African National Congress. Simon Zukas was one of only two Europeans who publicly identified themselves with the African nationalist cause at this time. The other was Commander Thomas Fox-Pitt, a recently retired and senior member of the Provincial Administration. Zukas attended two conferences of the congress in Lusaka as a delegate from Ndola. At the first of these, late in 1951, Godwin Mbikusita-Lewanika was replaced as president by Harry Nkumbula, a more forceful leader who had recently returned from the London School of Economics. Unlike Lewanika, who eventually became a member of the

Federal Parliament, he was unequivocal in his opposition to Federation, and had been active in the campaign against it in London. At the second conference in February 1952, a Supreme Action Council to coordinate mass action against Federation was established on the initiative of the Ndola delegates. Zukas was elected as one of the nine members of the council together with a number of trade unionists, including Lawrence Katilungu, Robinson Puta and Simon Kaluwa of the African Mineworkers' Union, and Dixon Konkola of the African Railway Workers Union. Zukas advocated a programme of civil disobedience, non-payment of poll tax and industrial strike action against the Federal proposals. His views were circulated in the *Freedom Newsletter* which, with Justin Chimba and Nephas Tembo, he had begun to publish from his home in Ndola in January 1952.[42]

Zukas was dismissed from his job with the Ndola Town Council before the end of 1951. On 31 March 1952 police raided his home in Ndola and confiscated the stencils of the April number of the *Freedom Newsletter* and other documents. He was not arrested, but was required to appear in the High Court in Livingstone where the Attorney-General sought a deportation order on three counts which included incitement, and conducting himself in such a way as to pose a threat to 'peace and good order in the territory'. The court upheld the last count and the deportation order was issued. It was clear that the government had come to see Zukas as the chief organiser of resistance to the Federal proposals. Roy Welensky, then leader of the unofficial members of the Legislative Council, writing on 7 April to his close friend and political mentor Stewart Gore-Browne, made it clear that Zukas was seen as part of an international communist conspiracy.[43]

Bill Epstein, who had never met Zukas, was surprised to be called out of a sitting of the Urban Native Court in Broken Hill to be questioned by two members of the Special Branch about his knowledge of him. He was even more surprised to discover later on that the investigation of his own possibly subversive links was extended to his parents' home in Northern Ireland.[44] There was a definitely anti-Semitic tone in contemporary newspaper reports which referred to Zukas as 'the Lithuanian Jew'. A columnist in the *Livingstone Mail* showed that both fascism and anti-Semitism were alive and well in Northern Rhodesia when he suggested that 'it is a great pity we could not have hired a mobile Gestapo unit to eliminate him without fuss, one dark night'.[45] The newspaper was fined £10 for criminal libel, but Zukas himself was fined £50 for contempt of court. His offence was to have sent a telegram to Julius Lewin, a lecturer in African law and government at the University of the Witwatersrand, who had written a report in 1940 on the Copperbelt disturbances of that year. In his telegram, Zukas had said that the government was determined to deport him, and that only mass action by the African trade unions would stop it.

Simon Zukas spent most of the next eight months in prison in Livingstone, while his legal team, which included a Queen's Counsel from London, Denis

Pritt, fought against his deportation order. Funds for his defence were collected from among working people on the Copperbelt, though in some cases, as in Luanshya, money was apparently misappropriated. He was finally deported to London in December 1952 and was to remain in exile for the next twelve years. The conventional Jewish population of Luanshya was embarrassed by his political activities and his parents felt compelled to close their small business and move to Salisbury, though his brother Jack, with his French wife, Yvette, remained in business in Ndola for many years. There was, of course, some irony in Simon Zukas's deportation to a country in which he had never lived, and with which he had no familial ties, though there was a wartime precedent in the case of Frank Maybank, the New Zealand-born communist leader of the mineworkers union who was also deported for alleged incitement to strike.[46]

Those who believed that Zukas was the key figure in the opposition to Federation must have received some support for their views from the failure of the Supreme Council of Action to organise an effective demonstration against the deportation order. A sympathy strike was called for 10 April 1952 by a mass meeting of workers on the Copperbelt. Lawrence Katilungu, who was a member of the Supreme Council, but who also took the view that unions should not be involved in purely political strikes, personally visited the mine compounds in Kitwe and Nkana on the night before the strike to campaign against it. He was successful, though Reuben Kamanga, James Chapoloko and Edward Mungoni Liso were among those who were imprisoned, fined or dismissed following protest actions in Ndola and at Nkana. Katilungu later opposed the African National Congress's call for a two-day strike, disguised as two 'Days of Prayer', against Federation in April 1953, and helped to ensure that this had only a limited success. These incidents were the first manifestations of a conflict between political parties and trade unions which was to be a feature of Northern Rhodesian and Zambian politics for many years to come.[47]

In the end the efforts of Simon Zukas and the other members of the Ndola Anti-Federation Action Committee appeared to have been in vain. The Federation was imposed in September 1953 regardless of African opposition to it in the northern territories. There can, however, be no doubt that they served an important role in the radicalisation and development of the African nationalist movement in Northern Rhodesia. The fact that Northern Rhodesia's first conspicuous political prisoner and exile in the cause of African nationalism was both white and Jewish had some lasting significance. Zukas's catalytic role at this time was a political asset on which, as we shall see, he was able to draw almost forty years later. He continued to be actively involved in politics through the Movement for Colonial Freedom, and the Labour Party, while he was based in London where he established his first civil engineering business. He wrote articles on trade union and political issues, and acted as an unofficial London representative of the African National

Congress and, latterly, of the United National Independence Party. He contributed to the economic section of UNIP's first manifesto. He returned to Northern Rhodesia on a visit on 15 February 1964, within weeks of the end of the Federation, and was given a hero's welcome by large crowds at the airports at both Ndola and Lusaka. In an interview with the *Central African Mail* a few days later he expressed views on the one-party state which were to become a hostage to fortune. He was quoted as saying that a one-party state was desirable in Zambia as 'opposition merely fragments the national effort'. He felt that in a multi-party system 'the government wastes a lot of time worrying about what the opposition might or might not do instead of going all out with development projects to uplift the whole country'.[48]

Simon Zukas returned for the independence celebrations in October 1964 with his wife, Cynthia Robinson, a South African-born artist with Rhodesian connections, whom he had met in London and married in 1954. They returned to live permanently in the country in the following year. He devoted the next twenty-five years of his life to the establishment of a successful civil engineering business. His first partner was Harry Chimowitz, with whom he had worked politically in Cape Town and professionally in London. Harry had been deported as a listed communist from South Africa to Southern Rhodesia with his wife, Marjorie, and four young daughters in 1953. He moved with his family from London to Lusaka in May 1964. He remained with the business until the late 1970s when he went into farming in partnership with Robert Dean, devoting his engineering skills to the irrigation of citrus fruit and other crops on Ellendsdale farm east of Lusaka. The Chimowitzes took no part in Zambian politics, but they remained close to many members of the southern African liberation movements which were based in Lusaka.[49]

Simon Zukas joined forces in the early 1980s with the late Peter Miller, son of one of the civil engineers who built the railway into Northern Rhodesia, and a contemporary of Zukas and Harry Chimowitz as a civil engineering student at the University of Cape Town. Among the more conspicuous of ZMCK Consulting Engineers' commissions, which include the National Assembly building in Lusaka and a large dam on the Kaleya river at Mazabuka, are the elegant flyover bridge over the railway on the Great East Road in Lusaka, and Wally Dobkins's Meridien Bank building.

On his return to Zambia, Zukas expected to be called back into active politics by President Kenneth Kaunda, whom he had first encountered as a delegate from Chinsali at the 1951 conference of the African National Congress. His first impression of Kaunda was of a tall and rather flamboyant personality with a serious speech impediment. Kaunda was also impressed by Simon's voice, recalling its curious pitch. He attended party congresses for a number of years, and was nominated to the council of the University of Zambia, serving for over twenty years. He was also appointed as a director of two parastatal companies, Indeco and the Zambia National Building

Society, but he was never offered a political appointment. He feels that Kaunda was wary of his reputation as a radical and that he was deliberately side-lined. The only white member of Kaunda's first Cabinet was James Skinner, a moderate Irish lawyer who had arrived in Northern Rhodesia in 1951. Simon Zukas was at first disappointed that he was not offered political preferment, but he soon became disillusioned with the nationalistic, and at times tribalistic, tendency in Zambian politics. Some of his closest political associates, such as Justin Chimba, split with UNIP to join Simon Kapwepwe in the formation of a new opposition party, the UPP, in 1971. Zukas had to wait for almost thirty years before he was able to enter the Cabinet under a new political dispensation.

Aaron Milner

There was, however, to be one son of Lithuanian Jewry in Kaunda's first Cabinet. Among the posts which Aaron Milner held between 1964 and 1980 were those of Minister of State for Cabinet Affairs and the Public Service, Minister of State for Presidential Affairs, Minister of State for Foreign Affairs, Secretary-General to the Government, and Minister of Home Affairs. He was also the first deputy secretary-general of the United National Independence Party. For most of this time he was close to President Kaunda, and was seen by many as his right-hand man and, by some, as his hatchet man.

In terms of 'Jewishness', Aaron Milner was the most marginal of the three sons of Lithuania who held high office in Northern Rhodesia and Zambia almost continuously between 1938 and 1996, though, with a Jewish father and a gentile mother, he was technically neither more nor less Jewish than Roy Welensky. Aaron Michael Milner was born in Bulawayo on 31 May 1932. His father, Joseph Milner, was one of two brothers who emigrated from Lithuania to Southern Rhodesia before the First World War and who eventually owned a farm and store in the Bubi district of Matabeleland. Aaron's mother, Esther, was a member of the Cele clan whose grandfather came from Zululand. Joseph Milner was unable to legalise his common-law marriage, but he registered each of his four children in his name. He was in partnership in a farm and store with his elder brother, Isaac, who also had a black wife and a mixed-race child. Joseph Milner died in February 1939, and his brother died two weeks later. Under the heading 'children', Aaron's father's death certificate recorded starkly: 'four illegitimate children, native mother, names unknown – minors'. The property of the two brothers was inherited by a third brother who lived in South Africa, and their wives and children were left destitute. Aaron remembers his father as a loving and caring man, but he was brought up by his mother and maternal uncles as an Ndebele by tribe, and a Roman Catholic by faith. He was educated at the Embakwe Coloured School, effectively an orphanage, near Plumtree in Southern Rhodesia.[50]

Given his early alienation from the Jewish side of his family, it is surprising how close Aaron Milner has remained to Jews and Jewishness. After leaving school, he was selected in 1953 for operatic training in Italy. Before leaving the country he decided to visit his sister, Rebecca, who was married and living on the Copperbelt. Her husband, Morrison Rosen, was also a Northern Rhodesian Coloured of Jewish descent. While Aaron was there, he met and fell in love with the woman who was to become his wife, Phyllis Lurie. She, too, was the child of a Jewish father, John Yankele Lurie, a well-known member of Ndola's Jewish community and his Coloured wife, Annie Bailes. Phyllis is the eldest of their six children. Her father was born in Lithuania and reached Luanshya, by way of South Africa, in 1932. He died in 1954, but their mother, who is still alive, brought up the children to have respect for Judaism. The youngest child, Johnny, went on *aliyah* to Israel, married a Jewish woman, and now lives in Canada.[51]

Aaron abandoned his operatic career and decided to settle in Chingola where he began work for 'George' Mandel at the Nchanga Trading Company. After a year or two with this business, he began work for David Marcus, another member of Chingola's small Jewish community. He continued to work for him as a store manager until he became a full-time political activist in the early 1960s. He found Marcus a liberal employer who was conscious of the 'Jewish experience of oppression', and was broadly sympathetic to the aspirations of the Zambian nationalist movement. He was tolerant of Aaron's early involvement in politics which was with a Coloured pressure group, the Euro-African Association of Northern Rhodesia, of which he became the first chairman in 1956. This association brought together earlier Eurafrican and Cape Coloured associations, and also involved Harry Thornicroft and Aldridge Adamson. It was a few years later that Milner realised that it was no longer 'beneficial to continue fighting for a separate Coloured identity'. It was decided to dissolve the association and to encourage its members to join the mainstream African nationalist parties. He threw in his lot with the United National Independence Party at its formation.

Aaron Milner was not the only person of Rhodesian Jewish descent to become involved with Coloured politics. Dick Snapper, who is described by Ibbo Mandaza as 'the main figurehead of "Eurafrican" politics' in central Africa, was the son of Egnatz Snapper, an early trader in Barotseland. He was born in Mongu in 1916 to a Lozi mother, and was educated from the age of seven at the Waddilove Training Institute in Southern Rhodesia. He was proud that his father visited him at school from Mongu, and commented that 'the relationship between me and my father was just as good as in any other marriage'. He became a journalist and editor of the *Rhodesian Tribune* in 1945. He had earlier founded the Eurafrican Provident and Burial Society, and went on to found in 1948 the Euro-African Federation of Central Africa. Its first conference was opened by the Prime Minister of Southern Rhodesia, Godfrey Huggins. He was also involved in a variety of commercial activities including a butchery, a printing works, hotels in Bulawayo and Salisbury, and a transport business. He later abandoned Coloured politics, and became prominent in nationalist political organisations, including ZAPU. He returned home to Northern Rhodesia as a political exile in 1963, and later became the first Registrar of Lusaka's polytechnic, the Evelyn Hone College.[52]

Aaron Milner clearly values his Jewish, Zulu and Ndebele roots, but he has also identified himself politically at different times as a Coloured, and as an African nationalist in both Zambia, his country of adoption, and Zimbabwe, his country of birth. It is probable that it was this ethnic versatility, and his lack of Zambian tribal affiliations, which made him useful to Kaunda. Among the highlights of his political career, which he himself recalls, are his role in the negotiations with the Chinese for the building of the Tazara railway. He is also proud of his role liaising between Kaunda and the leaders of the various southern African liberation movements which were based in Zambia, and as a 'roving ambassador' to the Front Line states before their formal identification as such. His knowledge of the Ndebele language, and indeed his Ndebele identity, were useful in dealings with Joshua Nkomo and ZAPU. He maintains his support for Joshua Nkomo and Jonas Savimbi, and may have influenced Zambia's controversial commitments to both ZAPU and UNITA. His reputation as Kaunda's strongman may stem from tough measures taken by the Zambian government in the mid-1970s against allegedly dissident members of both ZANU and SWAPO.

Milner now says that he was among the most open and accessible of the UNIP leaders and that he was prepared to argue against Kaunda in Cabinet. He says that he opposed two of UNIP's most controversial decisions: the nationalisation of the mines, and the establishment of the one-party state. There is no doubt that he was regarded in the late 1970s as Kaunda's most effective and powerful minister. His sudden dismissal from office early in 1980 was surprising and remains unexplained. The excuse was his alleged infringement of the Leadership Code through the purchase, which he denies, of a property in London. He feels that he was perceived by many of his colleagues to have become too powerful for his own good, and that Kaunda was under pressure to remove him. When close friends in the government, including John Mwanakatwe, protested at his dismissal, Kaunda apparently told them that Milner had been planning a coup.

Soon after his dismissal Milner moved, with the encouragement of Kaunda, to Zimbabwe to help Joshua Nkomo in his first election campaign. It was presumed at the time that he intended to capitalise on his Zimbabwean roots and that, in the event of a ZAPU victory, he would have had a place in the government. When Edward Shamwana, Valentine Musakanya and others were arrested in October 1980 in the wake of an alleged coup attempt, an effort was made to implicate Milner. Paramilitary police raided his farm at Makeni, near Lusaka, where his wife and children were still living. President Robert Mugabe advised him not to return to Zambia, but he did so on a Zimbabwean passport, and gave evidence in defence of Edward Shamwana and Valentine Musakanya. It is evident that Milner still feels bitter about the humiliating way in which Kaunda informed him of his dismissal. Nevertheless, he assisted Kaunda in 1996 in his ill-fated election campaign. He explains this apparent contradiction by saying that in politics 'people are subjected to abnormal pressures'.

While Jewishness is only one of several identities on which Aaron Milner has drawn in a varied career, it is clear that it has continued to fascinate him. He visited Israel, which he sees as his spiritual home, twice on political business and met Golda Meir. Len Pinshow, who knew him on the Copperbelt in the 1960s, has no doubt as to his commitment to 'Jewishness', volunteering a comparison with Welensky. He also recalls that Milner acted as a liaison between Kaunda and Jewish communal groups, and assisted them in securing the transmission of funds to Israel. One of Milner's sons, Philip, emigrated to Israel, lived on a kibbutz for three years, converted to Judaism, married a Jewish girl and now lives in Canada. In an extraordinary genealogical twist to this story, Aaron Milner's nephew, Owen Milner, who was brought up in Chingola, also went with a sister to Israel. While there, he met a member of another Chingola family, Saren, daughter of Wally and Vyv Dobkins, and granddaughter of Moss and Fay Dobkins. They later married and now live in Brisbane, Australia.[53]

South African Exiles

The story of the Jewish contribution to political life in Northern Rhodesia and Zambia would be incomplete without some reference to a number of Jewish exiles from South Africa and Southern Rhodesia who reached the country between the 1960s and the 1980s. The majority of these were socialists who had rejected the Jewish religion, but many of them continued to identify themselves, or to be identified by others, as Jews. One of those who was frequently identified by others as Jewish was Jack Simons. His influence as a teacher at the University of Cape Town on a variety of people, including Simon Zukas, Harry Chimowitz and Edwin Wulfsohn, has already been mentioned. His father, Hyman, was born in England of German Jewish descent. Jack was himself born at Riversdale in the then Cape Colony in 1907 and identified most strongly with his mother's mixed Afrikaner and English-speaking South African ancestry. He was brought up as an Anglican, but lost his faith at an early age. He had a life-long interest in religion from a secular point of view, but he rejected the Jewish label.[54]

Rachel Elizabeth (Ray) Alexander, whom Jack Sions married in Cape Town in 1942, also rejected identification as Jewish, though there could be no doubt about her ethnic identity and religious upbringing. She was born in the *shtetl* of Varkalan in what became Latvia, but was then a province of the Russian empire, on 31 December 1913 (Old Style), which happened to be

Chanukah, and was brought up in a large orthodox family. She attended school in Riga and learnt to speak Russian and German as well as Yiddish. Her youth was overshadowed by the rise of Latvian nationalism and anti-Semitism to which the Russian Revolution and communist internationalism seemed to provide some antidote. She joined an underground communist cell while at school, and was encouraged by her family to leave the country for South Africa in 1929. Her mother and other members of her family also settled in South Africa.

Jack and Ray Simons both played a major part in the resuscitation of the Communist Party of South Africa from the late 1930s until its banning in 1950. Ray made an unrivalled contribution to the development of trade unionism, especially through the establishment in 1941 of the Food and Canning Workers' Union. She was elected to Parliament in 1953 as a representative of Africans in the Western Cape, but was not allowed to take her seat. She was banned from trade union work in 1954, but continued to be politically active. It was only when Jack was banned from teaching after twenty-seven years on the staff of the University of Cape Town in 1964 that they were forced into exile.

They visited Zambia for several months in 1965 on their way to Manchester where Jack had secured a Simon Fellowship through the influence of Max Gluckman. On this visit they stayed with Barney and Sonia Gordon. Barney Gordon was a Jewish veteran of the Springbok Legion who had been in business as a clothing wholesaler in Lusaka for some time. He was in close touch with the leaders of the ANC in exile such as Oliver Tambo, as well as with Zambian political radicals such as Simon Kapwepwe, Justin Chimba and Nephas Tembo. His close association with Kapwepwe resulted in his deportation from Zambia as an alleged spy in September 1970.[55]

Jack was, on this visit, able to secure the prospect of employment as a professor of sociology at the new University of Zambia, which was still in the planning stages, and they bought a plot at 250 Zambezi Road in the then largely undeveloped Roma Township. The building of the house began during their absence of over a year in Manchester. Their resettlement in Zambia was facilitated by Ronnie Frankenberg, a social anthropologist and student of Max Gluckman, who acted as the first head of the Department of Sociology, and dean of the Faculty of Social Sciences, at the University of Zambia between 1966 and 1969. He and his then wife, Joyce Leeson, lived in the Lusaka 'compound' of Lilanda, and were engaged in a major socio-medical survey there. Joyce Leeson later married Archie Sibeko (also known as Zola Zembe) who was in the late 1960s based in Lusaka as a leading member of the ANC's armed wing, Mkhonto weSizwe.[56]

Jack and Ray Simons were to live in Lusaka for most of a quarter of a century between 1967 and their return to South Africa in 1990. During that time their house was an important social and organisational centre for the ANC of South Africa, the SACP, and the South African Congress of Trade

Unions. A cottage in the garden was built in the late 1960s to provide accommodation for Oliver Tambo, leader of the ANC in exile, on his frequent visits to Lusaka. There can be few leaders, or even rank and file members, of the ANC, SWAPO or ZAPU in exile in Zambia who did not visit their house at some time. From 1985 onwards, there was a steady flow of visitors from South Africa itself as the collapse of apartheid became imminent, though not necessarily obvious, and the movement towards the unbanning of the ANC and SACP gained momentum.

Jack and Ray Simons were primarily involved with the liberation of South Africa, but they also contributed to Zambian social and political life. Ray worked for some years as an administrative officer at the International Labour Organisation in Lusaka, and was actively involved with the local trade union movement. Jack worked at the University of Zambia for eight years, and succeeded Ronnie Frankenberg as head of the Sociology Department. He wrote important papers on urbanisation and on the position of women in the country, and became actively involved in political education within the ruling party, UNIP. In the late 1970s he worked tirelessly through lectures and other propaganda to promote 'scientific socialism' which was adopted at that time as the ideology of the party in conjunction with Kaunda's personal philosophy of humanism. This move caused controversy within UNIP and was opposed by the major Christian churches in an important pamphlet which was published in 1979. In the view of some people, this controversy contributed to the atmosphere in which the Shamwana coup attempt occurred in October of the following year. This was said to have had at least tacit support from some members of the Catholic clergy.

Joe Slovo

In global terms the most significant Jewish resident of Lusaka in the 1980s, and arguably at any time, was Joe Slovo, a leader of the ANC and the SACP, and chief of staff of the ANC's armed wing, Mkhonto weSizwe. He was born at Obel in Lithuania in 1926 and emigrated to South Africa with his mother and sister in 1936. His father had left Lithuania for Argentina in 1928 and Joe had no recollection of him before they were reunited in South Africa in 1936. His mother died two years later. Perhaps the most poignant section of his unfinished autobiography is the elegiac description of his return to Lithuania in 1981, and his attempt to rediscover his birthplace which he had not seen for forty-five years. He had then tried 'systematically to recollect his childhood memories of Obel'. His description must be typical of the experience of many less articulate people who feature in this book and left their homes in the Baltic states in their youth.[57]

Joe Slovo's life story belongs primarily to South African history. His roles as Treason Trial lawyer, founding member of Mkhonto weSizwe, and General Secretary of the SACP in exile, are well-known. After years of denigration by the South African government as the evil genius of the ANC, he is now recalled for his constructive role in the talks which ended apartheid, as the architect of the Government of National Unity, and as an effective Minister of Housing, whose life was tragically cut short in January 1995 within a year of taking office.

Slovo had been forced into a second exile in 1963. After many years in London he moved to Mozambique in 1976 to join his wife, Ruth First, who had started work there at the Eduardo Mondlane University in Maputo. He was a frequent visitor to Lusaka which became the headquarters of the ANC in the late 1970s, and spent longer periods there after the assassination of his wife by a parcel bomb in Maputo in August 1982. He was compelled to leave Mozambique after the signing of a non-aggression pact, the Nkomati Accord, between South Africa and Mozambique in March 1984. From then until after the unbanning of the ANC in February 1990, Lusaka was his home. For much of this time he lived in a house in the Ibex Hill suburb. He used to swim early in the morning in the pool at Harry and Marjorie Chimowitz's house in the neighbouring suburb of Kabulonga. Those who knew him would frequently see him driving alone, and apparently without bodyguards, on Lusaka's roads. It was at the Kabwe Conference of the ANC in April 1985 that he was elected as the first white member of the organisation's National Executive Committee following its opening to non-African members. In the following year he was joined in Lusaka by his second wife, Helena Dolny, who shared the last decade of his life.[58]

There was never any question as to Joe Slovo's ethnic identity. His autobiographical fragment provides an excellent account not only of his childhood in Lithuania, but also of immigrant life in the Doornfontein, Hillbrow and Yeoville districts of Johannesburg in the 1930s and 1940s. It also spells out his progress through membership in Lithuania of the Habonim to the Hashomeyr Hatzair, a Zionist organisation with Marxist pretensions, and finally to membership of the South African Communist Party. He had said kaddish as the only son on his mother's death, and recalled the professional 'minionites' whose presence was required to form a *minyan* on that occasion. He also remembered, however, that 'by the time that I stood on the *Bimah* of the Berea Synagogue to chant my allotted *barmitzvah* portion from the Bible, I had already begun to question whether He existed at all'.[59]

It defies statistical probability that Ronnie Kasrils, currently South Africa's deputy Minister of Defence, and the second white person to be elected to the National Executive Committee of the ANC in exile, is also a son or grandson of the Lithuanian *shtetl*. He was born in Johannesburg in 1938, was brought up in Yeoville, became an early member of Mkhonto weSizwe in Natal, and went into exile in 1963. After years in London, he moved in the late 1970s between the ANC's camps in Angola and Mozambique. Like Slovo, he was forced to leave Mozambique after the Nkomati Accord in 1984. After spending some time in Swaziland, he moved to Lusaka in 1985 where he became head of the ANC's Military Intelligence. Lusaka remained his base until his return to South Africa in January 1990, a few weeks before the unbanning of the ANC.[60]

Not all the Jewish members of the ANC in exile who spent time in Lusaka had the prominence of the Simonses, Slovo or Kasrils. Some, like Wolfie Kodesh, were rank and file members who had devoted much of their lives to the liberation movement. Wolfie spent much of the period between 1977 and 1985 in Lusaka and worked for the ANC's Treasury department. He is, perhaps, most famous as the man who acted as Nelson Mandela's 'minder' during his period 'underground' in South Africa in 1962 and has been represented as such in several films. One of his roles in Lusaka was to find temporary accommodation for prominent ANC members in Lusaka's better suburbs. Although Lusaka's permanent Jewish population was much reduced by the late 1970s and 1980s it did, nevertheless, provide a network which could be of use. Wolfie found Harvey Golson, a contemporary of Simon Zukas and Harry Chimowitz as a civil engineering student at Cape Town, who became the chief executive and co-proprietor of Lewis Construction, a useful source of vacant houses.[61]

One of the most poignant letters in the surviving files of the Council for Zambia Jewry is from Eli Weinberg, a frequent visitor to Zambia in the late 1970s, which was written under the letterhead of the South African Congress of Trade Unions in July 1981. Eli, who was born in Latvia in 1908, reached South Africa in 1930, but never acquired a South African passport. He is perhaps best known as the political photographer who created many of the most famous images of episodes such as the Defiance Campaign. After a period of imprisonment in the late 1960s, he was forced into exile following the Soweto uprising in 1976. In his letter, which was addressed to Abe Galaun, his Latvian Jewish compatriot and near contemporary, he requested the council to provide accommodation for himself and his wife, Violet, as they intended to move to Lusaka from Dar es Salaam. He ended his letter with the assurance that compliance with this request would be a *mitzvah* – a benevolent religious act. Sadly, he died a few weeks after writing this letter, rendering a reply redundant.[62]

There was at least one person who came to Zambia as a political refugee and rediscovered her Jewishness. Gesse Martin, who was born in South Africa to Lithuanian Jewish parents, arrived in Zambia shortly before independence with her Coloured fiancé, Les Martin. They were forced into exile both by his political involvement with the Non-European Unity Movement, a minor South African liberation movement, and by the country's notorious Immorality and Mixed Marriages Acts. They were married in Lusaka and had three daughters who attended school there. Gesse had trained in dance and drama in London and practised as a teacher in Lusaka. At the time of her arrival the Hebrew Congregation was still quite large and active, and she became involved with its communal life, seeking to make her children aware of their

Jewish heritage. After over twenty years in Lusaka she emigrated to Israel with her daughters in 1985 with the assistance of the Council for Zambia Jewry. Les Martin died in Lusaka in 1996, and Gesse Martin died in Israel in July 1997.[63]

While the majority of Jews in Zambia and elsewhere devoted themselves to business and, as Simon Zukas has pointed out, lacked the confidence to take political risks in countries where they were often insecure refugees, there was always a minority who were prepared to take political chances and who espoused radical causes. Jewish social networks were not usually divided along political lines and there were often social or familial links between the people who had devoted themselves to business or the professions and those who had become political activists. Ray Simons, for instance, recalls Goody Glasser as a 'friend' who was prepared to make contributions in cash or kind to the ANC. Wulfie Wulfsohn and his wife Millicent gave generous financial support to UNIP, and he was once asked to stand as a parliamentary candidate for the party. Cynthia Zukas, who had frequently provided accommodation and help to visiting Zambian nationalists and their wives, in London in the 1950s and early 1960s, gave financial support to the ANC's Solomon Mahlangu Freedom College at Mazimbu in Tanzania, which was the brainchild of Eli Weinberg. David Susman remained close to his friend Jimmy Kantor, one of the accused in the Rivonia Trial, and his sister, Anne-Marie Wolpe. He spoke at the funeral in Cape Town in 1996 of her husband, Harold Wolpe, a leading Marxist intellectual and member of the SACP, who was arrested at Rivonia and made a spectacular escape from Pretoria Central Prison in 1964. Networks such as these were particularly important for members of the liberation movements in exile who were always in need of accommodation and funds as well as, and perhaps more importantly, of social and moral support.[64]

A few people, such as Nathan Zelter, contrived with some success to combine political radicalism with commercial enterprise. He was a close friend of the novelist Doris Lessing, who stayed with him in Salisbury during her visit in 1956 which is described in her memoir, *Going Home*. She has described him in another memoir, *Under the Skin*, as an exponent of free love, and as a Quixotic and impossibly generous idealist. He had been one of the founders of Southern Rhodesia's minuscule Communist Party, was a supporter of the Southern Rhodesian Labour Party, and was later a sponsor of Guy and Molly Clutton-Brock's non-racial commune, Cold Comfort Farm. With the break-up of the Federation he left Southern Rhodesia and became for a while an exile in Zambia. After a period in England he returned to Zimbabwe after its independence in 1980 and succeeded in reviving Cold Comfort Farm before his death. Doris Lessing was herself one of the small circle of predominantly Jewish, and central African, radicals. She writes under the name of her second husband, Pieter Lessing, a German Jewish refugee in Southern Rhodesia, who later became an East German diplomat. In her

most recent memoir, *Walking in the Shade*, she has described her visit to
Northern Rhodesia in 1956, and her comradely role soon afterwards in
providing hospitality and support to Northern Rhodesian nationalist leaders
in London, including Harry Nkumbula, Kenneth Kaunda and Mainza Chona.[65]

Some exiles, or at least supporters of liberation movements, such as Leo
Baron, Joshua Nkomo's lawyer and a ZAPU supporter, were fortunate enough
to be able to carry on with their professions in their new homes. Baron
moved to Zambia following his detention in, and deportation from, Southern
Rhodesia after UDI. He became Deputy Chief Justice in Zambia in the early
1970s before returning to Zimbabwe in 1980 to take up a similar appointment.
Born in London in 1916, he had moved to Southern Rhodesia in 1952 where
he practised law in Bulawayo. An international bridge player, he was the
brother of Jacob Bronowski, the eminent scientist and British television
personality.[66]

Simon Zukas Returns to Politics

As we have seen, Simon Zukas devoted most of his energy in the years from
1965 to 1990 to the development of a successful civil engineering business.
He also became involved, initially in partnership with two other Zambian
Jews, Mark Zemack and Leslie Szeftel, in farming. They bought the Balmoral
farm in Makeni from John Roberts, the former leader of Welensky's United
Federal Party in Northern Rhodesia, in the late 1970s. He also became
chairman in 1986 of Zambezi Ranching and Cropping and, perhaps to his
own surprise, joined forces with the old Jewish business establishment. His
political radicalism now took a different form. He had become disillusioned
with the one-party state as practised by Kenneth Kaunda and UNIP since
1973, and was also converted by the failure of many of Zambia's parastatal
enterprises to economic liberalism. When he was interviewed, as an elder
statesman, by Philip Chirwa in the *Zambia Daily Mail* in April 1987, he was
outspoken in his support of the informal sector and of the productive
enterprise of the people who had recently begun to sell hand-crushed building
stones along Lusaka's Kafue Road. He was equally outspoken in his criticism
of the recent takeover of the last remaining private millers, following riots
on the Copperbelt. He was certain that there was 'need for competition
between parastatals and the private sector in the industry to maintain high
levels of production and quality'. He favoured the reduction of subsidies on
breakfast meal, and suggested that the riots were not caused by the attempt
to reduce subsidies, but by 'the inept way in which it was done'. When
pressed as to whether he still supported the one-party state, he was, however,
guarded. According to his interviewer, he smiled and asked: 'And what do
you think my views are?'[67]

By the later months of 1989, Zukas was prepared to be more outspoken,
and to indicate clearly his support for a return to multi-party democracy. He

was the first prominent person in Zambia to come out in public against the one-party state which had then been in place for sixteen years. He had clearly sensed earlier than most that the time for a change had arrived. He was aware of unfolding events in eastern Europe and of developments in South Africa. He was also influenced by the World Bank's important publication on the African economies, *Sub-Saharan Africa: from Crisis to Sustainable Growth*, which was published at that time. It placed a new emphasis on accountability and 'good governance' as conditions for future international assistance.

His statements were noticed by a small group of younger Zambian intellectuals, including Akashambatwa Mbikusita-Lewanika, son of an old adversary, and Derrick Chitala, who were beginning to develop similar ideas. By March 1990, at UNIP's Fifth National Convention in Lusaka, a number of political veterans, such as Sikota Wina, Vernon Mwaanga, Alex Chikwanda and Humphrey Mulemba, were critical of the government, and were outspoken in their demand for political reforms which included, for some, a return to multi-party democracy. The unbanning of the ANC, and the release on 11 February 1990 of Nelson Mandela, who visited Lusaka within two weeks, marked the end of Zambia's contribution to the liberation struggle in southern Africa, and prompted questions about internal democracy and the sacrifices which had been made for the freedom of others. Lusaka and the Copperbelt were again racked by food riots at the end of June, following the government's second mismanaged attempt to achieve a reduction of food subsidies, and to implement a policy of structural adjustment. When Lieutenant Luchembe's one-man coup attempt was greeted by public rejoicing, Kaunda sought to regain the political initiative by announcing that a referendum on the one-party state would be held in October.

Akashambatwa Mbikusita-Lewanika and others had been trying to organise a National Conference on the Multi-Party Option since March, but had found it difficult to raise funds or to find a venue. The way was now cleared by the announcement of the referendum, and the conference was held on 20–21 July at Theo Bull's Garden House Hotel in Lusaka. According to the organisers, Simon Zukas was the first of the elder statesmen to come out in positive support. He attended the conference and his public apology for his earlier support for the one-party state made headline news. Writing seven years after the event, it is difficult to recall that attendance at this conference seemed at the time to be a courageous act. It was by no means certain that the meeting would be allowed to take place at all, and some conspicuous political figures needed forceful persuasion to attend. Some arrived after the beginning of the meeting when it was clear that participants would not, after all, be detained. It was at the Garden House meeting that the Movement for Multi-Party Democracy was born. Arthur Wina chaired the meeting and was elected as interim chairman of the movement.[68]

Simon Zukas was among the main speakers at the first rallies of the movement which were held in Kabwe and at the Pope's Square in Lusaka in September. Enthusiastic crowds attended these meetings and it soon became clear that there was no need for a referendum. Kaunda announced that multi-party elections would be held late in the following year. When the new party held its first national conference, Zukas stood for the office of Deputy National Chairman and was elected. Frederick Chiluba, leader of the Zambia Congress of Trade Unions, was elected as president of the party, taking the leadership from Arthur Wina who had been an effective interim chairman. As the date of the general elections, October 1991, drew near, Simon Zukas, who had not originally intended to enter Parliament, agreed to stand in the remote Sikongo constituency west of Kalabo in the Western Province.

Members of his constituency party hoped that he could bring back Susman Brothers and Wulfsohn's stores to their remote and neglected area on the border with Angola. The people of the former Barotseland, whose economy had been so closely tied to the South, had suffered severely through nearly thirty years of UNIP rule. They had seen their province's special status eroded and its economy decline more dramatically than in most other regions. Simon was not able to bring back Susman Brothers and Wulfsohn, nor to revive WENELA, and he resisted suggestions that he should hand out bales of *salaula*, second-hand clothing, but he did do his best to improve roads in the area, and to bring back into use an abandoned canal.

Soon after the MMD's landslide victory over Kaunda and UNIP in the elections of October 1991, Simon was appointed as a Deputy Minister in the President's Office at State House. This enabled him to work closely with President Chiluba in a number of trouble-shooting roles. In April 1993 he joined the Cabinet as Minister of Agriculture, succeeding Guy Scott, a commercial farmer, who was the son of Dr Alec Scott, former editor of the *Central African Post*. Simon inherited a difficult situation in agriculture which resulted from the serious drought of 1991–92. This had fuelled inflation to 200 per cent a year, and problems for farmers had been compounded by the hasty abandonment of the old-established maize marketing mechanisms. The government had pledged that it would not print money, and did not have the funds to purchase a bumper maize crop. The decision to pay farmers in promissory notes, which they could either sell at a discount, or redeem at a later date, caused controversy though it proved an effective way of dealing with the crisis. Zukas devoted his two years at the ministry to the production of a master plan for agriculture, and was happy to work with what he saw as an excellent team. He was transferred in 1995 to the Ministry of Public Works where his portfolio, which included roads, suited his civil engineering background.

In the MMD's four years in government there had been a rapid turnover of ministers. One of the first to leave had been Simon's young friend Akashambatwa Mbikusita-Lewanika who, as one of the prime movers behind the MMD, was frustrated in the Ministry of Vocational Training. Some, such as Emmanuel Kasonde and Arthur Wina, had been seen as posing a threat to Chiluba's leadership and were removed from their posts. Others, such as Vernon Mwaanga and Sikota Wina, were forced out by donor pressure. Dipak Patel resigned over an issue of principle, as Simon himself was to do, in May 1996.

It fits well with the theme of this book, and with the story of Simon Zukas's life, that the issue over which he finally resigned concerned the political rights of immigrants and their children. He had indicated privately for some time that he would resign if the new constitution contained clauses debarring immigrants, or their children, from running for the office of President. As an immigrant refugee himself, and as the father of two sons, David and Alan, who intended to make their homes in Zambia, he had a personal interest. There were, however, broader issues. There was a sense in which Zambia, with its largely artificial boundaries with eight neighbouring countries, was a nation of immigrants and the new constitution would disqualify hundreds of thousands of people. It was clearly designed to prevent Kenneth Kaunda, whose parents were immigrants from Malawi, from running in the then forthcoming presidential elections. Zukas had not always agreed politically with Kaunda, but he did respect him as a man who had made a genuine contribution to the liberation of southern Africa as a whole. The press conference at which Simon Zukas announced his resignation marked the end of nearly fifty years of his own involvement in the political life of Zambia. It may also have marked the end of a distinctive Jewish contribution to the country's political history.

CHAPTER 14

Intellectuals and Some Professionals

Among the great achievements of the Jews of the Diaspora is the preservation of their religion, language, culture and identity. They have both sought and resisted assimilation to the cultures of the people among whom they have lived. They have been more conscious than most people of the possibility of multiple identities. People like Roy Welensky, Simon Zukas, Aaron Milner, and Joe Slovo, though they may have differed greatly in their political attitudes, were all involved in the articulation of new kinds of national consciousness. There were a number of Jewish intellectuals who, using Northern Rhodesia as a base of operations, concerned themselves with questions of identity and ethnicity, and contributed to the development of global ideas on these issues. Their Jewishness influenced the way in which they saw and interpreted Zambia to the outside world.

Max Gluckman

The most significant intellectual, regardless of origins, to live and work in colonial Northern Rhodesia was the social anthropologist Max Gluckman. He was associated with the Rhodes–Livingstone Institute, which was set up at Livingstone in 1937 to study social change in central Africa, and went on to be the founder of a distinct school of social anthropology, known from the university where he spent the climax of his career, as the 'Manchester School'.

Max Gluckman was born in Johannesburg in 1911, and was educated at the University of the Witwatersrand, and, as a Rhodes Scholar, at Oxford. His parents, Emmanuel and Kate Gluckmann (sic), were Lithuanian Jews who had reached South Africa as children in the first wave of immigration after the discovery of the Witwatersrand. His father was a lawyer who took what would today be called human rights cases. His mother was one of the founders and leaders of WIZO, and was in 1928 the first woman to be elected to the executive of the South African Zionist Federation. Max's parents and most of their family emigrated to Israel after 1948, and his brother, Philip Gillon, a founder of Habonim, became Attorney-General there.[1]

Sir Raymond Firth described Gluckman's relationship to Jewishness and Judaism in terms which might fit many people who see themselves as 'traditional' Jews:

> He came from a non-religious background in South Africa, and himself was of fundamentally agnostic temperament. His parents respected Jewish religious custom and held a Bar-Mitzvah ritual for Max, though perhaps primarily for social reasons. But the secular importance of Israel was very important for them, and Max himself was proud of being Jewish culturally and socially – though he never acquired any real knowledge of Hebrew. He visited Palestine in 1936 with his mother ... and worked for a time in a kibbutz.[2]

One of his former colleagues, Elizabeth Colson, recalls that he always said that he had a 'blind-spot' about religion, but she also notes that, contrarily, he wrote his doctoral dissertation on a religious topic, the hoe-cultural ritual of the Zulu. He maintained a life-long interest in aspects of ritual.[3]

Max Gluckman's experience of anti-Semitism may have sharpened his awareness of questions of ethnicity and conflict, and may have influenced the development of his ideas on these themes. He had a brilliant academic and sporting record at the University of the Witwatersrand and at Oxford. He was also a member of Bronislaw Malinowski's famous seminar at the London School of Economics. When he applied for a job as a social anthropologist at the Rhodes–Livingstone Institute in 1939 he did not, however, find immediate acceptance. The trustees of the Institute had, reflecting current anti-Semitic attitudes, introduced a nationality clause and specified that the job should be given to a candidate 'who is of British nationality and pure British descent'. It was only after the job had been offered to two men of British descent, including one, Louis Leakey, who was born in Kenya and was to achieve international fame as a palaeontologist, that Gluckman was offered the job.[4]

On his arrival in Northern Rhodesia, with his Anglo-Italian wife Mary Brignoli, shortly before the outbreak of the Second World War, he soon discovered the reasons for the delay in his appointment and became embroiled in more controversy resulting from his Marxism, and his apparently favourable response to the Nazi–Soviet Pact. When he did finally get into the field in Barotseland early in 1940, there were two further crises. He accidentally shot and killed a Lozi barge induna on his way up the Zambezi, and was charged with culpable homicide. He was compelled to return to Livingstone where the charges were eventually dropped. Within six months he was recalled to Lusaka to be interviewed by the Governor, Sir John Maybin, on his loyalty and commitment to the war effort. The Governor had taken seriously unfavourable reports on his activities from senior members of the Provincial Administration. According to Richard Brown, these reports stemmed from his practice of discussing the sensitive issue of the war with members of the Lozi *Kuta* or National Council.[5]

Godfrey Wilson, the first director of the Institute, clearly felt that anti-Semitism was an issue in these charges and, after living with Gluckman for several months, he had also reached the conclusion that it had an impact on his personality. In a lengthy confidential report to the Governor, which concluded with a passionate appeal for his retention, Wilson commented that Gluckman was 'a man of very great intellectual ability' who in South Africa 'was intellectually head and shoulders above most of his friends':

> The only challenge to his complacency was one particularly difficult for him to meet soberly, since it was unjust. He was a Jew and in South Africa he was constantly reminded of the fact in a humiliating way. It is because of this, I think, that he has retained his adolescent arrogance and aggressiveness longer than most men do.[6]

While Godfrey Wilson's amateur psychology may be open to question, there can be no doubt that Jewishness, and anti-Semitism, were real issues for Gluckman and for members of the government in Northern Rhodesia at this time.[7] It is astonishing that in spite of these inauspicious beginnings, and of the war, he was able to carry on fieldwork in Barotseland in the early 1940s which was to lay the foundation for many publications on the Lozi, and to contribute to the formation of a great academic reputation. He became acting director of the Rhodes–Livingstone Institute in April 1941, following the departure of Wilson, who had also fallen foul of the mining companies and of the administration, and, after a long delay, was finally confirmed as director early in 1943.

After Hitler's invasion of the Soviet Union, Gluckman's Marxism became more acceptable to the authorities, and he became a peripheral member of the colonial establishment. He became friendly with the new Governor, Sir John Waddington, and was also close to Roy Welensky and his family. His first major work was a study of *The Economy of the Central Barotse Plain* (1941) which drew on historical as well as contemporary sources to provide a detailed description of what Marxists would call 'the material base' of Lozi society.[8] In addition to his Lozi informants, he acknowledged the assistance in his economic research of one Barotseland trader, Frank Balme, and may well have drawn on the assistance of another, Abe Galaun, with whom he established a friendship at this time which lasted until his death. They shared an interest in socialism and in the Soviet Union.[9]

Gluckman became at this time an advocate of the Soviet 'collective farm' or *kolkhoz* as a model for African development. At the end of the war he was involved with his friends William Allan, the acting director of agriculture, and C. G. Trapnell, the government ecologist, in the 'Mazabuka Reconnaissance Survey'. This resulted in an attempt to establish a working 'collective farm' at Kanchomba, near Magoye. Gluckman's ideas, which may have drawn on his experience on a kibbutz, became quite widely accepted by members of the Provincial Administration and contributed in the long run to the development of the idea of 'African Socialism'.[10]

He also made proposals for the reform of the complex Lozi traditional system of local government and developed an interest in the Lozi legal system which was the subject of his two most influential books: *The Judicial Process among the Barotse of Northern Rhodesia* (1955) and *The Ideas in Barotse Jurisprudence* (1965). In these books he analysed and indexed Lozi cases according to the most rigorous standards of modern legal practice.[11] These books had a remarkable impact on students of jurisprudence in both Britain and the United States. According to Elizabeth Colson, his study of the Lozi courts was the inspiration for the establishment in these countries of 'small claims courts' which provide for the informal settlement of disputes by arbitration.[12]

Gluckman came to see that new kinds of ethnicity were being created by the interaction of people of diverse origins in towns. In much the same way as people who were not strictly Zulu might identify as Zulu in the towns of South Africa, so people who were not strictly Lozi might identify as Lozi on the Copperbelt. The identity of the Bemba in the Northern Province was different from the identity of the Bemba on the Copperbelt. These ideas were developed by his colleagues J. C. Mitchell and A. L. Epstein and gave rise to the now common notions of 'situational' and 'optional' ethnicity. People are not confined to one ethnicity, but may choose from a variety of possible ethnic identities according to their situations. It is probably not a coincidence that several of the members of the 'Manchester School' who developed these ideas, including Gluckman, Epstein and Abner Cohen, were Jewish. The idea that people might have multiple identities must have come fairly easily to a South African Lithuanian Jew, with Zionist parents, who was working in colonial Northern Rhodesia, and who was, according to Lewis Gann, 'far too loyal to the British Empire'.[13]

After eight years in Northern Rhodesia, Max Gluckman resigned his post and moved to Oxford University in 1947, and to Manchester in 1949. He left the institute with a 'Seven Year Research Plan' which was itself a remarkable work of scholarship, and ensured that his influence lasted long after his departure. The first fruits of this plan were brought together in 1951 in a book, *Seven Tribes of British Central Africa*, which he edited with Elizabeth Colson. Gluckman later wrote introductions to most of the monographs which were written by researchers at the institute and published by the Manchester University Press. He was proud of the Lozi soubriquet, 'Makapweka', meaning 'generous giver', which he had acquired, and he used it on the title page of his two big Lozi books. It was his academic generosity, and his enthusiastic personality, as much as a common point of view, which created the 'Manchester School' of social anthropology. Not all of its members had worked in Northern Rhodesia, but the influence of the Rhodes–Livingstone Institute within it was strong.[14]

Gluckman was unable to return to Northern Rhodesia for nearly twenty years after his departure. His sympathy with emergent African nationalism led him publicly to oppose the establishment of the Federation. He was informed by a senior member of the Federal government that he was a prohibited immigrant. In correspondence with his former friend Roy Welensky he sought, between 1955 and 1958, to have this embargo lifted. Welensky feigned surprise at the suggestion that he might be refused entry to the country, and said that he would take up the matter with the Minister of Home Affairs, but there was no positive result. His blacklisting by the Federation also led to his being refused permission by the Australian government to do research in New Guinea.[15] Gluckman finally returned to Zambia in 1965 and spent two weeks in Barotseland. He was shocked by what he saw as a serious deterioration in the agriculture of the Central Barotse Plain which he had first studied in 1940, and attributed this decline to the impact of increased labour migration.[16]

Thwarted in his attempts to return to Zambia, or to start a new field in New Guinea, Gluckman devoted the last decade of his life to the coordination of social anthropological research on the adaptation of immigrants from diverse cultural backgrounds to life in Israel. The Bernstein Israel Research Project was set up at the University of Manchester in 1963 with funds provided by Sidney Bernstein, later Lord Bernstein, and his family. They had the idea of studying the in-gathering of the Jews in Israel. Ten separate studies were sponsored and the majority of them were published by Manchester University Press with introductions by Gluckman in the years before his death. These included studies of *moshavim* (cooperative farming villages), kibbutzim (communal villages) and new towns. Gluckman's introductions constituted a significant contribution in themselves to the study of Israeli society. Although he was never a Zionist, and never lived permanently in Israel, he died in Jerusalem in April 1975 at the age of sixty-four.[17]

In the last years of his life, Gluckman lost some of the radicalism of his youth. The main thrust of his work on ethnicity was, however, liberal in its intent and in its impact. He emphasised that, while social anthropologists could study cultures as separate entities, the similarities between cultures were always greater than the differences. In the modern world, people everywhere were exposed to many different cultural influences, but the processes of cultural change were universal. Although he was sympathetic to the cause of African nationalism, he was opposed to exclusive nationalisms. The idea that people might have multiple identities clearly struck against the view of culture as primordial and innate. In his personal life he fought against prejudice. Lewis Gann recalls his openness to American scholarship, which was not always the case with intellectuals on the Left in the 1950s, and his kindness to Gann's German and gentile wife, only a few years after the Holocaust.[18]

A. L. Epstein

By no means all the Rhodes–Livingstone social anthropologists who took an interest in questions of ethnicity and identity were Jews. Important contributions in this field were also made by J. C. Mitchell and Elizabeth Colson among others. It was, nevertheless, A. L. Epstein who wrote most extensively on these issues and contributed most to the development of Gluckman's ideas on ethnicity. He also followed Gluckman in taking a specific interest in questions of Jewish ethnicity and identity.

Epstein was born in Liverpool in 1924 and was educated partly in Northern Ireland where he did a degree in law at Queen's University, Belfast. He served during the Second World War in the Royal Navy. After the war he was called to the English Bar and also studied social anthropology for a year at the London School of Economics. He arrived in Northern Rhodesia early in 1950 to do work as a legal anthropologist on the Urban Native Courts system which had recently been introduced. After some time in the Northern and Luapula Provinces, where he studied the Bemba language, he spent most of his first period of research, 1950–52, in Ndola which he described on this first visit as a sleepy colonial town. He was recruited in 1952 by the Rhodes–Livingstone Institute, and returned in 1953 to do research on African urban politics in Luanshya. Between 1950 and 1953 there had been a dramatic change in the political atmosphere on the Copperbelt as a result of the decision to impose the Federation in spite of African opposition to it. He described the atmosphere in Luanshya on his arrival there in July 1953 as 'nightmarish'.[19]

Epstein began his fieldwork in Luanshya at the very moment when the Federation was being imposed. He was able initially to get the cooperation and support of the District Commissioner in Luanshya, Tony Heath, of the resident director of the Rhodesian Selection Trust, Jack Thomson, and of Lawrence Katilungu, the president of the African Mineworkers Union. He soon found, however, that he was working in a political minefield. His research topic related to the emergence of African political leadership and necessitated working closely with both the African National Congress and the African Mineworkers Union. He had to overcome the suspicions of the African political leadership, which was itself divided, but in doing so he aroused the suspicion of the white community and of the Chamber of Mines.

As Epstein himself recalled :

> If one were to work successfully with Africans one had to win their confidence and support, and this was to put oneself in a position *vis-à-vis* the African that was entirely different from that of other Europeans: it was a relationship which demanded mutuality. In such circumstances even a public handshake, elsewhere scarcely to be regarded as a momentous event, here became a subversive act because it was an acknowledgement of the African's equality.[20]

His cause was hardly helped by a campaign against social anthropology which had been run for some years by Dr Alec Scott, the 'liberal' editor and proprietor of the *Central African Post*, and which was intensified at this time. In his view, 'European familiarity with Africans breeds contempt by Africans'. In an article which harked back to comments about Jews in the early years of the century, he accused sociologists of undermining 'deference' and disturbing the political atmosphere in the country. 'They can give Africans "wrong ideas". They treat them as if they were a responsible, grown-up community which they are not, and they teach them to hate and resent the Europeans whom they represent as their exploiters. They may not be complete communists, but they are uncommonly near being so.'[21]

It was the secretary of the Chamber of Mines, S. Taylor, who noted in September that Epstein's research was 'ill-timed and dangerous for obvious reasons'. It was his contacts with the Mineworkers Union which caused most alarm. Taylor put pressure on Mitchell, the director of the Rhodes–Livingstone Institute, to stop the research. Mitchell declined to stop it, but Epstein was, by a decision of the Chamber of Mines, denied access to the Roan Antelope mine compound. This made his research very difficult as he had access only to the municipal compound, but he was fortunate that African informants were prepared to come and see him at his house, even though some of them, including Lawrence Katilungu, were questioned about their contacts with him. He persisted with the research until May 1954 and completed an important book based on it. *Politics in an Urban African Community*, which was published in 1958, was the first major study of urban African politics to be completed in southern Africa.[22]

The book is of interest to the student of Zambian Jewry for the light it sheds on the Zukas affair, and also for its detailed, and at times entertaining, description of the politics behind the boycott of Werners Butchery and the Standard Butchery in Luanshya in February 1954.[23] Its main importance, however, lies in its description of the emergence of the African nationalist and trade union movements on the Copperbelt, and in its assessment of the interplay of class and tribalism, or ethnicity, as factors in African urban politics. Epstein indicated that there was an element of 'situational selection' which determined whether people stressed their ethnic or class loyalties. He realised that the emergence of class-based trade unions, replacing the old system of worker representation through Tribal Elders, did not mean that tribes had ceased to be a factor in urban politics.[24]

Epstein carried out further research in 1955–56 on the urban situation in Ndola. He found a marked difference between Luanshya, the mine and company town, and Ndola, which was not a mine town, but the commercial, industrial and administrative centre of the Copperbelt. In Luanshya he had concentrated on the political domain, but in Ndola he worked primarily on the domestic domain. Although he had at first found research in Ndola relatively easy, he was forced to end it a little prematurely by the series of rolling strikes which occurred on the mines during 1956, and culminated in the declaration of a state of emergency on the Copperbelt in September of that year. The first results of this work were published as an article in 1961: 'The Network and Urban Social Organisation'. This developed the idea of the social network – an idea which seems commonplace now but which had been invented by a colleague, John Barnes – in the context of the Copperbelt. He also developed at this time influential ideas about the social role of gossip. After a very long period of gestation the fruits of this period of research were published in 1981 as a book, *Urbanisation and Kinship*.[25]

Meanwhile Epstein, who had done further fieldwork among the Tolai people of New Britain before taking up an appointment as a professor at the University of Sussex, had in 1978 published another book, *Ethos and Identity: Three Studies in Ethnicity*. This was a comparative study in which he drew on his fieldwork in Northern Rhodesia, and his later work on the Tolai, as well as literary research on America Jewry, to develop his ideas on ethnicity and identity. Epstein, who was, in contrast to Gluckman and Gann, an 'observant' Jew, playing a part in the life of the local Jewish community, prefaced this work with a clear statement that his views on these subjects were profoundly influenced by his Jewish identity.

> I am keenly aware that if I achieved any insight into these situations it was because they touched some chord of response that echoed my own ethnic experience as a Jew of the Diaspora. Reflecting on all this, the one major conviction that emerged was the powerful emotional charge that appears to underlie so much of ethnic behaviour; and it is this affective dimension of the problem that seems to me lacking in so many recent attempts to tackle it.[26]

In this complex book he rejected the idea that ethnicity was primarily a matter of culture. He considered the suggestion that ethnic groups were primarily economic or political interest groups. He also considered the role of ethnicity in defining boundaries between peoples and in categorising people in increasingly complex societies, but he felt that none of these ways of looking at ethnicity took sufficient account of emotional and psychological factors.

The essential question which Epstein was examining was why 'tribalism' or ethnicity did not fade away with the erosion of traditional practices and cultural differences. Why was it that Jewishness survived the migration of Jews from the enclosed community of the ghetto, and the *shtetl*, to the towns and suburbs of America, or Southern Africa, in spite of the loss of the Yiddish language and, for many, of belief in Judaism? In the African context, why did a sense of Bemba identity survive, or even develop, in the Copperbelt towns where Bemba-speaking people were far removed from the rural centres of Bemba culture? Epstein differed from Gluckman in his emphasis on emotional and psychological factors, but he followed him in seeing that ethnicity functioned in much the same way among apparently very different people.

He stressed the differences between positive ethnic identity which comes from within, and negative ethnic identity which is imposed from the outside, as on the half-Jewish *mischlings* of America, or, we might add, on Roy Welensky in Northern Rhodesia. He also showed that for ethnicity to function in the public sphere of politics it must draw on what happens at the intimate level of the household. The erosion of custom and tradition in the public domain may be counter-balanced by the survival of less visible practices in the privacy of the family. In the final analysis, the importance of ethnicity depends on the universal tendency of most people to prefer the company of what they see as their own kind. For, paradoxically, it is only in the company of those whom we see as our own kind that ethnicity ceases to be an important issue.

Lewis Gann

Elizabeth Colson recalls that when she arrived in Northern Rhodesia to begin social anthropological fieldwork in 1946 there was no published history of the country. To discover the dates of an important event, such as the arrival of the railway on the north bank of the Zambezi, it was necessary to search in colonial reports or the archives. It is hardly surprising, therefore, that it was during her tenure as director of the Rhodes–Livingstone Institute that a professional historian was recruited. This was at a time when there was still some tension between social anthropologists and historians. Lewis Gann, a recent graduate from Oxford, was recruited in 1950 and became the first professional historian to work in Northern Rhodesia.

Lewis H. Gann was born Ludwig Hermann Ganz in Mainz, Germany, in 1924. He changed his name when he joined the British army during the Second World War. He was, as he has recalled in a fragment of autobiography, a German *marrano* whose 'grandparents converted from Judaism to the Lutheran religion while retaining a vestigial sense of Jewish identification'. His parents belonged to what he called the provincial *haute bourgeoisie*. His grandfather served in the German army in the First World War on the Western Front, but died at Auschwitz. Gann recalled: 'Until Hitler came to power I was not aware of my Jewish origin; we felt ourselves Germans, and were proud of it – until 1933.' He was brought up on the German classics, Schiller, Goethe, Heine and Kant, and, as he says: 'There was *Haltung* aplenty, that untranslatable German word indicating good form and stiff-backed rectitude, virtues that somehow seemed unattainable to myself.'[27]

Gann's family left Germany for Britain in 1938. After their house in London was bombed during the Blitz in 1940, they moved to Carlisle where he attended the grammar school. Among his teachers were other German Jewish refugees, including the distinguished classical scholar Victor Ehrenberg, father of the equally distinguished British historian, Sir Geoffrey Elton. By the time that Gann left school, after winning an open scholarship to Balliol College, Oxford, 'the King had no more loyal citizen than myself, Winston

Churchill no more enthusiastic supporter, the Empire no more devoted citizen'.[28] Gann joined the Royal Fusiliers in 1943, but became a sergeant in the Intelligence Corps. Because of his invaluable linguistic skills, he was required to remain in the army for two years after the end of the war and served in occupied Germany, mainly in Berlin. He witnessed the beginning of the industrial reconstruction of West Germany. He read widely in Marxist literature in German and English and learned about conditions in the Soviet zone of occupation from numerous interviews with refugees. By the time he left the army in 1947, he was a 'committed anti-communist. The Soviet empire seemed to me dangerous and detestable.'[29]

While at Oxford University between 1947 and 1950, he learned little about Africa, but his loyalty to the Labour Party was challenged by lectures on the disastrous East African groundnuts scheme given by S. Herbert Frankel, the newly appointed Professor of Colonial Economics, who has already featured in this book. After graduation, Gann looked for a job, 'preferably abroad, ideally in the Empire', and was offered the post of historian at the Rhodes–Livingstone Institute. His frank account of his attitudes on his arrival in Northern Rhodesia also reveals the pervasive influence on him of his Jewish background:

> I looked upon Africans, I suppose, in much the same way as my parents in the olden days would have looked upon poverty-stricken Jewish immigrants from eastern Europe, benighted *Ostjuden*, worthy folk no doubt, with their own time-honoured folklore and religious customs – but urgently in need of civic improvement to be effected by a thorough training in *Haltung*, German classics, cold baths and lots of Latin. It was only gradually that I discarded these particular prejudices. On the other hand my parents had also taught me something useful. When I was first introduced to a Lamba village in the backwoods of what is now Zambia, I realised that *Haltung* was in order. I tried to behave as I would have done in my grandmother's house, and was later told that, in the villagers' opinion, my manners had not been too bad, for a European.[30]

Gann did not spend long in Northern Rhodesia and spent most of his two years with the Institute doing archival work in Salisbury. After a further two years in Manchester, where his chief mentors were Max Gluckman and Sir Lewis Namier, a distinguished historian and leading Zionist whose intellectual interests included the history of the Austro-Hungarian empire, Gann returned to Africa to take up a job with the Central African Archives in Salisbury where he remained until 1963.

During this time he worked mainly on the history of Northern Rhodesia. His Oxford dissertation was the basis of his first book, *The Birth of a Plural Society: the Development of Northern Rhodesia under the British South Africa Company, 1894–1914*, which was published in 1958. It was the first scholarly work on the history of the country. It differed from most contemporary work in the field of imperial history in that it was mainly based on local archival sources, as well as on interviews with living informants, and was influenced by the work of social anthropologists. In his Introduction to the book, Max Gluckman humorously noted that the anthropologists at the Institute, who had been expecting little more than a list of dates from their historian, had got rather more than they had bargained for, as the book had a distinctly sociological slant to it. Gann had, however, provided them privately with their list of dates.[31]

The sociological aspects were not welcomed by his Oxford supervisors who delayed approval of the dissertation and its publication. He followed this with *A History of Northern Rhodesia, Early Days to 1953* which was published in 1964. This was an official history which was sponsored by the Northern Rhodesian and Federal governments. It remains the most comprehensive history of Northern Rhodesia in the colonial period, and is a mine of information and ideas, though its usefulness is reduced by a totally inadequate index. It is also a far from objective history. It is written from a white settler point of view and is a frank apology for the Federation. Gann had been the co-author, with Peter Duignan, of a short Penguin book, *White Settlers in Tropical Africa*, which was published two years previously and was also an apologetic work.

Gann differed from the majority of Jewish intellectuals, including Gluckman, Epstein and Zukas, in taking a distinctly pessimistic view of African nationalism. He was unusual in that he identified with the white settler minority, dedicating his first book to Sir Roy Welensky. He rejected what he saw as the belief of some liberal students of southern Africa that an objective study of the facts of history would necessarily be good for race relations. He cited the example of G. L. Reitlinger's *The Final Solution*, a scholarly study on the Holocaust, and commented that this work would not improve the relationship between Germans and Jews. Clearly he was greatly influenced by his own experience as an assimilated German Jew. Drawing on his knowledge of eastern Europe, especially the Austro-Hungarian and Ottoman empires, he had concluded that the colonial societies of Southern Africa were not unique.

Plural societies in which social and economic functions were performed by people of different ethnic and linguistic groups were common in eastern Europe. In Transylvania, for example, 'the landowner was a Hungarian, the peasant a Rumanian, the burgher perhaps a German, the trader a Jew'. Such societies were threatened by the rise of 'peasant intellectuals' who eventually demanded recognition of their languages and both political and economic power. In southern Africa the caste system was complicated by race and colour, but Gann saw essential similarities. In his view:

National-social transformations ... sometimes even led to the physical extinction of the minorities concerned. Such was the experience of the Anatolian Greeks and the Ottoman Armenians. The German Jews had a similar fate, when conditions after the world crisis in the slump-ridden Fatherland temporarily began to resemble those of an underdeveloped country. There was nothing the minorities could do in those circumstances but to emigrate; even the most thorough-going attempts at identifying themselves with their host-nations – as with Jews who intermarried and adopted German culture – were of little avail. The 'German citizen of Israelite faith', with his passionate German nationalism and his officer's commission, was never fully accepted as a German, and was liquidated in the end. Yet he was much more assimilated to the land of his birth than any European liberal in East or Central Africa who believes that he can safeguard his future by identifying himself with the forces of Bantu nationalism.[32]

Gann's views were extremely unfashionable in intellectual circles and his fears were greatly exaggerated, though some of his gloomy predictions of economic decline were borne out. In one passage he had compared the probable economic consequences of the departure of white settlers from central Africa with the effects of the expulsion of the Jews from Spain by the Inquisition. He moved in 1963 to the Hoover Institute at Stanford University and collaborated with Duignan on a large number of works on African history. They eventually abandoned African studies and in the years before his death in 1997 he had found intellectual satisfaction in work on the Americanisation of Europe. It is, perhaps, unfortunate that Gann's extreme views on African nationalism have led to an underestimation of the originality of his work. His Balkan analogies anticipated some of the much more recent work of radical scholars such as Benedict Anderson's *Imagined Communities* and Basil Davidson's *The Black Man's Burden*. He was, for instance, one of the first scholars to refer to the importance of the rise of 'peasant intellectuals' and to the tendency of emergent nationalist movements to 'invent' traditions and a glorious past.

Robert I. Rotberg

The second professional historian to work on the history of Northern Rhodesia was also Jewish. Robert I. Rotberg was an American scholar who was attached as an associate to the Rhodes–Livingstone Institute in 1959 and made annual visits to the country throughout the 1960s. He completed a doctoral dissertation at Oxford University which was published in 1965 as *Christian Missionaries and the Making of Northern Rhodesia, 1880–1924*. He also did pioneering work on Alice Lenshina and the Lumpa Rebellion. His second book, *The Rise of Nationalism in Central Africa: the Making of Malawi and Zambia, 1873–1964* was published in 1966. He became friendly with Sir Stewart Gore-Browne and published in 1977 a comprehensive, and controversial, biography of him which made extensive use of his private papers and was entitled: *Black Heart: Gore-Browne and the Politics of Multi-racial Zambia*. Although this book deals in great detail with the relationship between Gore-Browne and Roy Welensky, it does not comment on their attitudes towards Jewish immigration in the late 1930s. Rotberg, whose later works have included a massive biography of Cecil Rhodes, recalls that he had no contact with, or knowledge of, the Zambian Jewish community.[33]

The examples of Gluckman, Epstein, Gann and Rotberg, who all made significant contributions to the study of Zambia, indicate that their Jewishness influenced their perceptions of the country in different ways. In the cases of Gluckman and Epstein, it seems to have influenced them to take a liberal view of ethnicity and African nationalism. It influenced Lewis Gann in the opposite direction, and in the case of Robert Rotberg, there is no discernible influence at all.

Nadine Gordimer

No account of writing about Zambia, and African nationalism, by Jewish authors would be complete without a brief reference to the work of Nadine Gordimer, one of South Africa's most eminent novelists. She has been a regular visitor to the country since the early 1960s. Her husband, Reinhold Cassirer, a German Jewish refugee from a distinguished family, had become a partner in the early 1950s in an electrical engineering business on the Copperbelt which supplied the mines with switch gear and other electrical equipment. At one time, in the 1960s, she contemplated moving to live in Zambia. She later commented that this was 'a romantic idea' which she had rejected when she found that 'I was only a European there, just like any other white person. I took that very hard. At least in South Africa even if I get my throat cut, I am an African.'[34] A great deal of her work relates to African nationalism, and her main experience of an independent African country has been gained in Zambia. One of her best-known novels, *A Guest of Honour*, which was published in 1970, is set in an imaginary country which bears a close physical, and a less close political, resemblance to Zambia. The hero of the book is a liberal colonial official who returns to the country where he served ten years previously to work for the newly independent government. He is shocked by the rise of tribalism and corruption and his visit ends in disillusionment and violent death. The book is believed by many to have been at least partly inspired by the experience in Zambia of Thomas Fox-Pitt, a former colonial official, who, as we have seen, was involved with Simon Zukas as an early white supporter of the Zambian nationalist movement.

Another of Gordimer's novels with specifically Zambian, and strong Jewish, associations is *A Sport of Nature* which was published in 1987. This 'picaresque' novel, which she clearly did not intend to be taken too seriously, traces the roving career of Hillela Capran, a Southern African Jewish girl. In the course of the novel it emerges that Hillela's travels began as a child when she accompanied her father, Len, on his weekly journeys as a commercial traveller from Salisbury to Northern Rhodesia. He later takes a job as a mine storeman at Ndola, dies, and, unknown to Hillela, is buried in 'the North'. After a series of political liaisons, Hillela becomes involved with, and eventually marries, Whaila Kgomani, a leader of the African National Congress in exile. They are moved in the mid-1960s from Dar es Salaam to Lusaka, where Hillela leads for several years a relatively settled life with her husband and two children. Her closest friends outside the 'movement' are Selina and Russell Montgomery, another mixed-race couple.

Hillela's husband, Whaila, is assassinated by a parcel bomb in Lusaka and, like her father, is buried in Zambian soil. She goes on to marry a man who becomes president of another independent African country and the book ends with a colourful description of her attendance at the inauguration of South Africa's first black president in Cape Town. Although this is probably the least serious of Nadine Gordimer's works, and not a work of history, it does provide a good fictional description of exile life in Lusaka, as well as a highly evocative portrayal of the sights, sounds and smells of the city from the avenues of its middle-class suburbs to the vegetable stalls and metal workshops of Luburma market. It may also be seen as a book about a central African Jewess's search for roots and identity.

Michael Gelfand

An amateur historian who made a major contribution to the writing of the history of Northern Rhodesia was the distinguished physician, and first head of the medical school at what is now the University of Zimbabwe, Michael Gelfand. His book, *Northern Rhodesia in the Days of the Charter*, was published in 1961 and is both a general history of the country under British South Africa Company rule and a pioneering work on medical history, containing two chapters on medical services before 1924 and one on the campaign to eradicate sleeping sickness. Gelfand never lived in Northern Rhodesia, but he had a close association with the country through his marriage to Esther, daughter of Isadore, Kollenberg. His brother, Benny Gelfand, was also associated with the country: he was a chartered accountant who worked for Northern Caterers on the Copperbelt both before and after the Second World War. He later had his own firm which was based in Salisbury, and audited the accounts of the more important Northern Rhodesian Jewish businesses.[35] Lewis Gann, who collaborated with Michael Gelfand on a life of Godfrey Huggins, later Lord Malvern, gave a touching testimonial to this remarkable man:

> My collaborator ... was an excellent physician, a medical historian and anthropologist, and a very great authority on Shona religion. This South African was also a man of outstanding moral stature who devoted much of his life to unpaid work for African patients. Though an orthodox Jew, he was made a Papal knight; but I suspect that he may have been even more – one of the Thirty-Six Just Men, the *Lamed Vav* who, according to Jewish folklore, shoulder the world's weight until the Messiah comes.[36]

Michael Gelfand died not long after Zimbabwe's independence. His funeral at the Harare *shul* was attended by President Robert Mugabe – a tribute to his roles as a doctor, as a family friend, and as a writer on Shona religion. His widow, Esther, still lives in Harare.

Medicine

If there is one practical profession with which Jews have been most closely identified in Zambia in the course of this century, it is medicine. It would be impossible to mention all the Jewish doctors who have spent time in the country, but there is room for a sample of some of the most interesting of them. One who remains a legend on the Copperbelt, nearly forty years after her death, is Dr Manya (Marie) Damie. There is even a street, Dr Damie Street, in Ndola which still bears her name. She was in all probability the first woman to practise modern medicine in the country. She was born near Libau in Latvia at the beginning of the century and studied medicine at the University of Padua, Italy, one the oldest medical schools in Europe. She arrived in Ndola in the late 1920s with an Italian husband, Dr Tattoni, who stayed for only a few years. He left the country with another partner.

Marta Paynter, who knew her well, has provided a moving description of this remarkable woman:

> Dr Damie was for many years the 'Rhodesia Railways' doctor. She was a tall, big-boned, red-haired woman with a very tough, hoydenish manner – I suppose she had to be. In her early years she saved thousands from the very serious and often fatal blackwater disease, then rampant in NR. The tough railwaymen, mainly from South Africa and Rhodesia, were said to be terrified of her: she would receive them in the railway surgery, tell them roughly: 'Take off your trousers, I want to have a look at your rump.' These men were not used to being examined or treated by a woman.
>
> During her 40 years in NR she must have brought thousands of babies into the world. She had a tough and frightening manner, but her hands were warm and gentle and behind her rough exterior was a very soft heart. Her African patients adored her. Many times if patients could not afford medicines or drugs, she would provide them free of charge for them: also bed sheets and pillows and millions of nappies for 'her' babies. Some of them grew up to be ministers and high government officials, but they never forgot her.[37]

Dr Damie was a doctor at the Ndola hospital, and is said to have often been the only sober one there. Among the births she attended were those of Dr Mark Lowenthal and his sister, Isa Teeger. She acted as an unofficial *mohel* to many boys, and was godmother to Denise Scott Brown. After over thirty years in the country, she went on long leave in 1958 and never returned. She went to visit a sister in the United States, where she is said to have met one of 'her' babies on the New York subway. While in America, she was found to have breast cancer. She appeared to have made a good recovery after an operation and went on to visit her nieces in Israel, but she died there in 1961.[38]

Dr Damie was succeeded in Ndola by another remarkable Jewish woman doctor who also remained in the town for over thirty years. Sylvia Lehrer was born in Jassy, Romania, in 1917. She studied medicine at the University of Edinburgh and was a highly qualified gynaecologist and obstetric surgeon. She came on a visit to friends in Salisbury and was told that a 'women's doctor' was needed at Ndola general hospital. She lived for a while in Dr Damie's house, but later built her own. Like Dr Damie she brought thousands of children into the world and was very highly regarded as a surgeon.

In the early 1960s she married Gabriel Radson who had arrived in Northern Rhodesia during the war from Poland by way of Persia as one of the 'Merra' refugees. He was an accountant in Luanshya, but moved to Ndola where he established Piper Clothing, a menswear manufacturing company. He had left his wife and daughter in Poland and only discovered after many years that they had survived the war and were living in Israel. According to Marta Paynter, it was Sylvia who was instrumental in bringing him together with his daughter, who visited them several times in Zambia. After the break-up of her marriage, Sylvia Lehrer continued to live and work in Ndola. She died there of meningitis in 1989 and was buried in Jerusalem.[39]

There were, of course, also Jewish doctors on the Copperbelt who were men, such as Dr Leo Gottlieb, who was the Nkana mine doctor in the 1940s and 1950s. He was politically active and during the war was secretary of the Kitwe branch of Roy Welensky's Labour Party. There has also been a succession of Jewish doctors in Lusaka. The first of them, Dr Manning, met a tragic end. He arrived in about 1934 and is described by Jack Fischer as having been 'tall, dark and good looking'. He gave a party in the rooms which he rented from Sam Fischer to celebrate the end of the Yom Kippur fast in 1936. Jack Fischer recalls: 'One of his guests picked up a .22 rifle which was standing in a corner and, thinking that it was unloaded, pulled the trigger, killing him instantly.'[40] His grave has the largest stone in the Jewish section of the Old Cemetery in Rhodes Park, and bears the single name: 'Manneschevitz'. He was succeeded by Dr Dennis Fabian, a German Jewish refugee, who arrived in 1937 and stayed until 1950. He had some rabbinical training and, as Alf Metzger recalls, he also acted as a *mohel*.[41] Dr Fabian sold his practice to Dr Lazar Molk who remained in the town until 1966, and was highly regarded as a general practitioner. He is remembered especially for his devoted care for Ellis Mendelsohn who died of cancer at an early age. He emigrated with his family to the United States where he still practises in Colorado.[42]

Dr Michael Bush arrived in 1972 to work for the Kariba North Bank Company, but he moved to Lusaka soon afterwards. He has now been in charge of the Minbank Clinic, the best equipped private clinic in the town, for a quarter of a century and has maintained the almost unbroken succession of Jewish doctors in the town. He has also, as we have seen, played an important part as *baal tefilah* in the Hebrew Congregation. His services to medicine were recognised in 1993 by his appointment by Dr Michael Sata, the Minister of Health, as chairman of the General Medical Council. His wife, Ruth, made an important contribution to the artistic life of the town through her management of the Mpapa Gallery, a commercial but non-profit-making art gallery – the first in the town – from its establishment in 1979 until 1994.[43]

There were at least two sons of Jewish businessmen in Northern Rhodesia who returned to the country to work for long periods as doctors. The first of them was Eric (Ahron) Iljon. He was born in St Petersburg in 1919 at a time of great deprivation for the city's inhabitants as a result of revolution, civil war and outside intervention. He arrived with his family, and his sister's grand piano, the family's sole reminder of their pre-revolutionary affluence, in Mazabuka in 1928. He vividly recalls that what appeared from the train to be the bright lights of the city of Mazabuka turned out on closer examination to be a raging grass fire on the Kafue flats beyond the lagoon. He attended school in Mazabuka and in Southern Rhodesia. His miraculous survival in Lusaka's then primitive hospital after a ruptured appendix inspired him to study medicine, and he enrolled at the University of Cape Town's medical school in 1938.

When he qualified at the end of the war, Dr Iljon joined the Colonial Medical Service in Northern Rhodesia. His first appointment in 1946 was as the only medical officer at the newly opened Silicosis Bureau in Kitwe. After six months he was transferred to Balovale (now Zambezi) in the North-Western Province, one of the most remote of the Provincial Administration's bomas, then regarded as a punishment posting. He claims that he was the first civil servant to arrive in Balovale by car. When he asked Susman Brothers and Wulfsohn how to get there, he was told: 'Ndola, then Solwezi and ask for directions from there.' Solwezi was about 300 miles by bush tracks and footpaths from his destination.

When he arrived in Balovale, he found an empty hospital. There was no lack of potential patients, but the hospital had acquired a reputation as a place where people went to die. His first operations were performed by candlelight and the sterilising of instruments was done on an open hearth about 100 yards from the nearest ward to avoid setting the buildings on fire. During his three-year stay in Balovale the hospital was, as part of the first post-war ten-year development plan, enlarged from sixty to 240 beds. A maternity ward and dispensary were opened. The introduction of penicillin during this time had a dramatic effect on the recovery rate of patients, and on the reputation of the hospital. New treatments for leprosy, which was endemic, were also introduced. It was in Balovale that he met his wife, Betty Evans, a Welsh nurse. They were married in a civil ceremony in Mazabuka in 1950 and, after receiving the permission of Chief Rabbi Abrahams in

Cape Town, they had a religious wedding which was performed by Rabbi Clayman in Lusaka in 1952.

Dr Iljon's later postings were to Mazabuka, Lusaka, where he was involved in the introduction of TB testing and BCG vaccinations, and Mongu where he remained until 1957 as Provincial Medical Officer. A highlight of his time in Mongu was an invitation to accompany the Litunga Mwanawina III on the royal barge, the *Nalikwanda*, during the Kuomboka ceremony. After two years in Fort Jameson, he returned to Livingstone as the Provincial Medical Officer for the Southern Province. Among his duties was the medical supervision of the controversial removal of thousands of people from the Gwembe valley to make way for Lake Kariba. Losing faith in the Federation, he left Northern Rhodesia in the early 1960s, and went with his family on *aliyah* to Israel where he still lives and works as a farmer on a kibbutz in the north of the country.[44]

The second son of a prominent Northern Rhodesian Jewish businessman to return to work as a doctor in the country was Mark Lowenthal, son of Abe Lowenthal. He was born and brought up in Ndola and studied medicine at the University of Cape Town where he graduated in 1957. After postgraduate studies he returned to Ndola in 1960, a few months after his father's death. He first worked as a locum at the Pneumoconiosis Bureau, before working for a year, 1961–62, as a general duties medical officer at Ndola Hospital. In 1962 he was on duty when Harold Julien, a seconded member of the New York Police Department and the sole survivor of the air crash which killed Dag Hammarskjold, the United Nations Secretary-General, and all the other passengers, was brought into the hospital, still conscious and able to give some account of events. Lowenthal recalls:

> Julien was a strong young man and, with the best that modern care of the time could offer, would have survived. I was inexperienced, four years out of medical school and not in charge of the case. A maturer me would have unofficially told the Americans to send an aircraft to take him to the US quickly. The matter remains with me as a great regret.

Mark Lowenthal went on to work from 1964 to 1974 as the first Government Medical Specialist (consultant) at the Ndola Hospital. During this time the new Ndola Hospital was built and he was able to do research and to publish a number of articles in a variety of medical journals. His family had a strong Zionist commitment: two of his Lowenthal aunts had emigrated from Latvia to Palestine in the 1920s. In 1974 he too went with his family on *aliyah* to Israel where he still lives and works.[45]

The Media

Another area in which Jewish intellectuals and professionals have had a significant impact is in the media. No individual has made a greater contribution over a longer period to journalism in Zambia than Marta Trefusis-Paynter who has now lived in the country for over fifty years. For most of this time she has worked for *The Times of Zambia* and its predecessor, *The Northern News*. Marta Paynter was born in Vienna, Austria, and was educated there at college, language school and music academy. She left her home country in June 1938, three months after the *Anschluss* – the Nazi takeover. She left the country illegally and sailed to Palestine on a refugee ship, the *Artemissia*, which was organised by Betar, the youth wing of Vladimir Jabotinsky's Zionist Revisionist movement. She was required to work for two years at Rosh Pina, Galilee, as a field hand and quarry worker by day, and as a guard by night, receiving military training as a member of the Revisionist movement's military wing, Irgun. She went to Haifa in 1940 where she played the piano accordion in a girls' band. It was there that she met her future husband, Guy Trefusis-Paynter, an officer in the Natal Rifles, in 1942. It was also there that she hid Chaim Landau, Menachem Begin's deputy as commander of Irgun, under her bed, when he was on the run from the British.

Marta left Palestine on a South African troopship in November 1944, twelve days after her release from a short spell in Bethlehem Women's Prison (she was detained in a case of mistaken identity). She was married in February 1945 in Durban and arrived in Ndola, where her husband became district manager of African Oxygen, in April of the same year. When Menachem Begin and Yakov Meridor came to Ndola in 1953 to address the Jewish community, she sat on the platform and was introduced as 'an old fighter', though, as she says, she was then still young. After her husband's death in 1976 she went on re-*aliyah* to Israel, and stayed for eighteen months, but she was unable to settle down there, though she makes regular visits to the country.

Marta began work in November 1953 for *The Northern News*. Over the years she has worked as editorial assistant, general reporter, court reporter, senior court reporter and crime reporter, business editor, and, for the last ten years, as copy editor. She is well known for her television reviews, as a scourge of sloppy news reading and incorrect English pronunciation, and for her reflective column, 'From my Rocking Chair', as well as for features which enable her to display her unrivalled knowledge of Copperbelt history over the last fifty years. She has played an important behind-the-scenes role under a succession of editors in training journalists and helping to maintain *The Times of Zambia*'s high editorial standards. She has provided a unique element of continuity to the paper, bridging the colonial and post-colonial periods. Her services to journalism in the Commonwealth were recognised by the award of the MBE in 1986. Following the death of Harry Stern in the early 1990s, she is the last surviving member of the Jewish community in Ndola. Although not religious, she says that she acutely misses any communal life, but that this is 'the price I have to pay for living and working here in relative peace and comfort'. Her elder son, Michael, works in Australia, while her younger son, Geoffrey, is managing director of Gallo Music Publications in Johannesburg.[46]

Marta Paynter is not the only Jewish woman, and refugee from nazism, to have worked as a journalist on *The Times of Zambia*. Ruth Weiss also worked as business editor of the paper for five years from 1970. She was simultaneously the central African correspondent of the London *Financial Times* and reported for a number of German newspapers. She was born in 1924 near Nuremburg in Germany and travelled with her family as a refugee to South Africa in 1936. She finished school in Johannesburg, but could not afford to take up a place to study law at the University of the Witwatersrand. She began to practise journalism in South Africa, but became a refugee for a second time in 1966 after her husband's office was raided by the security police. She was in Zambia at a critical period and covered the end of the liberation wars in Mozambique and Angola. She was in touch with members of liberation movements from other southern African countries such as ZAPU, ZANU, SWAPO and the ANC which, she noted, had a relatively low profile in Zambia in the early 1970s. She came to see herself as a southern African and returned from London to work in Zimbabwe after its independence in 1980.[47]

Although he might be described as more of an amateur, in the best sense of the word, than a professional, Theo Bull, a great-nephew of Alfred Beit, deserves inclusion in this work as a journalist. He is the son of an Anglican clergyman, but he takes immense pride in the Jewish element in his ancestry. His 'German Jewish descent' was carefully noted in a Federal intelligence report submitted to Sir Roy Welensky in 1960. Nadine Gordimer maintains that she does not base her characters on real people: it is difficult to avoid the conclusion that in *A Sport of Nature* she has broken her own rules, as the characters of Selina and Russell Montgomery seem to owe a great deal to the lives of her friends, Theo Bull and his wife, Mutumba Mainga, a historian and a former Foreign Minister of Zambia. Although the character in the novel is an engineer of Scottish descent, Theo Bull could be described as a man

> whose family made a colonial fortune two generations earlier in those raw materials that were exported and sold back, transformed, to those who could afford them. He himself was transformed; he come back to Africa as the member of his family who married a black girl instead of paying her forbears a few British pence a day to labour in field, plantation or mine.[48]

After education at Harrow School and Trinity College, Cambridge, Theo Bull came to Southern Rhodesia in 1959 where he studied education at the University College of Rhodesia and Nyasaland. In the following year he became one of the proprietors, and the chairman of the board, in Salisbury of the *Central African Examiner*, a liberal periodical which was sponsored by Rhodesian Selection Trust and the Hochschild family. It was latterly edited by Eileen Haddon, and survived until Rhodesia's UDI in 1965. A man of diverse interests and enthusiasms, Theo Bull has for over thirty years been an irrepressible feature of Zambia's journalistic, social, business and, to a lesser extent, political scene. In the late 1960s he was the promoter of a chain of bookshops which made the latest Penguin paperbacks available in provincial centres such as Kasama. This was forced to close down following the ill-advised granting of a monopoly of school textbook publication and distribu-tion to the Kenneth Kaunda Foundation and Neczam. In recent years his main business activity has been in hotels where, with Enzio Rossi, he has run the Ndeke and Garden House Hotels in Lusaka as well as other enterprises.

Theo Bull's first love has, however, always been journalism, and he has used his pen to agitate on a number of issues. In 1990 he became a promoter, and chairman of the board, of the *Weekly Post*, the first independent news-paper to be established in the new wave of liberalisation which accompanied the move towards the restoration of multi-party democracy. More recently he has been a member of the editorial board of *Profit Magazine*, a business monthly, and has used its columns to lead a campaign for the privatisation and 'unbundling' of ZCCM, the parastatal mining group. He has also been a regular contributor to Johannesburg's *Business Day*.[49]

Peter Fraenkel who, as we have seen, arrived in Lusaka with his parents as a thirteen-year-old boy in 1939, made his mark in a different branch of the media. After education in Lusaka, at Milton High School in Bulawayo, and at the University of the Witwatersrand, he joined the Northern Rhodesian civil service in 1950 and served in the Department of Cooperatives for two years. Ever since his wartime visits to Lusaka's radio station it had, however, been his ambition to become a broadcaster. He joined the Central African Broadcasting Services in Lusaka in 1952 and worked there for four years. He published a vivid account of his experiences as a broadcaster in the early years of Federation under the title *Wayeleshi* in 1959. When he joined CABS he found that it was, under the inspiring leadership of Michael Kittermaster, an island of non-racialism. Among his early colleagues was Edwin Mlongoti, whose premature death in 1952 prompted an extraordinary public response and demonstrated that, within a few years of the introduction by Harry Franklin of the cheap 'saucepan' radio, broadcasting had become an important part of African life. Other colleagues included Alick Nkhata, the Nyasaland-born leader of the Lusaka Radio Band, whose compositions are still very popular, Stephen Mpashi and Sylvester (Andrea) Masiye, who were both early Zambian writers. With the encouragement of Kittermaster and his successor, Dick 'Sapper' Sapseid, who was also a gifted musician, Fraenkel spent much of his time collecting African music in remote areas of Northern Rhodesia and Nyasaland. He helped to build up what was thought at the time to be the largest collection of recorded African music on the continent. He married Merran McCulloch, a social anthropologist and member of the staff of the Rhodes–Livingstone Institute, who had worked on a social survey of the African population of Livingstone.

Although this work took him away from Lusaka, he could not conceal from himself the fact that CABS had become a propaganda organ for the Federation – an institution which no Northern Rhodesian African would defend. While he realised that it was unrealistic to compare the Federation with Nazi Germany, he was undoubtedly influenced by his own experience as a German Jewish refugee in deciding whether or not he should stay in the country.

> I had long been saying to myself that the increasing illiberalism could only be fought from inside, that it was people with views and contacts like mine who ought to stay. But in the end I decided that the argument was false, as false as history has shown the 'inner migration' to have been, the justification that many German non-Nazis made for carrying on the administration for a regime repugnant to them.

As he was drawn deeper into administration and away from actual broadcasting, he felt the danger of losing touch with African opinion. He resigned in 1956 and, apart from a short interlude in Malawi as Director of Broadcasting Services in the months after independence in 1964, he spent the next thirty years working for the BBC External Services in London. He became head of the European Service of the BBC before his retirement in 1986. He returned to Zambia as a consultant in that year to advise the government on a suitable media response to the then emerging HIV/AIDS epidemic. He recommended that the media avoid a confrontational approach and that discussion of HIV/AIDS should be introduced into existing radio drama series. He returned in the following year to make a television film on the same subject.[50]

Art and Architecture

While Peter Fraenkel had devoted at least part of his time in the country to the preservation of African music, Cynthia Zukas has devoted over thirty years of her life to the promotion of art. She is herself a gifted painter and trained at the Michaelis School of Art in Cape Town. On her arrival in the country in 1964–65 she found that there was a Lusaka Art Society which held an annual exhibition, but its membership was entirely white or expatriate and it was doing nothing to encourage local talent. She became secretary of the society and, with the help of her friend Bente Lorenz, the Danish potter who had arrived in Lusaka a year or two previously, she set out to broaden the scope of its activities. She was also associated with the establishment of the art department at Evelyn Hone College and was responsible, with Robert Loder, later founder of the annual Mbile workshops for artists from the region, for the inclusion of an art gallery in the Anglo-American Building which was designed by Erhardt Lorenz. The Arts Centre Foundation emerged out of this initiative and was later responsible for the construction of the

Henry Tayali Visual Arts Centre in the Lusaka Showgrounds. She worked closely with the late Henry Tayali, Zambia's best-known painter and sculptor, in several of these initiatives. She joined Joan Pilcher and Ruth Bush as a director of the Mpapa Gallery in 1979. Until its closure, at least temporarily, in 1996, this provided the most important outlet for the work of Zambian artists. Its last home was in Joseph Mwilwa Road, in the area of Lusaka once known as Fairview, where the former Little Nkhwazi School provided an ideal setting for many exhibitions. She served for twenty years on the National Museums Board and is currently a member of the newly formed National Arts Council and the advisory committee of the National Lusaka Museum.

Cynthia Zukas was the prime mover in the establishment in 1985 of the Lechwe Trust which, under the chairmanship of Edwin Wulfsohn, has raised funds in Zambia and abroad for the acquisition of work by Zambian artists and for scholarships. The Lechwe Trust's fine collection, including remarkable paintings by Henry Tayali and others, has formed the nucleus of a national collection and is now on show in the recently opened National Lusaka Museum. Among the artists who have received scholarships from the Lechwe Trust to study abroad are Godfrey Setti and Patrick Mumba. The trust has sponsored many other artists for short courses and visits.

Cynthia Zukas confesses that she enjoys committee work. She also served for twenty-five years, from 1965 to 1990, on the committee of the Zambia Red Cross. Her enjoyment of committees undoubtedly comes from the pleasure which she derives, as an artist who normally works alone, from working with people. She does not seek publicity and would be the last person to claim that she has made a contribution as an individual to the development of the artistic life of Lusaka. There can, however, be no doubt that her long-term commitment and consistent work with others, including Bente Lorenz and Henry Tayali, has helped to create in Lusaka an exciting artistic life which did not exist thirty years ago, and which deserves greater international recognition than it has hitherto received.[51]

Walter (known as Wally) Dobkins has made an important contribution to the Zambian artistic scene in the field of architecture. Born at Nchanga in 1937, the son of Moss and Fay Dobkins, he was educated in South Africa where he completed his degree in Architecture at the University of Cape Town. After postgraduate studies at the University of Edinburgh, he returned to Zambia in 1968, and worked on low-cost housing for the Zambian Housing Corporation before moving into private practice. He moved to Australia in 1976 after Kaunda's 'Watershed' speech of the previous year had put a temporary stop to private housing developments. He worked there on a low-cost housing project for the Aboriginal population of Alice Springs before moving to a post in the Department of Architecture at the University of Adelaide. He continued to think of himself as based in Zambia and made frequent return visits, both to see his mother in Chingola, and for professional reasons. He had done some work for Andrew Sardanis who invited him in

1987 to design the new headquarters building for his Meridien Bank group on a prime site at the south end of Lusaka's Cairo Road. The design was completed in outline in 1988. He returned to Zambia a few years later to supervise the construction of the building and stayed until 1996.[52]

The completed Meridien Bank building is a major addition to the architecture of central Lusaka. A low-rise building on an extensive site, its four levels and five wings, with intervening courtyards, are in marked contrast to the massive and alien tower blocks, rising, as in the case of the neighbouring Findeco House, to twenty-two storeys, which are typical of prestige buildings in the city centre. Wally says: 'The building is not post-modern, but I probably wouldn't have designed it in the same way if the post-modern movement hadn't existed.'[53] The diagonal pedestrian spine which links the courtyards at ground level was inspired by a footpath which crossed the undeveloped site and is intended to draw people into the building. The wings and courtyards reflect the best colonial architecture of Lusaka's 1930s New Town. The eccentrically circular first level Banking Hall with its eucalyptus pole roof trusses pays tribute to pre-colonial Zambian architecture. The building draws as far as possible for both economic and aesthetic reasons on local materials: sand, crushed stone, cement, hardwoods and eucalyptus poles. The red laterite colour of the building blends with the local soil. The complex includes an art gallery, and Flinto Chandia, a remarkable sculptor, was employed full-time on art works which are an integral part of the project. The building has no lifts and is exceptionally sensitive to the climate and to the influence of light, shade, summer heat and winter cold – factors which expatriate architects tend either to ignore or to misunderstand.

Wally Dobkins has succeeded in creating a large building on a human scale. It is a decorative and original contribution to central Lusaka's rather limited assortment of interesting buildings; they include Sam Fischer's house, Abe Galaun's Grand Hotel with its collegiate quadrangle, and the Synagogue complex itself. Sadly, the completion of the building coincided with the failure of the Meridien Bank, and it is not at the moment fully used.

While medicine and the law are the professions with which Jews are most frequently identified, Zambia has attracted a number of engineers. In addition to Simon Zukas, Harry Chimowitz and David Messerer, whose varied careers are described elsewhere, Harvey Golson, a younger contemporary of Zukas and Chimowitz at the University of Cape Town, worked in Lusaka from 1962 until his death in 1987. Born in England and brought up in South Africa, he had worked in Southern Rhodesia on the Lake McIlwain dam project near Salisbury before moving to Northern Rhodesia. He arrived as the managing partner of Lewis Construction, a company with Australian roots, and links with the Anglo-American Corporation. Under his leadership, it became one of the largest contracting firms in the country. Among his earliest projects was the expansion of the Arakan Barracks for the Zambian army in Lusaka. He was a public-spirited person who served for eighteen years as president of the Association of Civil Engineering Contractors and was a member of the committee of the Hebrew Congregation. He was especially noted for the help and encouragement which he gave to small contractors, and sub-contactors, in the always competitive and risky building business. Following his death his widow, Diana Bignell, took control of the business which has been carried on by their son, Paul.[54]

There are, of course, many other professions, and professionals, who could be considered in a chapter of this kind. There are surprisingly few Jewish lawyers who have been prominent in Zambia. The careers of Maurice Diamond, Val Magnus and Leo Baron are discussed elsewhere. Although we have noted a number of people, such as Simon Zukas, Eric Iljon, Mark Lowenthal and Wally Dobkins, who were all born, or brought up, in the country as the children of traders, and who then returned to work as professionals, there is an even larger number of people who were born and brought up in the country and went on to work elsewhere. Wally Dobkins can enumerate half a dozen relatives with Zambian connections who trained as architects and who work all over the world.

Zambia's most spectacular contribution to the world of architecture is Denise Scott Brown, daughter of Shim and Phyllis Lakofski, who was born at Nkana in 1931. With her husband, Robert Venturi, she is a partner in one of the world's best-known architectural practices, responsible for such land-mark buildings as the new Sainsbury Wing at London's National Gallery. She has also done the city plan for New York. She has published extensively on architectural topics and remains very conscious of her African and Jewish roots. Her most influential book, written jointly with her husband, is *Learning from Las Vegas: The Forgotten Symbolism of Architectural Form*, which was published in 1972. This took a fresh look at the apparently 'ugly and ordinary' archi-tecture of Las Vegas's neon-lit casino strip, and saw it as more democratic than architecture produced in the modernist style. The book became a post-modernist text, though Denise Scott Brown has little sympathy with the influence on architecture of that movement. It is tempting to speculate that her sympathy with the 'ugly and ordinary' in urban design may stem from her experience of southern African towns which, like Lusaka, Kitwe, and Johannesburg – to whose 'style' her father made such a significant contribu-tion – seem to have sprung out of the bush in much the same way as Las Vegas has sprung out of the desert. She has, indeed, said that 'mine is an African view of Las Vegas'.[55]

Another remarkable intellectual and professional who emerged out of Zambia and has cut a figure on the world stage is Stanley Fischer, son of Philip and Ann Fischer, of Mazabuka. We have already quoted his memoir of his experiences as a Jewish boy growing up in a small town on the Line of Rail in the 1940s and 1950s. He went on to study at the London School of Economics, and at the Massachusetts Institute of Technology. He has had a distinguished career as an academic economist and is the co-

author of a standard textbook on macro-economics. He has written extensively on the economy of Israel and has acted as an economic adviser to
successive governments. He has been director of research at the World Bank,
and is currently first deputy managing director of the International Monetary
Fund in Washington. He has been in the news a great deal recently as the
architect of the IMF's controversial recovery package for the economies of
East Asia and Brazil. He is convinced that 'growing up in a developing
country, albeit in a privileged position, has given me much greater understanding of developing countries than I would have had if I had grown up
in the USA'.[56]

The relationship between intellectuals and professionals, and the countries
in which they are brought up, or live and work, is complex and symbiotic.
The most interesting intellectuals in the Zambian context are, perhaps, those
social anthropologists and historians like Max Gluckman, A. L. Epstein and
Lewis Gann who not only built their academic careers on a Zambian foundation, but who also interpreted Zambia to the world and, to some extent, to
itself. They played an important, but often forgotten, role in creating the
idea of a nation and a culture. Others, like Cynthia Zukas, have sought to
create an enabling environment in which Zambian artists could express
themselves and communicate with a wider world. Wally Dobkins has drawn
on the Zambian experience, interpreted it in his own way, and put something
back into the country in a tangible shape and form. Even a short exposure
to the Zambian experience can have an impact on artists and writers, as can
be seen in the works of Nadine Gordimer.

A remarkable example of this can be seen in the life and work of Johnny
Clegg, co-founder of the musical groups Juluka and Savuka, and the creator
of 'a new cross-over music which fused traditional Zulu ethnic guitar and
accordion with bilingual lyrics and pop and rock progressions'.[57] Born in
England to a Zimbabwean Jewish mother of Lithuanian descent, and a British
father, he was brought up in South Africa, Zimbabwe and Zambia. He spent
only two years in Zambia where he lived in Lusaka and was a pupil at
Woodlands Primary School soon after independence, but he makes it clear
that this was the formative experience of his life. It made him unable to fit
into South Africa in the 1960s and led him on an extraordinary path of cross-
cultural exploration which started in the Zulu migrant workers' hostels of
Johannesburg and led through the academic study of social anthropology to
international fame as a rock/pop star. Of his Zambian experience he has said:

> When I came to Zambia I was confronted with a situation of an independent
> black country, a non-racial school with more black school kids than white, and
> more black teachers than white. I had to adjust to that, and I became part of a
> gang of young black boys in our area. We had a garage and we made these wire
> cars, they were incredibly well made ... coming back to South Africa was dif-
> ficult. It was a new environment, and, as a kid, I just adapted, but I do remember
> feeling a sense of displacement and dislocation ... a sense of isolation. I felt
> marginalised. I've been a marginal person ever since.[58]

Johnny Clegg's sense of marginalisation was reinforced by the discovery of his Jewish identity. Jews clearly do not have a monopoly of marginality, and they do not all experience a problem of identity. But as a minority within a minority in colonial Northern Rhodesia, and post-independence Zambia, some Jews have been unusually sensitive to cross-cultural currents. In examining her own Jewish and African roots, Denise Scott Brown also emphasises marginality as a potential strength:

> Seeing what was happening in Europe while we were growing up, my parents warned their children not to trust non-Jews. They said: 'We must conserve what is ours. We must not mix it with anything else.' So I lived with two contradictory desires: I wanted to conserve what was mine against persecution, but at the same time I did not want to be forced into a ghetto, I wanted to be part of the whole world. Being in and being out, I wanted both and felt in conflict. I have since come to regard that conflict as the sea of my being; what I exist in; it gives me strength and enables me to adapt.[59]

It is this often self-conscious search for identity, both for themselves and for the country, which has made a distinctive Jewish contribution to the political, intellectual and cultural development of Zambia. But this is not a one-way process. The Zambian experience of a multi-cultural and, at least since independence, an unusually non-racial society, has been of benefit to people who were brought up with it and who have moved on to work in a variety of professions all over the world.

CHAPTER 15

Conclusion

This book is about an immigrant ethnic group – the Jews – and their role in the history of one country – Zambia. It has been written in response to the desire of surviving members of the group, living in Zambia and outside it, to record for posterity their own history, and that of their parents and grandparents. They are proud of their contribution to the development of Zambia, and are grateful to Zambia for the home which it gave to people who usually arrived as refugees – the victims of economic discrimination, of political and religious persecution and of perverted racial theories. Neither Zambia, nor the Zambian Jews, existed at the beginning of the twentieth century. The making of a nation, and of this particular ethnic identity within it, went on simultaneously. The publication of this book is in itself a strong affirmation of the existence of an ethnic identity – that of the Zambian Jew – by people who may no longer all live in Zambia, but who are proud of their Zambian roots.

The Jews on the frontier in Northern Rhodesia/Zambia came from diverse sources: Yiddish-speaking people from the Baltic states of the Russian empire; Ladino-speaking people from the former Turkish empire; English-speaking people from Britain, Ireland and South Africa; and assimilated Germans. They defined themselves, and were defined by others, in terms of a common religion though, paradoxically, for many of them, religion was not in itself important. They were forged into a single ethnic group on the frontier both by the external pressure of anti-Semitism and by internal dynamics. These manifested themselves in the creation of religious institutions, such as Hebrew Congregations, in the building of synagogues, and in a commitment to Zionism – a secular nationalist movement. These institutions were usually part of wider regional organisations, but they did not prevent the emergence over time of a distinct Northern Rhodesian/Zambian Jewish identity.

In writing this book, we have tried to avoid ethnic stereotypes and generalisations about 'the Jews' or 'the Jew'. We have seen the Jews on the frontier in Northern Rhodesia/Zambia as unique in themselves, but as an example of a fairly common type: the immigrant ethnic group which special- ises, at first, in a particular kind of commercial activity. Similar books could

probably be written about Scots, Greeks, Hindus, Muslims and other immigrant groups in central Africa, who can be defined in terms of ethnicity
or religion. The nature, timing and significance of their involvement in the
history of the region would, in each case, be different. There is probably
nothing in Judaism, any more than there is in Christianity, Islam or Hinduism,
which predisposes people towards either involvement, or success, in trade.
For, as Adam Smith knew, the 'propensity to truck, barter and exchange' is
universal. What members of these groups had in common were both tightly-
knit and extended family networks, and membership of minority ethnic
groups or religions. Eric Hobsbawm, a leading historian of modern Europe,
has emphasised the role of the family in areas where the impersonal institutions of capitalism, such as banks and limited liability companies, are not
well established. He has noted that:

> the market itself makes no provision for that central element of private profit-
> seeking, namely trust; or, its legal equivalent, the performance of contracts ...
> thus international trading, banking or finance, fields of sometimes physically
> remote activities, large rewards and great insecurity, [have] been most successfully
> conducted by kin-related bodies of entrepreneurs, preferably with groups from
> special religious solidarities, like Jews, Quakers or Huguenots.[1]

There is a danger that any book which emphasises the economic role of
the Jews may provide material for anti-Semitic conspiracy theorists. This was
the effect, intended or not, of Werner Sombart's *The Jews and Modern Capitalism*
which was first published in German in 1911. It took the central idea of Max
Weber's *The Protestant Ethic and the Spirit of Capitalism* – that there was some
kind of relationship between the Protestant Reformation, Puritanism and the
development of capitalism – and distorted it. Sombart argued that it was not
Calvinism but Judaism which was the source of the Puritanism, asceticism
and 'commercial calculation', which he saw as the basis of capitalism. He
contrasted this with a Germanic, and heroic, type of entrepreneurialism.
While Weber had been interested in the influence of religious ideology on
economic history, Sombart used a racial theory to explain the development
of capitalism, with catastrophic consequences. He overemphasised the role,
for good or ill, of the Jews on European economic history, writing: 'Israel
passes over Europe like the sun: at its coming new life bursts forth; at its
going all falls into decay.' The great French historian of the Mediterranean
world in the sixteenth century, Fernand Braudel, took a more reasonable view
of the economic role of the Jews in world history, showing that their
relationship to places of economic growth was as much symbiotic as catalytic.
In a passage which seems to fit well with the theme of this book, he wrote:

> It is rather that the Jews were able to adapt to the geography as well as the
> changing circumstances of the business world. If Israel was a 'sun' it was a sun
> teleguided from the ground. Jewish merchants went towards regions of growth

and took advantage of their growth as much as they contributed to it. The services rendered were mutual.[2]

When the Dotsons wrote in the mid-1970s about the economic role of immigrant ethnic groups in colonial Africa, they found that the economist who had thought most deeply about the subject, and the cultural aspects of capitalist development, was S. H. Frankel.[3] He has already featured in this book as an early economic analyst of the Copperbelt, as a critic of agricultural settlement schemes for German Jewish refugees in tropical Africa, and as an organiser of relief for German Jewish refugees in Northern Rhodesia. As the son of a German Jewish immigrant grain trader in South Africa, and as the brother of a major entrepreneur – Rudy Frankel, founder of Tiger Oats, the South African food conglomerate – he was well equipped to write about the economic role of immigrant ethnic groups. In *Capital Investment in Africa*, he anticipated modern ideas about 'social capital', and emphasised that the investment of capital is not just a question of the mobilisation of money. Capital includes both material and 'non-material' things such as the knowledge, experience and relationships of people and of groups. Like Hobsbawm and Braudel, who wrote later, he was well aware of the importance of social networks to the spread of capitalism.[4]

While S. H. Frankel was aware that there was a cultural and, possibly, an ethnic dimension to the development of capitalism, and in the workings of imperialism, he was also acutely conscious of the danger of ethnic stereotypes. He was a great admirer of the efficient commercial networks of rural stores which were built up in East Africa by Asian traders who both bought and sold a wide range of commodities. He clearly identified with them, as fulfilling a similar role to his Jewish forebears, and defended them against the colonial accusation that they were responsible for the poverty of the African population. He pointed out that they were accused, contradictorily, of being so poor that they could undercut all their competitors, and so rich that they could freeze out competition by the size of their investments, while, simultaneously, sending their profits illegally to India. He provided an explanation for their achievement that also explains the early predominance of Jewish traders in Zambia: 'Actually they had, by being largely confined to commerce, developed the most efficient system of commodity distribution East Africa has known, ever, to the great advantage of the indigenous population.'[5]

In his old age, Frankel became involved in a debate with another distinguished liberal economist, Milton Friedman, on the theme of 'Modern Capitalism and the Jews'. Friedman had identified what he saw as the paradox that the Jews, who might be thought to be the main beneficiaries, as a group, of the free market and of capitalism, had also provided many of its Marxist and collectivist opponents. Friedman mounted a defence of Sombart, and concluded that the hostility of Jewish intellectuals to the free market stemmed, at least in part, from their subconscious attempt to refute the ethnic stereotype which portrayed them as 'money-grabbing, selfish and heartless'. Frankel saw in this argument a revival of the idea of the *Salon Kommunist*, the Jew who over-compensates, and of the 'fallacy that races and peoples can be regarded as having identifiable general social characteristics or attitudes which determine their behaviour'. He felt that this fallacy was based on the idea that 'there is a Jewish world, or one could add, a Protestant or Catholic world – as distinct from the real world'. He concluded:

> The world of the banker who happens to be a Jew is not a different banking world than that of the Protestant or Catholic. The physicist who is a black man is not engaged in a different type of physics from one who is white. The world of Jews who are capitalists or socialists does not differ from the world of capitalists or socialists who are Gentiles.[6]

Frankel's idea of 'non-material capital' illuminates a major theme of this book. Jews arrived on the frontier in central Africa with little cash, but with a variety of attributes. These included a high level of motivation which was imposed upon them by the knowledge that they did not usually have homes to which they could easily return. Of many of them it could be said, as it was of Barnett 'Bongola' Smith, that they arrived in central Africa 'poor in money, but rich in energy and experience'. This book has, we hope, demonstrated the importance of Jewish family and commercial networks in Barotseland, and on the Line of Rail, in the early decades of this century. These networks were important for the extension of credit, for recruitment and for commercial intelligence. Access to credit was probably the most important aspect of 'non-material' capital which was available to the otherwise impoverished young men who reached Northern Rhodesia in the early years of the century. The Bulawayo wholesalers extended credit to their *landsleit* (countrymen) on the basis of trust. This was dependent on a 'special religious solidarity', and, often, on ties of kinship and marriage. An important element in credit was the time factor. The extension of credit over ninety or 120 days by Bulawayo, Port Elizabeth or, later, London merchants was of vital importance to traders who had little or no working capital. A good trader could turn over his goods and make his profit within the period in which he had to pay.

The Bulawayo wholesalers were not always benevolently disposed towards new entrants in the market. They could combine as a cartel to freeze them out, and to protect existing customers, as they attempted to do in the case of Sid Diamond. They could also combine to bring to heel customers, like Moss Dobkins, who sought to break out of their control by establishing direct links with London merchants. Direct access to London agents, and the ninety-day credit which they provided, were vital to the success of Sid Diamond's business. The extension of credit was not confined to Jewish networks. The Susmans were saved from bankruptcy at a critical moment by the support of Tom Meikle, a South African Scot. Harry Wulfsohn was largely financed by the Susmans but, at a critical moment in his career, he was saved by a loan from an Afrikaner farmer. Although banks did not play an important role in the early days, both Shim Lakofski in the late 1920s and Abe Galaun in the 1940s owed their big breaks to sympathetic bank managers.

Jewish traders on the frontier were not only recipients of credit; they also gave it. The Susmans' ledgers show the credit lines which they extended to traders, and to the Lozi royal family, in the early years of the century. David Susman recalls their later role not only as suppliers of goods on credit to struggling farmers on the Line of Rail, but as lenders of oxen and of breeding stock. Stanley Fischer recalls his father's extension of credit to Mazabuka farmers in the 1940s and 1950s. Very little business in the early days was done for cash. Civil servants, and mine and railway workers, who were paid monthly, usually took all their supplies on credit and paid – even for cinema tickets – at the end of the month. This was a system which broke down only in the mid-1950s when, as Richard Sampson noted, the newspapers were filled with columns of advertisements in which traders sued their customers for debt.[7] By the 1970s, credit was almost non-existent for the customers of Zambian shops. Credit was also extended in a variety of ways by Jewish wholesalers and suppliers to Asian traders, who are described in the 1950s as credit-hungry at a time when the majority of Jewish traders had become cash purchasers. Loans in goods and in cash were also made to African hawkers and cattle buyers in the Southern and Western Provinces, and to fish buyers in the Luapula Province.[8]

As Hobsbawm points out, trust is particularly important in areas where banks, limited liability companies and the legal system are underdeveloped. In areas of high risk, losses, disputes over partnerships and bankruptcies are common. The first partnership involved in the Barotseland cattle trade, that of Gordon and Levitz, ended in apparent betrayal, acrimony, resort to the colonial courts and bankruptcy. The Susman brothers' providential escape from the threat of insolvency, which would have been caused by an unavoidable natural disaster, is a feature of their story. They prided themselves on their reputation for 'straight-forward dealing', and there is no reason to doubt that Elie Susman was 'without guile', and honest to a fault.[9] The names of unscrupulous traders, of undischarged bankrupts who went on to prosper elsewhere, such as the Glazer brothers, are recalled with distaste. Whether or not it is attributable to Judaism, there does appear to have been a prevailing ethic which placed greater value on commercial probity and reliability than on spectacular success. This emerges clearly from the diary of Moss Dobkins with its emphasis on hard work, honesty, the avoidance of debt and the fulfilment of family obligations. Maurice Thal's journal also provides clear evidence that he put greater value on keeping his family together during the depression than he did on preserving his capital.

Another major theme of this book has to be the role of Jews as entrepreneurs. It is difficult to avoid the impression that there was a disproportionate number of successful Jewish entrepreneurs in Northern

Rhodesia, and that they played an important role in the development of trade, towns and new industries. Elie Susman, Barnett 'Bongola' Smith, Harry Wulfsohn, Maurice Gersh, Shim Lakofski, Sid Diamond and Abe Gelman, and many others, stand out as exceptionally talented traders. It is, however, important to remember that they were the exceptions who proved the general rule, and that the majority of traders were men like Moss Dobkins who achieved a moderate competence after decades of hard work. There were many other people whose careers ended prematurely in death from blackwater fever, suicide or bankruptcy. There were also many people who never made the transition from shop assistant, hawker or commercial traveller to shop-keeper. It also has to be remembered that the incomes derived from shopkeeping were not always greater than could be obtained in employment by artisans. For much of our period, Jews found it difficult, if not impossible, to obtain employment on the mines, but, when the opportunity arose, they frequently gave up commercial activities for more profitable avenues of employment.

The functions of entrepreneurs include innovation and risk-taking. It becomes clear from this book that these two activities are closely related and, paradoxically, often involve risk-spreading. For the Susman brothers, for instance, the diversification of cattle supplies by the opening up of new sources was a way of reducing the risk from cattle disease. The purchase and development of farms and ranches was a way of creating fixed assets, and providing greater security than could be found in cattle or trade goods. The provision of venture capital to enterprising young men, and the taking of shares in other people's businesses, were also ways of spreading risk and insuring against the emergence of powerful competition. Some businesses were seen as 'cash cows', while others were seen as ways of creating capital assets. Jewish entrepreneurs undoubtedly did play an important role in the development of secondary industry in Northern Rhodesia at a time when official policy discouraged it. The involvement of Susman Brothers and Wulfsohn in the development of Northern Rhodesia Textiles, and of the Gersh brothers in a great variety of activities on the Copperbelt, are good examples of this.

There can also be no doubt that the same group of Jewish entrepreneurs did play an important role in the development of national capital. Although entrepreneurs like the Susmans and Harry Wulfsohn developed important interests outside the country, they continued to think of it as their home base, and developed a network of enterprises within the country which had no equal in the colonial period, and which has survived in a variety of forms until the present day. It is difficult to avoid the conclusion that the status of the Jews as economic or political refugees did give them a greater commitment to the development of national interests, and national capital, than most other settlers.

This may also be the explanation for the apparently catalytic role played by people of Jewish descent in a variety of political movements in the region. As we have seen, Roy Welensky, Simon Zukas and Aaron Milner were all deeply involved in the articulation of new kinds of national consciousness. In the intellectual sphere, Max Gluckman, A. L. Epstein and Lewis Gann were also involved, from different perspectives, with issues of ethnicity and identity. As victims of racial prejudice, and as people who were in the early decades of the century regarded by a deeply racist society as less than 'white', Jews had a special interest in these issues. It was not, however, always the case that this experience predisposed people of Jewish descent to take a liberal view on matters of race. Frankel's warnings as to the dangers of ethnic generalisations are well demonstrated by the evidence presented here. Roy Welensky, Simon Zukas, Max Gluckman and Lewis Gann were all of Jewish descent, but this did not determine that they would take the same line on issues of politics, culture and identity. As Frankel would lead us to expect, the Jews as a group were neither more nor less well disposed towards the rise of African nationalism and the ending of colour bars than the average member of the settler population. There is, however, still a paradox that, while only a small minority of the Jews in Southern Africa adopted radical positions on matters of race and politics, members of that minority, such as Joe Slovo and Ronnie Kasrils, were conspicuous among white people in rising to leadership roles within the ANC, and the broader southern African liberation movement.

Even in a book of this size, it is unavoidable that there remain a number of issues which would repay further research. Little has emerged from this study about African perceptions of Jews. It may be that, as Akashambatwa Mbikusita-Lewanika suggests, the people of Barotseland did not think of early traders as Jews, though they did distinguish between traders, missionaries and civil servants.[10] Not a great deal has emerged about the relationship between Jewish traders and their African customers on the Line of Rail, except at critical and, perhaps, rather untypical moments when political boycotts disturbed that relationship. The point of view of Jewish shop assistants has also been neglected, as well as that of the African shop assistants who, in Kitwe during the war, were the first African employees to begin the process of forming trade unions. It is clear that in that instance they had the support of the District Commissioner, but were opposed by the Jewish-dominated Chamber of Commerce.[11]

More could, perhaps, also have been said about 'ethnic succession'. This comes in a variety of forms. We have noticed the way in which children of Jewish traders often trained in the professions, and sometimes returned to work in the country. As Jews moved out of retail trade and into secondary industry, their places were often taken by Asian retailers. The same process of professionalisation, and movement into other economic sectors, has also occurred among the Asian population, though a large number of Asian traders have remained in the commercial front line as retailers. Jewish traders undoubtedly did play a role in the training of an indigenous capitalist class. In some rural areas, such as the Western Province, formerly Barotseland, where there never was Asian competition, African traders were the immediate successors of Jewish traders, but have recently been threatened by the emergence of new, and stronger, competition from South African retail chains.[12]

It would be conventional for a book of this kind to end with an assessment of the 'Jewish contribution' to the development of Zambia. We shall avoid doing that for two reasons. In the first place, following Braudel, we would like to emphasise the mutuality in the relationship between the Jewish community and the people of Zambia. As a German Jewish refugee, Helen Mohrer, recalled: 'Northern Rhodesia was very good to us, and as Northern Rhodesia grew, so we grew with the country.'[13] The last of the German Jewish refugees in the country, Hilda Caminer, recently died, and left a considerable sum, about £100,000, to Zambian charities. It was a way of saying thank you to a country which had given her and her husband a home when no other country would, and in which she had lived for almost sixty years. It seems right, therefore, to emphasise the gratitude of people of Jewish descent, including recent refugees from South Africa who were able to return home in the early 1990s, for the home which Zambia gave them.

In the second place, this is a story without an end. There are many Zambian Jews outside the country who look back on their time in it with nostalgia and affection, and who sometimes return, as Wally Dobkins has frequently done, and as Saul Radunski has recently done, to live and work in it. There are others, like the members of the Susman, Wulfsohn and Rabb families, who continue to be closely involved with the economy of Zambia through investments in commercial agriculture. Although it is now much smaller than it was in its post-war heyday, there is still a Jewish community with a functioning synagogue in Lusaka. As well as people such as Fay Dobkins and Dennis Figov whose family roots in the country go back towards the beginning of the century, there are also people like Simon Zukas and Abe Galaun who arrived in the late 1930s. There are also people of their children's generation, who were born in the country, and more recent arrivals, who show every sign of wishing to continue to live and work in Zambia for many more years.

Notes and References

All file references are to the Zambia National Archives unless otherwise stated.

1. Jews on the Frontier

1. F. and L. Dotson, *The Indian Minority of Zambia, Rhodesia and Malawi* (New Haven: Yale University Press, 1968); B. A. Kosmin, *Majuta: A History of the Jewish Community of Zimbabwe* (Gwelo: Mambo Press, 1980); J. McCracken, 'Economics and Ethnicity: The Italian Community in Malawi', *Journal of African History* 32 (2), 1991.

2. R. Oliver, *The African Experience* (London: Weidenfeld and Nicolson, 1991), 77–9.

3. N. Levtzion, *Ancient Ghana and Mali* (London: Methuen, 1973), 4; E. W. Bovill, *The Golden Trade of the Moors* (London: Oxford University Press, 1968), 108–9, 141–2; F. Braudel, *The Mediterranean and the Mediterranean World in the Age of Philip II* (London: Fontana/Collins, 1973), vol II, 818.

4. C. R. Boxer, *The Portuguese Seaborne Empire, 1415–1825* (London: Hutchinson, 1969), 88–9, 96–7, 103, 266–72; M. D. D. Newitt, *Portuguese Settlement on the Zambezi* (London: Longmans, 1973), 9–10; Braudel, *The Mediterranean and the Mediterranean World*, vol II, 814; David Brion Davis, 'The Jews and the Slave Trade', *New York Review of Books*, 22 December 1994; information from papers by J. A. Nunes da Silva Horta on the Inquisition in Angola in 1596–98 by courtesy of Professor Joseph Miller, University of Virginia, Charlottesville, USA.

5. J. Comay, *Who's Who in Jewish History* (London: Routledge, 1995), 137.

6. G. Saron and L. Hotz (eds), *The Jews in South Africa: A History* (Cape Town: Oxford University Press, 1956).

7. Robert I. Rotberg, *The Founder: Cecil Rhodes and the Pursuit of Power* (New York: Oxford University Press, 1988), 275, 286.

8. Kosmin, *Majuta*, 1–10.

9. R. Sampson, *The Man with a Toothbrush in His Hat: The Story and Times of George Copp Westbeech in Central Africa* (Lusaka: Multimedia Publications, 1972), 35; A. Schultz and A. Hammar, *The New Africa: Up the Chobe and Down the Okavango Rivers …* (London: Heinemann, 1897).

10. H. W. Macmillan, 'The Origins and Development of the African Lakes Company, 1878–1908', PhD dissertation, University of Edinburgh, 1970; S. E. Katzenellenbogen, *Railways and the Copper Mines of Katanga* (Oxford: Clarendon Press, 1973).

11. L. H. Gann, *A History of Northern Rhodesia: Early Days to 1953* (London: Chatto and Windus, 1964), 87; L. Vail and L. White, *Capitalism and Colonialism in Mozambique* (London: James Currey, 1980), 212–13, 235–6.

12. Gann, *A History of Northern Rhodesia*, 87–8; H. W. Langworthy (ed.), *Expedition in Central Africa, 1888–91: A Report by Carl Wiese* (London: Rex Collings, 1983), 3. Langworthy casts some doubt on Wiese's Jewishness, saying that 'although it was possible that he was of Jewish ancestry, it is unlikely that he was brought up as a Jew'. W. V. Brelsford, *Generation*

of Men: The European Pioneers of Northern Rhodesia (Salisbury: Stuart Manning, for Northern Rhodesia Society, 1965), 146; F. Macpherson, *Anatomy of a Conquest* (London: Longman, 1981), 36. See also J. A. Barnes, *Politics in a Changing Society: A Political History of the Fort Jameson Ngoni* (London: Oxford University Press, 1954), 68–101.

13. *British Central Africa Gazette*, 30 April, 30 June 1900, 31 May 1902; H. St A. Gibbons, *Africa from South to North through Marotseland* (London: John Lane, 1904), vol 2, 117–21.

14. Macmillan, 'The Origins and Development of the African Lakes Company', 397; E. D. Morel, 'Another Stokes Affair', *West Africa*, 22 July 1902; Public Record Office, London, FO 2/972; Langworthy, *Expedition in Central Africa*, 184; *British Central Africa Gazette*, 31 October 1900, 31 May 1902; J. B. Thornhill, *Adventures in Africa* (London: John Murray, 1915), 164, 199; *Livingstone Mail*, 25 April 1913.

15. G. Shimoni, *Jews and Zionism: The South African Experience, 1910–67* (Cape Town: Oxford University Press, 1980), 1–10.

16. M. Gelfand, *Northern Rhodesia in the Days of the Charter* (Oxford: Blackwell, 1961), 240–2.

17. G. Prins, *The Hidden Hippopotamus* (Cambridge: Cambridge University Press, 1980), 85–7.

18. A. von Oppen, *Terms of Trade and Terms of Trust* (Munster: Lit, n.d. [1993]), 202–3.

19. Livingstone Museum, Sampson Papers. Notes of interview by R. Sampson with E. Susman, Lusaka, 1 August 1955, by courtesy of Palma Russell.

20. M. I. Cohen, 'The Jewish Communities of Rhodesia and the North', in *The South African Jewish Year Book* (Johannesburg: Jewish Board of Deputies, 1929), 135–6; B. Nidlog, (B. Goldin), 'Early Days in Northern Rhodesia' (based on interview by B. Goldin with H. Susman), *Rhodesian Jewish Times*, January 1948, 11–15.

21. 'North Western Rhodesia: Report of the Administrator, 1901–2', in BSA Company, *Reports on the Administration of Rhodesia*, 1900–2 (no place, n.d.), 450.

22. RHL: Rhodes Papers, 'Report on North Western Rhodesia for 1900', 16 February 1901.

23. M. Gluckman, *The Economy of the Central Barotse Plain* (Manchester: Manchester University Press, 1968, first published 1941), 77.

24. 'North Western Rhodesia: Report of the Administrator, 1901–2', 451, 458.

25. Thornhill, *Adventures in Africa*, 8, 78.

26. P. Clark, *Autobiography of an Old Drifter* (London: George Harrap, 1936), 119, 163–4, 157–8.

27. Interviews with Molly Diamond and Lilian Chow; Ronald Alistair Dick Snapper, entry in *Who's Who of the Federation of Rhodesia and Nyasaland for 1957* (Salisbury: Who's Who Publications [Central Africa] Limited).

28. L. H. Gann, *The Birth of a Plural Society* (Manchester: Manchester University Press, 1958), 153.

29. Clark, *Autobiography of an Old Drifter*, 148–9.

30. Zambia National Archives (ZNA). All file references hereafter are to the ZNA unless otherwise specified. H1/2/1 (vol 1): F. Levitz and R. Gordon and Company, Bankruptcy Proceedings, May 1908. Evidence of F. Levitz, David Wersock, Sam Peimer, E. Snapper.

31. Cohen, 'The Jewish Communities', 135–6; information from Dennis Rosenfield, grandson of A. B. Diamond, by courtesy of Jack Fischer.

32. Interview with Zena Berold.

33. Cohen, 'The Jewish Communities', 135–6.

34. Kosmin, *Majuta*, 18–19, 39, 56–7; biographies in *South African Jewish Year Book*, 1929.

35. Kosmin, *Majuta*, 35, 49; interviews with P. Lakofski-Hepker, D. Scott Brown and I. Teeger.

36. Macpherson, *Anatomy of a Conquest*, 162–3; ZNA H1/2/4(vol 2): J. R. Rollnick versus H. Stern, June 1909; *Livingstone Mail*, 16 December 1911, 1 June 1912; interview with F. Wulfsohn.

37. P. J. Pretorius, *Jungle Man* (Sydney: Australian Publishing Company, 1948), 50; W. V. Moroney, 'Vereker's Diary: Cattle Buying in 1904', *Northern Rhodesia Journal* 6, 1965; *North Eastern Rhodesia Government Gazette*, 15 June 1904.

2. The Susman Saga: the Early Years, 1901–30

1. Natie Grill, born 1896, son of Marcus Grill, transcript of recorded memoir, no date; Susman Papers. Maurice Gersh to David Susman, 24 September 1993; interview with David Susman.

2. M. Sonnenberg, *The Way I Saw It* (Cape Town: Howard Timmins, n.d. [1958]), 63.

3. M. Gersh, 'The Susman Saga', *Northern Rhodesia Journal* 6, 1965, 266; Livingstone Museum, Sampson Papers. Notes of interview by R. Sampson with E. Susman, Lusaka, 1 August 1955.

4. Nidlog (Goldin), 'Early Days in Northern Rhodesia', 11.

5. Stenham PLC, London (SPLC), F. Sykes to E. Susman, 4 October 1901, with trading and gun licence on reverse.

6. SPLC. E. Susman, 'Last Will and Testament', 28 July 1902.

7. SPLC. 'Articles of co-partnership between Elie Susman and John Austen', 1 July 1903.

8. SPLC. Agreement with R. Gordon and inventory of stock, 21 July 1904.

9. Clark, *Autobiography of an Old Drifter*, 142.

10. SPLC. General Dealer's licence for Sesheke store, 4 January 1906; Prince Litia Lewanika to E. Susman, 19 September 1906.

11. G. Clay, *Your Friend Lewanika: Litunga of Barotseland, 1842–1916* (London: Chatto and Windus, 1968), *passim*; Gluckman, *Economy of the Central Barotse Plain*, 77–82; Thornhill, *Adventures in Africa*, 95–6.

12. Clay, *Your Friend Lewanika*, 129; interview with Maurice Rabb; T. Ranger, 'The Ethiopian Episode in Barotseland', *Human Problems in Central Africa* 38, 35–6.

13. G. Caplan, *The Elites of Barotseland, 1878–1969* (London: C. Hurst, 1970), *passim*; SPLC. Debtors' Ledger, 1912, for evidence of their business relationship with members of the Lozi royal family; interviews with Akashambatwa Mbikusita-Lewanika.

14. G. Sterling, quoted in Moss Dobkins's diary. See below, Chapter 4.

15. SPLC. Coryndon to E. Susman, 1 August 1902.

16. Gersh, 'The Susman Saga', 266.

17. Nidlog (Goldin), 'Early Days in Northern Rhodesia', 12–13.

18. BS3/242: Criminal Investigations Department to Secretary, Administration, 28 August 1917; J. Coxhead, Memorandum, September 1917.

19. Gann, *The Birth of a Plural Society*, 153, quoting E. Susman, *Livingstone Mail*, 2 November 1907.

20. SPLC. All references in this section are to balance sheets and other accounts of the Susman Brothers' business, 1907–12.

21. L. Van Horn, 'The Agricultural History of Barotseland, 1840–1964', in R. Palmer and N. Parsons, *The Roots of Rural Poverty in Central and Southern Africa* (London: Heinemann, 1977), 153.

22. J. Smith (ed. T. Bagnall Smith), *Vet in Africa: Life on the Zambezi, 1913–33* (London: Radcliffe Press, 1997), 137.

23. Thornhill, *Adventures in Africa*, 260–3.

24. KDE2/41/1: Assistant Native Commissioner, Nalolo, 2 December 1908, commenting on the opening of a Susman Brothers branch there in the previous year: 'With their big stock they would defy competition.'

25. Van Horn, 'Agricultural History of Barotseland', 153.

26. Thornhill, *Adventures in Africa*, 174; Cohen, 'The Jewish Communities', 136; *Livingstone Mail*, 22 June 1912; SPLC. Balance sheets, 1912.

27. SPLC. Captain H. P. Eason to E. Susman, 23 October 1912; interview with D. Susman.

28. SEC3/565/1: Director of Veterinary Services (J. Smith) to CS, 27 August 1929; Director of Veterinary Services (J. P. A. Morris) to CS, 23 May 1933; Gersh, 'The Susman Saga', 267.

29. Smith, *Vet in Africa*, 206.

30. Ibid., 217.

31. Interview with D. Susman; R. Sutherland (ed. June Lawson), *The Memoirs of Robert 'Katembora' Sutherland* (Bulawayo: privately printed, 1956), 101. Reference by courtesy of Dick Hobson.

32. Cohen, 'The Jewish Communities', 133.

33. Nidlog (Goldin), 'Early Days in Northern Rhodesia', 13.

34. SEC3/565/1: Director of Veterinary Services (J. Smith) to CS, 27 August 1929; Director of Veterinary Services (J. P. A. Morris) to CS, 23 May 1933; Gersh, 'The Susman Saga', 267.

35. I. Phimister, *Wangi Kolia: Coal, Capital and Labour in Colonial Zimbabwe, 1894–1954* (Johannesburg: Witwatersrand University Press, 1994), *passim*; Van Horn, 'Agricultural History of Barotseland', 149–66.

36. SPLC. Correspondence with the Lands Department, 1911–12, 1927; Susman Papers. M. Gersh to D. Susman, 24 September 1993.

37. SPLC. E. Susman, transcript of diary for 1920.

38. The material in these paragraphs on the career of Bongola Smith has been gathered from a variety of sources. These include Viscomte Roger d'Hendecourt's book, *L'Élevage au Katanga* (Brussels: Desclée de Brouwer, 1953), 24–50; and an MS memoir of the life of Smith's daughter entitled 'Dora Lazarus: a memoir'. We are grateful to her son, Charles Lazarus, for providing a copy of the memoir. Further information comes from Charles Lazarus, Sam Gelman and Anne Rief, all grandchildren of Barnett 'Bongola' Smith, as well as from interviews with I. Teeger, G. Glasser and D. Scott Brown.

39. SPLC. Balance sheets and accounts, 1920, 1921.

40. SPLC. Balance sheets and accounts of main business and subsidiary companies, 1921–26.

41. Susman Papers. M. Gersh to D. Susman, 24 September 1993.

42. Nidlog (Goldin), 'Early Days in Northern Rhodesia', 12.

43. Susman Papers. M. Gersh to D. Susman, 24 September 1993.

44. SPLC. Richard Goode, Secretary to the Administration, Northern Rhodesia, to Secretary for the Interior, Pretoria, 28 December 1916.

45. Nidlog (Goldin), 'Early Days in Northern Rhodesia', 13.

46. Interview with D. Susman.

47. SPLC. E. Susman, 'Last Will', 7 March 1909.

3. Jewish Networks, the Line of Rail and the Growth of Towns

1. Cohen, 'The Jewish Communities', 137.

2. W. Rybko, 'A Zionist Lecture Tour: Northern Rhodesia', *Zionist Record*, 18 July 1947.

3. The concept was first used by S. H. Frankel in *Capital Investment in Africa: Its Course and Effects* (London: Oxford University Press, 1938). See below, Chapter 15.

4. Interview with A. Kaplan.

5. Cohen, 'The Jewish Communities', 137.

6. A. M. Kanduza, *The Political Economy of Underdevelopment in Northern Rhodesia, 1918–60: A Case Study of Customs, Tariff and Railway Freight Policies* (Lanham: University Press of America, 1986), *passim.*

7. Gann, *A History of Northern Rhodesia*, 117–24; R. Murray-Hughes, 'Edmund Davis', *Northern Rhodesia Journal* 6(1), 1965.

8. G. Pauling, *The Chronicles of a Contractor* (London: Constable, 1926), 206–13; H. F. Varian, *Some African Milestones* (Wheatley and Oxford: George Ronald, 1953), 125–6; Thornhill, *Adventures in Africa*, 256–8.

9. Cohen, 'The Jewish Communities', 136.

10. W. Rybko, 'A Zionist Lecture Tour: Livingstone', *Zionist Record*, 24 October 1947.

11. K. Ese, *An Historical Guide to Livingstone Town* (Livingstone: Livingstone Tourism Association, n.d. [1996]), *passim*; RHL: Welensky Papers. Welensky to S. G. Millin, 13 May 1966; interviews with R. Welensky, T. Bagnall Smith and D. Susman.

12. C. Mansfield, *Via Rhodesia* (London: Stanley Paul, n.d., *circa* 1910), 146.

13. Ibid.

14. Ese, *Livingstone*, 28.

15. *Livingstone Pioneer and Advertiser* (cyclostyled), vol 1, no. 1, 13 January 1906; no. 2, 20 January 1906; no. 4, 3 February 1906; no. 5, 10 February 1906. Copies in RHL: Coryndon Papers.

16. Interview with Adella Kamionsky.

17. *Livingstone Pioneer*, nos 1 and 2, January 1906; interview with Michael Gelman, grandson of Abraham Gelman.

18. Most of the following information on the Grill family comes from Beverley Olsberg (Sossen)'s pamphlet, 'Marcus and Faiga Grill Family History', produced for the Grill family reunion which was held 9–11 August 1996 at the Victoria Falls to celebrate the centenary of the arrival of Marcus Grill in Africa. For an account of the reunion which was attended by 108 members of the Grill family, see Beverley Olsberg, 'Grill Family Centenary Reunion', in *Centre* (North Western Reform Synagogue Magazine), October 1996.

19. SPLC. Natie Grill, transcript of interview, no date; Kosmin, *Majuta*, 28, quoting *Bulawayo Chronicle*, 2 December 1908.

20. Interview with H. Wolffe.

21. Ibid.

22. Interview with Norma Davidov, daughter of Harry Wasserson.

23. Interviews with N. Davidov and Bertha Barenblatt.

24. NRGG. Naturalisation applications for L. and M. Jacobs and A. H. Troumbas; I. M. Nzila, 'The Zambezi Sawmills: A History of Forest Exploitation in the Western Province of Zambia, 1910–68', MA dissertation, University of Zambia, 1987.

25. ZIF. Meyer Flax.

26. Interviews with Cecilia Krasner and Doreen Tow.

27. D. Hobson, *Show Time* (Lusaka: Agricultural and Commercial Society of Zambia, 1979), 67; R. Sampson, *So This Was Lusaaka's* (Lusaka: Multimedia Publications, 1982), 24; interview with Arthur Kaplan.

28. M. McCulloch, *A Social Survey of the African Population of Livingstone* (Lusaka: Rhodes-Livingstone Institute, 1956), 3.

29. F. Dotson and L. Dotson, 'The Economic Role of Non-indigenous Ethnic Minorities in Colonial Africa', in P. Duignan and L. H. Gann, *Colonialism in Africa, 1870–1969*, vol IV, *The Economics of Colonialism* (Cambridge, Cambridge University Press, 1975), 565–631.

30. McCulloch, *A Social Survey*, ix, 3. She acknowledges Elias Kopelowitz as an informant. SEC3/53: 'Report on Immigration into NR', 7 February 1939, draft.

31. Pauling, *Chronicles of a Contractor*, 206–13: Varian, *Some African Milestones*, 125–6: Thornhill, *Adventures in Africa*, 256–8.

32. A3/8/3. This file includes a petition on the demarcation of a township at Broken Hill, 12 August 1909.

33. KSD4/1–2: Mpika District Notebook.

34. See above, Chapter 1.

35. Harry Beemer was among the creditors of Gordon and Levitz in 1908. See above, Chapter 1; Moss Dobkins's diary, see below, Chapter 4; interviews with H. Kuper and S. Jacobs.

36. Interview with G. Glasser.

37. Interview with G. Jacobson.

38. Interview with S. Lakofski by D. Scott Brown, R. Venturi etc., 9–10 August 1983. Communications from S. Lakofski.

39. Newitt, *Portuguese Settlement on the Zambezi*, 309–11.

40. See below, Chapter 4.

41. Biographical material on M. Thal from 'Notes from Maurice Thal's journal and miscellaneous letters' then in the possession of his daughter, Sheilagh Matheson, made by Leonard Thal, Bulawayo, April 1992. Copy by courtesy of D. Scott Brown.

42. Interviews with S. Matheson and Sir Roy Welensky.

43. M. Thal journal, transcript, 22 September 1935, courtesy of D. Scott Brown.

44. Ibid., 28 September 1935.

45. Thal family tree, by courtesy of D. Scott Brown; personal information.

46. Eileen Bigland, *The Lake of the Royal Crocodiles* (New York: Macmillan, 1939), 213.

47. Rybko, 'A Zionist Lecture Tour: Broken Hill', *Zionist Record*, 18, 25 July 1947; SEC3/53: 'Report on Immigration into NR', 1939.

48. Sampson, *So This Was Lusaaka's*, 14–16; Rybko, 'A Zionist Lecture Tour: Lusaka', *Zionist Record*, 26 September 1947. See also Dotson and Dotson, 'The Economic Role of Non-indigenous Ethnic Minorities', 587, f.n. 54.

49. G. J. Williams, 'The Early Years of the Township', in G. J. Williams (ed.), *Lusaka and its Environs* (Lusaka: Zambia Geographical Association, 1987), 138–54.

50. Sampson, *So This Was Lusaaka's*, 14–16, 23; interview with G. Glasser.

51. Rybko, 'A Zionist Lecture Tour: Lusaka', quoting interview with Frieda Glasser.

52. Sir Percy Sillitoe, *Cloak Without Dagger* (London: Cassell, 1955), 25.

53. Interviews with Gerald Kollenberg, Doris Bryer and Doreen Tow.

54. Sampson, *So This Was Lusaaka's*, 23.

55. Williams, 'The Early Years of the Township', 74.

56. ZIF. D. Kollenberg and E. Herr; interviews with Molly Diamond and Deirdre Leibowitz, daughter of Teddy Herr; Rybko, 'A Zionist Lecture Tour: Lusaka'.

57. See below, Chapter 5.

58. Sampson, *So This Was Lusaaka's*, 23.

59. See above, Chapter 2; SPLC. E. Susman diary, 1920; Hobson, *Show Time*, 137–8.

60. Information from Dennis Rosenfield, by courtesy of Jack Fischer; Williams, 'The Early Years of the Township', 85–6; Hobson, *Show Time*, 74.

61. Interview with A. Kamionsky. Rybko, 'A Zionist Lecture Tour: Lusaka'. Aberman's son, Gerald, remained in Bulawayo and was in the 1950s the publisher of the *Rhodesian Jewish Journal* and the *Rhodesian Jewish Year Book*.

62. RHL: Welensky Papers. S. Fischer to Welensky, enclosing *curriculum vitae*, n.d., *circa* February 1954; ZIF. Assia Fischer (first wife of Sam Fischer); Rybko, 'A Zionist Lecture Tour: Lusaka'; interview with and communications from Jack Fischer.

63. Williams, 'Early Years in the Township', 82.

64. RHL: Ms. Afr. s. 348. Wakefield Papers. 'Impressions and experiences of Northern Rhodesia', 1924.

65. SEC3/53: 'Report on Immigration into NR', 1939.

66. J. Collins, 'Lusaka: the Historical Development of a Planned Capital, 1929–1970', in Williams (ed.), *Lusaka and its Environs*, 95–137.

67. Sampson, *So This Was Lusaaka's*, 59; Kanduza, *The Political Economy of Underdevelopment*, 136.

68. SEC3/199 (vols 1–4): 'Brick and tile-making at Lusaka – agreement with Mr Shapiro', 1933, various correspondence. ZIF. A. Shapiro; communications from Winston Shapiro and Wulfie Wulfsohn.

69. RHL: Welensky Papers. S. Fischer to Welensky, enclosing *curriculum vitae*, n.d., *circa* February 1954; ZIF, Assia Fischer (first wife of Sam Fischer); Rybko, 'A Zionist Lecture Tour: Lusaka'; interview with and communications from Jack Fischer.

70. D. Hobson, *Food and Good Fellowship* (Lusaka Lunch Club, n.d.), 42–3; interview with John Hudson.

71. Interview with and communications from J. Fischer.

72. H. M. McKee, 'Northern Rhodesia and the Federation', *African Affairs* 284, 1952, 323–35.

73. Interviews with F. Wulfsohn and Doreen Marcus.

74. Interview with 'Moggy' Mendelsohn; entries for S. and A. Mendelsohn in *Central African Who's Who* (Salisbury: Central African Who's Who), 1953.

75. Interview with Berjulie Press; Sampson, *So This Was Lusaaka's*, 65–6; Lyndall Gordon, *Shared Lives* (Cape Town: David Phillip, 1992). The Press brothers were cousins of the Grills.

76. Information on Baitz family from Jack Baitz by courtesy of Beverley Olsberg. See also ZIF. Klein.

77. ZP2/1/8: Evidence to Bledisloe Commission by B. Iljon, 4 June 1938. Reference by courtesy of Robin Palmer.

78. Interviews with Eric (Aron) and Nicky Iljon.

79. C. Mkunga, 'The Development of the Asian Trading Class, 1900–80', MA dissertation, University of Zambia, 1992.

80. Smith, *Vet in Africa*, 24–5.

81. F. Braudel, *Capitalism and Material Life, 1400–1800* (London: Fontana/Collins, 1974), 373.

4. A Wandering Jew: Moss Dobkins's Story

1. Morris (Moss) Dobkins's manuscript autobiography and transcript of his diary of his 1922 trek through the Congo and Angola, with preamble dated 9 August 1974. Copy in possession of Wally Dobkins, Adelaide, Australia. Unless otherwise stated, all references in this chapter are to the manuscript.

2. Mankoya District, now the Kaoma District.

3. For the history of the Northern Rhodesia Volunteer Force, see W. V. Brelsford (ed.), *The Story of the Northern Rhodesia Regiment* (Lusaka: Government Printer, 1954).

4. George Sterling who, as we have seen, had accompanied A. B. Diamond on his first journey to the Congo in 1909, died at the Kansanshi mine, where he was working as a fitter, in 1938.

5. Interview with Fay Dobkins.

6. Interviews with A. Kaplan and W. Dobkins.

7. Kosmin, *Majuta*, 16; Cohen, 'The Jewish Communities', 134.

8. 'Copy of draft of letter (or address) in handwriting of Bro. B. Pollon presumably intended for Bro. H. S. Palmer', 2 February 1943. Copy by courtesy of W. Shapiro.

9. Interview with W. Dobkins.

5. The Copperbelt: Boom, Bust and Recovery

1. See *Dictionary of South African Biography*, vol iv. L. H. Gann indicates incorrectly that Stanley had changed his name from Cohen and that he was 'of partially German Jewish descent'. See his *A History of Northern Rhodesia*, 192. Interviews with Norma Davidov and Bertha Barenblatt.

2. Gann, *A History of Northern Rhodesia*, 204–11, 251–6; L. H. Gann, 'The Northern Rhodesian Copper Industry and the World of Copper, 1932–52', *Rhodes–Livingstone Journal* 18, 1955, 1–18.

3. *Zambia's Mining Industry: the First Fifty Years* (Ndola: Roan Consolidated Mines Limited, 1978), 33–4.

4. Gann, *A History of Northern Rhodesia*, 251–6; K. Vickery, 'Roy Welensky and the World of Central African Labour', unpublished seminar paper, University of Zambia, 1989, folio 6; J. A. Bancroft, *Mining in Northern Rhodesia* (n.p.: British South Africa Company, 1961), 114, 118–20, 139–41.

5. Bancroft, *Mining in Northern Rhodesia*, 66, 145–8; interview with Joseph Susman; SPLC. Accounts for 1917–18.

6. Susman Papers. M. Gersh to D. Susman, 24 September 1993; communication from Shim Lakofski.

7. P. Lakofski-Hepker MS, 'Memories of my Childhood and Youth', September 1989, folio 20, reference by courtesy of P. Lakofski-Hepker and D. Scott Brown.

8. Susman Papers. M. Gersh to David Susman, 24 September 1993; Lakofski-Hepker, 'Memories of my Childhood and Youth', folios 17–20.

9. CRL. Northern Caterers Limited, File 37 (1930).

10. Carolyn Baylies, 'The State and Class Formation in Zambia', PhD dissertation, University of Wisconsin, Madison, USA, 1978, 188–9, 200, drawing on joint project with Morris Szeftel on company files in the CRL. The Copperfields Cold Storage file, no. 38, 1931, is no longer available.

11. Interviews with G. Kollenberg, D. Bryer and D. Tow; Susman Papers. M. Gersh to D. Susman, 24 September 1993.

12. Susman Papers. M. Gersh to D. Susman, 24 September 1993; interviews with H. Gersh and M. Gersh.

13. S. Lakofski, transcript of interview, 9–10 August 1983, folios 1–63. Copy by courtesy of D. Scott Brown. All references in this section are to this source.

14. Bancroft, *Mining in Northern Rhodesia*, 152.

15. Communications from S. Lakofski; interview with D. Scott Brown; communications from A. Lipman; C. Chipkin, *Johannesburg Style* (Cape Town: David Philip, 1994), viii, 114–19, 249–51.

16. Interview with P. Lakofski-Hepker.

17. Lakofski-Hepker, 'Memories of my Childhood and Youth', folios 1–26. All the information in this section comes from this source.

18. Herman Blumenthal was a major cattle buyer in Northern Rhodesia in competition with Barnett 'Bongola' Smith in the 1920s. See Sampson, *So This Was Lusaaka's*, 47, quoting unpublished notes on the history of the Standard Bank, Lusaka, by Colonel N. O. Earl-Spurr (1955). Blumenthal was apparently ruined in the depression, though according to

one source he was 'the man who broke the bank at Monte Carlo' and his failure was due to gambling. Interview with Jeannette Cohen, whose father worked for him in the Congo.

19. ZCCM. NCCM/RC/HO 522/1: Various correspondence on establishment of Kitwe Closed Township and minutes of meeting between Nkana traders, including M. Gersh, H. Figov, H. Kollenberg, S. Diamond and M. Barnett with DO, Nkana, 14 November 1935, and minutes of meeting with traders' representatives including Kollenberg and Diamond with Gov, 6 December 1935 and 25 February 1936. See also ZNA. SEC1/1520 vol I: Closed Township Commission, 1948, correspondence and papers.

20. Interview with M. Diamond; ZCCM. NCCM/RC/HO 522/1: G Rodgers, Rhokana, Nkana, to Secretary, Rhokana, London, 7 January 1936.

21. NRGG. 1940; interview with Simon Zukas.

22. 'Report on Immigration into NR', 1939.

23. Interview with M. Diamond.

24. Brochure in possession of M. Diamond, Kitwe.

25. ZCCM. NCCM/HO/102: Census of aliens at Nkana, 27 July 1938.

26. U8/1/1: Max Thal, Luanshya Trading Company, Bankruptcy Proceedings, 1931.

27. Philip Rosen, entry in *Central African Who's Who*, 1953.

28. Interview with D. Figov.

29. ZIF. I. Zlotnik and A. Stiel; CRL. NR Native Produce Company, File 105; interview with W. Dobkins. Zlotnik's fine for smuggling razor blades in 1943 was £450.

30. Communications from K. T. Hansen and B. Mumba, Mansa.

31. ZIF. Joseph Minchuk; interviews with S. Kroll, D. Figov and D. Messerer.

32. ZIF. Uri Iljion; interviews with Eric Iljon, Isa Teeger and David Messerer; communication from Karen Meyerowitz (Illion).

33. ZIF. A. J. Mendelsohn.

34. Interviews with L. Schulman and I. Port; Rybko, 'A Zionist Lecture Tour: Ndola', 25 July 1947, interview with H. Schulman; SEC1/696: H. Schulman to Provincial Commissioner, Ndola, 12 July 1940.

35. Interviews with D. Figov, nephew of Nathan Schulman; Lily Schulman, sister-in-law of Nathan Schulman, widow of Hyam Schulman; Isadore Port, brother of Lily Schulman. SEC1/1520 vol I: Closed Township Commission, 1948, correspondence.

36. Interview with D. Figov.

37. Interview with H. Lowenthal; interview with and communication from I. Teeger; entries for the three Lowenthal brothers in *Central African Who's Who*, 1953.

38. Lakofski-Hepker, 'Memories of my Childhood and Youth'; interview with D. Messerer.

39. RHL: Welensky Papers. 590/2, Intelligence report, Glazer Brothers, 17 June 1955; interview with Joe Teeger; Jack Halpern, *South Africa's Hostages: Basutoland, Bechuanaland and Swaziland* (Harmondsworth: Penguin Books, 1965), 325.

40. Rudy Frankel (assisted by Marian Robertson), *Tiger Tapestry* (Cape Town: Struik, 1988), 177–8.

41. Frankel, *Tiger Tapestry*, 216–18; interview with H. I. (Victor) Menashe. See also P. Bonner and R. Lambert, 'Batons and Bare Heads: The Strike at Amato Textiles, 1958', in S. Marks and S. Trapido, *The Politics of Race, Class and Nationalism in Twentieth Century South Africa* (London: Longman, 1987), 336–65.

42. ZIF. H. I. Menashe; interview with H. I. Menashe.

43. Cohen, 'The Jewish Communities', 144. Cohen commented on the Rhodes Islanders: 'These stand on an altogether different plane from the rest of the Jewish population, and unless they are going to adopt our standards their influence may be unfortunate.'

44. Interview with H. I. Menashe.

45. ZIF. H. I. Menashe.

46. SEC1/696. H. Schulman to PC, Ndola, 12 July 1940; ZIF. H. I. Menashe. Director of Military Intelligence and Censorship to PC, Ndola, 25 August 1940, containing Gov's authorisation for release of most of the internees. Interview with H. I. Menashe.

47. ZIF. M. D. Capelluto. He was born on Rhodes Island in 1906 and entered NR in 1931. His wife, Violette Galante Capelluto, was born in Cairo in 1918 and entered NR in 1939. According to Gov, NR (Maybin) to Gov, SR (Stanley), 24 September 1940, he was not released 'as there was evidence that at any rate prior to the crisis of September 1938, his conversation had a definite anti-British bias'. See also letters from Welensky to CS, 13 January 1941, 22 October 1941, and further correspondence.

48. ZIF. V. Capelluto. He was born on Rhodes Island in 1921 and entered NR in 1938. His appeal for release (2 September 1940) from Koffyfontein internment camp, SA, was rejected on 11 October 1940. Prompted by E. Susman, Superintendent Brodie wrote to the Director of Intelligence on 16 August 1944: 'The majority of people in this category were released at Ndola shortly after internment and I have no knowledge as to why these two were not released as there is nothing against them as far as I am aware.' The reply, dated 18 August, gave no explanation, but simply stated that the Governor was opposed to their return to NR.

49. Interviews with H. I. Menashe and W. Dobkins.

50. Kosmin, *Majuta*, 92–3.

51. ZCCM. NCCM/RC/HO/102: S. Taylor to R. Parker, 21 July 1938; Census of aliens, Nkana, 17 July 1938.

6. 'Land of Milk and Honey': Settlement Schemes and Immigration Debates

1. L. Hotz, 'South Africa and the Refugees en Route: Restrictions on Immigration', in F. Sichel (ed.), *From Refugee to Citizen* (Cape Town: Balkema, 1966), 12–25. This chapter also draws on H. Antkiewicz, 'Zion on the Zambezi: The Problem of German-Jewish Settlement Schemes in NR', unpublished seminar paper, University of Zambia, January 1980.

2. Shimoni, *Jews and Zionism*, 117–18; Sichel (ed.), *From Refugee to Citizen, passim*.

3. Kosmin, *Majuta*, 67–86.

4. NR LegCo Debates, 1, 8 June 1938; SEC3/53/1: 'Report on Immigration into NR', draft, and correspondence.

5. 'Report on Immigration into NR', 14–15.

6. 'Report on Immigration into NR', 16; SEC3/54/5: Boyd, CO, to FO, 16 February 1939, asks for British Consulates to be informed of changes in the immigration requirements.

7. SEC3/54/1: Maffey to Young, 20 March 1934, encloses Montefiore, 'List of Specialists', 2 March 1934.

8. SEC3/54/1: Parkinson to Young, 15 December 1937.

9. SEC3/54/1: Young to Parkinson, 23 May 1938.

10. SEC3/54/1: MacDonald to Logan, 3 June 1938; Parkinson to Logan, 3 June 1938; NR ExCo minute, 27 June 1938; Logan to Parkinson, 27 June 1938; Logan to MacDonald, 28 June 1938; MacDonald to Logan, 28 June 1938; Cartmel-Robinson to Logan, 28 June 1938; Allan, memorandum, 28 June 1938.

11. SEC3/54/1: Logan to MacDonald, 29 June 1938; Logan to MacDonald, 15 July 1938; Logan to Parkinson, 21 July 1938; SEC3/54/2: 'Proceedings of the Intergovernmental Conference at Evian, 6–15 July 1938', speech of Lord Winterton.

12. *Bulawayo Chronicle*, 1 August 1938; Kosmin, *Majuta*, 74.

13. SEC3/54/2: MacDonald to Maybin, 16 November 1938. See also Antkiewicz, 'Zion on the Zambezi', folios 18–19.

14. SEC2/54/2: Stephenson to Stanley, 21 July 1938, enclosed in Cohen to Maybin; Stephenson to CS, 5 March 1939, referring to his unacknowledged letter to Gov of 27 November 1938.

15. SEC2/54/2: Cohen to Maybin, 13 December 1938.

16. SEC3/54/2: Melland, 'Memorandum on a suggested area for settlement by refugees in the Muchinga Highlands of NR near Mpika', n.d.; SEC3/54/3: Minutes of ExCo, 3 February 1939, including statement of views of all unofficial members; Gore-Browne to Maybin, 12 February 1939, encloses Trapnell to Gore-Browne, 2 February 1939.

17. SEC3/54/5: Gore-Browne to Maybin, 10 February 1939; de Rothschild to Gore-Browne, 1 February 1939. See also E. de Rothschild, *A Gilt-edged Life* (John Murray, 1998), 88–9.

18. SEC3/54/3: Prentice to PC, Eastern Province, 3 January 1939; SEC3/54/1: Logan to Parkinson, 21 July 1938; Logan to Shuckburgh, 21 July 1938.

19. SEC3/54/2: MacDonald to Maybin, 31 October 1938; MacDonald to Maybin, 16 November 1938; Maybin to MacDonald, 18 November 1938; MacDonald to Maybin, 3 January 1939; SEC3/54/5: MacDonald to Maybin, 7 March 1939.

20. SEC3/54/5: Maybin to MacDonald, 10 March 1939; MacDonald to Maybin, 14 March 1939; Maybin, minute, 15 March 1939; Maybin to MacDonald, 16 March 1939. SEC3/54/3: Minutes of ExCo, 3 February 1939.

21. SEC3/54/5: Branch Sec, RRWU, to CS, April 1939; SEC3/53/1: Diamond, interview with CS, Mufulira, 28 February 1938.

22. SEC3/54/2: Mrs Catherine Olds to Gov, 10 July 1938.

23. SEC3/54/5: Maybin, minute, 15 March 1939; MacDonald to Maybin, 16 March 1939; Maybin to MacDonald, 25 March 1939.

24. SEC3/54/5: CS, Communiqué, 10 June 1939; Dunnett, 'Abstract of present views of the Commission', handed to Maybin, 10 June 1939; SEC3/54/4: Lewin, Director of Agriculture to CS, 4 July 1939, encloses copies of reports of Dunnett Commission and of Local Committee on Refugee Settlement.

25. SEC3/54/4: de Rothschild to Shuckburgh, 28 June 1939; Boyd to Maybin, 30 June 1939.

26. S. H. Frankel, *An Economist's Testimony* (Oxford: Centre for Postgraduate Hebrew Studies, 1992), *passim*.

27. Ibid., 152–3.

28. Ibid., 138–40, 152–3.

29. SEC3/53/1: 'Report on Immigration into NR', 14.

30. SEC3/54/5: Hudson to Maybin, 6 February 1939; Logan to Campbell, 13 February 1939; Campbell to Logan, 18 February 1939.

31. NRGG. December 1939.

32. 'Memorandum Submitted by the South African Jewish Board of Deputies to the Anglo-American Committee of Inquiry on Palestine', printed as a supplement to the *Zionist Record*, 12 April 1946.

33. SEC3/54/4: Brodie to CS, 3 February 1940; SEC3/54/2: Immigration Office to CS, 1 November 1938.

34. SAJBD. Council for Refugee Settlement in Africa Outside the Union, Rhodesian Sub-Committee, Minutes, 12 January 1940, report from Sonnabend.

35. Interview with M. Gersh; Susman Papers. M. Gersh to D. Susman, 12 November 1994.

36. SEC3/54/1: Brodie to Chief Secretary, 21 April 1939.

37. NR LegCo Debates, 1 June 1939, CS, 218–19.

38. NR LegCo Debates, 8 June 1939, CS, 418–19; Sichel, *From Refugee to Citizen*, 109; Susman Papers. M. Gersh to D. Susman, 12 November 1994; SEC3/54/1: Brodie to CS, 21 April 1939.

39. NR LegCo Debates, 1, 8 June 1939, 218–19, 400–18.

40. SAJBD. Council for Refugee Settlement Outside the Union, papers.

41. SEC3/54/1: Read to Brodie, 17 April 1939, in Brodie to CS, 21 April 1939.

42. SAJBD. Council for Refugee Settlement Outside the Union, Papers.

43. SEC3/54/4: Frankel and Sonnabend to Acting FS, 29 June 1939.

44. Interview with G. Glasser.

45. Interviews with H. Caminer and P. Fraenkel.

46. SEC3/54/4: Max Witzenhausen to CS, 3 October 1939; ZIF. M. Witzenhausen; SEC1/696: Brodie Memo on Witzenhausen, 1947.

47. SEC3/54/4: Frankel and Sonnabend to Acting FS, 29 June 1939.

48. Interview with A. Metzger.

49. SEC3/54/4: Frankel to Acting FS, 12 July 1939; Acting CS to Frankel, 25 July 1939; SEC353/1: Brodie to CS, 2 September 1939, enclosing 'Return of Jewish immigrants', 21 August 1939, 12 January, 5 April 1940; interview with A. Metzger.

50. SEC3/54/4: Hudson, minute, 20 December 1939, reports meeting of Sonnabend and Wulfsohn with Maybin.

51. SEC3/54/4: Wright to Brodie on behalf of Robert Simon, 30 November 1939; Brodie to CS, 3 February 1940.

52. SEC3/54/4: Minute by unidentifiable civil servant, 9 February 1940.

53. SEC3/54/4: Stammreich to CS, 6 April 1940; Wulfsohn to CS, 6 May 1940, on behalf of Metzger; Metzger to CS, 14 March 1941; CS to Metzger, 25 March 1941. ZIF. Stammreich.

54. SEC1/1700/1: CONF GOV, Nairobi, to Gov, NR, 7 June 1941; Gov, NR to CONF GOV, Nairobi, 8 June 1941; ExCo minute, 8 June 1941; CONF GOV to Gov NR, 14 June 1941, indicated that Tanganyika was prepared to take the Jews.

55. SEC1/1700/1: Minute, 3 July 1942, indicates that 462 Poles (including some Jews) had arrived by that date.

56. ZM/1/1/1: Department of War Evacuees and Camps, Chief Inspector to DC, Mazabuka, 24 December 1941; Levine to CS, NR, 12 December 1941. Council for Refugee Settlement Outside the Union, Rhodesian sub-committee, 5 January 1942, and later minutes.

57. SEC1/1700/1: Extract from Report on Public Opinion, PC, Western Province (then the Copperbelt), July 1942.

58. ZM/1/1/2: Report of visit of delegate of ICRC to Northern Rhodesia, June 1943, G. C. Senn, 11 September 1943. For the extraordinary life of Gottfried Senn, ICRC representative in SR, 1941–58, and founder of Red Cross in NR, 1949–50 see RHL: Welensky Papers. 692/6. See also H. Antkiewicz, 'Sikorski's Tourists in Tropical Africa: the World War II Polish Evacuees in Northern Rhodesia', unpublished seminar paper, University of Zambia, no date.

7. Escape from the Holocaust

1. Interview with H. Caminer.

2. Interview with P. Fraenkel; ZIF. Sommer, Aufochs, Fried, Jacoby, Stammreich, Mayer; and communication from E. Mayer.

3. Interviews with H. Caminer and P. Fraenkel.

4. Interview with H. Caminer.

5. Interview with P. Fraenkel; ZIF. P. Fraenkel; interview with A. Metzger.

6. T. Robins, unpublished memoir.

7. Interview with T. Robins.

8. ZIF. A. Fischer.

9. ZIF. H. Rowelsky; interview with Sigrid Fischer.

10. Interview with Helen Mohrer; ZIF. Mohrer.

11. Interviews with David and Rose Messerer.

12. Interview with R. Messerer.

13. ZIF. Mohrer; interviews with H. Mohrer and D. Messerer. See also Chapter 13.

14. ZIF. S. Israel. B. Baron, Bulawayo, to CS, 12 December 1938; N. Iljon to Brodie, 21 June 1939; Brodie to Iljon, 22 June 1939; Oertel to Brodie, 17 August 1939; Brodie to British Passport Officer, Berlin, 22 August 1939.

15. Ibid. S. Israel to Brodie, 20 September 1939; Brodie to Israel, 21 September 1939; Israel to Brodie, 6 January 1940; Brodie to British Consul, Geneva, 8 January 1940.

16. Ibid. Israel to Brodie, 17 May 1940; Brodie to British Consul, Beira, 23 May 1940; British Consul, Beira, to Brodie, 30 May 1940, sanctions entry.

17. Ibid. H. and E. Israel immigration form, Livingstone, 5 June 1940.

18. Interview with E. Israel.

19. ZIF. Z. Fichs. British Passport Officer, Riga, to Chief Immigration Officer, NR, 17 November 1939.

20. Interview with Ellen Israel.

21. ZIF. M. Hamburger; interviews with John Hudson and Morris Szeftel.

22. ZIF. A. J. Behrens.

23. G. Rosenberg, unpublished memoir; interview with G. Rosenberg; ZIF. S. Rosenberg.

24. Interview with W. Dobkins.

25. Interviews with J. Goldberg and D. Figov.

26. Interview with B. Szeftel; ZIF. S. Szeftel. He entered NR, 29 December 1938.

27. Interviews with B. Amoils, C. and B. Katz; W. V. Brelsford, *Fishermen of the Bangweulu Swamps* (Livingstone: Rhodes–Livingstone Institute, 1946), 115–16.

28. Interview with W. Dobkins.

29. Interviews with T. Bull and H. Caminer; Council for Zambia Jewry. Papers relating to death of A. Bornstein.

30. SAJBD: Council for Refugee Settlement in Africa Outside the Union, Rhodesia sub-committee minutes, 5 January 1942.

31. SEC1/1771: Reports on Public Opinion in Western Province (Copperbelt), H. F. Cartmel-Robinson, PC, 2 July 1943.

32. SEC1/1771: H. A. Watmore, PC, 11 July 1945.

33. SEC1/1970: Reports on Public Opinion in Central Province, Broken Hill, 4 October 1944.

8. Bigger Business: from the Depression to Independence

1. D'Hendecourt, *L'Elévage au Katanga*, 41–51, 70–71.

2. C. Rey (eds N. Parsons and M. Crowder), *Monarch of All I Survey: Bechuanaland Diaries, 1929–37* (London: James Currey, 1988) 89–90.

3. SPLC. J. Smith to E. Susman, 22 November 1932; Rey, *Monarch of All I Survey*, 131–2; SEC3/548/1. Conference on Cattle Trade with Representatives of NR, SR and BP, Victoria Falls, 16–18 December 1932, Synopsis of Proceedings.

4. SEC3/548/1: Minutes of meeting between E. Susman and Director of Veterinary

Services, 26 August 1933; minutes of meeting of Deputy Gov, NR, with H. Susman, 11 October; minutes of meeting between Gov, NR and PM, SR, 27 December 1933; Huggins to CS, 27 December 1933; Gov, NR to Acting Gov, NR, 28 December 1933; minutes of meeting with Captain Murray, NR Farmers Association, 11 January 1934; Morris to CS, 11 January 1934. Evidence of E. Susman to the Hilton Young Commission in letter to the secretary of the commission, 20 March 1928. Reference by courtesy of Robin Palmer.

5. Interview with David Susman; M. Kaplan (assisted by Marian Robertson), *Jewish Roots in the South African Economy* (Cape Town: Struik, 1986), 349–51.

6. SPLC. H. Susman, 31 July 1941.

7. ZCCM. WMA 24: Minutes of Cattle Marketing and Control Board, 30 December 1937; Minutes of meeting under the chairmanship of the CS on the supply of meat to the mines, attended by I. Kollenberg for Copperfields Cold Storage and Dechow for Werners, Nkana, 24 February 1938. A. P. Wood, *Report on a Socio-economic Study of the Feasibility of Removing the Western Province Cattle Cordon Line to the International Boundary* (Rural Studies Bureau, University of Zambia, 1983), 7–9.

8. ZCCM. WMA 24: Minutes of meeting attended by Dechow and I. Kollenberg representing the mines meat contractors and H. Susman and L. Deaconos representing the Bechuanaland cattle traders, Livingstone, 1941; Cattle Marketing and Control Board statistics on cattle purchases in Northern Rhodesia and imports for 1941.

9. Interview with W. Wulfsohn.

10. Interviews with H. Lowenthal, I. Teeger and I. Port.

11. T. Robins, unpublished MS 'Memoir', and interview; interviews with M. Dorsky; D. Susman.

12. KSF1/8/4: Land at Namwala: DC, Kalomo, to DC, Namwala, 13 December 1934; DC, Namwala (J. Gordon Read) to PC, 20 December 1934; PC to Messrs Dorsky and Wulfsohn, 29 December 1934; L. S. Diamond, Northern Produce and Livestock Co., to DC, Namwala, 11 April 1937; PC, Livingstone, to DC, Namwala, 21 May 1937; title deed to plot 3, Namwala, registered 17 August 1937.

13. Interview with T. Robins; K. Vickery, 'Saving Settlers: Maize Control in Northern Rhodesia', *Journal of Southern African Studies* 11(2), 1985, 212–34.

14. Robins, unpublished 'Memoirs'.

15. Interviews with T. Robins and M. Dorsky.

16. Robins, unpublished 'Memoirs'.

17. Interview with H. Wolffe.

18. Baylies, 'The State and Capital Formation in Zambia', 287. According to M. Rabb, 'Recollections' (unpublished MS, n.d.), Wulfsohn's original partnership in Kala ranch was with Geoffrey Beckett.

19. Baylies, 'The State and Capital Formation in Zambia', 288; Rabb, 'Recollections'. CRL. Indexes. The Susman Brothers and Wulfsohn file is no longer available. It appears that Harry Wulfsohn Ltd changed its name to Susman Brothers and Wulfsohn Ltd in 1946–47, but it is not possible to confirm this.

20. Rabb, 'Recollections'; SPLC. A. W. Crombie memorandum, 4 February 1976.

21. CRL. Werners, Local Company File 91, 1937 (now Concorde Agricultural Development Ltd); Rabb, 'Recollections'; interview with Len Pinshow.

22. Rabb, 'Recollections'; interview with David Susman.

23. All information in this section is from Rabb, 'Recollections', folios 1–39.

24. Interview with Len Pinshow.

25. Rabb, 'Recollections'; K. D. Kaunda, *Zambia Shall be Free* (London: Heinemann, 1962), 73–4.

26. KSX/4/1: Mankoya District Notebook; Rabb, 'Recollections'; interviews with Alex Freedman, Isa Teeger and Tim Barnett.

27. CRL. Werners File; Rabb, 'Recollections'.

28. Interview with Tim Barnett; Sylvia Barnett scrapbook, by courtesy of Tim and Carol Barnett; interviews with M. Fisher and M. Sanderson.

29. Interview with E. Faerber; communication from E. Colson.

30. Pinshow interview; ZCCM. NCCM/RC/HO 522/2: Bennett to Etheridge, 19 January 1959.

31. P. Brownrigg, *Kenneth Kaunda* (Lusaka: Kenneth Kaunda Foundation, 1989), 29; F. Macpherson, *Kenneth Kaunda of Zambia: The Times and the Man* (Lusaka: Oxford University Press, 1974), 149.

32. K. Makasa, *March to Political Freedom* (Nairobi: Heinemann Educational Books, 1981), 85; RHL: Welensky Papers. 237/6: 'Visit to Northern Rhodesia', May 1956, probably by B. M. de Quehen.

33. ZCCM. NCCM/RC/HO 522/2: Bennett to Etheridge, 19 January 1959.

34. Interview with L. Pinshow.

35. Dick Hobson, 'Profile: Len Pinshow', *Horizon*, 1965, 26–8.

36. Interview with L. Pinshow; RHL: Welensky Papers. 650/6: Pinshow to Welensky, 26 July 1960, referring to the views of I. Kollenberg on the Cold Storage Board.

37. *Report of the Commission of Inquiry into the Beef Cattle Industry of Southern and Northern Rhodesia* (Salisbury: Federal Government, 1963), 17; SEC6/1126: Minutes of the Cattle Marketing and Control Board; interview with L. Pinshow.

38. Marianne MacDonald, 'King of the Blockbuster', *Sunday Times: Inside Magazine* (Johannesburg), 11 May 1997. Lochinvar ranch had been established by Major Robert Gordon's Rhodesia Land and Cattle Company in 1913. SPLC. Lochinvar Guest House Visitors' Book, 1953–66; Rabb, 'Recollections'; Zambezi Ranching and Cropping Ltd Papers; interviews with D. Susman and L. Pinshow. For the history of Lochinvar, see also A. H. Mulongo, 'Land Use Conflicts on Lochinvar National Park: an Example of Contradictions in Environmental Policy, 1950–75', *Zambia Journal of History* 1, 1981, 61–75.

39. Rabb, 'Recollections'; SPLC: Werners Papers. G. Beckett, entry in *Central African Who's Who*, 1953; Gann, *A History of Northern Rhodesia*, 348.

40. 'On the Farming Front: Recipe for Success – the Jew, the Scot and the Afrikaner', *Central African Post*, 20 April 1956.

41. Rabb, 'Recollections'; CRL. NR (now Zambia) Textiles Ltd, File 191; SPLC. NR Textiles Ltd, Minutebook, 1946–52; Baylies, 'The State and Capital Formation in Zambia', 291.

42. Rabb, 'Recollections'; NR Textiles Ltd, Minutebook.

43. Rabb, 'Recollections'; CRL. Zambesi Saw Mills (1948) Ltd (later Redwood Investments Ltd), File 258; Baylies, 'The State and Capital Formation in Zambia', 290.

44. Rabb, 'Recollections'; interview with E. Wulfsohn.

45. Robins, 'Memoirs'.

46. Rabb, 'Recollections'.

47. Susman Papers. M. Gersh to D. Susman, 24 September 1993; CRL. African Commercial Holdings Ltd, File 308; Baylies, 'The State and Capital Formation in Zambia', 288–92; interviews with M. Gersh and N. Molver.

48. Kaunda, *Zambia Shall be Free*, 33–5; Macpherson, *Kaunda of Zambia*, 217–18.

49. Interviews with D. Susman and E. Wulfsohn.

50. Robins, 'Memoir'; communication from D. Susman; interview with I. Teeger; SPLC. Wulfsohn Papers.

51. Rabb, 'Recollections'; interviews with E. Wulfsohn and D. Susman.

52. Rabb, 'Recollections'.

53. ZIF. N. Zelter; SPLC. N. Zelter to E. Wulfsohn, 9 June 1980.

54. Rabb, 'Recollections'.

55. Interview with D. Susman.

56. Gersh, 'The Susman Saga'; interview with D. Susman; *Livingstone Mail*, 16 January 1952.

57. Kaplan, *Jewish Roots in the South African Economy*, 352–9; interviews with D. and A. Susman.

9. The Climax of the Community

1. Interviews with W. Dobkins and Aviva Ron.

2. Rybko, 'A Zionist Lecture Tour: Northern Rhodesia'.

3. Gann, *History of Northern Rhodesia*, 443; Cohen, 'The Jewish Communities', 141; M. Wagner, 'A Picture of Rhodesian Jewry', *Zionist Record*, November 1954, 12.

4. Cohen, 'The Jewish Communities ', 136; Gann, *History of Northern Rhodesia*, 443.

5. Gann, *History of Northern Rhodesia*, 441–4; L. H. Gann and P. Duignan, *White Settlers in Tropical Africa* (Harmondsworth: Penguin Books, 1962), 159–61.

6. Gann, *History of Northern Rhodesia*, 332–3.

7. Interviews with W. Dobkins, B. Press and D. Messerer.

8. Rybko, 'A Zionist Lecture Tour: Livingstone'.

9. Interview with Harry Sossen; interview with and communications from Beverley Sossen; *Central African Motor Trader*, November 1956.

10. Interview with and communications from B. Olsberg.

11. Interview with C. Krasner; ZIF. K. Aufochs, H. Jacoby, A. Fried, E. Mayer; communication from E. Mayer; interview with and communication from W. Wulfsohn.

12. Interview with S. Radunski.

13. Interview with R. Slutzkin.

14. Interviews with Nicky and Helga Iljon.

15. M. Wagner, *Zionist Record*, 6 July 1956; interviews with H. Sossen and B. Olsberg; Rabb, 'Recollections'; interviews with Saul Radunski, I. McKillop and A. Anderson.

16. Communication from Stanley Fischer.

17. Rybko, 'A Zionist Lecture Tour: Lusaka'.

18. Interview with G. Glasser.

19. Interview with J. and S. Fischer, and communications from Jack Fischer; RHL. Welensky Papers. S. Fischer to Welensky, n.d. [February 1954] and 11 June 1956.

20. Interview with J. and S. Fischer; communications from J. Fischer.

21. Interview with Frieda Wulfsohn.

22. Interview with and communications from Wulfie Wulfsohn.

23. Interviews with H. Caminer, Helen Mohrer, J. and S. Fischer; communications from J. Fischer; interview with 'Moggy' Mendelsohn.

24. Interview with B. Press; K. Kaunda, 'The Watershed Speech, 30 June–3 July, 1975' (Lusaka: Zambian Information Service), 44.

25. ZIF. A. J. Behrens; interview with Wendy Berman; communication from J. Fischer; interview with and communications from G. Rosenberg.

26. SEC1/1771: G. W. A. Bloomfield, District Commissioner, Chingola, 29 December 1942.

27. NR LegCo Debates, January 1948; *Bulawayo Chronicle*, 15 January 1948; SEC1/1520/1: Closed Township Commission Report, 16 April 1948.

28. SEC1/1520/1: Evidence to Closed Township Commission by Mrs Sarah Taylor Zaremba.

29. Doris Lessing, *Going Home* (London: Michael Joseph, 1957), 83–4; *Northern News*, 3 October 1959; Dotson and Dotson, *The Indian Minority*, 79; Rabb, 'Recollections'.

30. Interviews with Maurice and Reevee Gersh; Gertie Gersh, Wendy Berman, and Estelle Levinson. D. Jacobson, *The Electronic Elephant* (London: Hamish Hamilton, 1994) and *Heshel's Kingdom* (London: Hamish Hamilton, 1998).

31. ZIF. D. Kollenberg and E. Herr; interviews with Deirdre Leibowitz, Nathan Leibowitz, L. Pinshow and D. Tow.

32. Interviews with Molly Diamond and A. Kaplan; 'Profile: Maxine Diamond', *Horizon*, February 1966.

33. Interviews with D. and M. Figov; K. G. Mlenga, *Who is Who in Zambia 1967–8* (Lusaka: Zambia Publishing Company), 1968.

34. SEC1/1521: Closed Township Commission evidence; RHL. Welensky Papers. B. I. Menashe to DC, Chingola, 6 January 1954; Menashe to Welensky, 12 May 1962 and subsequent correspondence; interviews with A. Israel, A. Kaplan and H. I. Menashe.

35. Interviews with A. Israel, W. Dobkins, M. Dorsky and D. Marcus.

36. Rybko, 'A Zionist Lecture Tour: Nkana-Kitwe, Luanshya, Mufulira, Chingola', *Zionist Record*, 15, 29 August, 19 September 1947; interviews with Lilianne Benigson and E. Levinson.

37. ZIF. F. Buch; interviews with D. Messerer and E. Levinson.

38. Interviews with D. Messerer, and A. and F. Messerer.

39. See below, Chapter 15, for A. L. Epstein.

40. Interviews with Hessie Lowenthal and I. Teeger; communication from I. Teeger. See below, Chapter 15.

41. Interviews with H. Elkaim, Aviva Ron, and Avner and Ronnie Elkaim.

42. Communication from Marta Trefusis-Paynter; interview with W. Dobkins.

43. Interviews with D. Messerer and D. Figov.

44. Interviews with Alan Feigenbaum and Avner Elkaim.

45. Interviews with Deirdre Leibowitz, L. Benigson and M. Dorsky.

46. Gann, *A History of Northern Rhodesia*, 377.

47. Communication from Bright Mumba, Mansa.

10. The Galaun Story

1. Most of the information in this chapter comes from interviews with Abe, Vera and Michael Galaun.

2. Interview with Chaim Katz.

3. NRGG, 1945.

4. CRL. Lusaka Cold Storage Ltd (now G and W Holdings Ltd), File 166.

5. Ibid.

6. Interviews with Ben, Morris and Leslie Szeftel.

7. Macpherson, *Kaunda of Zambia*, 147–9.

8. SEC1/1970: H. L. Bright, District Commissioner, Lusaka, 7 December 1942.

9. Brownrigg, *Kenneth Kaunda*, 29; *Northern News*, 22 February 1954.

10. Macpherson, *Kaunda of Zambia*, 148; I. M. Manda, 'Women and Mass Mobilisation in Nationalist Politics in Zambia: the Case of Lusaka, 1951–64', MA dissertation, University of Zambia, 1992.

11. *Northern News*, 22 January, 12 February 1954.

12. *Northern News*, 5, 20 February 1954; Sampson, *So This Was Lusaaka's*, 72–3.

13. *Northern News*, 1 March 1954. The agreement was published in *Central African Post*, 1 March 1954.

11. Bigger Business Continued: Independence and After

1. SPLC. N. Zelter to E. Wulfsohn, 9 June 1980; D. Lessing, *Under My Skin* (London: Flamingo, 1995), 388. Her account of his experience in Zambia does not appear to be accurate. See also below, Chapter 14, for the relationship between N. Zelter and D. Lessing.

2. SPLC. H. Wulfsohn, 'Memorandum re staff', 23 February 1967.

3. K. D. Kaunda, 'Zambia: Towards Economic Independence' (19 April 1968), in B. de Gaay Fortman (ed.), *After Mulungushi* (Nairobi: East African Publishing House, 1969), 34–74.

4. Ibid., 63.

5. Interview with E. Wulfsohn; Rabb, 'Recollections'; CRL. Redwood Investments File.

6. Kaunda, 'Zambia: Towards Economic Independence', *passim*.

7. Rabb, 'Recollections'.

8. Interview with E. Wulfsohn; Rabb, 'Recollections'.

9. K. D. Kaunda, *Towards Complete Independence* (Lusaka: Zambia Information Services, 1969), 14.

10. Interview with E. Wulfsohn; Rabb, 'Recollections'.

11. Rabb, 'Recollections'.

12. SPLC. Werners Papers. CRL. Werners File; interview with G. Kollenberg.

13. SPLC. M. Barnett to Ministry of Agriculture, 2 April 1965.

14. SPLC. Zambezi Ranching and Cropping Papers; Rabb, 'Recollections'; interview with D. Susman.

15. Rabb, 'Recollections'; SPLC. Zambezi Ranching and Cropping Papers; *Times of Zambia*, 17 August 1973.

16. Rabb, 'Recollections'; interview with N. Molver.

17. Interview with E. Wulfsohn; V. J. Mwaanga, *An Extraordinary Life* (Lusaka: Multimedia Publications, 1982), 273–4.

18. Rabb, 'Recollections'; interview with D. Susman.

19. Interview with E. Wulfsohn; Baylies, 'The State and Class Formation in Zambia', 703–4.

20. TZI Ltd, Annual Report, 1993.

21. Interview with E. Wulfsohn; TZI Ltd, Prospectus, 1996.

22. TZI Ltd, Annual Report, 1995.

23. Interview with E. Wulfsohn.

24. TZI Ltd Prospectus, 1996; TZI Ltd, Annual Reports, 1995, 1996; communications from Edwin Wulfsohn and Hillary Duckworth.

12. Religion

1. Rybko, 'A Zionist Lecture Tour: Luanshya', *Zionist Record*, 15 August 1947.

2. Interviews with G. Gersh, 'Moggy' Mendelsohn and I. Teeger.

3. Nidlog (Goldin), 'Early Days in Northern Rhodesia', 15.

4. Rybko, 'A Zionist Lecture Tour: Livingstone'.

5. *Zionist Record*, 5 October 1928.

6. Rybko, 'A Zionist Lecture Tour: Livingstone'.

7. Interviews with E. Wulfsohn and B. Olsberg.

8. Rybko, 'A Zionist Lecture Tour: Lusaka'.

9. Interview with A. Metzger.

10. Interview with 'Moggy' Mendelsohn.

11. Interview with J. and S. Fischer.

12. Interview with A. Metzger.

13. M. Konviser, 'Tour of the Northern Rhodesian Jewish Community undertaken by the Rev. M. Konviser and Mr D. Shapiro, 3 March to 13 March 1946', copy by courtesy of Winston Shapiro.

14. Interview with M. Szeftel.

15. Interviews with R. Moss and M. Bush.

16. Interviews with E. Wulfsohn and M. Bush.

17. Interview with D. Rankow.

18. Rybko, 'A Zionist Lecture Tour: Broken Hill'; interviews with G. Rosenberg and N. Molver.

19. H. Gersh, 'Speech on handover of Kitwe-Nkana *Sefer Torah* to Cape Town Synagogue', 31 October 1972, copy by courtesy of Wendy Berman.

20. Konviser, 'Tour of the Northern Rhodesian Jewish Community'; interview with H. Elkaim.

21. Kitwe-Nkana Hebrew Congregation, 'Consecration of the Synagogue', 19 July 1946; Mufulira Hebrew Congregation, 'Consecration of the Synagogue', 21 July 1946, copies of Orders of Service by courtesy of, and interview with, D. Messerer; *Zionist Record*, 2 August 1946.

22. Konviser, 'Tour of the Northern Rhodesian Jewish Communities'; Rybko, 'A Zionist Lecture Tour: Chingola and Mufulira'; 'Nkana'; David S. Klein (brother-in-law of A. J. Mendelsohn), letter to editor, *Zionist Record*, 19 September 1947; interview with D. Messerer.

23. Konviser, 'Tour of the Northern Rhodesian Jewish Communities'; Rybko, 'A Zionist Lecture Tour: Luanshya'; interview with D. Figov.

24. Rybko, 'A Zionist Lecture Tour: Chingola and Mufulira'.

25. Interviews with W. Dobkins and D. Marcus.

26. Konviser, 'Tour of the Northern Rhodesian Jewish Communities'.

27. Rybko, 'A Zionist Lecture Tour', *passim*; interview with D. Messerer.

28. Konviser, 'Tour of the Northern Rhodesian Jewish Communities'.

29. Rybko, 'A Zionist Lecture Tour: Nkana'.

30. W. Rybko, 'The Reverend', in J. Sherman (ed.), *From a Land Far Off* (Cape Town: Jewish Publishing, 1987), 148–9.

31. Rybko, 'The Reverend', 150; communications from A. Ron.

32. H. Gersh, speech, 31 October 1972; M. Wagner, 'Wanted: Minister-Teachers for the Copperbelt', *Zionist Record*, 6 July 1956; interview with D. Messerer.

33. M. Wagner, 'Wanted: Minister-Teachers'.

34. Kosmin, *Majuta*, 119; 'Rhodesian, Zambian Jews Face Grave Difficulties', *South African Jewish Times*, 18 July 1969.

35. 'Zambian Jews Face Problem of Dwindling Communities', *South African Jewish Times*, 24 December 1970.

36. Rabb, 'Recollections'.

37. Interviews with D. Figov and D. Messerer; communications from V. Galaun and A. Ron; interview with M. Galaun; Council for Zambia Jewry Files.

38. J. Loeb, 'Zambia's Resilient Jews', *SA Jewish Report*, 19 June 1998; interviews with C. Krasner and M. Galaun.

39. Maurice Thal Papers, by courtesy of D. Scott Brown.

40. Interview with D. Messerer.

13. Politics

1. Shimoni, *Jews and Zionism*, *passim*; Kosmin, *Majuta*, *passim*.

2. R. G. Weisbrod, *African Zion* (Philadelphia: Jewish Publications Society of America,

1968), *passim*. The Governor of NR in the early 1930s, Sir Ronald Storrs, had served as Britain's first Governor of Jerusalem under the mandate. He hated Livingstone and left the country as soon as he could.

3. Cohen, 'The Jewish Communities', 144. We are grateful to Robin Palmer for a reference to an undated letter in the papers of Philip Gell, a director of the BSA Company, from the company to A. Spielmann of the Jewish Territorial Organisation on the possibility of Jewish settlement in North-Eastern Rhodesia.

4. Interview with A. Galaun.

5. *Zionist Record*, 14 June, 15 September 1912, 26 February 1913; Rybko, 'A Zionist Lecture Tour: Livingstone'.

6. *Zionist Record*, 21 April 1920, quoting obituary in *Zionist Bulletin* (London), 24 March 1920; letter from Oscar Susman to 'a Rhodesian friend', and tribute by Reverend M. I. Cohen.

7. Susman Papers. M. Gersh to D. Susman, 12 November 1994; Kosmin, *Majuta*, 157; *Zionist Record*, 29 June 1928.

8. *Zionist Record*, 7, 21 September 1928.

9. Susman Papers. M. Gersh to D. Susman, 12 November 1994; *Zionist Record*, May 1932; Rybko, 'Zionist Lecture Tour: Livingstone'; interview with B. Barenblatt.

10. *Zionist Record*, 21, 28 August, 4 September 1942; Cohen, 'The Jewish Communities', 137; Rybko, 'A Zionist Lecture Tour'; interviews with A. and V. Galaun and B. Press and communication from A. Ron.

11. Interviews with H. Oza, A. and V. Galaun; Rabb, 'Recollections'; communication from A. Ron.

12. C. Gertzel, 'Two Case Studies in Rural Development', in W. Tordoff (ed.), *Administration in Zambia* (Manchester: Manchester University Press, 1980), 244–5; interview with D. Figov; communication from A. Ron.

13. Interview with Monica Fisher.

14. Rabb, 'Recollections'.

15. Ibid.

16. Interview with Shmuel Magnus.

17. Interview with L. Pinshow.

18. Interview with Roy Welensky; D. Taylor, *The Rhodesian: The Life of Sir Roy Welensky* (London: Museum Press, 1955); G. Allighan, *The Welensky Story* (London: MacDonald, 1962), 18–23; Gann, *History of Northern Rhodesia*, 262–4.

19. Taylor, *The Rhodesian*, 32–5.

20. Gann, *History of Northern Rhodesia*, 262.

21. Allighan, *The Welensky Story*, 105–6.

22. Ibid., 109.

23. R. I. Rotberg, *Black Heart: Gore-Browne and the Politics of Multiracial Zambia* (Berkeley: University of California Press, 1977), 170–5.

24. RHL. Welensky Papers. Welensky to Millin, 13 May 1966.

25. Kosmin, *Majuta*, 106.

26. SEC1/1970: H. L. Bright, Public Opinion Report, Central Province, 5 September 1942.

27. Gann, *History of Northern Rhodesia*, 426.

28. Kosmin, *Majuta*, 120.

29. R. Welensky, 'Africans and Trade Unions in Northern Rhodesia', *African Affairs* 181, 1946, 185–91.

30. Gann, *History of Northern Rhodesia*, 352–9, 397–404.

31. Ibid.

32. L. H. Gann and M. Gelfand, *Huggins of Rhodesia* (London: Allen and Unwin, 1964), 144–7; H. Franklin, *Unholy Wedlock: The Failure of the Central African Federation* (London: Allen and Unwin, 1963), 105–20; Peter Fraenkel, *Wayeleshi* (London: Weidenfeld and Nicolson, 1959), 192–4; interview with A. Galaun.

33. Communication from L. H. Gann; P. Fraenkel, *Wayeleshi*.

34. Interview with D. Susman.

35. RHL: Welensky Papers. File 711/5, Correspondence, Programmes etc. Communication from Andrew Roberts.

36. Zukas Papers. *Rhodesia Study Club Newsletter* I, 1, October 1948; 13, October 1949.

37. Interviews with Simon Zukas; S. B. Zukas, 'Independence – The Role of the Anti-Federation Action Committee (AFAC)', unpublished paper, no date.

38. A. L. Epstein, 'Retrospect: an Anthropologist on the Copperbelt in the 1950s', in *Scenes from African Urban Life* (Edinburgh: Edinburgh University Press, 1992), 3–4.

39. Zukas, 'Independence – the Role of the AFAC'.

40. J. H. Chimba and S. B. Zukas, *The Case Against the Federal Proposals* (Ndola Anti-Federation Action Committee on behalf of the Ndola Federal Proposals Examination Group, 20 August 1951), Chapter 6.

41. Ibid.

42. E. L. Berger, *Labour, Race and Colonial Rule: the Copperbelt from 1924 to Independence* (Oxford: Clarendon Press, 1974), 119, 138; *Freedom Newsletter* 1 (1–4), January–April 1952; 2(5), May 1952.

43. RHL: Welensky Papers. Welensky to Gore-Browne, 7 April 1952.

44. Epstein, 'Retrospect', 4.

45. N. Tembo, *The Lilian Burton Killing: The Famous Trials of Zambian Freedom Fighters* (Lusaka: Apple Books, 1986).

46. Berger, *Labour, Race and Colonial Rule*, 64–5; ZIF. F. Maybank.

47. H. S. Meebelo, *African Proletarians and Colonial Capitalism* (Lusaka: Kenneth Kaunda Foundation, 1986), 418–19.

48. Quoted in *Zambia Daily Mail*, 29 April 1987.

49. Interviews with H. and M. Chimowitz.

50. Interview with A. Milner; communications from Juliette Milner Thornton, including copy of death notice for Joseph Milner, 13 March 1939.

51. Communications from Juliette Milner Thornton, Nicola Sharpe and Aviva Ron.

52. *Who's Who in the Federation of Rhodesia and Nyasaland in 1957* (Salisbury, 1957); Ibbo Mandaza, *Race, Colour and Class in Southern Africa* (Harare: Sapes, 1997), 497, 814; interview with Lilian Snapper Chow.

53. Interviews with L. Pinshow, and W. and V. Dobkins.

54. 'H. J. Simons: A Biographical Note', in H. J. Simons, *Struggles in Southern Africa for Survival and Equality* (Basingstoke: Macmillan Press, 1997), xi–xiv.

55. Interviews with R. Simons; and published interview in I. Suttner (ed.), *Cutting Through the Mountain: Interviews with South African Jewish Activists* (London: Viking, 1997), 23–47.

56. Communication from R. Frankenberg; A. Sibeko (Z. Zembe), *Freedom in Our Life Time* (Durban: Indicator Press, 1996), *passim*.

57. J. Slovo, *Slovo: the Unfinished Autobiography* (Randburg: Ravan Press, 1995), 4–5.

58. H. Dolny, 'Introduction', in J. Slovo: *The Unfinished Autobiography*, xi–xviii; interviews with H. and M. Chimowitz.

59. Slovo, *The Unfinished Autobiography*, 17–22.

60. R. Kasrils, *Armed and Dangerous* (Oxford: Heinemann Educational, 1993), 258–68.

61. Interview with W. Kodesh.

62. Personal knowledge; Council for Zambia Jewry correspondence, July 1981.

63. Interviews with G. Martin and T. Bull; Council for Zambia Jewry correspondence, 1984–85.

64. Interviews with R. Simons, W. Wulfsohn, C. Zukas and D. Susman; A. Wolpe, *The Long Way Home* (Cape Town: David Philip, 1994), 274.

65. Lessing, *Under My Skin*, 260, 384–9; *Going Home*, 83–5; *Walking in the Shade: Volume Two of My Autobiography* (London: HarperCollins: 1997), 172–89.

66. Kosmin, *Majuta*, 119; communication from Eileen Haddon.

67. *Zambia Daily Mail*, 29 April 1987; interviews with Simon Zukas, and personal knowledge.

68. A. Mbikusita-Lewanika and D. Chitala (eds), *The Hour Has Come! Proceedings of the National Conference on the Multi-Party Option* (Lusaka: Zambia Research Foundation, 1990).

14. Intellectuals and Some Professionals

1. M. Gluckman, 'The Tribal Area in South and Central Africa', in L. Kuper and M. G. Smith (eds), *Pluralism in Africa* (Berkeley: University of California Press, 1971), 373–4; Sir R. Firth, 'Max Gluckman, 1911–75', *Proceedings of the British Academy* 61, 1976, 479–96.

2. Firth, 'Max Gluckman', 486.

3. Communication from Elizabeth Colson.

4. Richard Brown, 'Passages in the Life of a White Anthropologist: Max Gluckman in Northern Rhodesia', *Journal of Southern African History* 20, 1979, 527–8.

5. Ibid., 529.

6. Ibid.

7. M. Gluckman, *Analysis of a Social Situation in Modern Zululand* (Lusaka: Rhodes–Livingstone Institute Papers, 28, 1958), 43. See also H. Macmillan, 'Return to the Malungwana Drift: Max Gluckman, the Zulu Nation and the Common Society', *African Affairs* 94, 1995, 39–65.

8. M. Gluckman, *The Economy of the Central Barotse Plain* (Livingstone: Rhodes–Livingstone Institute Papers, 7, 1941).

9. Firth, 'Max Gluckman', 482–3; interview with A. Galaun.

10. M. Gluckman, 'Individual Rights of Ownership in Land and its Products', in *Essays on Lozi Land and Royal Property* (Livingstone: Rhodes–Livingstone Institute Papers, 10, 1943), 61–4; W. Allan, M. Gluckman and others, *Land Holding and Usage among the Plateau Tonga of Mazabuka District: a Reconnaissance Survey, 1945* (Livingstone: Rhodes–Livingstone Institute Papers, 14, 1948), 8–9.

11. M. Gluckman, *The Judicial Process among the Barotse of Northern Rhodesia* (Manchester: Manchester University Press, 1955); *The Ideas in Barotse Jurisprudence* (New Haven: Yale University Press, 1965); Firth, 'Max Gluckman', 491.

12. E. Colson, 'The Relevance of Irrelevant Studies: the Future of Anthropology in Development Research', *Zambia Journal of History* 5, 1992, 9.

13. Communication from L. H. Gann.

14. E. Colson, 'The Institute under Max Gluckman', *African Social Research* 24, 1977, 285–95.

15. RHL: Welensky Papers. Box 616/6, Gluckman–Welensky correspondence, 1955–58.

16. M. Gluckman, 'Introduction', in F. Coillard, *On the Threshold of the Zambezi* (London: Frank Cass, 1971).

17. E. Marx, 'Introduction', in E. Marx (ed.), *A Composite Portrait of Israel* (London: Academic Press, 1980), 1–28.

18. Communication from L. H. Gann.

19. Epstein, 'Retrospect: an Anthropologist on the Copperbelt in the 1950's', 3–4.

20. Ibid., 19.

21. J. C. Mitchell, 'The Shadow of Federation, 1952–5', *African Social Research* 24, 1977, 315–18, quoting editorial and subsequent correspondence in *Central African Post*, 10, 17 April 1953. News of Epstein's appointment and research topic had been greeted by a satirical article in the *Central African Post*, 8 December 1949. See Epstein, 'Retrospect', 3–4.

22. ZCCM. NCCM/HC/HO/171: J. C. Mitchell to Secretary, Chamber of Mines, 22 September 1953; S. Taylor (secretary) to committee members, Chamber of Mines, 28 September 1953; Mitchell, 'The Shadow of Federation', 313; Epstein, 'Retrospect', 9–12, 17–18.

23. A. L. Epstein, *Politics in an Urban African Community* (Manchester: Manchester University Press, 1958), 163–4; 171–93.

24. Ibid., 224–34.

25. Epstein, 'Retrospect', 12–16; *Urbanisation and Kinship* (New York: Academic Press, 1981).

26. A. L. Epstein, *Ethos and Identity: Three Studies in Ethnicity* (London: Tavistock Press, 1978), xi.

27. L. H. Gann, 'Ex Africa: an Africanist's Intellectual Autobiography', *Journal of Modern African Studies* 31(3), 1993, 477–9.

28. Ibid., 480.

29. Ibid., 481.

30. Ibid., 481–2.

31. M. Gluckman, 'Introduction', in Gann, *Birth of a Plural Society*, vii–xiv.

32. Gann and Duignan, *White Settlers in Tropical Africa*, 124–5 (both quotes). See also: L. H. Gann, 'Liberal Interpretations of South African History: A Review Article', *Human Problems in Central Africa* 25, 1957, 40–58.

33. Communications from Robert Rotberg.

34. S. R. Clingman, *The Novels of Nadine Gordimer: History from the Inside* (Johannesburg: Ravan Press, 1986), 112 and 241 note 48.

35. ZIF. Benny Gelfand; interview with Esther Gelfand.

36. Gann, 'Ex Africa', 485.

37. Communication from M. Trefusis-Paynter.

38. Ibid.; communications from M. Lowenthal; interviews with I. Teeger and D. Scott Brown.

39. Communication from M. Trefusis-Paynter.

40. RHL: Welensky Papers. 516/10: Welensky–Gottlieb correspondence, 1943–45; communication from J. Fischer.

41. Interview with A. Metzger.

42. Communication from Dick Hobson; interview with 'Moggy' Mendelsohn.

43. Interview with M. Bush.

44. Interview with Aron (Eric) Iljon.

45. Interview with, and communications from, M. Lowenthal.

46. Communication from M. Trefusis-Paynter.

47. Interview with Ruth Weiss in H. Bernstein (ed.), *The Rift: The Exile Experience of South Africans* (London: Jonathan Cape, 1994), 40–6.

48. Personal information; RHL: Welensky Papers. Box 279/4, Intelligence Report for PM, 1 December 1959; Nadine Gordimer, *A Sport of Nature* (London: Jonathan Cape, 1987), 237.

49. Interviews with T. Bull.

50. Fraenkel, *Wayeleshi, passim*; personal information.

51. Interview with C. Zukas.

52. Interviews with and communications from W. Dobkins.

53. 'Meridien: an Impressive New Structure', *Profit Magazine* November,1993.

54. Interview with Diana Golson.

55. D. Scott Brown, 'Learning from Africa', interview with Evalina Francia, *Zimbabwean Review* 1(2), 1995; R. Venturi, D. Scott Brown and S. Izenour, *Learning from Las Vegas: The Forgotten Symbolism of Architectural Form* (Cambridge: Massachusetts Institute of Technology Press, 1972), 161; J. A. Hannigan, 'The Postmodern City: A New Urbanization?', *Current Sociology* 41(1), 1, 1995, 170; interview with D. Scott Brown; Chipkin, *Johannesburg Style*, 316.

56. Communication from S. Fischer.

57. Suttner (ed.), *Cutting Through the Mountain*, 74.

58. Ibid., 82–3.

59. Scott Brown, 'Learning from Africa'.

15. Conclusion

1. E. Hobsbawm, *Age of Extremes: The Short Twentieth Century, 1914–91* (London: Abacus, 1995), 338.

2. Braudel, *The Mediterranean and the Mediterranean World*, vol II, 816; and quotation from W. Sombart, *The Jews and Modern Capitalism* (translated by M. Epstein, London, 1913), 13.

3. Dotson and Dotson, 'The Economic Role of Non-indigenous Ethnic Minorities', 658–9.

4. Frankel, *Capital Investment in Africa*, 4, 28.

5. S. H. Frankel, *Modern Capitalism and the Jews* (Oxford: Centre for Postgraduate Hebrew Studies, 1983), 7.

6. Ibid., 11.

7. Sampson, *So This Was Lusaaka's*, 78.

8. Interview with A. Kaplan.

9. Interview with D. Susman.

10. Interview with A. Mbikusita-Lewanika.

11. Meebelo, *African Proletarians and Colonial Capitalism*, 176–84.

12. Interview with A. Mbikusita-Lewanika.

13. Interview with H. Mohrer. See above, Chapter 7.

Sources

One article in a quasi-learned journal, Maurice Gersh's 'The Susman Saga', published in the *Northern Rhodesian Journal* in 1965, deals with an aspect of the history of the Jews in Zambia. There are also a few articles which have appeared in Jewish publications which refer to this topic. The first was the Reverend M. I. Cohen's article, 'The Jewish Communities of Rhodesia and the North', which was published in the *South African Jewish Year Book* in 1929. Only one Jewish intellectual, Wolf Rybko, took a specific interest in the history and religious experience of the Jewish community in Northern Rhodesia. His series of seven short articles appeared in the *Zionist Record* between 18 July and 24 October 1947. Almost the only other source which claims to be historical is a rather unreliable article by B. Nidlog (Goldin), 'Early Days in Northern Rhodesia', which was based on an interview with Harry Susman and appeared in *The Rhodesian Jewish Times* in January 1948.

Only one academic paper has been written on an aspect of the history of the Jews in Zambia. Henry Antkiewicz's 'Zion on the Zambezi' is an unpublished seminar paper which was given at the University of Zambia in 1980. It deals with the pre-war schemes for Jewish refugee settlement in Northern Rhodesia. There is also half a paragraph on Jewish traders in Northern Rhodesia in L. and F. Dotson's chapter on 'The Economic Role of Non-indigenous Ethnic Minorities in Colonial Africa' in P. Duignan and L. H. Gann, *Colonialism in Africa*, vol IV. There is one dissertation, Carolyn Baylies's 'The State and Capital Formation in Zambia', which deals with a much wider topic, but touches on aspects of Jewish business history. It is an important source because it draws on a joint project which she conducted with her husband, Morris Szeftel, in the Companies Registry in Lusaka on the ownership of Zambian companies. Many of the files which they used are now lost or inaccessible.

In view of this dearth of published primary and secondary material relating specifically to the topic under investigation, this study has had to rely on archival and oral sources, and on occasional references in books which deal with other topics.

The most important archival source is the Zambia National Archives. It has not been possible to trawl through the whole of this vast archive looking for references to Jews. Given unlimited time, greater use could have been made of the District Notebooks. Unfortunately, some of the most relevant, such as those for Mongu and Senanga, are unavailable. The most important sources in the archives are the five volumes of documents relating to Jewish immigration and settlement schemes in the 1930s, and the immigration files. A large number of these survive for people who entered Northern Rhodesia between the 1920s and the 1950s. They have been particularly useful for German Jewish refugee immigration in the late 1930s, but they are incomplete. Files for some of the most interesting immigrants, such as Cantor Feivel Metzger, are not available. The Companies Registry in Lusaka should also be an important source on business history, but the files there are in a chaotic state. The ZCCM Archives in Ndola were also consulted.

The Jewish communities in Zambia do not appear to have been great keepers of records. The only files relating to the community to which we have had access are two relating to the Council for Zambia Jewry since its establishment in 1969. If the individual Hebrew Congregations kept minutes of meetings, they do not appear to have survived in Zambia, though some may exist outside the country.

The most useful sources outside the country have been the archives of the South African Jewish Board of Deputies in Johannesburg, which are largely unsorted, and the Welensky Papers at Rhodes House, Oxford. The latter collection is enormous, and has only recently been opened to the public. It provides an unrivalled source of information on settler society in Northern Rhodesia from the 1930s to the 1960s.

The most important private collection of documents relating to this topic is Edwin Wulfsohn's collection kept at the offices of Stenham Plc in London which includes the Susman Brothers' accounts from 1907 to 1928, a transcript of Elie Susman's diary for 1920, and papers relating to various companies, especially Werners, Northern Rhodesia Textiles, and Zambezi Ranching and Cropping. We are very grateful to Edwin Wulfsohn and David Susman for access to these documents.

Another important source has been Denise Scott Brown's collection of papers relating to the Lakofski, Hepker and Thal families. We are very grateful to her for copies of an interview with her father, Shim Lakofski; an autobiography by her mother, Phyllis Lakofski-Hepker; and extracts from the writings of Maurice Thal.

We are also very grateful to Wally Dobkins for access to his father's unpublished memoir and diary of his Great Trek from Likasi to Lobito Bay in 1922, and to Trude Robins and Gert Rosenberg for access to their unpublished autobiographies.

Interviews have been a very important source for this work. The first group of about one hundred interviews were conducted by Frank Shapiro in Israel, the United Kingdom, Zambia, Zimbabwe and South Africa in 1989–90. A further seventy-five interviews, sometimes with the same people, were conducted by Hugh Macmillan in Zambia, South Africa and the United

Kingdom, and by phone with people in the United States, Spain, Switzerland and Zimbabwe in 1995–99. The interviews vary in formality from transcripts of tape-recordings to notes of international telephone calls and chance encounters on aeroplanes. The greatest problem encountered in using interviews is the tendency for people to confuse dates, people and the sequence of events. Every effort has been made to check interviews not only against each other, but also with docmentary sources.

The most important single primary source for this purpose has been the *Northern Rhodesian Government Gazette*, from 1911 to 1964. In order to avoid cluttering the text with footnotes, we have not given individual citations to this source which rarely provides substantial information, but has been invaluable for confirming the movements of people. It provides a record of: all general dealers, hawkers and gun licences issued 1911–33; all new general dealers' licences, and transfers of licences, 1940–64; the registration of cattle brands; bankruptcies and deaths; the registration and liquidation of companies, and the dissolution of partnerships; applications for, and grants of, naturalisation; electoral rolls; civil service establishment lists, and so on.

There is one other source of information to which we have not always given references and that is biographical entries in various *Who's Who*s. The most useful of these have been *The Central African Who's Who for 1953* and its successor, *Who's Who in the Federation of Rhodesia and Nyasaland for 1957*. These were edited and produced by Victor Michelson, the son of a rabbi, and contain short entries on many Rhodesian Jews.

I. Interviews conducted during 1989–90 and 1995–98, with some indication of relationships

Amoils, Bella (daughter of Aryeh Zemack); Anderson, Andy

Barenblatt, Bertha (daughter of Harry Wasserson); Barnett, Carol (wife of Tim); Barnett, Tim (son of Max); Barrow, Charlie (nephew of Feiga Grill); Benigson, Lilianne; Benigson, R. L.; Berman, Wendy (daughter of Harry Gersh); Berold, Zena (daughter of Max Kominsky); Boyer, Amos; Bryer, Doris (daughter of Isadore Kollenberg); Bull, Theo (great-nephew of Alfred Beit); Bush, Michael

Caminer, Hilda; Chimowitz, Harry and Marjorie; Chow, Lilian Snapper (granddaughter of Egnatz Snapper); Cohen, Ellen (daughter of Solly Israel); Cohen, Jeannette

Davidov, Norma (daughter of Harry Wasserson); de Goede, Minda (daughter of Elias Kopelowitz; Diamond, Molly (widow of Sid); Dobkins, Fay (widow of Moss); Dobkins, Maurice (son of Andrew); Dobkins, Ray (widow of Andrew); Dobkins, Vyvian (wife of Walter); Dobkins, Walter (son of Moss); Dorsky, Morris (son of Harry)

Elkaim, Avner (nephew of Hanan); Elkaim, Hanan; Elkaim, Ronnie (daughter of Joe Furmanowsky)

Faerber, Esther (widow of Jack; sister of Sylvia Barnett); Feigenbaum, Alan; Figov, Dennis (son of Harry); Figov, Maureen (wife of Dennis); Fischer, Jack (nephew of Sam); Fischer, Sigrid (wife of Jack; daughter of Hans Rowelsky); Fisher, Monica; Fraenkel, Peter; Frankel, Sally Herbert; Frankenberg, Ronnie; Freedman, Alex (son-in-law of Maurice Rabb); Friedman, Liebe (daughter of Henrie Kollenberg)

Galaun, Abe; Galaun, Michael; Galaun, Vera; Gelfand, Esther (widow of Michael; daughter of Isadore Kollenberg); Gelman, Michael (grandson of the elder Abraham Gelman); Gelman, Sam (son of the younger Abraham Gelman); Gersh, Gertie (widow of Harry); Gersh, Harry; Gersh, Maurice; Gersh, Reevee; Glasser, Goodman; Goldberg, Joseph; Golson, Diana (widow of Harvey Golson); Greenberg, Frieda (daughter of Eli Lurie); Grill, Tilly (daughter of Marcus)

Horton, G. T.; Hudson, John; Hyman, Frieda (daughter of S. B. Wulfsohn)

Iljon, Aron (Eric, son of Oscar); Iljon, Nicholas (son of Oscar) and Helga (Sonnabend)

Jacobs, Sonia (daughter of Joseph Beemer); Jacobson, Gerald (son of Myer)

Kamionsky, Adella (daughter of Isadore Aberman); Kaplan, Arthur; Katz, Chaim and Becky; Katz, Zena; Kodesh, Wolfie; Kollenberg, Gerald (son of Isadore); Kopelowitz, Minda (see de Goede); Krasner, Cecilia (daughter of Elias Kopelowitz); Kroll, Suzanne (daughter of Joseph Minchuk); Kuper, Hilda (daughter of Joseph Beemer, interviewed in 1983)

Lakofski, Shim; Lakofski-Hepker, Phyllis (wife of Shim; daughter of William Hepker); Lazarus, Charles (grandson of Barnett 'Bongola' Smith); Leibowitz, Deirdre (wife of Nathan; daughter of Edward Herr); Leibowitz, Nathan; Levinson, Estelle (daughter of Morris Goldstein); Lowenthal, Hessie (widow of Abe; sister of Harry Wulfsohn); Lowenthal, Mark (son of Abe)

McKillop, Ian; McKillop, Leslie; Magnus, Shmuel (Val); Marcus, David; Marcus, Doreen (wife of David; daughter of Henry Herbstein); Martin, Gesse; Matheson, Sheilagh (daughter of Maurice Thal); Mbikusita-Lewanika, Akashambatwa (grandson of King Lewanika); Menashe, Haim Isaac (Victor); Mendelsohn, 'Moggy' (son of Sam); Messerer, Alex and Fanny; Messerer, David and Rose; Metzger, Alf (son of Feivel); Milner, Aaron; Mohrer, Helen (widow of Julius); Molver, Neil; Moss, Reuben

Olsberg, Beverley (daughter of Harry Sossen); Oza, H.

Pinshow, Len; Port, Isadore; Press, Berjulie (daughter of George Lipschild)

Rabb, John (son of Maurice); Rabb, Maurice; Radunski, Saul; Rankow, Dvora; Reif, Ann (granddaughter of Barnett 'Bongola' Smith); Robins, Trude (widow of Harry Wulfsohn); Robinson, Charlie; Robinson, Ella (widow of Harry; daughter of Harry Susman); Ron, Aviva (daughter of Hanan Elkaim); Rosenberg, Gert (son of Siegfried)

Sanderson, Murray; Schulman, Lilian (widow of Hyam); Scott Brown, Denise (daughter of Shim and Phyllis Lakofski); Seider, Ray; Simon, Heinz (son of Benno); Simons, Ray Alexander (widow of Jack); Slomowitz, Zoe; Slutzkin, Riva (widow of Alex); Sossen, Beverley (see Olsberg); Sossen, Harry; Sossen, Marion (daughter of Harry); Surdut, B. Z. (son of Samuel); Susman, Ann (wife of David); Susman, David (son of Elie); Susman, Joseph (son of Harry); Szeftel, Ben; Szeftel, Leslie (son of Ben); Szeftel, Morris (son of Ben)

Teeger, Isa (daughter of Abe Lowenthal); Teeger, Joseph (husband of Isa); Tow, Doreen (widow of Max; daughter of Henrie Kollenberg); Trefusis-Paynter, Marta

Weinberg, Eli (interviewed in 1976–81); Weisenbacher, Freddie; Welensky, Roy; Wide, Renée (daughter of Moss Dobkins); Wolffe, Hymie (nephew of Marcus Grill); Wright, Patrick (son of Hannah Grill and Trevor Wright); Wulfsohn, Edwin (son of Harry); Wulfsohn, Frieda (see Hyman); Wulfsohn, Wulfie and Millicent

Zukas, Cynthia; Zukas, Simon

II. Manuscript Sources

A: Public Archives

Lusaka: Zambia National Archives (ZNA)

Immigration Files (prefix IMMI/1/)

Aufochs, K. L. I.: A/83 1939

Baitz, P.: B/7 1928; Bardavid, C.: 128 1938; Behrens, A. J.: B/221 1939; Bryn, M.: B/165 1925

Capelluto, M. D.: G/131 1938 (with V. Galante); Capelluto, V.: C/94 1938; Cavadia, K. T.: C/1 1924

Epstein, A. L. E/28 1949

Fichs, Z.: F/144 1940; Fischer, A.: F/42 1922; Flax, M.: M/21 1932: Fraenkel, P.: F/246 1939; Fried, A. M.: F/113 1939

Gelfand, B.: G/84 1938; Glasser, L.: E/15 (with Ross, E.)

Hamburger, M.: H/132 1939; Heilbronn, S.: H/136 1939; Herr, T.: T/7 1927

Illion, U.: I/43 1926; Israel, S.: I/17 1939

Jacoby, H.: H/198 1939

Kacas, N.: K/54 1930 (Katz); Kollenberg, D.: D/418 1919

Liptz, C.: L/234 1932

Marcus, S. A.: M/293 1939; Maybank, F.: F/112 1939; Menashe, H. I.: H/128 1937; Mendelsohn, A. J.: M/64 1934; Meyer, E.: M/286 1939; Minchuk, J.: J/193 1928; Mohrer, J.: M/180 1938; Mortge, S.: M/271 1939

Roetgen, H.: R/92 1938; Rosenberg, S.: R/98 1939; Rowelsky, H.: R/89 1938

Shapiro, A.: A/144 1926 ; Sommer, M.: S/184 1939; Stammreich, M.: M/301 1939; Stern, L.: S/261 1939; Stiel, A.: S/272 1939; Strauss, H.: S/269 1939; Sussman, S.: S/291 1930; Szeftel, S.: S/188 1938

Traubas, C.: T/44 1940 (Traube)

Weiss, M.: W/138 1939; Welensky, D.: W/263 1940; Witzenhausen, M.: W/127 1939

Zelter, N.: Z/10 1938; Zlotnik, I.: Z/6 1929

Other Administrative Files

A3/8/3	Broken Hill Township
BS3/242	Lobengula's Treasure
H1/2/1/1	Bankruptcies
H1/2/4/2	Bankruptcies
KDE/2/41/1–3	Barotseland Traders
KSD4/1–2	Mpika District Notebook
KSF1/8/4	Namwala Township Plot
KSX/4/1	Mankoya District Notebook
KTA/3	Sesheke District Notebook
SEC1/696	Rhodes Island Internees
SEC1/1520/1	Closed Townships Commission

SEC1/1521	Evidence to Closed Township Commission
SEC1/1700/1	Middle Eastern Refugee Administration
SEC1/1771	Wartime Public Opinion Reports: Western Province
SEC1/1970	Wartime Public Opinion Reports: Central Province
SEC3/53/1	Report on Immigration into Northern Rhodesia
SEC3/54/1–5	Jewish Immigration
SEC3/199/1–4	Brick and Tile-making for Lusaka Capital Development
SEC3/548/1	Conference on Cattle Trade
SEC3/565/1	Bovine Pleuro-pneumonia
SEC6/1126–7	Cattle Marketing and Control Board
U8/1/1	Bankruptcies
ZMM/1/1/1–2	Wartime Evacuees and Camps

Lusaka: Companies Registry (CRL)

African Commercial Holdings Ltd. File 308, 1949
Concorde Agricultural Developments Ltd. *See* Werners
G and W Holdings. *See* Lusaka Cold Storage Ltd
Hide Holdings. *See* Northern Hide and Produce Company
Lusaka Cold Storage Ltd. File 166, 1946
Northern Caterers Ltd. File 37, 1930
Northern Hide and Produce Company. File 218, 1947
Northern Rhodesia Native Produce Company. File 105, 1940
Northern Rhodesia Textiles Ltd. File 191, 1946
Redwood Investments Ltd. *See* Zambesi Saw Mills (1948) Ltd
Werner and Company Ltd. File 91, 1938
Zambesi Saw Mills (1948) Ltd. 1948

Ndola: ZCCM Archives

NCCM/HC/HO/171	Rhodes–Livingstone Institute
NCCM/RC/HO/102	Prevention of Sabotage on the Mines
NCCM/RC/HO 522/1–2	Closed Townships
NCCM/RC/HO 533/2	Closed Townships
WMA 24–5 Cattle	Marketing Board
WMA 176–81	Luanshya Management Board

Johannesburg: South African Jewish Board of Deputies Archives (SAJBD)

Council for Refugee Settlement Outside the Union
Press Cuttings – Zambia
Rhodesia Sub-committee Minutebook and Correspondence

Oxford: Rhodes House Library (RHL)

Coryndon Papers; Rhodes Papers; Wakefield Papers; Welensky Papers

B: Private Collections

Dobkins, W., Adelaide, Australia. Autobiography/diary of Moss Dobkins

Olsberg, B., London. Grill and Sossen family papers

Rabb, J., Cape Town. M. Rabb, MS 'Recollections'

Rosenberg, G., Tenerife, Canary Islands. 'My Autobiography'

Scott Brown, D., Philadelphia, USA. S. Lakofski, transcript of interview; P. Lakofski-Hepker, MS 'Memoirs'; M. Thal Papers (transcripts); Hepker, Lakofski, Thal family trees

Shapiro, W., London. Family papers

Stenham PLC (SPLC) London. Northern Rhodesia Textiles Minutebook; Robins, T., MS 'Memoirs'; Susman Brothers accounts 1907–28; E. Susman diary 1920; Susman Papers; Werners Papers; Wulfsohn Papers; Zambezi Ranching and Cropping Papers

Susman, D., Cape Town letters from M. Gersh

Zukas, S., Lusaka. *Rhodesia Study Club Newsletter*; *Freedom Newsletter*; Anti-Federation Action Committee, 'Report on the Federal Proposals'; Zukas, S., MS on Anti-Federation Action Committee

III. Periodical Publications

British Central Africa Gazette, 1900–3

Livingstone Mail, occasional volumes

Livingstone Pioneer and Advertiser, 1906

North Eastern Rhodesia Government Gazette, 1903–7

Northern News, occasional volumes

Northern Rhodesia Government Gazette, 1911–64

Zionist Record, 1911–50

IV. Books and Articles

Allan, W., Gluckman, M. and others, *Land Holding and Usage among the Plateau Tonga of Mazabuka District: a Reconnaissance Survey, 1945* (Livingstone: Rhodes–Livingstone Institute Papers, 14, 1948).

Allighan, G., *The Welensky Story* (London, 1962).

Bancroft, J. A., *Mining in Northern Rhodesia* (no place, 1961).

Barnes, J. A., *Politics in a Changing Society: A Political History of the Fort Jameson Ngoni* (London, 1954).

Berger, E. L., *Labour, Race and Colonial Rule: The Copperbelt from 1924 to Independence* (Oxford, 1974).

Bernstein, H. (ed.), *The Rift: The Exile Experience of South Africans* (London, 1994).

Bigland, E., *The Lake of the Royal Crocodiles* (New York, 1939).

Bovill, E. W., *The Golden Trade of the Moors* (London: Oxford University Press, 1968).

Boxer, C. R., *The Portuguese Seaborne Empire, 1415–1825* (London: Hutchinson, 1969).

Braudel, F., *The Mediterranean and the Mediterranean World in the Age of Philip II* (London, 1973).

— *Capitalism and Material Life, 1400–1800* (London, 1974).

Brelsford, W. V., *Fishermen of the Bangweulu Swamps* (Livingstone, 1946).

— *Generation of Men: The European Pioneers of Northern Rhodesia* (Salisbury, 1965).

Brelsford, W. V., (ed.), *The Story of the Northern Rhodesia Regiment* (Lusaka, 1954).

Brion Davis, David, 'The Jews and the Slave Trade', *New York Review of Books*, 22 December 1994.

Brown, R., 'Passages in the Life of a White Anthropologist: Max Gluckman in Northern Rhodesia', *Journal of Southern African History* 20, 1979.

Brownrigg, P., *Kenneth Kaunda* (Lusaka, 1989).

BSA Company, *Reports on the Administration of Rhodesia, 1900–2* (no place, no date).

Caplan, G., *The Elites of Barotseland, 1878–1969* (London, 1970).

Central African Who's Who for 1953 (Salisbury, 1953).

Chipkin, C., *Johannesburg Style* (Cape Town: David Philip, 1994).

Clark, P., *Autobiography of an Old Drifter* (London, 1936).

Clay, G., *Your Friend Lewanika: Litunga of Barotseland, 1842–1916* (London, 1968).

Clingman, S. R., *The Novels of Nadine Gordimer: History from the Inside* (Johannesburg, 1986).

Cohen, M. I., 'The Jewish Communities of Rhodesia and the North', in *The South African Jewish Year Book* (Johannesburg, 1929).

Collins, J., 'Lusaka: the Historical Development of a Planned Capital, 1929–1970', in Williams (ed.), *Lusaka and its Environs*.

Colson, E., 'The Institute under Max Gluckman', *African Social Research* 27, 1977.

— 'The Relevance of Irrelevant Studies: the Future of Anthropology in Development Research', *Zambia Journal of History* 5, 1992.

Comay, J., *Who's Who in Jewish History* (London: Routledge, 1995).

D'Hendecourt, R., *L'Élevage au Katanga* (Brussels, 1953).

Dotson, F., and Dotson, L., *The Indian Minority of Zambia, Rhodesia and Malawi* (New Haven, 1968).

— 'The Economic Role of Non-indigenous Ethnic Minorities in Colonial Africa', in P. Duignan and L. H. Gann, *Colonialism in Africa, 1870–1969*, vol IV, *The Economics of Colonialism* (Cambridge, 1975), 565–631.

Epstein, A. L., *Politics in an Urban African Community* (Manchester, 1958).

— *Ethos and Identity: Three Studies in Ethnicity* (London, 1978).

— *Urbanisation and Kinship* (New York, 1980).

— 'Retrospect: an Anthropologist on the Copperbelt in the 1950s', in *Scenes from African Urban Life* (Edinburgh: Edinburgh University Press, 1992)

Ese, K., *An Historical Guide to Livingstone Town* (Livingstone, n.d. [1996]).

Firth, R., 'Max Gluckman, 1911–75', *Proceedings of the British Academy* 61, 1976.

Fraenkel, P., *Wayeleshi* (London, 1959).

Frankel, R. (assisted by Marian Robertson), *Tiger Tapestry* (Cape Town, 1988).

Frankel, S. H., *Capital Investment in Africa: Its Course and Effects* (London, 1938).

— *Modern Capitalism and the Jews* (Oxford, 1983).

— *An Economist's Testimony* (Oxford, 1992).

Franklin, H., *Unholy Wedlock: The Failure of the Central African Federation* (London, 1963).

Gann, L. H., 'The Northern Rhodesian Copper Industry and the World of Copper, 1932–52', *Rhodes–Livingstone Journal* 18, 1955.

— 'Liberal Interpretations of South African History: A Review Article', *Human Problems in Central Africa* 25, 1957.

— *The Birth of a Plural Society* (Manchester, 1958).

— *A History of Northern Rhodesia: Early Days to 1953* (London, 1964).

— 'Ex Africa: An Africanist's Intellectual Autobiography', *Journal of Modern African Studies* 31, 1993.

Gann, L. H. and P. Duignan, *White Settlers in Tropical Africa* (Harmondsworth, 1962).

Gann, L. H. and M. Gelfand, *Huggins of Rhodesia* (London, 1964).

Gelfand, M., *Northern Rhodesia in the Days of the Charter* (Oxford, 1961).

Gersh, M., 'The Susman Saga', *Northern Rhodesia Journal* 6, 1965.

Gertzel, C., 'Two Case Studies in Rural Development', in W. Tordoff (ed.), *Administration in Zambia* (Manchester, 1980).

Gibbons, H. St A., *Africa from South to North through Marotseland* (London, 1904).

Gluckman, M., *Essays on Lozi Land and Royal Property* (Livingstone, 1943).

— *The Judicial Process among the Barotse of Northern Rhodesia* (Manchester, 1955).

— *Analysis of a Social Situation in Modern Zululand* (Lusaka: Rhodes–Livingstone Institute Papers, 28, 1958).

— *The Ideas in Barotse Jurisprudence* (New Haven, 1965).

— *The Economy of the Central Barotse Plain* (Manchester, 1968).

— 'The Tribal Area in South and Central Africa', in L. Kuper and M. G. Smith (eds), *Pluralism in Africa* (Berkeley: University of California Press, 1971).

— 'Introduction', in F. Coillard, *On the Threshold of the Zambezi* (London: Frank Cass, 1971).

Gordimer, N., *Guest of Honour* (London, 1970).

— *A Sport of Nature* (London, 1987).

Gordon, L., *Shared Lives* (Cape Town, 1992).

Halpern, J., *South Africa's Hostages: Basutoland, Bechuanaland and Swaziland* (Harmondsworth, 1965).

Hannigan, J. A., 'The Postmodern City: A New Urbanization?', *Current Sociology* 41(1), 1995.

Hobsbawm, E., *Age of Extremes: The Short Twentieth Century, 1914–91* (London, 1995).

Hobson, D., *Food and Good Fellowship* (Lusaka, no date.)

— *Showtime* (Lusaka, 1979).

Jacobson, D., *The Electronic Elephant* (London, 1994).

— *Heshel's Kingdom* (London, 1998).

Kanduza, A. M., *The Political Economy of Underdevelopment in Northern Rhodesia, 1918–60: A Case Study of Customs, Tariff and Railway Freight Policies* (Lanham: University Press of America, 1986).

Kaplan, M. (assisted by Marian Robertson), *Jewish Roots in the South African Economy* (Cape Town, 1986).

Kasrils, R., *Armed and Dangerous* (London, 1993).

Katzenellenbogen, S. E., *Railways and the Copper Mines of Katanga* (Oxford, 1973).

Kaunda, K. D., *Zambia Shall be Free* (London, 1962).

— 'Zambia: Towards Economic Independence', (19 April 1968) in B. de Gaay Fortman (ed.), *After Mulungushi* (Nairobi, 1969).

— *Towards Complete Independence*, (Lusaka, 1969).

Kosmin, B. A., *Majuta: A History of the Jewish Community of Zimbabwe* (Gwelo, 1980).

Langworthy, H. W. (ed.), *Expedition in Central Africa, 1888–91: A Report by Carl Wiese* (London, 1983).

Lessing, D., *Going Home* (London, 1957).

— *Under My Skin* (London, 1995).

— *Walking in the Shade: Volume Two of My Autobiography, 1949–62* (London, 1997).

Levtzion, N., *Ancient Ghana and Mali* (London: Methuen, 1973).

McCracken, J., 'Economics and Ethnicity: the Italian Community in Malawi', *Journal of African History* 32(2), 1991.

McCulloch, M., *A Social Survey of the African Population of Livingstone* (Lusaka, 1956).

McKee, H. M., 'Northern Rhodesia and the Federation', *African Affairs* 284, 1952.

Macmillan, H., 'Return to the Malungwana Drift: Max Gluckman, the Zulu Nation and the Common Society', *African Affairs* 94, 1995.

Macpherson, F., *Kenneth Kaunda of Zambia: The Times and the Man* (Lusaka, 1974).

— *Anatomy of a Conquest* (London, 1981).

Makasa, K., *March to Political Freedom* (Nairobi, 1981).

Mandaza, I., *Race, Colour and Class in Southern Africa* (Harare, 1997).

Mansfield, C., *Via Rhodesia* (London, no date).

Marx, E. (ed.), *A Composite Portrait of Israel* (London, 1980).

Mbikusita-Lewanika, A. and Chitala, D. (eds), *The Hour Has Come! Proceedings of the National Conference on the Multi-Party Option* (Lusaka: Zambia Research Foundation, 1990).

Meebelo, H., *African Proletarians and Colonial Capitalism* (Lusaka, 1986).

Mitchell, J. C., 'The Shadow of Federation, 1952–5', *African Social Research* 24, 1977.

Morel, E. D., 'Another Stokes Affair', *West Africa*, 22 July 1902.

Mulongo, A. H., 'Land Use Conflicts on Lochinvar National Park: an Example of Contradictions in Environmental Policy, 1950–75', *Zambia Journal of History* 1, 1981.

Murray-Hughes, R., 'Edmund Davis', *Northern Rhodesia Journal* 6(1), 1965.

Mwaanga, V. J., *An Extraordinary Life* (Lusaka, 1982).

Newitt, M., *Portuguese Settlement on the Zambezi* (London, 1973).

Oliver, R., *The African Experience* (London: Weidenfeld and Nicolson, 1991).

Pauling, G., *The Chronicles of a Contractor* (London, 1926).

Phimister, I., *Wangi Kolia: Coal, Capital and Labour in Colonial Zimbabwe, 1894–1954* (Johannesburg, 1994).

Pretorius, P. J., *Jungle Man* (Sydney, 1948).

Prins, G., *The Hidden Hippopotamus* (Cambridge, 1980).

Rey, C. (eds N. Parson and M. Crowder), *Monarch of All I Survey: Bechuanaland Diaries, 1929–37* (London, 1988).

Rotberg, R. I., *Black Heart: Gore-Browne and the Politics of Multiracial Zambia* (Berkeley, 1977).

— *The Founder: Cecil Rhodes and the Pursuit of Power* (New York, 1988).

Rybko, W., 'A Zionist Lecture Tour' (7 parts), *Zionist Record*, 18 July–24 October 1947.

— 'The Reverend', in J. Sherman (ed.), *From a Land Far Off* (Cape Town, 1987).

Sampson, R., *The Man with a Toothbrush in His Hat: The Story and Times of George Copp Westbeech in Central Africa* (Lusaka, 1972).

— *So This Was Lusaaka's* (Lusaka, 1982).

Saron, G. and L. Hotz (eds), *The Jews in South Africa: A History* (Cape Town, 1955).

Schulz, A., and A. Hammar, *The New Africa: Up the Chobe and Down the Okavango Rivers ...* (London, 1897).

Scott Brown, D., 'Learning from Africa', interview with Evalina Francia, *Zimbabwean Review* 1(2), 1995.

Shain, M., *The Roots of Anti-Semitism in South Africa* (Johannesburg, 1994).

Shimoni, G., *Jews and Zionism: The South African Experience, 1910–67* (Cape Town, 1980).

Sibeko, A. (Z. Zembe), *Freedom in Our Life Time* (Durban: Indicator Press, 1996).

Sichel, F. (ed.), *From Refugee to Citizen* (Cape Town, 1966).

Simons, H. J., *Struggles in Southern Africa for Survival and Equality* (Basingstoke, 1997).

Slovo, J., *Slovo: The Unfinished Autobiography* (Randburg, 1995).

Smith, J. (ed. T. Bagnall Smith), *Vet in Africa: Life on the Zambezi, 1913–33* (London, 1997).

Sonnenberg, M., *The Way I Saw It* (Cape Town, n.d.).

Suttner, I. (ed.), *Cutting Through the Mountain: Interviews with South African Jewish Activists* (London, 1997).

Taylor, D., *The Rhodesian: The Life of Sir Roy Welensky* (London, 1955).

Tembo, N., *The Lilian Burton Killing: The Famous Trials of Zambian Freedom Fighters* (Lusaka, 1986).

Thornhill, J. B., *Adventures in Africa* (London, 1915).

Vail, L., and L. White, *Capitalism and Colonialism in Mozambique* (London, 1980).

Van Horn, L., 'The Agricultural History of Barotseland, 1840–1964', in R. Palmer and N. Parsons, *The Roots of Rural Poverty in Central and Southern Africa* (London, 1977).

Varian, H. F., *Some African Milestones* (Wheatley and Oxford, 1953).

Venturi, R., Scott Brown, D. and Izenour, S., *Learning from Las Vegas: The Forgotten Symbolism of Architectural Form* (Cambridge: Massachusetts Institute of Technology Press, 1972).

Vickery, K., 'Saving Settlers: Maize Control in Northern Rhodesia', *Journal of Southern African Studies* XI(2), 1985.

Wagner, M., 'A Picture of Rhodesian Jewry', *Zionist Record*, November 1954, 12.

— 'Wanted Minister-Teachers for the Copperbelt', *Zionist Record*, 6 July 1956.

Weisbrod, R. G., *African Zion* (Philadelphia, 1968).

Welensky, R., 'Africans and Trade Unions in Northern Rhodesia', *African Affairs* 181, 1946.

Who's Who in the Federation of Rhodesia and Nyasaland for 1957 (Salisbury, 1957).

Williams, G. J. (ed.), *Lusaka and its Environs* (Lusaka, 1987).

Wood, A. P., *Report on a Socio-economic Study of the Feasibility of Removing the Western Province Cattle Cordon Line to the International Boundary* (Rural Studies Bureau, University of Zambia, 1983).

Wolpe, A., *The Long Way Home* (Cape Town, 1994).

Zambia's Mining Industry: the First Fifty Years (Ndola: Roan Consolidated Mines Limited, 1978).

V. Dissertations, Unpublished Papers etc.

Antkiewicz, H., 'Sikorski's Tourists in Tropical Africa: The World War II Polish Evacuees in Northern Rhodesia', seminar paper, University of Zambia, n.d.

— 'Zion on the Zambezi: The Problem of German-Jewish Settlement Schemes in Northern Rhodesia', seminar paper, University of Zambia, 1980.

Baylies, C., 'The State and Capital Formation in Zambia', PhD dissertation, University of Wisconsin, Madison, 1978.

Macmillan, H. W., 'The Origins and Development of the African Lakes Company, 1878–1908', PhD dissertation, University of Edinburgh, 1970.

Manda, I. M., 'Women and Mass Mobilisation in Nationalist Politics in Zambia: the Case of Lusaka, 1951–64', MA dissertation, University of Zambia, 1992.

Mkunga, C., 'The Development of the Asian Trading Class, 1900–80', MA dissertation, University of Zambia, 1992.

Nzila, I. M., 'The Zambezi Sawmills: A History of Forest Exploitation in the Western Province of Zambia, 1910–68', MA dissertation, University of Zambia, 1987.

Vickery, K., 'Roy Welensky and the World of Central African Mining', University of Zambia, 1989.

Index

ABC Bazaar (Livingstone), 122, 163
Abercorn Trading Company, 14
Aberman, Adella, 61
Aberman, Fanny, 207
Aberman, Isadore, 43–4, 61, 62
Aberman's store, 62
Abrahams, Chief Rabbi, 275
Abrahams, Mark, 37, 226
Adamson, Aldridge, 247
Africa, Jan, 4
African Agricultural Enterprises Ltd, 148
African City Investments Ltd, 99
African Commercial Holdings Ltd, 153, 196, 200
African Jewish Congress, 222
African Lakes Corporation, 5, 6, 50, 52, 68, 90, 92, 93, 142, 180
African Mineworkers' Union, 79, 144, 243, 264, 265
African National Congress (ANC): Northern Rhodesia, 144, 145, 187, 188, 189, 225, 244–5; South Africa, 251, 252, 253, 254, 256, 272
African nationalism, 145–6, 159, 187–9, 225, 239–42
African Railway Workers' Union, 243
Agriflora Ltd, 204
Akananisa (or Akanangisa), Mulena Mukwae, of Sesheke, see Mulena Mukwae
Alexander II, Tsar, 7
Alexander, Ray, see Simons, R.E.
Aliens' Act, South Africa (1937), 111
Allan, William, 105, 261
Allighan, Garry, 235
Alter, Israel, 116
Amato family, 101, 176, 228
Amato, Benny, 99
Amato, Ruben, 99, 150
Amato Frères company, 100
Amenhotep IV, Pharaoh, 2
American Metal Company, 83
Amiran Ltd, 213
Anglo-American Corporation, 83, 85, 92, 104, 135–6, 139, 144, 147, 163, 191, 204, 282
anti-Semitism, 10–11, 42–3, 73, 80, 100–101, 103, 116, 117, 118, 120, 132, 136, 145, 151, 158, 182, 211, 143, 261, 286
Appleby, Jill née Bensusa, 90
Arthur, Prince, Duke of Connaught, 34
Asian traders, 50–1, 56, 62–3, 93, 167–8, 171, 172–3, 180–1, 288, 292–3
Associated Printers Ltd, 177
Astra Cinema (Kitwe), 152

Attala, Antoine (Tony), 98
Attenborough, David, 148
Aufochs family, 122, 163
Aufochs, Frieda, 122
Aufochs, Ilse, 163
Aufochs, Kurt, 163
Aukstolker, M., 225

B.I. Stores (Chingola), 176
Bach, Rabbi, 209
Bailes, Annie, 247
Baitz family, 165
Baitz, Florrie, 66
Baitz, Jack, 66, 158
Baitz, Lewis, 158
Baitz, Pesach, 66
Balme, Frank, 261
Bancroft, J.A., 85, 89
Bardavid, C., 101
Barkly, Sir Henry, 3
Barnes, John, 266
Barnett, Isaac, 143
Barnett, J.M., 113, 128
Barnett, Joyce, 222
Barnett, Max, 87, 130, 143–6, 147, 148, 154, 158, 174, 186, 189, 194, 198
Barnett, Sylvia née Emdin, 143, 174
Barnett, Tim, 143
Baron, Ben, 127
Baron, Leo, 255, 283
Baron, Rachel, 229
Barotse Transport Company, 142
Barotseland Trading Company, 183
Bata Shoe Company, 111
Baylies, Carolyn, 187
Beau, Alec, 165
Beau, Esther née Rubenstein, 165
Bechuanaland Exploration Company, 99
Beckett, Geoffrey, 148, 149, 150
Beemer, Harry, 52–4, 68, 75
Beemer, Joseph, 52–4, 68, 75
Begin, Menachem, 229, 277
Behrens family, 49, 129
Behrens, Cilla née Scher, 49, 163
Behrens, Fritz, 170–1
Behrens, Heinz, 49, 163
Behrens, Joe, 170–1
Beit, Alfred, 1, 4, 278
Benatar, Isaac, 100, 235
Benatar, Sylvia née Schulman, 97

Benguela Railway Company, 97
Benigson family, 50, 180
Benigson, Lazar, 177
Bennett, O.B., 146
Benson, Sir Arthur, 168
Benton, Kenneth, 128
Berelowitz, Philip, 59
Berger and Cohen (partnership), 43
Berlin, Sir Isaiah, 229
Bernstein, Alex, 143
Bernstein, Dianne née Barnett, 221
Bernstein, Herbert, 143, 221
Bernstein, Molly née Martin, 143
Bernstein, Sidney (later Lord), 263
R.J. Bernstein (builder), 43
Bernstein and Barnett (partnership), 143
Berold, Zena née Kominsky, 13
Berro family, 101
Bigland, Eileen, 56
Bijou cinema, 99
Bloch, Chaim, 58, 207
Bloch, Mr, 208
Bloch Brothers company, 43
Blumenthal, Annie née Goldberg, 130
Blumenthal, Herman, 54, 92
Blumenthal, Johanna née Rubenstein, 92
W. Bolus and Company, 22
Booth, Harold, 68
Bornstein, Abraham, 131
Boyd, Robert, 32, 36, 37, 148
Brander, Bishop S.J., 22
Brattle, Miss, 36
Braude, Louis, 13, 14
Braudel, Fernand, 69, 287, 288, 293
Brin, Myer, 54, 171
British South Africa Company, 3–6, 11, 16, 18, 42, 82, 106, 107, 155, 224, 225, 238
British Union of Fascists, 55, 80, 235
Brodetsky, Professor Selig, 228
Brodie, Israel, Chief Rabbi, 207
Brodie, Superintendent Norman, 112–13, 114, 116, 117, 127
Bronowski, Dr Jacob, 255
Brown, Dr, 55
Brown, Richard, 260
Buch, Frank, 143, 177
Buchanan, George, 9, 33, 37
Bull, Theo, 278–9
Burton, Len, 204
Bush, Dr Michael, 212, 222, 274–5, 274
Bush, Ruth, 275, 281
Busschau, W.J., 149
Butts family, 144
Bwana Mkubwa Hotel, 85, 98
Bwana Mkubwa Trading Company, 98

Cable and Wireless Ltd, 153
Caminer family, 169
Caminer, Hilda née Herman, 120–3, 125, 170, 293
Caminer, Horst, 120–3, 170
Campbell, Bobby, accountant, 143

Campbell, Captain R.E. 'Skipper', 110, 111, 113
Campbell Brothers Ltd, 90
Cantor, Reverend, 220
Capelluto, M.D, 101
Capelluto, V.G., 101
Capelouto, Nic, 100, 228
Capital Dry Cleaners (Lusaka), 122
Caravaghia family, 101
Carlton Cinema (Lusaka), 171
Cartmel-Robinson, H.F. (later Sir Henry), 105, 132
Cassirer, Reinhold, 271
Cattle Marketing and Control Board, 136, 147
cattle diseases: anthrax, 25; bovine pleuro-pneumonia, 25–7, 33, 144; east coast fever, 30; foot-and-mouth, 134; rinderpest, 8, 19
cattle trade from: Barotseland, 8–15, 16–29, 135, 184; Bechuanaland, 27–9, 30–4, 86, 133–4, 144, 147; Line of Rail, 29–34, 66–7, 147, 203, Tanganyika, 14–15; cattle trade to: Angola, 12, 29; Congo, 20, 14, 30–2, 133–4; Southern Rhodesia, 8–10, 13–14, 26
Cavadia family, 137
Cavadia, Kosta, 66
Cavadia, Pangos, 66
CBC (Campbell, Booker, Carter) Ltd, 167, 196
Central African Airways Ltd, 153
Central African Broadcasting Services, 279–80
Central African Examiner, 278
Central African Jewish Board of Deputies, 221, 232
Central African Motors Ltd, 152, 200
Central African Post, 257, 265
Central Garage, Lusaka, 61
Chalmers, J.A., 30
Chamberlain, Joseph, 224
Chamberlain, Neville, 107
Chandia, Flinto, 282
Changufu, Lewis, 188
Chapoloko, James, 244
Charelik Salomon and Company, 22, 40, 43–4
Chartered Butchery (Bulawayo), 14
Chemin de Fer du Bas Kongo (railway company), 100
Chester Beatty, Alfred, 82–3
Chibote Meat Corporation, 203
Chibuku Breweries Ltd, 200
Chikerema, Robert James, 240
Chikwanda, Alex, 256
Chileshe, Safeli, 188
Chiluba, Frederick, 257, 258
Chimba, Justin, 241, 242, 243, 246, 250
Chimowitz, Harry, 240, 245, 249, 252, 253, 282
Chimowitz, Marjorie, 245, 252
Chipkin, Clive, 90
Chirwa, Philip, 255
Chitala, Derrick, 256
Chloride (CA) Ltd, 204
Cholmeley, E.H., opponent of Jewish immigration, 113
Chona, Mainza, 255
Clark, Percy, 11, 18

Clarke, Frederick J. 'Mopani', 42, 68, 74, 164
Clay, Gervase, 233
Clayman, Reverend Sidney, 211, 212, 213, 220, 276
Clegg, Johnny, 284–5
Cloete, Hermanus, 149
Clutton-Brock, Guy, 254
Clutton-Brock, Molly, 254
Coca-Cola franchise, 153, 200
Cohen, Abner, 262
Cohen, Andrew (later Sir), 106, 237
Cohen, Ellen née Israel, 127–8
Cohen, Ephraim, 178
Cohen, Reverend Moses Isaac, 13, 34, 38, 40, 41,
    100, 106, 159, 208, 209, 225, 227, 229
Cohen, Victor, 180
Coillard, Reverend François, 4
Colson, Elizabeth, 260, 262, 264
Commercial Press Ltd, 169
Commonwealth Jewish Council, vii
Compagnie d'Elevage et d'Alimentation du
    Katanga (Elakat), 32, 133, 147, 149
Concorde Agricultural Development Ltd, 198
Concorde Investments Ltd, 203
Congo-Rhodesia Ranching Company, 86, 133
Consolidated Textiles Ltd, 201
Copperfields Cold Storage Ltd, 86–7, 93, 129, 130,
    131, 133, 136, 139, 143, 144, 145, 146, 147, 172,
    174, 186, 196, 198, 199
Copperbelt, the, 82–102, 171–9, 214–20, 229, 264–6
Copperbelt Co-operative Society, 172
Coryndon, Robert (later Sir), 9, 18, 21
Council for Refugee Settlement in Africa beyond
    the Union, 114, 118
Council for Rhodesian Jewry, 217, 219, 220
Council for Zambia Jewry, vii, 192, 221, 222, 253,
    254
Creed, R.N.P., 68
Critchley, Erica, 164
Croad, Hector, 108
T. A. Crombie and Company, 197
Cuninghame, Major Boyd, 57, 74
Cypin, M., 216
Cyprus, evacuees from, 118–19

Dagan, M., 221
Damie, Dr Manya (Marie), 179, 273–4
Davidov, Norma née Wasserson, 47
Davis, Sir Edmund, 40–1, 51, 52, 57, 82, 83
Davis, Frank, 44
Davis, 'Ma', 214
Davis, Norman, 214
Dayan, General Moshe, 229
De Beer's Consolidated Mining Company, 4, 83
Dean, R.B., 57
Dean, Robert, 245
Dechow, E.W., 139, 185
Deuss, Ludwig, 6, 7, 14–15, 52, 68
Diamond, Aaron Barnett, 13, 17, 20, 22, 24, 60,
    191, 207, 225
Diamond, Cissy (later Rosenfield), 61
Diamond, Louis Solomon, 13, 137

Diamond, Reverend Maurice, 209, 228
Diamond, Maurice, QC, 212, 283
Diamond, Maurice, of Siavonga, 175
Diamond, Maxine, 175
Diamond, Molly née Hamilton, 94, 175
Diamond, Sidney, 11, 92, 93, 94–5, 98, 131, 174–5,
    289, 291
Diamond, Victor Solomon, 61, 108
Diamond, W.H., 13
Dobkins family, 161, 217
Dobkins, Aaron Samuel, 71
Dobkins, Andrew, 76, 79, 97, 176
Dobkins, Fay née Steinberg, 79, 81, 221, 249, 281,
    293
Dobkins, Len, 72, 179
Dobkins, Moss, 54, 70–81, 93, 97, 130, 158, 176,
    208, 221, 249, 281, 289
Dobkins, Sarah Rachel née Liptz, 81
Dobkins, Vyv, 249
Dobkins, Walter (Wally), 79, 80, 158, 160, 245, 249,
    281–2, 283, 284, 293
Dolny, Helena, 252
Dombie, Millicent see Wulfsohn
Donin, Shaya, 169
Dorsky family, 217
Dorsky, Harry, 97, 137, 176, 180
Dorsky and Wulfsohn (partnership), 138
Dotsons, F. and L., 1, 51, 173, 288
Drake, Paddy, 156
Dublon, Dr, 113, 166
Duckworth, Hillary, 202, 203, 205
Dufferin and Ava, Marquess of, 102
Duly, Captain, 75
Duncan, Sir Patrick, 232
Duncan-Little, Major, 128
Dunell, Ebden and Company, 22
Dunnett, Sir James, 108
Dunnett Commission, 114
Dutch East India Company, 3

Eason, Captain H.P., 24
Economy Stores Ltd, 87, 92, 93, 133, 151, 153, 172,
    174
Edgars Stores Ltd, 66
Edward VII, King, 19
Ehrenberg, Victor, 267
Elizabeth, Queen Mother, 169
Elizabeth II, Queen, 168
Elkaim, Aviva see Ron
Elkaim, Avner, 179, 180
Elkaim, Hanan, 80, 178–9, 215, 218, 222, 224
Elkaim, Ronnie née Furmanowsky, 179
Elkaim, Yona, 218
Ellenbogen, Henry, 36
Elton, Sir Geoffrey, 267
Epstein, Arnold L. (Bill), 34, 178, 241, 243, 262,
    264–7, 269, 271, 284, 292
Epstein, Barry, 177, 218
Epstein, Gabriel, 27, 34
Epstein, Reverend Moshe, 214
Espinosa, A., 98

Esra, Sam (formerly Esrachovitch), 218
Ettinger, Sigismund, 129

Fabian, Dr Dennis, 274
Faerber, Esther *née* Emdin, 143
Faerber, Jack, 143, 144, 231
Favish, Harry, 177, 216
Federal Cold Storage Board, 198, 203
Federation of Meat Distributors, 147
Feigenbaum family, 47, 213
Feigenbaum, Alan, 47, 180, 240
Feigenbaum, Bill, 47, 56
Ficks, Sam (formerly Zalmans Fichs), 128, 165
Ficks, Herta *née* Iljon, 128, 165
Field, H.H., 149
Figov family, 175, 180
Figov, Dennis, 95, 174, 175, 221, 222, 230, 231, 293
Figov, Harry, 85, 94, 98, 130, 175, 217
Figov, Maureen, 175
Findlay, George, 9, 27
Finkelstein, Joseph, 9, 12, 17, 226
First, Ruth, 56, 252
Firth, Sir Raymond, 260
Fischer family, 49, 67, 167, 168, 171, 192
Fischer, Ann *née* Kopelowitz, 158, 166, 283
Fischer, Assia, 61, 125
Fischer, Jack, 64, 168, 170, 212, 231, 274
Fischer, Lazar, 165
Fischer, Paula *née* Kopelowitz, 166
Fischer, Philip, 49, 67, 165, 166, 231, 283
Fischer, Sam, 49, 61–2, 64, 114, 122, 125, 165, 168, 210, 231, 274, 282
Fischer, Sigrid *née* Rowelsky, 125, 169, 211
Fischer, Stanley, 166, 167, 283, 290
Fischer's Building (Lusaka), 64
Fischer's Store (Lusaka), 62
Fisher, Ffoliot, 105
Fisher, Dr Monica, 230
Fisher, S., 221
Fix Outfitters (Livingstone), 165
Flax, Meyer, 48, 165
Forjaz, Moira *née* Matheson, 56
Forjaz, Ze, 56
Forman, Lionel, 241
Fox-Pitt, Lieutenant-Commander, Thomas, RN, 242, 271
Fraenkel family, 170
Fraenkel, Hans, 121–3, 206
Fraenkel, Margot, 121–3
Fraenkel, Peter, 121, 123, 238, 239, 240, 279–80
Frame, Philip, 149, 201
Frame group, 180
Frankel, Professor Sally Herbert, 109, 110, 114, 115, 116, 268, 288–9, 292
Frankel, Rudy
Frankenberg, Ronnie, 250, 251
Franklin, Harry, 188, 279
Fredman, Alex, 142
Fredman, Willy, 46
Freedman, Barney, 90
Freedom Newsletter, 243

Freeman, John, 235
Freemasonry, 79–80
Fried family, 122
Friedman, Milton, 288
Frykberg, W., 14
Furmanowsky, Joe, 46, 179

Galaun family, 161, 181
Galaun, Abe, 131, 144, 171, 182–93, 198, 212, 220, 221, 225, 253, 261, 282, 290, 293
Galaun, Jack, 192
Galaun, Michael, 190, 191, 192, 193, 222
Galaun, Vera *née* Harris, 185, 190, 192, 193, 221
Gama, Gaspar da, 3
Gama, Vasco da, 3
Gann, Lewis Henry, 6, 11, 180, 239, 262, 263, 266, 267–70, 271, 272, 284, 292
Garden House Hotel (Lusaka), 279
Gavronsky, Helen (later Suzman), 140
Gee, Malcolm, viii
Gelfand, Benny, 212, 272
Gelfand, Esther *née* Kollenberg, 272, 273
Gelfand, Michael, 272–3
Gelman family, 228
Gelman, Abraham (elder), 44
Gelman, Abraham (younger), 32, 133, 147, 149, 150, 151, 291
Gerber family, 170
Gerber, David, 158
Gerber, Jack, 80, 170, 210
Gersh (formerly Gershowitz) family, 92, 95, 111, 151, 157, 174, 196, 200, 224, 291
Gersh, Bernard, 200
Gersh, Errol, 214
Gersh, Gertie *née* Baron, 214
Gersh, Harry, 35, 80, 87, 152–3, 214, 222
Gersh, Maurice, 17, 33, 35, 86, 87, 112, 114, 143, 149, 150, 152–3, 172, 173, 194, 199, 200, 216, 227, 228, 231, 291
Gersh, Reevee *née* Melamed, 173, 200
Gershowitz, Emmanuel, 35
Gibbons, Major H. St A., 57, 224–5
Gillon, Philip (formerly Gluckman), 260
Gladstone, Viscount, 35, 82
Glass, Samuel, 12
Glasser family, 57–60, 61, 168
Glasser, Benjamin, 53, 57, 58, 59, 62
Glasser, Frieda, 58, 168, 207
Glasser, Goodman ('Goody'), 53, 58, 114, 115, 158, 188, 206, 210, 254
Glasser, Louis, 53, 60, 168
Glasser's store, 62
Glasstone family, 228
Glasstone, Robert, 14, 65
Glazer, Bernard, 99, 290
Glazer, Sam Lieb, 99, 290
Gluckman, Mary *née* Brignoli, 185, 260
Gluckman, Max, 184–5, 250, 259–63, 266, 268, 269, 271, 284, 292
Gluckmann, Emmanuel, 259
Gluckmann, Kate, 259

Goldberg, Israel, 130, 230
Goldberg, Jack, 13
Goldberg, Joseph, 130, 230
Goldschmidt family, 129
Goldstein, Dr Alexander, 227, 229
Goldstein, Morris, 158, 174
Golson, Diana née Bignell, 283
Golson, Harvey, 253, 282–3
Golson, Paul, 283
Goodman's Store (Lusaka), 168
Gordimer, Nadine, 271–2, 278
Gordon, Barney, 250
Gordon, Lyndall, 66
Gordon, Nathan, 97, 179
Gordon, Robert 'Zambezi, 9, 12–15, 18
Gordon, Major Robert, of Lochinvar, 31, 75
Gordon, Rose née Dobkins, 81
Gordon, Sonia, 250
Gordon and Levitz (partnership), 290
Gore-Browne, Lorna née Goldman, 236
Gore-Browne, Sir Stewart, 107, 108, 113, 235–6, 238, 243, 270
Gottlieb, Dr Leo, 274
Grand Hotel (Lusaka), 190, 282
Greek traders, 67, 137, 181, 287
Green, Stuart, 148
Greenberg and Kriegler (partnership), 85, 88, 97
Grey, George, 19
Grill family, 44–7, 162, 227
Grill, Abe, 46
Grill, Annie see Susman
Grill, Bella see Sossen
Grill, Bennie, 46
Grill, Ephraim, 170
Grill, Faiga (Fanny) née Bruch, 44, 45, 46, 207
Grill, Gertrude see Merber
Grill, Hannah (later Wright), 46
Grill, Harry, 46, 125
Grill, Harry (nephew), 46
Grill, Hymie, 46
Grill, Laura née Sommer, 46, 122, 125
Grill, Lily (later Fredman), 46
Grill, Marcus, 16, 34, 44, 45, 46, 75, 207, 208, 209, 225
Grill, Natie, 45, 46, 75
Grill, Solly, 45, 46
Grill, Tilly, 46
Grunfeld, Dr, 131
Guttman family, 49
Guttman, Ann née Fischer, 170
Guttman, Heinz, 170
Gwembe Valley Development Project, 212

Habonim (Zionist youth organisation), 167, 230, 252, 260
Hailey, W.M., Lord, 109
Halberg, Murray, 233
Hamburger family, 170
Hamburger, Jacob, 128, 129
Hamburger, Max, 129
Hammarskjold, Dag, 276

Hanon family, 101
Harding, Colin, 9, 18
Harris, Kennedy, 94
Harris, Vera see Galaun
Harrison Clark, James 'Changa Changa', 54
Harvey, Laurence, 163
Haslett, Sam, 9, 26, 32, 36, 37, 59, 136, 185–6
Hazan family, 101
Heath, Tony, 264
Hebrew congregations: Broken Hill, 54, 55, 213–14; Bulawayo, 13, 34, 47, 207, 225; Chingola, 217; Elisabethville, 24, 207; Gwelo, 234; Harare, 124; Kitwe, 130, 221; Livingstone, 47, 49, 208–9, 229; Luanshya, 229, 230; Lusaka, 116, 119, 123, 192, 203, 207, 210–13, 221, 253, 275, 293; Mufulira, 177; Ndola, 81, 178, 179, 214, 230, 277; Salisbury, 14; Witten (Germany), 129
Heenen, Gaston, 31
Heilbronn, Solly, 170
de Hemptinne, Monsignor, 31
Hepker family, 14, 23, 91, 92, 98, 99
Hepker, Adolph, 14
Hepker, Hermann, 14
Hepker, Julius, 14
Hepker, Willie, 14, 54, 85, 91
Herbstein family, 213, 228
Herbstein, Basil, 158
Herbstein, Henry, 65, 176
Herbstein, Miriam (Mary) née Wulfsohn, 65
Herman, Gustav, 120
Herman, Isadore, 45
Herr, Deirdre (later Leibowitz), 174
Herr, Shirley, 174
Herr, Teddy, 174, 180
Herzl Zionist Society (Livingstone), 49, 225, 226
Herzl, Theodor, 55, 224
Herzliya Zionist Youth Movement, 125
Heslop, Karl, 145
Hilfsverein (German Jewish Emigration Agency), 104
Hirschfeld, Glicka see Kollenberg
Hirschfeld, Isadore, 59
Hirschmann, S., 229
Hitchcock, Alfred, 163
Hitler, Adolf, 103
HIV/AIDS epidemic, 280
Hobsbawm, Eric, 287, 288, 290
Hobson, Dick, 146
Hochschild family, 83
Hochstein family, 54, 171, 213, 214
Hochstein, Chaim (Harris), 54, 55, 70, 72, 77, 78
Hochstein, Lewis, 54, 228
Hochstein, Rebecca, 54, 73
Hoffman, Eric, 131
Hornby, George, 77
Hotel Victoria (later Fairview Hotel) (Lusaka), 131
House of Mansa (shop), 180
Huggins, Godfrey (later Viscount Malvern), 238, 247, 272
Human, N.M., 9, 17
Hurwitz family, 170

Hurwitz, George, 66, 165, 185
Huxley, Elspeth, 91, 148

Iljon family, 49, 67, 165
Iljon, Benjamin (Benny), 67, 79, 80, 164, 231
Iljon, Betty née Evans, 275
Iljon, Eric (Ahron), 67, 97, 166, 275–6, 283
Iljon, Helga née Sonnabend, 164–5
Iljon, Johanna, 67
Iljon, Nicholas (Nicky), 67, 127, 158, 164–5
Iljon, Oscar, 67
Iljon, Paula née Kopelowitz, 166
Illion family, 49, 67, 126, 129
Illion, Eli, 49, 97, 216
Illion, Lazar, 49, 67, 128
Illion, Mike, 97
Illion, Uri, 49, 67, 96, 132, 177, 216, 231
immigration debates (NR), 111, 113
Immigration Ordinance (NR, 1931), 104, 112
Imperial Cold Storage Ltd, 140
Imwiko, Prince (later Litunga), 20
Industrial Development Corporation (Indeco),
    195, 245
International Red Cross, 118–19
Irwin, Carl, 203
Irwin, Oliver, 203, 204, 233
Israel family, 126–30, 177, 217
Israel, Albert, 176, 177
Israel, Henny, 127–8
Israel, Joseph, 216
Israel, Nahman, 97, 100, 101, 176
Israel, Rica, 218
Israel, Solly, 126–30, 214

Jablonski, H., 171
Jabotinsky, Vladimir, 277
Jack, Chisholm, 218
Jacobs, Cecil, 36, 53
Jacobs, Jehiel (also Michael), 47–8, 183
Jacobs, John (Witbooi), 21, 22
Jacobs, Lewis, 47–8
Jacobs, Saul, 226
Jacobs, Sonia née Beemer, 53
Jacobson and Kiehl (Livingstone shop), 43
Jacobson family, 213
Jacobson, Dan, 173, 174
Jacobson, Gerald, 53
Jacobson, M., 208
Jacobson, Meyer, 53, 228
Jacoby family, 122, 163
Jemmy's Stores (Lusaka), 190
Jewish communities in NR/Zambia: Broken Hill
    (Kabwe), 51–6, 171, 213–14, 234–5; Chingola
    (Nchanga), 78, 81, 96–7, 100, 176–7, 217; Kitwe
    (Nkana) 92–95, 171–7, 144–6, 214–16, 222–33;
    Livingstone, 42–51, 68–9, 74, 162–5, 208–9, 221,
    225–6, 231; Luanshya, 95–6, 144, 145, 175–6,
    216–17; Lusaka, 56–66, 166–71, 210–13;
    Mufulira, 96–7, 144, 145, 175–6, 216–17, 222;
    Ndola, 97–9, 101, 178–9, 215–17, 222
Jewish emigrants from Zambia to: Australia, 164,

249, 281; Botswana, 169; Canada, 249; Chile,
171; Great Britain, 165, 169, 197, 230, 280;
Greece, 175; Israel, 169, 230, 249, 274, 276;
South Africa, 168, 230; United States, 230, 283;
Zimbabwe, 165, 167
Jewish immigrants/refugees in NR/Zambia from:
Germany, 103–117, 120–30, 131–2, 160, 164,
169–70, 267–8; Great Britain and Ireland, 61,
70–3, 94, 95, 97–8, 264; Palestine, 63–4, 95,
131, 178; Poland, 65, 118–19; Romania, 43–4,
61; Russian Empire (Lithuania/Latvia), 7–8,
16, 30–1, 47–8, 49–50, 54, 57–8, 58–9, 66, 67,
70, 99, 130–1, 136, 140, 165, 182–3, 233–4, 240;
South Africa, 88, 143–4, 146, 160, 164, 249–55,
259; Turkish Empire (Rhodes), 99–102
Jewishness (identity), 1, 37, 66, 70, 73, 76–8, 120,
206, 222–3, 234–7, 247, 249, 252, 260–1, 266–8,
271, 272, 285
Jewish Territorial Organisation, 225
Johnston, Sir Harry, 5, 6, 224
Judaism, 36–7, 55–6, 77–8, 91, 123, 206–23, 260,
266, 267, 287, 290
Judelman, Lazar, 163
Julien, Harold, 276

Kabulonga Farm, 28, 30
Kafue Polder Pilot Project, 199
Kaldis and Company, 146
Kaluwa, Simon, 243
Kamanga, Reuben, 241, 244
Kantor, Jimmy, 254
Kaplan, Arthur, 39, 50, 79, 175
Kaplan Foundation, vii
Kapulsky, Akiva, 130
Kapulsky, Yonah, 130, 218
Kapwepwe, Simon, 177, 246, 250
Kasomo, Israel, 241
Kasonde, Emmanuel, 258
Kasrils, Ronnie, 252–3, 292
Katenga, Bridger, 241
Katilungu, Lawrence, 243, 244, 264, 265
Katz family, 50, 218
Katz, Chaim, 131, 183
Katz, Jacob, 95, 131, 179, 214, 221
Katz, Zena, 221
Katz, Max 'Mottel', 131, 217, 218
Katz, Zena, 179, 221
Kaunda, Kenneth, 49, 142, 144–5, 152, 170, 179,
187, 188, 189, 192, 195, 201, 213, 230, 232, 239,
245, 246, 248, 249, 251, 255, 256, 257, 258, 281
Kay's Ladies Outfitters (Lusaka), 65, 170
Kaye, Danny, 163
Kazunga, Abnor, 241
Khama III, King, 4, 5, 59
Khruschchev, Nikita, 130
Kiehl, Mr, of Livingstone, 208
Kirschner, Alec, 89
Kisch, Colonel, 227
Kisch, Daniel, 4
Kittermaster, Michael, 279
Kitwe Stores Ltd, 90, 93, 172

Klein family, 165
Klein, Max, 66
Klein, Myer, 66
Knight, C.S., 48
Kodesh, Wolf (Wolfie), 253
Kofie, Best, 240
Kolherr company, 174
Kollenberg family, 49, 57–60, 61, 92, 139, 192, 228
Kollenberg, David, 59, 75, 174, 216
E. Kollenberg and Sons Ltd, 62, 93
Kollenberg, Edward, 57, 59, 67, 210
Kollenberg, Glicka née Hirschfeld, 59
Kollenberg, Henrie, 59, 80, 110, 137, 168, 174, 210
Kollenberg, Herman, 59, 92
Kollenberg, Isadore, 59, 86, 110, 146, 147, 174, 272
Kollenberg, Joan, 174
Kollenberg, Johanna, 59, 67
Kominsky, Max, 9, 12, 13
Konkola, Dixon, 243
Konviser, Reverend Maurice, 179, 211, 213, 215–20, 223
Kopelowitz, Cecilia see Krasner
Kopelowitz, David, 163
Kopelowitz, Elias, 42, 48–50, 51, 61, 67, 79, 80, 96, 122, 128, 163, 165, 208, 209, 227, 229
Kopelowitz, Elias (of Cape Town), 166
Kopelowitz, Henne née Illion, 48–50, 163, 207, 208
Kopelowitz, Paul, 48, 166
Kopelowitz, Rosa (later Scher), 49
Koslowsky (later Kelly), Sam, 95, 131
Kosmin, Barry, 1, 221, 224
Kowalsky brothers, 131
Kramer, Rabbi, 209
Krasner, Cecilia née Kopelowitz, 222, 230
Kuper, Hilda née Beemer, 52
Kuritzky, Leon, 213

Lakofski, Barney, 88
Lakofski, Izzy, 89
Lakofski, Max, 89
Lakofski, Rose née Kirschner, 88
Lakofski, Simon (Shim), 53–4, 88–92, 94, 227, 283, 290, 291
Lakofski-Hepker, Phyllis née Hepker, 85, 90, 91, 92, 95, 99, 283
Lambert, Baron Henri, 133
Landau, Chaim, 277
Landau, David, 17, 54, 91
Landau, Reverend Dr. J.L. (Chief Rabbi), 88
Landau, H.D., 114
Landau, Harry, 17
Landau, Louis, 36
Landau Brothers Ltd, 14, 17, 22, 50
Laski, Nathan, 225
Leakey, Louis, 260
Lechwe Trust, 281
Lee, William, 85
Leeson, Joyce (later Sibeko), 250
Lehrer, Dr Sylvia, 179, 221, 274
Leibowitz brothers, 221
Leibowitz, Nathan ('Gus'), 174

Leopold's Hill Ranch, 28, 30, 87
Lesser and Company, 9–10, 18
Lessing, Doris, 172, 254, 254, 255
Lessing, Pieter, 254
Lessing, Rabbi, 209
Lever Brothers Ltd, 100
Levi, Reverend Maurice (Moise), 220
Levin, Israel ('Der Alter'), 208
Levin, Max, 9
Levin, Schmaryahu, 228
Levin, Wolf, 17
Levine, Isaac, 16
Levine, Reverend I., 118
Levinson, Abraham, 71, 72
Levinson, Leah, 71
Levisohn, Mr, a teacher, 218
Levitz, Fishel, 9, 10, 12–15, 18
Levitz, Michael, 225
Lewanika, King, 4, 5, 9, 10, 12, 17, 18–21, 22, 23, 25, 34, 77
Lewin, C.J., 108
Lewin, Julius, 243
Lewinson family, 35
Lewinson, Bertha see Susman
Lewis Construction Ltd, 253
Leyland Motors Ltd, 153
Line of Rail, the, 29–30, 38–69, 162–71
Lion Tile Ltd, 153
Lipowsky family, 60
Lipschild, Barnett ('Sonny'), 170
Lipschild, George ('Lippy'), 65, 170
Lipschild, May née Davis, 66, 170
Liptz, Annie see Mendelsohn
Liptz, Gertrude see Osrin
Liptz, Sarah Rachel (Ray) see Dobkins
Liso, Edward Mungoni, 244
Litia, Prince, 19, 20, 22, 185 see also Yeta III
Litungas of Bulozi (Barotseland) see Lewanika, Yeta III, Imwiko, Mwanawina III and Yeta IV
Livestock Cooperative Society Butchery (Lusaka), 136
Livingstone Cold Storage Ltd, 136, 144, 199
Livingstone Dress Factory, 122
Livingstone Industrial Holdings Ltd, 201
Livingstone Motor Works, 46
Livingstone Saw Mills, 48
Livingstone, Dr David, 38, 77, 78, 79
Lobengula, King, 4, 21–2
Lochinvar Ranch, 148
Loder, Robert, 280
Logan, William, 105
Longsberg, Robert, 90
Lonrho Ltd, 200
Lorenz, Bente, 280, 281
Lorenz, Erhardt, 280
Lowe, Chris, 200
Lowenthal, Abe, 91, 95–6, 98–9, 136, 178, 179, 276
Lowenthal, Conrad, 99
Lowenthal, Hessie née Wulfsohn, 99, 178
Lowenthal, Dr Mark, 178, 273, 276, 283
Lowenthal, Marlie née Wulfsohn, 99, 136

Lowenthal, William, 91, 99
Luchembe, Lieutenant, 256
Lurie, Eli, 95, 174, 214, 216
Lurie, Johnny, 247
Lurie, John Yankele, 247
Lusaka Cold Storage Ltd, 185–7
Lusaka Meat Market, 186
Lusaka Playhouse, 193
Lusaka Trading Company, 60
Lyttelton, Oliver (later Viscount Chandos), 187

MacDonald, Malcolm, 105, 108
Macleod, Iain, 239
Macmillan, Harold (later Earl of Stockton), 239
Macmurgas Drapery (Livingstone), 122
Magnus, Shmuel ('Val'), 220, 221, 232, 233, 283
Mainga, Mutumba, 278
Maisel, Max, 58
Maize Marketing Board (NR), 137
Malcolm, Sir Dougal, 83
Malinowski, Professor Bronislaw, 260
Manchester Trading Company, 13
Mandaza, Ibbo, 247
Mandel, 'George', 130, 217, 247
Mandela, Nelson, 253, 256
Mann, Thomas, 1
Manning, Dr, 274
Mansfield, Charlotte, 42–3
Mapanda Transport Company, 33
Marcus, David, 176, 217, 247
Marcus, Doreen née Herbstein, 176, 217
Margot's Dress Shop (Lusaka), 122
Marks and Spencers Ltd, 155–7
Marks, Simon (later Lord), 156, 157
Marrapodi, G.B., 57
Martin, Gesse, 253–4
Martin, Les, 253–4
Masiye, Sylvester (Andrea), 279
Matabeleland Trading Association, 13, 22
Matheson, Sheilagh née Thal, 55, 56
Mattos, Mauricio Teixeira de, 6, 7, 52
Maybank, Frank, 172, 244
Maybin, Sir John, 106, 107, 108, 260
Mayer, Edmond, 122
Mbikusita-Lewanika, Akashambatwa, 20, 256, 257, 292
Mbikusita-Lewanika, Godwin, 241, 242
McCracken, John, 1
McCulloch, Merran, 279
McKee, Major Hugh, 62
McKillop, Ian, 165
Meikle, Tom, 26, 27, 289
Meikle Brothers Ltd, 22
Meir, Golda, 229, 249
Melamed family, 174
Melamed, Max, 173
Melland, Frank, 106, 107
Menashe, Boaz Israel, 97, 100, 101, 102, 176
Menashe, Haim I. (Victor), 100, 101, 176
Menashe, Rebecca née Alhadeff, 100
Mendelsohn, A.J. (Jack), 97, 216

Mendelsohn, Annie née Liptz, 65, 81, 211
Mendelsohn, Ellis, 274
Mendelsohn, Moggy, 170, 207, 210
Mendelsohn, Samuel, 65, 81, 97, 170, 211
Mendelssohn, Moses, 55
Mendy's Outfitters (Lusaka), 170
Mennell, A., 114
Merber, Gertrude née Grill, 45–6, 145–6, 165
Merber, Joe, 45, 75
Meridien Bank, 203, 204, 245, 282
Meridor, Yakov, 277
Messerer, Alex, 177, 230
Messerer, David, 99, 126, 161, 177, 179, 215, 216, 218, 220, 221, 222, 223, 229, 230, 231, 282
Messerer, Fanny, 177, 230
Messerer, Ron, 230
Messerer, Rose née Mohrer, 126, 216, 218, 229
Messina (Transvaal) Copper Mines Ltd, 85
Metzger, Alf, 116, 169, 211, 274
Metzger, Reverend Cantor Feivel, 116, 117, 118, 119, 123, 124, 132, 210, 211, 212, 214
Meyer, Rose, 82
Micholls, Colonel, 108
Middle East Relief and Refugee Administration (Merra), 118–19, 274
Mike's Kitchen Ltd, 97
Milady's Dress Shop (Lusaka), 122, 170
Miller, P.S., 57
Miller, Peter T.S., 245
Millin, Sarah Gertrude, 236
Milner, Aaron Michael, 1, 233, 246–9, 259, 292
Milner, Esther née Cele, 246
Milner, Isaac, 246
Milner, Joseph, 246
Milner, Owen, 249
Milner, Philip, 249
Milner, Phyllis née Lurie, 247
Milner, Rebecca (later Rosen), 247
Milner, Saren née Dobkins, 249
Minchuk, Joseph, 96, 171, 175, 216, 217
Minchuk, Julius (Yudel), 96, 97, 177, 221
Mitchell, J.C., 262, 264
Mlongoti, Edwin, 279
Moffat, Reverend Malcolm, 77
Moggy's Milk Bar (Lusaka), 170
Mohrer family, 125–6, 169, 230
Mohrer, Helen née Guttman, 125, 229, 293
Mohrer, Julius, 125, 129, 220, 229
Mokalapa, Willie, 19
Molk, Dr Lazar, 274
Molver, Neil, 200
Momba, Patrick, 281
Moore, Sir Leopold, 42, 50, 105, 106, 108, 236
Morel, E.D., 6
J.P. Morgan and Company, 203
Morgan Stanley and Company, 203
Morton, Percy, 57
Mosenthals (Port Elizabeth importers and exporters), 22
Mosley, Sir Oswald, 235
Moss, Reuben, 212

motor franchises: Chevrolet, 61; Ford, 75, 89; General Motors, 98, 162; Hudson, 172; Land-Rover, 152; Volkswagen, 152
Mow, Len, 158
Mpapa Gallery (Lusaka), 275, 281
Mpashi, Stephen, 279
Mpezeni, King, 5, 6
Mtine, Thomas, 241
Mugabe, Robert, 248–9, 273
Mulemba, Humphrey, 256
Mulena Mukwae, Akananisa, of Sesheke, 20
Mulena Mukwae (Matauka), of Nalolo, 12, 21, 22
Muleya, Yotham, 233
Mulungushi Reforms, 195, 196
Musakanya, Valentine, 248, 249
Mussolini, Benito, 110, 140
Mwaanga, Vernon, 200, 256
Mwaiseni Stores Ltd, 196
Mwanakatwe, John, 248
Mwanawina III, Litunga, 20, 276

Nahman family, 177
Naicker, agent of Gustav Rabinek, 14
Nalumango, Nelson, 183, 225
Namier, Sir Lewis, 268
Naparstock, Smerl, 49
National Milling Company, 169
National Union of South African Students, 140
Ndeke Hotel, 279
Ndola Anti-Federation Action Committee, 242–4
Ndola Milling Company, 96, 179
Ndola Supply Stores, 99
Ndonyo Stores, 142
Ngamiland Trading Company, 147, 155
Nkana Trading Company, 89
Nkhata, Alick, 279
Nkomo, Joshua, 248, 255
Nkumbula, Harry, 152, 189, 236, 242, 255
Northcote, Hon. H.A., 209
Northern Bakeries Ltd, 86
Northern Caterers Ltd, 86, 93, 97, 129, 133, 143, 172, 174, 199, 272
Northern Cattle Exporters' Pool (Bechuanaland), 147
Northern Copper Company, 40–1, 57
The Northern News, 173, 237
Northern Produce and Livestock Company, 137
Northern Rhodesia Meat and Provision Company, 146
Northern Rhodesia Music Association, 164
Northern Rhodesia Native Produce Company, 96
Northern Rhodesia Textiles Ltd, 153, 162, 291
Northern Rhodesia Trading Company, 52
Northern Rhodesian Defence Force (Home Guard), 129, 158
Northern Rhodesian Farmers' Association, 134
Northern Rhodesian Industrial Development Corporation, 153
Northern Rhodesian Labour Party, 237, 274
Northern Rhodesian Livestock Co-operative Society, 148

Northern Rhodesian Mineworkers' Union, 108, 172
Northern Rhodesian Regiment, 168, 240
Northern Rhodesian Volunteer Force (Northern Rhodesia Rifles), 74
Northern Suppliers Ltd, 85

Olsvanger, Dr, 228
Oppenheimer, Sir Ernest, 83, 86, 87, 89, 147
O'Riordan, Father, 144
Osrin family, 228
Osrin, Alec, 90
Osrin, Gertrude née Liptz, 81, 211
Osrin, Isaac, 53, 88
Osrin, Sam, 80, 81, 89, 210, 211, 214
Ossewa Brandweg (SA paramilitary organisation), 132
Oury, Libert, 5
Oza, H., 229

Palace Cinema (Lusaka), 190
Palestine National Fund, 37
Parkinson, Sir Cosmo, 105
de Pass, Aaron, 4
Patel Brothers, 93, 180
Patel, Dinesh, 195
Patel, Dipak, 258
G. Pauling and Company, 51, 76
Paynter, Marta see Trefusis-Paynter
Peimer, Michael, 9, 43, 208, 225
Peimer, Samuel, 9, 43, 208
Pentopoulos, M.S., 141
Phiri, David, 203
Pieters, A., 13
Pieters, Isadore, 9, 13, 22
Piha, M., 101
Pilcher, Joan, 281
Pinhassovith family (formerly Pinhassovitch), 224
Pinhassovith, David and Shoshanna, 64, 227–8
Pinshow, Len, 146–7, 148, 174, 199, 203, 232–3, 249
Pinshow, Nina née Kollenberg, 146, 174
Pioneer Butchery and Bakery (Livingstone), 44
Piper Clothing Company, 274
Pirie, Gordon, 233
Pollon, B., 80
Port, Max, 98
Poswell, Rabbi, 211
Prain, Sir Ronald, 199
Premier Bakery (Broken Hill), 129, 171
Premier Milling Company, 100
Prentice, Reverend Dr George, 107
Press, Berjulie née Lipschild, 66, 160
Press, Hubert, 66
Press, Sydney, 66
Pretorius's Butchery (Livingstone), 138
Price, Jack, 153, 214
Price, Mrs, of Kitwe, 221
Prins, Moritz, 212, 221
Pritt, Denis, 243–4
Public Services Association (PSA) (Livingstone), 46, 162
Puta, Robinson, 243

Quinlan, Kate *née* Gersh, 200
Quota Act, South Africa, 103

Rabb family, 165, 203, 205, 293
Rabb, Anne, 140
Rabb, John, 140, 202
Rabb, Maurice, 139–43, 150, 151, 154, 155, 162,
    173, 194, 197, 201, 202, 221, 231, 232
Rabb, Peggy *née* Susman, 140, 141, 202, 231
Rabb, Tessa, 140
Rabinek, Gustav, 6, 7, 14
Rabinowitz, Joseph, 140
Rabinowitz, Uri, 222
Radson, Gabriel, 274
Radunski family, 164, 165, 180
Radunski, Paddy *née* Kleinman, 164
Radunski, Raymond, 158, 164
Radunski, Saul, 164, 293
Raine, E.R., 149
Raine Engineering Ltd, 149, 153
Rand Cold Storage Company, 140
Rankow, Dvora, 213, 230
Rankow, Tuvia, 213
Rayner family, 175
Rayner, Harry, 98, 175, 216, 231
Read, Gordon, 184
Red Robe Dress Shop (Lusaka), 125, 169
Refugee Assistance Committee (Lusaka), 114, 123
Refugee Assistance Committee (Copperbelt), 114
Refugee Farm (Lusaka), 115–17
refugee settlement schemes, 103–19
Reitlinger, G.L., 269
Rey, Colonel (later Sir) Charles, 133
Rhodes (island of), Sephardi Jews from, 75, 99–102
Rhodes, Cecil, 4, 5, 40
Rhodesia Bottling (later Copperbelt Bottling), 153
Rhodesia Cold Storage Commission, 149
Rhodesia Congo Border Concession Company, 83
Rhodesia Congo Oil and Soap Industries, 101–2,
    176
Rhodesia Railway Workers' Union, 108, 234, 235,
    237
Rhodesia Railways Ltd, 150, 151
Rhodesian Board of Jewish Deputies, 220, 232
Rhodesian Copperfields Trading Company, 92, 93,
    97
Rhodesian Lakes Trading Company, 131
Rhodesian Mercantile Holdings Ltd, 155
Rhodesian Native Labour Bureau, 28
Rhodesian Native Timber Concessions, 14
Rhodesian Selection Trust, 83, 139, 177, 199
Rhokana Corporation, 93, 146
Rietfontein Ranch, 149, 201
Riley, C., 24
Riley, Jim, 33
Roberts, John, 255
Robins, Sir Ellis (later Lord), 155
Robinson and Schwarz Ltd, 155
Robinson, Cynthia, 245
Robinson, Ella *née* Susman, 155
Robinson, Harry, 154, 189

Rockefeller Foundation, 203
Roetgen, Hans, 129
Rollnick, J.R., 32, 36, 52, 57
Ron, Aviva *née* Elkaim, 158, 206, 218, 219, 222,
    229, 230
Rosen family, 175, 213
Rosen, Isaac, 53, 54, 88
Rosen, Maurice, 95, 175, 217, 231
Rosen, Morrison, 247
Rosen, Philip, 95, 158, 175
Rosenberg, Fritz, 121
Rosenberg, Gert, 129, 171, 213
Rosenberg, Hedwig, 129
Rosenberg, Marianne *née* von Geldern, 171
Rosenberg, Siegfried, 129, 171
Rosenblatt, Meir, 95, 131
Rosenfield, Nicholas, 61
Rossi, Enzio, 279
Rotberg, Robert I., 270–1
Rothschild family, 129
Rothschild, Anthony de, 107, 108, 109
Rothschild, Nathaniel, Lord, 4
Rotter, Bertie, 171
Rotter, Josef, 171
Rovell Fashions (Lusaka), 170
Rowelsky family, 49, 169
Rowelsky, Hans, 170
Rowelsky, Max, 125, 211
Rowelsky, Sigrid *see* Fischer
Rowland, Tiny, 200
Rubenstein, Esther *née* Beau, 165
Rubin, J., 208
Rubinstein, Celia (later Thal), 54
Rubinstein, Louis, 35
Rumor, Max, 89
Rybko, Wolf, 39, 58, 61, 159, 162, 167, 169, 171,
    176, 207, 209, 213, 215, 216, 219, 223, 226, 227,
    228, 229
van Ryneveld, Pierre, 30

Sacher, Harry, 156
Salisbury, Marquess of, 4
Salomon and Kaufman Ltd, 40, 50
Messers Salomon and Rollnick (Broken Hill), 52
Salomon, Charelik, 52
Sampson, Richard, 188, 290
Samter, Ernst, 129
Sandford, T.F., 137
Sapseid, Dick ('Sapper'), 279
Sardanis, Andrew, 195, 196, 197, 203, 281
Sata, Dr Michael, 275
Savimbi, Jonas, 248
Scaw Ltd (formerly Scaw Tow Ltd), 163
Schatz, Harry, 216
Schatz, Mrs Israel, 216
Scher family, 49
Scher, Cilla *see* Behrens
Scher, Zalkind, 49
Schlesinger family, 49
Schlesinger, John, 163
Schlesinger, Minda *née* Kopelowitz, 230

Schlesinger Organisation, 64, 90, 163, 171
Schlitner, Florence (Flossie) *née* Dobkins, 81
Schlitner, Julius (later Slater), 81, 95, 96, 179
Schulman family, 98
Schulman, Hyam, 97, 101, 178, 214, 215, 231
Schulman, Lily *née* Port, 98
Schulman, Mrs Nathan, 228
Schulman, Nathan M., 80, 97, 98, 174, 216
Schwartz, Rabbi Z., 229
Scots traders, 8, 9, 27, 181, 287
Scott Brown, Denise *née* Lakofski, 273, 283, 285
Scott, Dr Alec, 257, 265
Scott, Guy, 257
Senn, Gottfried, 119
Serrano, A.F. ('Ndonyo'), 141, 142
A.F. Serrano Ltd, 195
Setti, Godfrey, 281
Shamwana, Edward, 248, 249
Shapiro family, 47, 192, 227
Shapiro, Absolom, 64
Shapiro, David, 63, 80, 169, 210, 211, 217, 220, 224
Shapiro, Ivie *née* Diamond, 210
Shapiro, Jenny *née* Feigenbaum, 47, 82, 163
Shapiro, Max, 47, 56, 82, 163, 208, 209
Shapiro's Milling Company, 122, 169
Sharett, Moshe, 229
Sharrer's Zambezi Traffic Company, 5
Sharrer, Eugene, 5, 6, 7
Shelmerdine, W., 33
Sher, H.D., 209, 226
Sher, Helene, 226
Shimoni, Gideon, 224
ships: *Artemissia*, 277; *Gerusalemme*, 116; *Stuttgart*, 103; *Watussi*, 126
Shoniwa, John, 240
Shoprite Checkers Ltd, 203
Sibeko, Archie (Zola Zembe), 250
Sibeko, Joyce *see* Leeson
Sieff, Israel (later Lord), 156
Silberhaft, Rabbi Moshe, 222
Sillitoe, Sir Percy, 58
Silverberg, Jimmy, 130
Simon, Benno, 129
Simon, Robert, 117
Simons, Hyman 249
Simons, Jack, 196, 240, 241, 249–51, Rachel Elizabeth (Ray) *née* Alexander, 249, 254, 249
Skinner, James, 246
Slomowitz, Dr Harold, 230
Slomowitz, Zoe, 230
Slovo, Joe, 251–5, 259, 292
Slutzkin, Alex, 164, 231
Slutzkin, Riva, 164
Smith, Barnett 'Bongola', 24, 30–2, 32–4, 36, 76, 86, 133, 134, 149, 289, 291
Smith, Herbert, 148
Smith, John, 19, 23, 25, 26, 68, 134
Smith, Wilbur, 148
Smuts, General (later Field Marshal) Jan Christian, 210
Snapper, R.A.D. 'Dick', 11, 247

Snapper, Egnatz, 9, 11, 12, 94, 247
Snapper, John, 11
Sokolow, Nahum, 226, 227
Solanki Brothers Ltd, 197
Solar Investments Ltd, 170
Solomon, C., 135
C. Solomon and Co., 16
Solly's Bakery (Lusaka), 170
Sombart, Werner, 287
Sommer, Laura *see* Grill
Sommer, Max, 122
Sonnabend, Dr Henry, 109, 111, 114, 115, 117, 164
Sonnenberg, Max, 16, 135, 156
Sonnenberg, Richard, 156, 157
Sonnenthal (later Stanley), Sigismund, 82
Sossen, Bella *née* Grill, 46, 162, 163, 165
Sossen, Harry, 46, 90, 162, 163
Sossy's Motors Ltd, 162
Soy Nutrients Ltd, 191
Speck, Eric, 143, 198
Stalin, Josef, 165
Stammreich, Max, 117, 122
Standard Butchery (Luanshya and Ndola), 96, 145, 265
Standard Trading Ltd, 92, 93, 131, 175
Stanley, Sir Herbert James, 82, 106
E. Stenham Ltd, 197
Stephenson, Colonel Arthur, 113
Stephenson, J.E. ('Chirupula'), 49, 106
Sterling, George, 20, 76
Stern family, 129
Stern, Harry, 14, 277
Stern, Major, 107
Stiel, Alex, 96
Storrs, Sir Ronald, 134
Surdut, Fanny, 177
Surdut, Samuel, 177
Susman (formerly Susmanovitch) family, 43, 44–7, 48, 54, 59, 60, 74, 84–6, 111, 136, 148, 151, 182, 185, 190, 194, 203, 205, 208, 231, 289, 290, 293
Susman, Ann *née* Laski, 156
Susman, Annie *née* Grill, 34, 46, 207, 208
Susman, Bertha *née* Lewinson, 35, 36, 135
Susman, Bruna, 36
Susman, David, 36, 135, 137, 154, 155–7, 194, 202, 205, 206, 239, 254, 290
Susman, Dora (later Gersh), 35
Susman, Elie, 9, 15, 16–37, 47, 60, 85, 98, 134, 135, 139, 140, 146, 149, 151, 154, 155, 204, 209, 225, 226, 290, 291
Susman, Harris (Harry), 9, 15, 16–37, 44, 45, 113–14, 135, 138, 140, 155, 204, 208, 209, 225, 226, 228
Susman, Joseph, 35, 84, 140
Susman, Oscar (elder), 35, 36, 37, 75, 226–7
Susman, Oscar (younger), 158
Susman, Peggy, 36, 140
Susman Brothers (partnership), 22–30, 133–6
Susman Brothers Ltd, 139
Susman Brothers and Davis (partnership), 44
Susman Brothers and Riley (partnership), 27
Susman Brothers and Smith (partnership), 32–4

Susman Brothers and Wulfsohn Ltd, 124, 139, 141–2, 143, 148, 149, 150, 151, 154, 155, 157, 162, 164, 173, 194, 195, 196, 197, 198, 200, 201, 239, 257, 275, 291
Susmanovitch family, 214
Susmanovitch, Behr, 16, 34, 35, 36, 45, 207
Susmanovitch, Marcia (later Rubinstein), 35
Susmanovitch, Taube née Diamond, 16, 35
Sussman family, 84–6
Sussman, Cyril, 96, 97, 145, 177, 216, 217
Sussman, Dr Otto, 83
Sussman, George, 86
Sussman, H.P., 217
Sussman, Philip, 86
Sussman, Sam, 86
Sussman, Sydney, 96, 175, 217
Sussman, Willie, 86
Sutherland, Robert 'Katembora', 33, 37, 156
R.F. Sutherland Ltd, 33, 142
Suu, Francis, 185
Sykes, Frank, 9, 10, 17, 18
synagogues: Bulawayo, 79; Cape Town, 4, 222; Kimberley, 3; Livingstone, 37, 208–9; Luanshya, 217; Lusaka, vii, 192, 210, 211–12, 222, 282, 293; Maputo, 222; Mufulira, 215, 216, 222; Ndola, 215, 217, 222; Nkana-Kitwe, 215, 216
Szeftel, Benjamin, 130–1, 171, 186–7, 188, 212
Szeftel, Gutel, 187
Szeftel, Leslie, 187, 255
Szeftel, Morris, 187, 211, 212
Szeftel, Sam, 131, 171, 186–7
Szlapak, Rabbi, 209

Tafuna, Chief, 241
Tambo, Oliver, 250, 251
Tanganyika Concessions Ltd, 40, 75
Tarica, Joe, 100
Tarica, Nissim, 101
J.W. Tarry Ltd, 68
Tas, Adam, 3
Tate and Lyle Ltd, 200
Tattoni, Dr, 273
Taube, Max, 183, 209, 228
Tayali, Henry, 191, 281
Taylor, S., 265
Teeger, Isa née Lowenthal, 142, 178, 208, 273
Teicher, Mort, 212
Tembo, Nephas, 241, 243, 250
Thal family, 98, 213
Thal, Basil, 56
Thal, Louis, 54
Thal, Maurice, 54, 91, 158, 213, 223, 290
Thal, Max, 95
Thal, Rebecca (later Hepker), 54, 91
Thatcher Hobson Airways Ltd, 153
Thom, John, 68, 142
Thomson, Jack, 264
Thomson, Joseph, 6
Thornhill, J.B., 10, 19, 23, 51
Thornicroft, Harry, 247
Tiger Oats Ltd, 100, 288

The Times of Zambia, 277, 278
Tongue and Knight (partnership), 150, 151
Tongue, W.E., 48
Totman, Chief Inspector William, 112
Tow family, 49, 174
Tow, Doreen née Kollenberg, 174
Tow, Harry, 163, 165, 214
Tow, Max, 158, 163, 165, 174
Tow Brothers Iron Works, 163
Trans Zambezi Industries Ltd, 157, 202–4
Trapnell, C.G., 107, 261
Traub, Chaim, 131
Traub, Rachel, 131
Trefusis-Paynter, Geoffrey, 278
Trefusis-Paynter, Guy, 277
Trefusis-Paynter, Marta, 179, 273, 277–8
Trefusis-Paynter, Michael, 277
Troumbas, Aristotle Hippocrates ('Hippo'), 47–8
Trout, Jim, 98
Truworths Ltd, 157
Tuch, Hans, 102, 216
Tuffin, Jack, 200, 202
Twentieth Century Cinema (Lusaka), 171
Twentieth Century-Fox, 90

Ullman, Adolph 'Tambalika', 24
Union Congo Oil and Soap Industries, 100
United Hebrew Congregation of the Copperbelt, 219, 232
Ussishkin, Menachem, 228

van der Post, Laurens, 28
Venturi, Robert, 281
Victoria Falls Hotel, 162–3
Vilinsky (also Wilensky), David, 95

Wacks, Abraham, 33
Waddington, Sir John, 151
Wagner, M., 220
Wankie Colliery Company, 28, 40, 234
Wasserson family, 47, 227, 228
Wasserson, Bertha (later Barenblatt), 228
Wasserson, Ethel née Feigenbaum, 47
Wasserson, Harry, 47, 209
Wasserson, Jack, 47
Wasserson, Norma see Davidov
Watmore, H.A., 132
Weber, Max, 287
Weinberg, Eli, 253, 254
Weinberg, Reverend A., 209, 214
Weinberg, Violet, 253
Weiss, Ruth, 278
Weizmann, Chaim, 156, 226, 228
Weizmann, Vera, 228
Welensky, Ben, 234
Welensky, David, 95, 234
Welensky, Leah née Aletta Ferreira, 234
Welensky, Liz née Henderson, 234
Welensky, Michael, 234
Welensky, Sir Roy (Roland), 1, 55, 80, 84, 101, 108, 113, 129, 130, 162, 168, 172, 176, 189, 206,

233–9, 243, 246, 259, 261, 263, 267, 269, 270, 274, 278, 292

Werner, H.C., 98, 139

Werner and Company, 129, 136, 142, 143, 144, 146, 147, 185, 186, 196, 198, 203, 204, 265

Wersock, David, 9, 12, 208

Westbeech, George, 4, 5

wholesale traders: Bulawayo, 22, 40, 44, 50, 79, 94, 289; Livingstone, 49, 163; London, 22, 40, 79, 94, 289; Port Elizabeth, 22, 40

Wide, Renee Dobkins, 230

Wiese, Carl, 5, 6, 7, 54

Wiesenbacher family, 123–5

Wiesenbacher, Freddy, 124

Wiesenbacher, Trude see Wulfsohn

Williams, Sir Robert, 40, 75

Wilson, Godfrey, 261

Wina, Arthur, 185, 256, 257, 258

Wina, Ngambela (traditional prime minister) Kalonga, 185

Wina, Sikota, 256

Winnicott, H.C., 84

Winterton, Earl of, 105

Wischnitzer, Mark, 104

Witwatersrand Native Labour Association (WENELA), 197, 257

Woest, Ben, 148

Wolffe, Hymie, 47, 50

Wolfsohn, Reverend, 220

Wolpe, Anne-Marie, 254

Wolpe, Harold, 254

Wolpowitz, Mr, store manager, 88

Wolpowitz, Sam, 64

Women's International Zionist Organisation (WIZO), 94, 178, 229, 231, 259

Wooltru Ltd, 157, 203, 204

Woolworths Ltd, 134–5, 140, 155–7

World Zionist Organisation, 226, 227, 228

Wright, Patrick, 46

Wright, Trevor, 46

Wulfsohn family, 180, 203, 205, 228, 293

Wulfsohn, Chaya, 136

Wulfsohn, Edwin, 151, 154, 195, 196, 197, 198, 200, 202, 203, 205, 249, 281

Wulfsohn, Floretta née Glasstone, 65, 124

Wulfsohn, Frieda, 169

Wulfsohn, Harry (born Hozias Vulfsohns), 99, 124, 136–9, 140, 141, 143, 149, 150, 151, 152, 154, 162, 163, 169, 189, 194, 195, 196, 289, 291

Wulfsohn, Isaac, 136

Wulfsohn, Marlie see Lowenthal

Wulfsohn, Millicent née Dombie, 169, 254

Wulfsohn, Samuel Barnett ('Tubby'), 65, 124, 127, 137, 169, 185, 210

Wulfsohn, Trude née Wiesenbacher (later Robins), 124, 138, 139, 151

Wulfsohn, Wolf (Wulfie), 80, 114, 136, 163, 169, 254

Yeta III, Litunga, 20 see also Prince Litia

Yeta IV, Litunga, 164

Young, Sir Hubert, 104, 105

Zaloumis, Dennis, 198

Zaloumis, Paul, 138, 149

Zambesi Saw Mills Ltd, 48, 87, 122, 135, 150–2, 153, 162, 163, 195, 197

Zambezi Ranching and Cropping Ltd, 157, 191, 198–9, 200, 202, 203, 204, 255

Zambezi River Transport Company, 33

Zambezi Trading Company, 42, 74, 164

Zambia Association of Chambers of Commerce and Industry (ZACCI), 192

Zambia Sugar Company, 200

Zambia Textiles Ltd (formerly Northern Rhodesia Textiles), 180, 196, 197, 201, 204

Zambian Women's Zionist Council, 221

Zambian Zionist Council, 221

Zangwill, Israel, 224, 225

Zaremba, Sarah Taylor, 172

ZCBC Ltd, 62, 175

Zelter, Nathan, 155, 194, 254

Zemack family, 224

Zemack, Aryeh, 131

Zemack, Mark, 255

Zemack, Rivka (Katz), 131

Zionism, 35, 37, 125, 156, 183, 192, 222–3, 224–30, 240

Zionist Record, 216, 219, 227

Zlotnik, Isaac, 95, 96, 175, 224

Zlotnik, Rabbi, 227

ZMCK Consulting Engineers, 245

Zukas, Alan, 258

Zukas, Chaim, 240

Zukas, Cynthia, 254, 280–1, 284

Zukas, David, 258

Zukas, Jack, 244

Zukas, Simon, 1, 93, 158, 202, 233, 239–46, 249, 253, 255–8, 259, 269, 271, 282, 283, 292, 293

Zukas, Yvette, 244

Zwick, O., 225